# Asian Century… on a Knife-edge

John West

# Asian Century... on a Knife-edge

A 360 Degree Analysis of Asia's Recent Economic Development

palgrave
macmillan

John West
Center for Global Discovery
Sophia University
Tokyo, Japan

ISBN 978-981-10-7181-2      ISBN 978-981-10-7182-9   (eBook)
https://doi.org/10.1007/978-981-10-7182-9

Library of Congress Control Number: 2017961555

© The Editor(s) (if applicable) and The Author(s) 2018 This book is an open access publication
**Open Access** This book is licensed under the terms of the Creative Commons Attribution 4.0 International License (http://creativecommons.org/licenses/by/4.0/), which permits use, sharing, adaptation, distribution, and reproduction in any medium or format, as long as you give appropriate credit to the original author(s) and the source, provide a link to the Creative Commons license and indicate if changes were made.
The images or other third party material in this book are included in the book's Creative Commons license, unless indicated otherwise in a credit line to the material. If material is not included in the book's Creative Commons license and your intended use is not permitted by statutory regulation or exceeds the permitted use, you will need to obtain permission directly from the copyright holder.
The use of general descriptive names, registered names, trademarks, service marks, etc. in this publication does not imply, even in the absence of a specific statement, that such names are exempt from the relevant protective laws and regulations and therefore free for general use.
The publisher, the authors and the editors are safe to assume that the advice and information in this book are believed to be true and accurate at the date of publication. Neither the publisher nor the authors or the editors give a warranty, express or implied, with respect to the material contained herein or for any errors or omissions that may have been made. The publisher remains neutral with regard to jurisdictional claims in published maps and institutional affiliations.

Cover illustration: © Creative Crop / Getty Images

Printed on acid-free paper

This Palgrave Macmillan imprint is published by Springer Nature
The registered company is Springer Nature Singapore Pte Ltd.
The registered company address is: 152 Beach Road, #21-01/04 Gateway East, Singapore 189721, Singapore

# Acknowledgments

This book is dedicated to my students at Tokyo's Sophia University.

Through our discussions and debates over the years, they inspired me to research many aspects of Asia's development, and motivated me to write this book. Naturally, I am responsible for any remaining errors and shortcomings.

I would also like to extend my sincere gratitude to the Asian Century Institute for its generous support that enables this book to be available through Open Access.

# Contents

| | | |
|---|---|---|
| **1** | **Introduction** | 1 |
| | *US Reboots Post-war Asia* | 1 |
| | *From Asian Renaissance to Asian Century Hype* | 2 |
| | *From Asian Century Hype to Donald J. Trump* | 4 |
| | *Trump Administration Moves into Action* | 5 |
| | *Taking Stock of Asia's Economic and Social Development* | 8 |
| | *Seven Challenges for an Asian Century* | 9 |
| | *What Next for the Asian Century?* | 12 |
| | | |
| **Part I** | **Taking Stock of Asia's Economic and Social Development** | **17** |
| | | |
| **2** | **Asia's Stunted Economic Development** | 19 |
| | *What Is the Outlook for Asia's Catch Up Economies?* | 21 |
| | *Size Matters, But Not 100%* | 23 |
| | *Japan Almost Made It!* | 25 |
| | *Korea: The Chaebol Republic* | 30 |
| | *China's Conundrums* | 35 |
| | *India: A Slow Burner* | 41 |
| | *Indonesia's Oligarchy* | 45 |
| | *Vietnam, the Next China?* | 49 |
| | *Concluding Comments* | 52 |

## 3 Asia's Mythical Middle-Class Society — 57
*Asia's Stunted Middle Class* — 58
*Middle Class in Manila* — 59
*Escaping Extreme Poverty* — 60
*Inequality Holds Back Asia's Poverty Reduction* — 61
*Asia's Precariat* — 62
*Surviving on the Threshold of Poverty in Bangladesh* — 64
*Poverty in the Midst of Prosperity: The Case of Singapore* — 66
*Japan's Two-Track Job Market and Vulnerability* — 67
*A Deeper Look at Poverty Reduction and Asia's Toilet Crisis* — 69
*A Deeper Look at Poverty Reduction and the Impact of Natural Disasters* — 71
*Asia's Education Divide* — 73
*Asia's Digital Divide* — 75
*Asia's Appalling Human Rights* — 77
*Happiness and Asia's Middle Class* — 82
*The Rise of Asia's Super Rich* — 83

## Part II  Seven Challenges for an Asian Century — 89

## 4 Getting Better Value Out of Global Value Chains — 91
*Birth of GVCs* — 93
*GVCs, a Fast Track to Development* — 96
*Hooking on to GVCs* — 98
*Asian Trade and Investment Liberalization* — 99
*Trans-Pacific Partnership* — 100
*Trump Trade Policy* — 101
*Regional Comprehensive Economic Partnership* — 103
*Climbing GVCs* — 105
*China's Efforts to Climb GVCs* — 106
*Asia's Weak Participation in GVCs for Services* — 111
*Risks and Challenges of GVC-Based Development* — 113
*The Quest for Socially Responsible GVCs* — 115

## 5 Making the Most of Urbanization's Potential — 125
*Insights from Sir W. Arthur Lewis* — 127

| | |
|---|---|
| Labor Unrest in China | 129 |
| China's Urban Apartheid | 130 |
| Urban Poverty and Slums | 133 |
| Dharavi, India's Most Famous Slum | 135 |
| Indonesia's Infrastructure Crisis | 138 |
| Asia's Urban Environmental Disaster | 140 |
| Urbanization and Asia's Innovation Imperative | 143 |
| Asia's Best City: Singapore Versus Hong Kong | 147 |

## 6 Giving All Asians a Chance! — 153

| | |
|---|---|
| LGBT Rights in Asia | 154 |
| The Many Trials of Womanhood in Japan | 156 |
| The Plight of South Asia's Women | 159 |
| Asia's Missing Women | 160 |
| Forced Child Marriage in South Asia | 161 |
| Pakistan's Dishonorable Honor-Killing Epidemic | 162 |
| Asia's Indigenous Peoples | 165 |
| Indonesia's West Papuans | 167 |
| China's Tibetans | 169 |
| Dire Situation of China's Uighurs | 171 |
| Sri Lanka Needs National Reconciliation | 174 |
| India's Caste System Is Still Alive and Well | 177 |

## 7 Solving Asia's Demographic Dilemmas — 183

| | |
|---|---|
| Asia's Demographic Transitions | 185 |
| India's Demographic Destiny | 187 |
| East Asia's Fading Fertility | 189 |
| China's "Two-Child Policy" | 192 |
| Economic Costs of Asia's Aging Populations | 194 |
| Social Policy Challenges of Asia's Aging Populations | 197 |
| Korea's Shameful Demographic Drama | 198 |
| Japan's Silver Democracy | 200 |
| Japan's Immigration Imperative | 202 |
| Toward a Multicultural Korea | 205 |

## 8 Fixing Asia's Flawed Politics — 213

| | |
|---|---|
| Asia's Democracy Deficit | 213 |

| | | |
|---|---|---|
| | *What's Holding Back Asia's Democratization?* | 215 |
| | *Will China Democratize?* | 218 |
| | *Korea's Corrupt Democracy* | 222 |
| | *Japan's Oligarchic Democracy* | 225 |
| | *Philippines' Populist Temptation* | 228 |
| | *Thailand, the Land of a Thousand Coups* | 232 |
| | *Military Hangs on in Myanmar* | 235 |
| | *Naïve Appeal of Authoritarian Government* | 240 |
| | *Why Democracy Matters, Even in Asia* | 242 |
| 9 | **Combating Asia's Economic Crime** | 247 |
| | *Counterfeiting and Piracy* | 248 |
| | *Illegal Drug Production and Trafficking in Asia* | 251 |
| | *Environmental Crime* | 254 |
| | *Human Trafficking in Asia* | 256 |
| | *Human Smuggling* | 260 |
| | *Corruption in Asia* | 262 |
| | *Japan's Institutionalized Corruption* | 264 |
| | *Malaysia's Crime of the Century* | 265 |
| | *China's Cancerous Corruption* | 267 |
| | *Mongolia's Corruption Curse* | 271 |
| | *Lessons from Clean Singapore* | 272 |
| | *Money Laundering in Asia* | 273 |
| | *Cybercrime* | 274 |
| 10 | **Can Asian Countries Live Together in Peace and Harmony?** | 279 |
| | *US and Asia During the Cold War* | 281 |
| | *Rehabilitation of China* | 284 |
| | *Japan, from Chinese Friend to Foe* | 286 |
| | *Taiwan and China: It's Complicated* | 288 |
| | *Hong Kong and China: It's Even More Complicated* | 291 |
| | *North Korean Imbroglio* | 293 |
| | *China Snaffles the South China Sea from Its Southeast Asian Neighbors* | 297 |
| | *China Fractures ASEAN* | 301 |
| | *China's Leadership for Asian Infrastructure* | 304 |

| | |
|---|---|
| *Belt and Road Initiative for a Sinocentric Asia* | 305 |
| *Chinese and Indian Frictions* | 308 |
| *Obama's Pivot to Asia* | 310 |
| *Trump's Potshots at Asia* | 312 |
| *The Future of Peace and Harmony in Asia* | 315 |

## Part III  Looking Ahead   321

## 11  What Next for the Asian Century?   323
*Can Asia Rise to the Challenge?*   324
*The Donald Trump Collision*   325
*A World with Increasingly Divergent Interests*   326
*Risks of Conflict and Crisis*   327

**Index**   329

CHAPTER 1

# Introduction

Asia, the continent just across the Pacific Ocean from the US, has been pushed into unchartered waters with the election of Donald Trump to the presidency of the US. The challenge of navigating this "new normal" comes just as Asia's own economies and politics are more vulnerable and fragile than they have been for a very long time.

How well prepared is Asia for this new phase in its renaissance following almost two centuries in an economic and political abyss? What are the major challenges that Asia faces? In short, what next for the Asian Century?

## US Reboots Post-war Asia

In the aftermath of World War 2 and the Korean War, the US planted the seeds for an "Asian Century" being realized in the twenty-first century. It remade its arch-enemy Japan into a democracy with a pacifist constitution. It offered security alliances and partnerships to Japan, Korea, the Philippines, Taiwan, Thailand and Singapore. It provided financial assistance to rebuild war-torn economies. America's open markets enabled these countries to pursue export-driven development. And the post-war liberal international order led by the US, which includes the United Nations, the International Monetary Fund (IMF), the World Bank and the World Trade Organization (WTO), formerly the General Agreement on Tariffs and Trade, underpinned an open and secure international system which facilitated Asia's development.

© The Author(s) 2018
J. West, *Asian Century... on a Knife-edge*,
https://doi.org/10.1007/978-981-10-7182-9_1

To be sure, sound domestic policies and strong leadership in many Asian countries played an important role. But the contribution of the US was crucial.

There were of course periods of tension. By the 1970s and 1980s, the US and other Western countries pushed Japan to open its highly protected markets and to invest in their own economies. It was time for Asia's export giant to allow more imports. And the US even felt under threat as Japan seemed to be taking over its mantle as the world's leading economy. This apparent threat faded from view with Japan's subsequent financial crisis in the 1990s.

When China began opening its economy from 1978, the US was also there to welcome Chinese exports, students, migrants and more recently Chinese investors. China's economy would experience a dramatic wave of economic growth following its membership of the WTO in 2001, which was supported by the US Clinton administration and business community. True, the US and other Western countries benefited handsomely from growing economic linkages with China and other Asian countries, even if they have been partly responsible for widening income inequality. And it has been hoped that closer economic relations would promote peace and security through the mutual interdependence that they create.

## From Asian Renaissance to Asian Century Hype

Speculation that the twenty-first century could belong to Asia reached a crescendo around the period 2010–2012. The US had been flattened by its Wall Street crisis. Europe was knocked out by its sovereign debt crisis and the side effects of America's financial crisis.

At the same time, China became the growth center for the world economy, thanks to a mega stimulus package from the Chinese government. This boosted economic growth worldwide, especially for China's Asian trading partners and for commodity exporters like Australia, Brazil and Indonesia, along with many African and other Latin American countries.

Many saw an Asian Century as a foregone conclusion. Certainly, the Chinese leadership adopted an air of triumphalism, and a period of assertive Chinese foreign policy began with the main targets being Japan and the US.

Singaporean intellectual Kishore Mahbubani set the tone for Asian Century "hype" when he announced that "the last two centuries of Western domination of world history have been a major historical aberration. From the years 1 to 1820, the two largest economies of the world were those of China and India … All historical aberrations come to a natural end. Therefore the Asian Century is irresistible and unstoppable."[1]

Some of the many signposts of Asian Century hype were:

- US President Barack Obama's comments in 2011 when he announced his administration's "pivot" (or "rebalance") to Asia—"As the world's fastest growing region—and home to more than half the global economy—the Asia Pacific is critical to achieving my highest priority, and that's creating jobs and opportunity for the American people … as a Pacific nation, the United States will play a larger and long term role in shaping this region and its future."[2]
- Australian Prime Minister Julia Gillard's declaration at the launch of her government's 2012 White Paper on the Asian Century—"Whatever this century brings, it will bring Asia's return to global leadership, Asia's rise. This is not only unstoppable, it is gathering pace … Asia will become home to most of the world's middle class by as early as 2025. Not only becoming the world's largest producer of goods and services; becoming the world's largest consumer of them."[3]
- After being blackballed by China for meeting with the Dalai Lama in 2012, British Prime Minister David Cameron committed one of the biggest kowtows in modern history, when he announced in 2015 that the UK would join the China-led Asian Infrastructure Investment Bank, in defiance of the wishes of the US. White House spokesmen could only bemoan the UK's "constant accommodation" of the Chinese government. Around the same time, Cameron declared that the UK is "China's best partner in the West", while at the same time it had seemingly abandoned its responsibilities to Hong Kong, its former colony, which is suffering from Beijing's abuses of the "One Country, Two Systems" regime.
- Chinese President Xi Jinping's press article, on the occasion of a 2014 visit to India, in which he wrote—"I am confident that as long as China and India work together, the Asian century of prosperity and renewal will surely arrive at an early date."[4]
- A 2006 speech by Indian Prime Minister, Manmohan Singh, in which he said—"The most important development, I believe, of the twenty-first century will be the rise of Asia. China has already trebled its share of world GDP over the past two decades and India has

doubled it. Both these giant economies of Asia are bound to gain a considerable part of their share of world GDP that they had lost during the two centuries of European colonialism."[5]
- In 2011, the Asian Development Bank projected, under an "Asian Century" scenario, that Asia could account for over half the world economy by 2050, and an additional 3 billion Asians could enjoy living standards similar to those in Europe today.[6]

## From Asian Century Hype to Donald J. Trump

As with most bubbles of hype, things have since come back down to earth, and the mood has fundamentally changed. The US economy has rebounded and become the strongest point of a weak global economy. China is struggling under the weight of its massive debt, large capital outflows, rapidly aging population and other challenges. And many other Asian countries have lost their economic mojo, in no small part due to the slowdown of world trade and concerns about "deglobalization". In other words, the likelihood that the twenty-first century might belong to Asia has greatly diminished.

Despite the return to economic growth, full employment and financial stability under the Obama presidency, a wave of popular discontent saw the election of Donald Trump to the US presidency, rather than Hillary Clinton, Obama's anointed successor. While there were many factors behind Trump's success, his anti-Asia and especially anti-China rhetoric was a key element of his "Make America Great Again" mantra.

Indeed, during the election campaign and before his inauguration, Donald Trump had much to say about Asia. He accused China of raping the US. He threatened to label China a currency manipulator, to levy an import tariff of 45% on American imports from China, to implement a "border-adjustment tax" on all imports and to penalize companies that locate manufacturing investments in China rather than the US. He called the Trans-Pacific Partnership (TPP) a "disaster" and a "rape" of the American people.

Trump criticized China for its island-building program and militarization in the South China Sea, and for not helping control North Korea. He argued that "the concept of global warming was created by and for the Chinese in order to make U.S. manufacturing non-competitive." He threatened to withdraw the US from the Paris Climate Change Agreement, which was forged through US–China leadership. Trump also threatened to make Japan and Korea pay more for the US military troops and assets that are defending them and suggested that they could acquire nuclear weapons. Trump also questioned the "One-China Policy" and spoke by telephone with Taiwan President Tsai Ing-wen.

## Trump Administration Moves into Action

The Trump administration moved quickly into action on the Asian front. To the dismay of the US business community, Trump withdrew the US from the TPP. This was after all a trade agreement designed by US business, for the benefit of US business, pushed onto allies and partners, and then rejected by a businessman president. Above all, the TPP was a manifestation of US leadership to establish modern rules of the game for trade and investment in the Asia Pacific. China was not a signatory, as it could never have signed up for the agreement's conditions for state-owned enterprises, intellectual property and labor rights. (Under Japanese leadership, the remaining 11 TPP signatories are discussing the possibility of pursuing with the TPP without the US.)

Trump's rhetoric on trade policy has been evolving and softening from the defiant protectionist messages during the election campaign and in his inaugural speech. Trump is now emphasizing his support for both free and fair trade. According to the president's 2017 Trade Policy Agenda,[7] America has not benefited from its trade deals over the past couple of decades due to the lack of reciprocity in trading relations. Trump would now like US trade policy to focus on bilateral, rather than multilateral, deals, to secure better market access. He plainly has China, Japan and Korea in his sights.

While the US Treasury has backed off from Trump's claims of Chinese currency manipulation, it has established a "Monitoring List" of major trading partners that merit close attention to their currency practices, which includes four Asian economies, namely China, Japan, Korea and Taiwan.[8] Despite some softening in Trump's trade rhetoric, there remains a strongly protectionist undercurrent, as Trump's overriding trade policy goals are reducing the US' bilateral trade deficits (notably with China, Japan and Korea) and bringing manufacturing jobs back to America. Trump has also threatened to disregard WTO dispute settlement rulings. While Trump is promising to shake up trade relations with Asia, China is actively seeking to foster trade within Eurasia through its Belt and Road Initiative.

Trump had a successful first summit with Chinese President Xi Jinping in April 2017 and seemed to have enlisted his support to help control North Korea. However, it only took a couple of months for Trump to realize that China is reluctant to seriously tackle North Korea for fear of destabilizing the regime. The Xi–Trump honeymoon was then over, as quickly as it started, when the Trump administration announced sanctions on Chinese entities for their dealings with North Korea, also announced actions against China's alleged dumping of steel exports, gave a green light for a $1 billion arms sale to Taiwan and sailed a US destroyer through the Chinese-occupied South China Sea. And Trump's launching in August 2017 of an investigation into China's alleged theft of US intellectual property has deeply troubled the Chinese government and raised the specter of a possible trade war between China and the US.

To the great disappointment of China and the rest of the international community, President Trump has also withdrawn the US from the Paris Climate Change Agreement and rolled back Obama-era clean energy regulations. China and the European Union are now positioning themselves as global leaders in the fight against climate change, despite China's appalling domestic environment and the bad environmental performance of Chinese investors in Africa and Latin America.

Trump officials reaffirmed the US commitment to its alliances with Japan and Korea, while Trump himself indicated his support for the "One-China Policy" in a telephone conversation with Chinese President Xi Jinping. This is seen to have been a big back down for Trump, as Xi reportedly refused to talk with him until Trump honored the One-China Policy.

It also seems that Donald Trump's administration is planning to defy Winston Churchill's advice that "to jaw-jaw is always better than to war-war". His 2017 budget proposal involves increasing funding to the US military by 9%, while cutting the State Department's diplomacy and foreign aid by a combined 28%, and also the Environment Protection Agency by 31%. "There is no question that this is a hard-power budget; it is not a soft-power budget," said Mick Mulvaney, the director of the Office of Management and Budget. While the US Congress is seeking to restore funding for these agencies, Trump's budget proposals certainly set the tone for his administration's approach to international relations.

Trump's hard-power approach to international relations was soon evident in its approach to North Korea. Administration leaders were quick to dismiss the Obama administration's "strategic patience" approach and announce that all options, including military options, were now on the table. Various administration comments have gyrated between advocating military intervention and regime change, and dialogue and diplomacy. It is hardly surprising that the paranoid North Korean regime, which is convinced that the US wants to remove it, should accelerate its missile and nuclear weapon development. As Trump's foreign policy becomes mired in a series of mixed messages, and the administration becomes increasingly chaotic in Washington, China appears a much steadier hand on the international stage.

Overall, Asia is now faced with a likely deterioration in key factors that have driven its development—an open US market, a relatively benign security environment and a stable global economic system. It is not surprising that the US credibility and standing in the region are now taking a beating. For example, in an interview before the US elections, Singapore's Prime Minister Lee Hsien Loong said that a failure to ratify the TPP "would be a very big setback for America." Former *Washington Post* reporter, Paul Blustein, has remarked that "this administration has no respect for international institutions."[9] And Australia's former foreign minister Gareth Evans has said that Donald Trump is "manifestly the most ill-informed, under-prepared, ethically challenged and psychologically ill-equipped president in US history" and that Australia should reduce its dependence on the US alliance and accept China as a legitimate "global rule maker".

This sea change across the Pacific is colliding with a raft of major challenges, as virtually all Asian countries have moved into middle-income status. The evidence shows that graduation from low-income to middle-income status can be relatively easy. By getting just a few things right, countries can achieve rapid economic growth, as even Bangladesh has shown. But transitioning through the middle-income group and graduating to high-income status requires a vastly more sophisticated set of policies and dealing with a complex range of challenges, notably the seven highlighted in this book. Countries can fall into a "middle-income trap", meaning that they are unlikely to graduate from middle-income to high-income status, unless they tackle such challenges.

The arrival of "Trumpism" only highlights the need for a dispassionate and realistic assessment of where we are in terms of realizing an Asian Century and what are the main challenges facing Asian economies if they are to realize their immense potential. This is the mission of this book. In the first section, we take stock of Asia's economic and social development.

In the following section, we analyze seven challenges for an Asian Century, before speculating about what's next for the Asian Century.

## Taking Stock of Asia's Economic and Social Development

Most Asian countries have achieved stunning economic growth over the past half century or more, starting with Japan, followed by the four Asian tigers of Hong Kong, Korea, Singapore and Taiwan, and then the Southeast Asian economies of Indonesia, Malaysia and Thailand, and China, India and Vietnam. But despite the hype of Asia's economic miracle, the harsh reality of our assessment in Chap. 1 is that Asia is suffering from stunted economic development. No major Asian economy has caught up with global leaders like the US and Germany in terms of GDP per capita and living standards, and there is little likelihood of such catch-up occurring over the foreseeable future. The city-states of Hong Kong and Singapore stand out for having the highest GDP per capita in Asia. But when they are compared with cities like London, New York or Zurich, their performance is much less remarkable.

What is the cause of Asia's stunted development? What is holding it back? While Asia's dynamic economies are a diverse bunch, they are all similar in the sense that, apart from Hong Kong and Singapore, none of them could be considered open market economies. The heavy hands of government and business elites played an important role in their economic development, but all too often they are now the main factor holding them back today. There are many other more specific challenges facing Asia, seven of which are examined in Chaps. 4, 5, 6, 7, 8, 9 and 10.

Size does matter, however. And countries like China, India and Indonesia, thanks in large part to their enormous populations, have some of the world's biggest economies. Today, China has the world's biggest economy in purchasing power parity terms, ahead of the second-placed US and third-placed India. Japan is the fourth placed, while Indonesia is eighth, just ahead of the UK and France. China, India and Indonesia have been able to transform economic weight into economic, political and military power, even though their GDP per capita, and their levels of economic, business and technological sophistication are modest (China's GDP per capita is only one quarter of that of the US). Without further economic, social and political development, these countries will remain fragile superpowers. It is no coincidence that China's increasing repression at home, and aggressive attitude toward its neighbors, has come at a time of fragility in its domestic economy.

The importance of size among Asian economies will be highlighted during the second half of this century, when India's total GDP could overtake China's. Factors driving this transition will be population, with India's projected to be some 50% higher than China's by 2100, and economic growth, if India can maintain its edge on China thanks to more ambitious reforms. Needless to say, such a transition could have great geopolitical implications in Asia.

The hype about Asia's dramatic economic rise has only been matched by similar hype about the emergence of Asia's middle class. And while it is true that Asian lives have improved immeasurably in tandem with economic development, only a small share of Asian citizens could be described as middle class, and the middle class is receding in Japan and Korea along with rising inequality and poverty. Today, half of Asia's population is stranded between poverty and the middle class, living in a zone of vulnerability and precarity, based on their income and consumption possibilities. And there are factors other than raw money which are also holding Asians back from joining the middle class, as we examine in Chap. 2: the vulnerability and precarity of informal/non-regular employment; deprivations like the lack of clean drinking water, inadequate health facilities and sanitation (i.e., clean, safe and hygienic toilets); the impact of Asia's all-too-frequent natural disasters; poor access to education and the Internet; and above all, Asia's appalling human rights.

The realization of a middle-class Asia would be a commendable achievement. But while economic growth may have been the most important driver of better Asian lives, the future will require a more active contribution of government, which has not been very effective in providing their citizens with the basic social services, rights and freedoms. And given the flawed politics of most Asian countries, civil society and trade unions will need to become much more assertive to ensure that governments are working for all citizens, not just entrenched elites.

## SEVEN CHALLENGES FOR AN ASIAN CENTURY

Asia faces an enormous array of challenges in its quest to catch up to world leaders in terms of GDP per capita, and economic, business and technological sophistication, and in creating true middle-class societies for its citizens. In Chaps. 4, 5, 6, 7, 8, 9 and 10, we examine seven of these challenges.

Global value chains (GVCs) have provided Asia's emerging economies with a fast track to development, as we discuss in Chap. 4. Perhaps the most well-known GVC is that of Apple's iPhone which is designed, marketed and branded in California, uses high-tech components from Japan, Korea, Taiwan and elsewhere, and is assembled in China by Foxconn, Taiwanese company. But despite the immense benefits of participating in GVCs, most Asian countries are still capturing very little value from GVCs. Much greater efforts are required to get better value by opening markets, and strengthening human capital, and technological and innovative capacities. President Trump's decision to withdraw the US from the TPP, his rejection of multilateral trade and investment deals, and his protectionism will undermine the further development of Asia's GVCs. There is no sign that any Chinese efforts, such as through the Regional Comprehensive Economic Partnership, would be an effective replacement for the TPP. Labor rights abuses have also been frequent in many GVCs. Asian governments need to more actively promote socially responsible GVCs in order to foster decent middle-class societies.

The movement of Asians from the countryside to towns and cities (urbanization), and from low-productivity jobs in the rural sector to higher-productivity jobs in factories for GVCs and the urban service sector, has also been a key driver of Asia's economic development, as we examine in Chap. 5. But Asia's model of urbanization is flawed in many respects. In China, migrants from rural areas are denied access to social services. In all emerging Asian economies, too many people leave rural poverty only to live in urban slums with poor infrastructure, while most of Asia's cities are environmental disasters. President Trump's withdrawal of the US from the Paris Climate Change Agreement will only exacerbate the vulnerability of Asian cities to the impact of global warming. In the case of Asia's advanced countries, very few cities offer an "ecosystem" which fosters innovation-driven development. Asian governments face a raft of challenges to make the most of urbanization's immense potential.

Economies and societies will realize their full potential only when all citizens are given a chance to participate. But discrimination, prejudice and persecution are rife in Asia, as our review shows in Chap. 6 which highlights the cases of: the LGBT community; Japanese women; South Asian women who suffer gendercide, forced child marriages and honor killing; Asia's indigenous peoples like West Papuans, Tibetans and China's Uighurs;

Sri Lanka's Tamil community; and India's lower castes. President Trump's proposed slashing of the budgets of the State Department and USAID will likely affect the US leadership in the promotion of the rights of the LGBT community, women and other minority rights in Asia and elsewhere.

Most Asian countries face intractable demographic dilemmas, as we analyze in Chap. 7. In much of East Asia, fertility has plummeted below replacement rates, populations are aging, workforces declining, and in Japan the population has begun falling. And yet governments are slow to react. At the same time, in South Asia, Indonesia and the Philippines, a youth bulge is bursting into the workforce, but much of this youth is not well educated and there are not enough jobs on offer. A potential demographic dividend could easily morph into an explosion of social frustration. Connecting these two demographic realities is the potential for mutually beneficial migration, and yet ethnocentric Asia is barely open to migration. Asia's skilled emigrants go to Australia, Canada, New Zealand and the US, while many of Asia's lower skilled migrants go off to the Middle East to suffer. Countries like China, India and the Philippines which rely heavily on migrants' remittances could suffer from President Trump's tightening of migration policies. These three countries account for almost all of America's 1.5 million illegal migrants coming from Asia, and 13% of all illegal migrants. And India has been the main beneficiary of the US H1-B temporary visa program.

Asia is crying out for democracy and better governance to improve the foundations for stronger economies and decent middle-class societies. And yet, according to some measures, there would not be even one mature democracy in Asia, as we explore in Chap. 8. Contrary to the hopes of political scientists, economic development has fostered too few democracies in Asia. Asia's political landscape is deeply flawed with: oligarchic democracies in Japan and Korea; pro-business soft dictatorships in Hong Kong, Malaysia and Singapore; Chinese client states in Cambodia and Laos; weak and fragile democracies in India, Indonesia, the Philippines, Mongolia, Sri Lanka, Bangladesh and Nepal; military-dominated governments in Thailand, Pakistan and Myanmar; and staunchly authoritarian states in China, North Korea and Vietnam. Asia will never have decent middle-class societies and innovative economies while repression, propaganda, censorship and human rights abuses occur in too many of its countries. And President Trump is not helping as he cozies up to some of Asia's authoritarian leaders, and has made it clear that promotion of democracy and human rights is not a priority of his administration.

One of the many consequences of these flawed politics is that, as Asia has moved toward the center of the global economy, it has also moved to the center of the global criminal economy, as we examine in Chap. 9. Asia is a major player in many aspects of economic crime like counterfeiting and piracy, illegal drug production and trafficking, environmental crimes, human trafficking and smuggling, corruption and money laundering, and cybercrime. And while flawed politics is one of the causes, this criminality is eating away at the integrity of the state, as state actors are very often criminals themselves or are colluding with criminals.

While many factors have underpinned Asia's renaissance over the past half century or more, the relative peace that the region has enjoyed has been perhaps the most important. And cooperation between Asian countries has also made a positive contribution, especially through the Association of Southeast Nations (ASEAN), which has become a fulcrum for broader Asian cooperation. Looking ahead, as we analyze in Chap. 10, the ability of Asia to continue to live together in peace and harmony will perhaps be the most important determinant of a successful Asian Century.

But today, the relative stability of post-war Asia, led by the US, is being shaken by the rise of China, as China is now engaged in a bitter power struggle with the US and its Asian allies for the political leadership of Asia. There is much debate about whether this will lead to military conflict between China and the US. In any event, the US seems to be losing its hold over Asia, something which will likely accelerate under the Trump administration. This means that it will become ever more necessary for Asian countries to cooperate better together. But this will be a great challenge in light of the tensions involving China, North Korea, Japan, Taiwan, Hong Kong, South Korea and India.

## What Next for the Asian Century?

The prospects for Asia overcoming stunted economic and social development, and realizing an Asian Century with advanced economies and middle-class societies, depend on how Asia responds to the seven challenges identified in this book. Unfortunately, there is too little evidence of Asia's major countries seizing the moment. Indeed, the cases of Japan, and more recently Korea and China, are salutary, where governments have avoided and postponed difficult reforms.

Trump's America will also shape the contours of a possible Asian Century. As argued, we will likely see a deterioration in key factors that have driven Asia development—an open US market, a relatively benign security environment and a stable global economic system. This is a tragedy for Asia, as China, the US' competitor, is not a promoter of open markets, good governance and the international rule of law.

Many observers speculate that Trump will not survive a year or two or beyond his first term. This is far from certain. His rise to the presidency was equally improbable. Even post-Trump, we should not assume a return to the US as a promoter of open markets and globalization, and a friend of democratic partners and the liberal international system. America has been struck by a wave of populism, and in particular nationalism (make America great again), nativism (secure our borders) and protectionism (protect American workers),[10] which is unlikely to go away anytime soon.

But if Asia continues to muddle through, in some decades time, the region could account for over half the world economy, far outstripping the West in total economic size. In these circumstances, no major Asian economy would have approached world leaders like the US and Germany in terms of GDP per capita, or economic, business and technological sophistication. Moreover, Asia could remain a democratic desert, with not one full democracy, and with continuing widespread human rights abuses and restrictions on personal freedoms. In other words, Asia would have the world's greatest economic weight, and be a leading economic and political power, but would remain a pygmy in terms of economic, social and political development. Asia's main power comes from its enormous population, currently about 55% of the world's total, compared with only 18% for the West.

Needless to say, the incongruities of such a scenario could generate even greater geopolitical tensions than we see today.

These incongruities would test the capacity of the international community to cooperate on issues like open trade and investment, democracy and human rights, the global environment, protection of intellectual property rights, economic crime, international rule of law, law of the sea and natural disasters. Why? Because forging consensus and working together requires shared interest and values, and a culture of cooperation and trust.

Beyond these incongruities, there are endless possibilities of economic, social, political and military crises in Asia—mostly due to the likely failure to deal with our seven challenges for an Asian Century.

Economic crisis is stalking several Asian countries, most notably Japan and China with their massive debt problems. And anti-globalization populism could break one of the most important drivers of Asia's rapid development, namely open trade and investment. Social crisis could be on the cards for India, Indonesia and the Philippines with their bulging youth populations, if they are unable to find decent jobs. Multi-ethnic countries like India and Indonesia could easily descend into violence as groups suffering from discrimination, prejudice and persecution mobilize themselves against dominant elites. And as natural disasters and environmental problems increasingly hit Asia's overcrowded and badly planned cities, social crises will also accelerate.

Continued authoritarian politics and social repression in China, North Korea and Vietnam could provoke political crises as citizens demand cleaner government and democratic government. Social unrest is already rampant in China, and North Korea has thousands of regime opponents locked away in secret gulags. The corruption crisis that engulfed the South Korean President Park Geun-hye and Samsung shows how fragile even Asia's most advanced countries can be.

The future of peace in Asia could be threatened by the great power struggle between China and the US. The US and China are unlikely to engage in a traditional military conflict, although the naval collisions involving the US Navy in 2017 show how easily accidents can occur, and possibly spiral out of control. They seem destined to remain "frenemies", that is both friends and rivals, with conflicts taking place in the areas of trade, intellectual property, international rule of law and cyber, rather than on the battlefield.

As China progressively displaces the US as Asia's hegemon, it will become ever more necessary for Asian countries to cooperate better together. In a region which is bristling with tensions involving China, North Korea, South Korea, Japan, Taiwan, Hong Kong, the South China Sea, ASEAN and India, this will be a great challenge. And while China's rise has been shaking Asia, the prospect of India's economy overtaking China's in the second half of the twenty-first century will require further adjustments by all. Any conflicts between Asian countries could do much to derail the prospects for an Asian Century. And the great risk for the US is being dragged into these conflicts between Asian countries, more than a straight head-on conflict with China.

Today, Asia is sitting on a knife edge. The potential of the region to generate good and happy lives for its citizens is enormous. But the requirements of success and the risks of failure are equally enormous. We cannot be sure of "what's next for the Asian Century". Indeed, anything could happen, and complacency of Asia's elites could be the Asian Century's greatest enemy.

## Notes

1. Schibotto, Emanuele, and Gabriele Giovannini (2015). Singapore's Role in the Asian Century—interview with Kishore Mahbubani. Asian Century Institute, 12 February 2015.
2. Obama, Barack (2011). Remarks by President Obama to the Australian Parliament, 17 November 2011.
3. Gillard, Julia (2012). Prime Minister's Speech at the launch of the White Paper on Australia in the Asian Century. Lowy Institute, 28 October 2012.
4. Xi, Jinping (2014). Towards an Asian Century of Prosperity. The Hindu, 17 September 2014.
5. Manmohan Singh, "Remarks at the LSE Asia Forum", (New Delhi, 7 December 2006).
6. Asian Development Bank (2011). Asia 2050: Realising the Asian Century.
7. The Office of the United States Trade Representative. President Trump's 2017 Trade Policy Agenda.
8. US Treasury, Treasury Releases Report on Foreign Exchange Policies of Major Trading Partners of the United States, 14 April 2017.
9. Lowy Institute. Conference on "Two decades after the Asian Financial Crisis: Have the world's financial firefighters learned anything?" Paul Blustein, former Washington Post reporter and Senior Fellow at the Centre for International Governance Innovation, 4 July 2017.
10. McGann, James G. 2016 Global Go to Think Tank Index Report.

**Open Access** This chapter is licensed under the terms of the Creative Commons Attribution 4.0 International License (http://creativecommons.org/licenses/by/4.0/), which permits use, sharing, adaptation, distribution, and reproduction in any medium or format, as long as you give appropriate credit to the original author(s) and the source, provide a link to the Creative Commons license and indicate if changes were made.

The images or other third party material in this chapter are included in the chapter's Creative Commons license, unless indicated otherwise in a credit line to the material. If material is not included in the chapter's Creative Commons license and your intended use is not permitted by statutory regulation or exceeds the permitted use, you will need to obtain permission directly from the copyright holder.

PART I

# Taking Stock of Asia's Economic and Social Development

CHAPTER 2

# Asia's Stunted Economic Development

"Yes, China is slowing down, but compared to the West, its GDP growth is enviable," once said Jon Copestake of the Economist Intelligence Unit.[1] This is a familiar refrain in media reports, international conferences and business discussions.

But all economies which are behind world leaders (like the US and Germany) have great potential for rapid, catch up growth. And the further they are behind, the faster they can grow, just by absorbing knowledge and technology from world leaders. This is the "benefit of backwardness".

It is thus not surprising that China should still be growing so quickly. Its GDP per capita is still only one-quarter of that of the US. It would be much more surprising if China were not growing so quickly. The real disappointment is that so many other countries cannot get their act together to achieve fast, catch up growth.

The main question facing China today is whether it can stay the course in catching up to world leaders, because other Asian economies like Japan, Korea and Taiwan have not managed to do so.

Indeed, the post-war waves of high-growth Asian economies, beginning with Japan, have been arrested. Asia's major economies now face the prospect of permanently stunted development. There is now very little prospect of full catch up to the world's leading economies in terms of GDP per capita, and economic, business and technological sophistication.

© The Author(s) 2018
J. West, *Asian Century... on a Knife-edge*,
https://doi.org/10.1007/978-981-10-7182-9_2

Japan's very rapid recovery from the ashes of World War 2 took the world by surprise. Many economists were then pessimistic about the prospects for Asia, which suffered greatly from the War. The continent had few natural resources and an enormous population compared with Africa and South America. But as Japan's growth continued, many then believed that Japan would overtake the US, in much the same way that the US overtook the UK in the nineteenth century.

Japan's economic dynamism inspired the four Asian Newly Industrializing Economies—Hong Kong, Korea, Singapore and Taiwan—on a similar path of rapid development. This gave rise to talk of an "Asian miracle" by the World Bank[2] and others, and the group was labeled the Asian tigers.

Much ink has been spilt in analyzing the rise of these Asian economies. The main factors were their export-orientation, good education, macroeconomic stability and strong government leadership. But as Ian Buchanan has argued,[3] geopolitics also played an important role in the context of the Cold War, as the US offered official assistance and open markets to its friends in Asia. And all of these successful economies were motivated to become strong in the face of their threatening neighborhoods, as they faced Mao's China, North Korea and the USSR.

But the shortcomings of the Japanese model became all-too-apparent following a financial crisis in the early 1990s. Japan (and Korea and Taiwan) has since failed to both reform its economy and deal with demographic decline. The prospect of these economies catching up to world leaders now seems remote.

Singapore and Hong Kong are rare birds in Asia, in that they have caught up to the US and Germany, and in Singapore's case well overtaken them. There are some very simple reasons. Both are Asia's only two genuine open market economies, with large immigrant populations, in contrast to Japan, Korea and Taiwan. They are also financial centers and tax havens, which allow Asia's super rich to hide their (often ill-gotten) wealth from the taxman. When these city economies are compared with other financial centers like London, New York or Switzerland's Zurich, their success seems much less surprising.

The next group of Asian economies to take off in the region's "flying geese" pattern[4] of development included Malaysia, Thailand and Indonesia. Their rapid development was mainly driven by a wave of investment from Asia's advanced countries, which offshored lower-value-added activities as they climbed the development ladder. But the education and technological capacities of these countries are relatively weak, and their economic catch up to date remains modest. These countries would seem to be caught in a "middle-income trap", meaning that they are unlikely to graduate from middle-income to high-income status.

China stunned the world with three decades of 10% growth rates, following its opening up, which began in 1978 (more recently, Vietnam launched a similar opening to the world economy). Today, the future of the Chinese economy is problematic, as the government seems almost paralyzed by the social and political risks of undertaking reform. China may well have the world's biggest economy, but it remains a relatively poor country, with an enormous population. It also faces a grave risk of getting stuck in a middle-income trap.

India is the other Asian giant, with an enormous population. It began its reform in the early 1990s and has since achieved good economic growth. While there is a lot of positive momentum in the Indian system, it also faces immense challenges.

## What Is the Outlook for Asia's Catch Up Economies?

All things considered, most Asian economies have been losing some of their economic mojo, as the Asian Development Bank has argued.[5] Emerging Asia's "potential economic growth rate" has fallen by almost 2 percentage points in less than a decade. The region can now only grow by about 6½%, not the 8½% of yesteryear. And looking into the future, the downward slide will only continue. How could this happen?

You only have to look back to the transitory nature of some of the factors driving emerging Asia's high-growth period to glean some insights. As populations are aging in East Asia, there will be less energetic, youthful populations to drive growth. Now that many countries are already highly urbanized, there will be less new movements of people from the country to the city. Over time, the benefits of backwardness also fade as countries have copied the easy lessons from world leaders. The slowdown in China, the most important trading partner for virtually all other Asian economies, is also dragging down the economic growth potential of everyone. And the arrival of Donald Trump at the leadership of the US will likely result in a deterioration of some of the key factors that have driven Asia's development—an open US market, a relatively benign security environment and a stable global economic system.

How to revive Asia's growth potential? There are many obvious suggestions to make like investing in human capital, technology and infrastructure; providing more opportunity to all Asians; responding effectively to Asia's poor demographics; and fully opening economies to domestic and international competition.

But digging behind the mechanical story of economic growth is a deeper story of institutions and politics. What is required for successful economic development are "inclusive economic institutions", as argued by Daron Acemoglu and James A. Robinson. Such institutions "allow and encourage participation by the great mass of people in economic activities that make best use of their talents and skills and that enable individuals to make the choices they wish". They "require secure property rights and economic opportunities not just for the elite, but for a broad cross-section of society".[6] And behind inclusive economic institutions are inclusive political institutions.

The enemy of economic development is "extractive political institutions" which "concentrate power in the hands of a narrow elite and place few constraints on the exercise of this power". This elite then usually structures economic institutions in order to extract resources from the rest of society.

The analysis of Acemoglu and Robinson provides many insights into Asia's changing political economy. In the early post-war period, Asia's success stories (Japan, Hong Kong, Korea, Singapore and Taiwan) all had a great incentive to build strong economies through inclusive economic institutions. They faced threatening neighborhoods surrounded by communist regimes in China, North Korea and the USSR, and instability in Southeast Asia. They were also dependent on imports to supply their energy and other natural resources—this meant that export-oriented growth was necessary to finance imports.

In more recent decades, there has been a waning of these geopolitical threat factors. And many of the winners of economic development—big business, state-owned enterprises (SOEs) and banks—have been able to exert a strong influence over Asia's politics to keep the cards stacked in their favor.

The classic example is that of Japan where corporate and government elites, and gerrymandering of politics in rural areas, have kept the economy closed from international competition. This is a key factor behind Japan's weak productivity and failure to fully catch up to the US. Regrettably, some 70 years after Japan began its post-war recovery, democracy and inclusive politics still have very shallow roots. New players have great difficulty breaking through.

Similarly, Korea's enormous conglomerates ("chaebol") like Samsung and LG have a stranglehold over the nation's economy and politics, and are now holding the economy back. In China, Communist Party elites fear the creative destruction that would result from deep reform of China's grossly inefficient SOE and banking sectors. At this stage, there is little sign of reforms to ensure that market will play a "decisive" role in allocating resources, as promised in the Third Plenum in 2013.

In short, the permanence of inclusive economic institutions cannot be taken for granted. As Acemoglu and Robinson argue, "fear of creative destruction is often at the root of the opposition to inclusive economic and political institutions." One of the most visible signs of this problem is the income gap between the rich and the poor, which continues to widen in Asia.[7]

In conclusion, a successful Asian century will require civil society, trade unions and youth becoming much more assertive to ensure that governments are working for all citizens, not just entrenched elites. In some cases, this may require democratization and even political revolutions. In other cases, enlightened elites may respond positively to fears for their political survival. Whatever the case, without important political change, Asia will not realize its full economic and human potential, and its economic development will remain stunted.

## SIZE MATTERS, BUT NOT 100%

Despite Asia's stunted economic development, it has enormous economic size. With 55% of the world's population, Asia's rapid economic growth has enabled it to grow its share of the world economy from 13% in 1960 to 31% in 2015 (the West, represented by the OECD member countries, accounts for only 18% of the world's population, and has seen its share of world GDP decline commensurately). And there are a plethora of projections from organizations like the Asian Development Bank, the OECD and PWC which predict that in the coming decades, Asia will account for more than half of the world economy.[8]

China is already the world's biggest economy in purchasing power parity terms, even though on a per capita basis America's GDP is still four times higher than China's. India has the world's third biggest economy, but America's GDP per capita is nine times higher than India's. One recent set of projections by PWC shows that by 2050, China's total GDP could be 70% higher than America's, while India's could be 30% higher. At the same time America's GDP per capita could still be double that of China and triple that of India.

This shift in economic weight from the West to Asia has led many analysts to argue that there has also been a shift in economic and political power, even if Asia lags behind in terms of productivity and living standards, and economic, business and technological sophistication. It is true that their enormous economic size gives countries like China, India and Indonesia "market power" which attracts Western and other businessmen. China has large pools of investible funds that can be used for both economic and political purposes like establishing the Asian Infrastructure Investment Bank, and the Belt and Road Initiative. Large economic resources can also finance militaries which can project power and intimidate smaller neighbors, as reflected in the arms race presently underway in Asia. China, India, Japan and Korea all figure among the world's top ten for military expenditure.[9]

But equating economic weight with economic and political power is also too simplistic. Many Asian elites still prefer to send their children to Western universities, to migrate to Western countries in search of freedom and clean air, to buy Western companies because of their technological superiority and to invest in Western markets because of their better governance. A diminishing West still has great power, especially soft power, meaning the attractiveness of its values and culture. Without further economic, social and political development, Asia's largest economies will remain partial and fragile superpowers. It is no coincidence that China's increasing repression at home, and aggressive attitude toward its neighbors, has come at a time of fragility in its domestic economy.

An illustrative comparison of relative power in Asia is that of Indonesia and Singapore. Indonesia's total GDP is some six times bigger than Singapore's, even though on a per capita basis Singapore's GDP is some eight times bigger than Indonesia's. But the relative power of Singapore should not be underestimated. Indeed, it is not underestimated by Indonesian elites themselves who prefer to invest their savings in Singapore's vastly superior financial system, who send their children to study in Singapore's excellent schools and universities and who run to Singapore's hospitals whenever they are sick. Poorer Indonesian citizens are very happy to migrate to Singapore in search of work. And Singapore is strategically located at a vital access point for maritime trade routes connecting East Asia with South Asia, the Middle East, Europe and Africa.

Perhaps the greatest limit on Asia's power comes from the poor relations between very many Asian countries—for example, China–Japan, Japan–South Korea, Vietnam–China, India–Pakistan, India–China, and North Korea and very many countries. Asian countries may together account for half of the world economy in a few decades time, but they are unable to join forces in a way that they can become a dominant force. The very low trust among Asian countries means that they have difficulty cooperating together to such a point that it is questionable whether Asia even exists. Asia's power equation will also be tested over the course of the twenty-first century, with the rise of India relative to China. India's population will overtake China's in 2022, and could be some 50% higher by 2100. And if current trends continue, India's total GDP could be bigger than China's before century's end.

After this brief diversion into what economic size means for power, in the following six sections, we will examine in greater detail the cases of Japan, Korea, China, India, Indonesia and Vietnam, Asia's most successful big economies.

## JAPAN ALMOST MADE IT!

Japan was Asia's original miracle economy. It rose dramatically from the ashes of military defeat in 1945. In the 1950s and 1960s, Japan's annual economic growth rate was around 10%, the same as China in the first three decades of its reform period. In the 1970s and 1980s, Japan's annual growth rate slipped down to the still respectable 4%.

Already in 1964, less than two decades after the war, Tokyo hosted the Olympic Games and showed off to the world its high-speed train from Tokyo to Osaka (the shinkansen). Today, more than half a century later, countries like the US, Canada and Australia can still only dream of having such impressive transportation infrastructure.

Japan's high-growth, catch-up period was engineered by partnership between business, bureaucrats and politicians, the "iron triangle"[10] (the "developmental state"). Infant industries were protected from imports and inward foreign investment, and given preferential access to finance, to give the export-oriented manufacturing sector the breathing space for industrial upgrading.

Japanese companies conquered world markets, especially for motor vehicles and electronics. Companies like Toyota and Sony were the envy of the world, as were Japanese business practices like "kaizen" (continuous improvement), lean manufacturing and just-in-time inventory management. By 1990, Japan's GDP per capita had risen to 80% of the US level.

But in the late 1980s, a real estate and stock market bubble took hold, fueled by easy money policies in response to a rising yen. The bubble was also driven by hubris and irrational exuberance. Many believed that Japan was becoming the leading global power, and that the US was set for decline. Japanese companies went on an international spending spree, as Mitsubishi bought the Rockefeller Center in Manhattan and Sony bought Columbia Pictures. And during the height of the property bubble, Tokyo's imperial palace grounds were believed by some to be worth more than all the real estate in California.

But then the bubble burst, and real estate and stock prices came crashing down again. Many banks, companies and citizens were thus saddled with large debts. The government responded sluggishly, in part due to disbelief. But the iron triangle also sought to protect enterprises and banks from the consequences of their follies. The Japanese economy would stagger through the 1990s, burdened by "zombie" or loss-making enterprises and banks that were kept afloat to ease the pain of the crisis. But in reality they only weakened the economic fundamentals by wasting finance that could have been used by new dynamic startups.

The early 1990s proved to be a major turning point in Japan's history—something which was not fully appreciated at the time, as Japan was preoccupied by the aftermath of its bubble economy. Several tectonic plates underlying Japan were shifting. Strategic, systemic adaptation was required for many reasons.

Japan's developmental state model resulted in lopsided development. While its manufacturing sector was a world leader, Japan's services and agricultural sectors were highly inefficient. Even today, productivity in Japan's services sector is only half that of the manufacturing sector. When it comes to services like finance, education, health and tourism, Singapore and Hong Kong are Asia's leaders.

Japan desperately needed fresh competition from trade and investment liberalization and deregulation to stimulate productivity in these inefficient sectors. But the very success of the iron triangle, and the constellation of interests that coalesced around it, made subsequent reform difficult, as Mark Beeson has argued.[11] This includes corporate–government collusion through the parachuting of retired officials into high-level corporate positions, known as amakudari. And corporate governance characterized by cozy relationships fostered numerous financial scandals, most notably at Olympus and Toshiba.

Another tectonic shift was the offshoring of much of Japan's labor-intensive manufacturing to other Asian countries like China, Thailand, Singapore and Indonesia, in response to the higher value of the yen, and new opportunities in these countries.[12] But while the manufacturing sector was being "hollowed out", Japan remained closed to inward foreign direct investment (FDI), which even today remains at only 4% of GDP, even lower than North Korea's inward investment. This has robbed the economy of lots of opportunities to improve productivity and create decent, high-paying jobs.

Today, Japan is not a closed market for inward FDI, according to the OECD.[13] And the current government has an ambitious target for doubling FDI.[14] But there are very many "social practice" hurdles for foreign investors, especially constraints on labor mobility, an insular and consensual business culture which resists mergers and acquisitions, a lack of independent directors on many company boards, and cultural and linguistic barriers.[15]

The corporate landscape of East Asia has also changed radically. Japanese companies were once undisputed leaders in Asia, but they gradually began to struggle in the face of stiff regional competition. For example, Korea's Samsung and Taiwan's contract manufacturer Foxconn have become leaders in mobile technology, while China's Huawei and Xiaomi occupy a large slice of the low end of the market. Fortunately, Japan has developed a niche in high-tech components for many industries like mobile telephony and airplanes.

In the automobile field, Hyundai has become a challenger for Toyota, while the Chinese automobile industry is now the world's largest and is developing rapidly. Strangely, Japan does not seem to be a major player in the rapidly emerging driverless car sector. And Japanese banks are no longer globally powerful. True, Japanese companies like Softbank, Uniqlo, Muji, Nintendo and Rakuten are making their mark. But Japanese companies no longer dominate, as they once did. And this country that once boasted some great entrepreneurs is now one of the weakest performers in the OECD group when it comes to entrepreneurship.

Japan's unfolding demographic drama is perhaps the country's most important shifting tectonic plate. Japan's fertility rate has been below the replacement rate of 2.1 children per woman since 1975. Thus, Japan's long-awaited decline in its workforce began in 1995, while its population began its inevitable decline around 2010. This has a direct hit on the potential GDP growth rate. Indeed, the OECD reports that the economy is now only capable of growing at half a percent a year over the medium term.[16] Needless to say, Japan's aging population is also giving a big hit to the government's budget deficit. And while Japan's demographic drama has been looming for decades, the government's response in terms of facilitating greater economic participation by women and admitting more migrants has been woefully inadequate. To this day, Japan remains sadly xenophobic and sexist, notwithstanding Prime Minister Abe's impressive chanting of "womenomics".

Japan's education system also desperately needs reinvention. It was very effective at promoting the literacy and numeracy of its population, things that were certainly very important when Japan was catching up to world leaders. But Japan's education system still emphasizes rote-learning, memorization and passing tests, rather than critical thinking and creativity—at a time when Japan needs to become more innovation-driven.

And while globalization has been the dominant feature of the past few decades, the Japanese are very poor at the world's global language, English. According to one survey, Japan's English-language proficiency is only "average", and behind Asian neighbors like Singapore, Malaysia, India, Korea and Vietnam, and only on par with Taiwan and Indonesia.[17] This has many consequences from making life difficult for visiting tourists to isolating Japanese scholars from global networks and preventing Japan's multinational companies from becoming globally integrated enterprises.[18]

Japanese Nobel Prize winning scientist Susumu Tonegawa[19] had some insightful comments on Japan's education: "Having spent a half century abroad since I went to the United States to study, I now regard Japan as a society rather dictated by rules. Within a fixed framework, the Japanese are able to produce things with extreme precision." In making a comparison with the US, Tonegawa argues that "A climate that respects individualistic thinking—thinking not bound by conventional wisdom—will produce revolutionary discoveries that shatter the framework. Unlike the Japanese, Americans put their own ideas first, and what others think of them is secondary. It is essential to have education that respects individual abilities and preferences."

These tectonic shifts have haunted Japan for over two and a half decades. Economic growth has been very sluggish, averaging only about

1% a year. Reforms to open the economy to more domestic and international competition have been proposed and discussed, but their implementation has never been serious. Japan's economy and society have been dragged down as a consequence.

Japan's GDP per capita, at $41,470 in 2016, has fallen back to only 72% of that of the US. Further, the country's once egalitarian society is now fracturing, as the share of people living in relative poverty has leapt from 12% in 1985 to 16% in 2012, putting it just behind the US, with the second highest poverty of the advanced OECD countries, while income inequality is above the OECD average.[20] When it comes to child poverty, Japan now has a higher rate than the US, and 50% of single parent households live in poverty. At the same time, corporate profits are riding high at record levels.

Many visitors to Japan are shocked to hear of stories of Japanese poverty, because you do not see any beggars and street crime is virtually non-existent. But much poverty is hidden, as it can be a subject of public shame and discrimination. And many urban homeless live in tents in public parks or on river banks.

Japan's public debt has reached world record levels at 220% of GDP, as government spending has been continuously used to keep the economy afloat. This has kept the government's friends in the construction industry happy, but also led to much wasteful spending and white elephants. Social spending on Japan's rapidly aging population has been the other factor driving debt.

As desperate as the public debt situation might seem, the government has no meaningful plan to bring it under control. Proposals to increase the consumption tax keep being postponed. The OECD has projected that it could well skyrocket to over 600% of GDP by 2060, in the absence of decisive action.[21] But before that date, markets will surely lose confidence in Japan, leading to a sharp increase in interest rates, a surge in capital flight and a crash in the yen. Japan has also suffered from deflation for much of the past two decades. Such falling prices weaken the economy, but it also exacerbates the debt problem, as the value of debt does not change, while the value of incomes and GDP are falling.

In short, Japan is caught in a "stagnation trap". But it is not too late for Japan to get its act together. After all, in recent history it has performed two miracles—one following the Meiji Restoration in the nineteenth century and the other following World War 2. But "Abenomics", the program of economic revitalization of the current government led by Prime

Minister Shinzo Abe, is a case of too little, too late. Its monetary and fiscal stimulus arrows have achieved little. After more than four years of easy money, the goal of lifting inflation to 2% remains out of reach. Japan is now suffering from a "deflationary mindset".

The structural reform "arrow" of Abenomics, the key to improving productivity, is still sitting in the quiver. In the words of the polite and diplomatic IMF, "structural reform remains the lagging element of Abenomics."[22] Its most courageous initiative was to sign up to the Trans Pacific Partnership (TPP), but this has since been shot down by US President Donald Trump. Japan is now leading the charge to keep the TPP alive with its 11 remaining members. But it is unclear if this will happen. And the TPP without the giant US economy would be a much less important deal.

Abe and Trump have since agreed to establish a new framework for economic dialog, which could lead to a bilateral free trade agreement. But despite the chummy relations between Abe and Trump, Japan is also subject of Trump's wrath in light of its large trade surplus with the US. It is now one of four Asian countries to be put on a "Monitoring List" of major trading partners "that merit close attention to their currency practices".

One very bright spot that holds promise for Japan and indeed the international trading system is the 2017 free trade deal between Japan and the European Union which will open up Japan's agricultural sector to European farmers, and improve access to the European market for Japanese motor vehicle manufacturers. But much more bold reform will be necessary to revitalize the Japanese economy.

In conclusion, it is difficult to see anything other than a real open crisis, rather than continually creeping decline, moving this cautious and conservative country into action.

## Korea: The Chaebol Republic

Heather Cho, vice-president of Korea Air, provoked a storm of controversy when she delayed the takeoff of a Korean Air flight in December 2014, over her dissatisfaction with the service of macadamia nuts. This ridiculous incident reminded the whole world that Korea is not a people's republic. It is still a "chaebol republic".

Today, the dominant role of Korea's chaebol (large and sprawling, family-controlled conglomerates) in the nation's politics, economy and society is seriously questioned by many—and not just because of the "nut-gate" incident. But it is still without question that the chaebol played a crucial role in Korea's rags-to-riches development miracle.

The "miracle on the Han River" was perhaps the most unlikely of all the Asian economic miracles.[23] The three-year Korean War, which ended in 1953, killed 2 1/2 million of the combined population of North and South Korea of 30 million. The peninsula's infrastructure of roads, buildings, bridges and so on was almost completely destroyed. And one-third of the population was left homeless.

At the end of the 1950s, Korea's situation still remained bleak. Then, in the space of two decades, the 1960s and 1970s, President Park Chung-hee laid the foundations for the comprehensive transformation of the Korean economy, society and politics through his "guided capitalism" (he was the father of President Park Geun-hye who was impeached in March 2017).

President Park was no believer in free markets or democracy. On the contrary, he was a ruthless dictator who came to power in 1961 following a military coup. He corralled the nation's leading businessmen into his economic development project. They were offered access to cheap finance and foreign technology, protection from imports and foreign investment, export subsidies, tax breaks, cheap labor and other favors, if they would develop industries like fertilizers, cement, chemicals, oil refining and textiles. Anticompetitive behavior like cartels, collusion and price-fixing was also tolerated. And corruption was widespread, as it still is today. Korea ranks 52nd on Transparency International's Corruption Perceptions Index (out of 176 countries), way below Japan's 20th place.[24]

Those who live by the sword all too often die by the sword, and President Park was assassinated in 1979. But his ruthless economic nationalism put the country on an irreversible path to prosperity and democracy, and ultimately membership of the OECD, the "rich man's club", in 1996. Within a year, Korea would be a victim of the 1997 "Asian financial crisis". The chaebol had gone an international borrowing spree, ignoring the risks of short-term, dollar-denominated debt. When international lenders then lost confidence in the Asian-miracle hype of the time, and withdrew their capital, Korea was left in financial crisis.

Korea recovered very quickly. Reforms imposed by the IMF, notably for corporate governance, opening to FDI and deregulation laid the foundation for a return to strong economic growth. But once the crisis passed, the chaebol vested interests regrouped and reasserted their influence over national policymaking.

Electronics giant Samsung has been the star chaebol, and is now ranked the world's 10th most valuable brand by Forbes magazine,[25] on a list headed by its nemesis, Apple. But Samsung is not the only one. Automobile company Hyundai is ranked 68th.

The chaebol completely dominate the Korean economy, with Samsung accounting for one-fifth of Korea's exports, and the 30 biggest chaebol for over four-fifths of exports. The chaebol's penchant for empire-building is symbolized by Samsung's 70 subsidiaries, which cover a vast array of unrelated industries like electronics, insurance, shipbuilding and petrochemicals. But they have been successful in upgrading the Korean economy from a producer of low-end manufactures to high-tech electronics and automobiles.

Overall, Korea was able to defy both history and its resource-poor geography to become the world's 14th largest economy and 7th biggest exporter. Its GDP per capita leapt from $8276 in 1990 to $35,751 in 2016. But it still has a long way to go in its economic catch up, as GDP per capita is only 62% of that of the US. Like Japan, Korea has a lopsided economy, where service sector productivity is less than half that of the manufacturing sector, and small enterprises are much less productive than larger ones.

The OECD estimates that Korea's potential economic growth rate has fallen from over 9% in 1990 to only 3% today, and since 2011 Korea's economy has been trundling along at only 2¾% annually. In other words, Korea faces a raft of challenges to lift its potential economic growth rate, and complete its catch up to world leaders like the US and Germany—and also to prepare the country for the possibility of having to suddenly absorb North Korea.

For one, Korea has the fastest aging population among the advanced OECD countries, as the fertility rate has plummeted from over six children per woman in 1960 to 1.2 today. This will impose an enormous drag on the economy as Korea's workforce started declining in 2016, and overall population decline could set in from 2035. In contrast to Japan, Korea has at least had the wisdom to open up significantly to immigration.

One area where Korea performs even worse than Japan is in its treatment of women.[26] This is indeed a great tragedy, as providing greater opportunity to women could help Korea cope with population aging. Anyone who doubts the ability of Korean women need only look at the Ladies Professional Golf Association rankings which are dominated by Korean lady golfers.[27]

Korea also needs to transform itself from a copycat nation to a creative and innovative economy to climb further up the development ladder. Korea has indeed great potential to become an innovation nation. It leads the world in R&D spending as a share of GDP. It has invested greatly in information technology, and is now ranked top of the world in terms of ICT development, way ahead of 10th placed Japan.[28] Koreans also have a great passion for studying English, the language of the global economy. And the "Korean wave" of K-pop, television drama and cinema that has conquered East Asia, is evidence of a very creative culture.

But Korean companies are facing stiff competition from Chinese and other emerging economy companies, as well as from advanced countries. As the OECD highlights, Korea needs to strengthen international collaboration, the role of universities, venture capital, and openness to domestic and international competition to improve the foundations for innovation. And like Japan, school and university students are too focused on rote-learning, memorization and passing exams, rather than critical thinking, creativity and analytical skills.

At the heart of many of Korea's challenges is the dominant position and continued favored treatment of the chaebol, which are squeezing out the emergence of new players, which could rejuvenate the economy for new wave of productivity growth.[29] The chaebol often use their market power to make it difficult for new entrants to gain a foothold. And even when new entrants do succeed, they are often acquired in takeovers by chaebol.

There is much that should be done to expose the chaebol to more healthy international and domestic competition by eliminating trade and investment barriers. Korea's market restrictions are some of the worst among the OECD group of countries, and even worse than Japan's.[30]

The US State Department has also highlighted Korea's weakness in the area of competition policy in noting that "the practical impact of Korea's laws and policies regulating monopolistic practices and unfair competition, however, has been limited by the long-standing economic strength of the chaebol ... Chaebol-government relations can also sometimes influence the business-government dialogue, to the detriment of foreign and small and medium-sized enterprises (SMEs)."[31]

Despite the reforms following the Asian financial crisis, Korea's corporate governance is still among the weakest in Asia, with complex webs of cross-shareholdings and pyramidal chaebol shareholdings, which enable owner families to exert control, but inhibit its economic efficiency and innovation performance. The Asian Corporate Governance Association

(ACGA) ranks Korea only 8th on its list of 11 Asian countries, behind Singapore, Hong Kong, Japan, Taiwan, Thailand, Malaysia and India, and ahead of only China, the Philippines and Indonesia.[32]

Over the years, there has been a series of chaebol scandals related to various financial crimes. Seven of the leaders of Korea's ten largest chaebol have been convicted of crimes such as breach of trust, corruption, embezzlement and large-scale accounting fraud. While prosecutions and court cases follow, they invariably lead to official pardons, thanks to the corrupt and cozy ties between the chaebol and government. The most recent corruption scandal involved Samsung chief Lee Jae-yong, who was sentenced to five years in prison in August 2017.

Overall, it is widely acknowledged that the Korean economy needs a more level-playing field, and that the chaebol should be brought to heel. Various governments have made some efforts to do so under the banner of economic democratization, but to little effect. Given their economic dominance, it is easy for the chaebol to scaremonger about the possible adverse effects of any reforms.

In May 2017, Mr Moon Jae-in was elected president to replace President Park Geun-hye who was impeached because of corruption and abuse of power. President Moon faces an enormous set of challenges, in addition to those outlined above. First, it is necessary to restore stability and order to a deeply polarized nation which was wracked by scandal for over six months. Second, he needs to deal with the North Korean crisis on his doorstep.

The new Korean administration also faces geopolitical fallout from its high dependence on the US and Chinese export markets. In light of Korea's large trade surplus with America, Donald Trump's US Treasury has put Korea on a "Monitoring List" of major trading partners that merit close attention to their currency practices. The US has also informed the Korean government that it wants to renegotiate their free trade agreement to remove more barriers to US business. But as the Asian Development Bank has argued, given the opposition on both sides, there is a serious risk that the free trade agreement could be annulled, despite the undeniable benefits that both sides have enjoyed.[33] Meanwhile, China imposed economic sanctions on Korea as an expression of its displeasure regarding Korea's agreement with the US for the installation of Terminal High Altitude Area Defence (THAAD) system. The THAAD is designed to help protect South Korea from North Korean missiles, but China fears that it will enable the US to spy on its military.

This vast list of challenges may seem daunting, and indeed they are. But unless the President Moon and his administration tackle them head-on, the "hermit kingdom" will become another Asian country that achieves moderate success, but is unable to realize its full potential by catching up to world leaders.

## China's Conundrums

The Chinese economy of today is riddled with a collection of conundrums.

The Chinese Communist government would like to open up the economy to more market forces, but at the first sign of inevitable volatility, its knee-jerk reaction is to impose anti-market controls. It would also like innovation to become the new driver of economic growth, but repression of voices of dissent, who are often the most innovative, has only been ramped up under President Xi Jinping. It is proud of having a strong and effective state, but cannot manage seemingly basic issues like food safety. And very few other countries have benefited as much from the post-war system of multilateral cooperation, and yet China is now regularly flouting and challenging this system.

China's conundrums are the inevitable consequence of its particular development model. The Chinese Communist government gradually opened up its state-owned and centrally planned economy from 1978. The main elements were opening up to foreign investment and trade, permitting private enterprise and privatizing many SOEs. China thus stunned the world with three decades of 10% growth rates.

At the same time, the government kept an important stable of SOEs, especially in the energy, telecommunications and banking sectors. These SOEs benefit from government protection and assistance, some of which is designed to help China improve its technological capacity. These SOEs also act as agents of the Chinese state through their foreign investment activities, and through helping manage the domestic economy ("state capitalism").

There has been much debate over the role of these SOEs, especially how independent that might be of government control. Their relative share in the economy has declined in tandem with the development of the private sector, and they lag the private sector in terms of productivity and efficiency. But their importance and links to the Chinese government have only grown under President Xi Jinping's leadership. Indeed, the close link between SOEs and politics is evident by the fact that the Communist Party appoints senior SOE executives, whose career paths usually involve time in the government administration.

Overall, China is not at all an open market economy, as evident by the OECD's research which highlights stringent state controls on the economy and barriers to trade and investment, which have only been getting worse.[34] While private entrepreneurship is vibrant in China, especially in the technology space, when firms become large and successful, they are usually coopted into the government's sphere of influence and punished if they fall out of favor with the Party. The Chinese Communist Party does not relish the development of other sources of power. Indeed, the Party keeps firm control over the private sector and foreign enterprises through "Communist Party committees" which are embedded in their management structures.

One important instrument of industry protection through much of China's development was exchange rate manipulation. The value of the Renminbi (RMB) was kept artificially low to help exports and discourage imports. This generated balance of payments surpluses and resulted in a massive accumulation of foreign exchange reserves. This reserve accumulation was very costly to Chinese citizens who were deprived of access to imports. It also meant that there was less pressure on the Chinese industry to become more competitive and productive. But these reserves, which today are still around $3 trillion, provide the Chinese government with financial firepower for international diplomacy (like the Asian Infrastructure Investment Bank and the Belt and Road Initiative) and foreign investment.

US President Donald Trump has called China a currency manipulator, because he believes that it is still artificially undervaluing the exchange rate. In fact, Trump is several years late in his accusation. In recent times, China has been intervening to prevent its exchange rate from falling for fear of the instability that might cause. This has not stopped Trump's US Treasury placing China on a "Monitoring List" of major trading partners that merit close attention to their currency practices.

As early as 2007, Premier Wen Jiabao warned that the Chinese economy may have looked extremely strong, but was increasingly "unbalanced, unstable, uncoordinated, and unsustainable" (the "four uns"). In particular, the environmental cost of China's development has been massive. According to the World Bank, "The costs of environmental degradation and resource depletion in China are estimated to approach 10 percent of GDP, of which air pollution accounts for 6.5 percent, water pollution 2.1 percent, and soil degradation 1.1 percent."[35] The OECD estimates that there were 670 premature deaths per million people in China from exposure to particulate matter and ozone concentrations in 2010.[36]

When the US was struck down by the financial crisis in 2008, triumphalism was the reaction of Chinese leaders. They interpreted this as a sign of the decline of the US, and the ascendancy of Asia. This period also saw the beginning of a new Chinese assertiveness in international relations and against America and Japan, in particular.

But the Chinese government also panicked. The Chinese economy had long been dependent on exports to the US and other Western markets, and there was fear of the adverse impact on the economy. So the Chinese government launched a massive stimulus package, by pushing state-owned banks to lend money to SOEs and local governments. And all the strictures of state-owned bank dominated financial system paved the way for a boom in China's risky shadow banking sector.

As a result, China's total public and private debt rose from 150% of GDP in 2008 to over 250% in 2016.[37] China's rapid debt buildup is about double than that in the US before the global financial crisis or in Korea before the Asian financial crisis. The IMF has remarked that "such large increases have internationally been associated with sharp growth slowdowns and often financial crises."[38]

Much of China's debt is in the SOE sector, with corporate debt representing 125% of GDP. Many of China's SOEs are zombie companies which are de facto bankrupt. China's government debt of 55% of GDP could jump quickly if the government were obliged to bailout SOEs or to recapitalize financial institutions. Many local government infrastructure projects are not capable of generating financial returns to enable debt repayment. And nearly half of China's total debt is directly or indirectly related to the volatile real estate sector. According to Chinese real estate magnate, Wang Jianlin, China's real estate market was the "biggest bubble in history".

Another consequence of the stimulus package is industrial overcapacity which has reached astronomical proportions across a wide range of industries like steel, aluminum, cement, chemicals, refining, flat glass, shipbuilding, and paper and paperboard. For example, China's steel production "has become completely untethered from real market demand, and is now more than double the combined production of the four next leading producers: Japan, India, the US and Russia".[39]

The Third Plenum of November 2013 announced a new phase of widespread reforms, with market forces set to play a "decisive role" in the economy. The goal was to wean the Chinese economy off its investment- and export-led growth model toward one based on domestic consumption and services. With little meaningful efforts toward these ambitious goals, "supply-side structural reform" (SSSR) was adopted as the new economic policy framework in December 2015. The ambitions are cutting excess industrial capacity, destocking property inventory, corporate deleveraging, lowering corporate costs and improving innovation capacities. But there are too few signs of decisive action in pursuit of these lofty ambitions. As the Economist Intelligence Unit has argued, SSSR could be more effective if the government would only let market forces drive structural reform, rather than being a "top-down, government-driven process".[40]

Today, the Chinese economy has reached a major turning point, as reflected in its current slowdown. According to the country's dodgy statistics, the economy is still growing in the 6–7% range, although the reality is probably much weaker. And this growth is being heavily doped by government spending, rather than any inherent dynamism. Exports, a key driver of China's high-growth period, have been sluggish for a few years now.

China may have the world's biggest GDP in purchasing power parity terms, but its GDP per capita is only one-quarter of that of the US. While poverty has been slashed from 89% of the population in 1990 to 27% in 2010 (based on a poverty line of $3.10 a day), only 20% of the population live on more than $10 a day. And China only has one company, Huawei, on Forbes' list of "The World's Most Valuable Brands", while its nemesis, Japan, has five.[41]

The only way that China can continue to climb the development ladder and global value chain (GVC) and become an advanced economy is by reigniting its productivity genie. But since 2007, China's productivity growth has been on a sharp downward trend, after having been a key driver of economic growth during much of the reform period. This is all the more worrying now that China's labor force has also been falling these past few years, the result of the sharp decline in the country's fertility rate. With less and less workers, China must lift its productivity. China's labor productivity is only 15–30% of the level in OECD countries.[42]

To meet its productivity challenge, China must remove more of the shackles of central planning and communism, and become an open market economy, which it is not at all today. It's high time for the Chinese government to let market forces play a decisive role in the economy.

As the European Chamber of Commerce has argued "China is not yet an open and domestic market, but rather a patchwork of regional markets, each with its own unique trade and investment barriers." Indeed, local protectionism is widespread. Local governments promote favored firms. SOEs have access to subsidized credit, energy and other inputs. They are often tasked with political objectives like maintaining employment. Corporate bankruptcies are avoided by banks rolling over company loans and using local subsidies.

The World Economic Forum has highlighted the structural weaknesses of China's financial sector.[43] This is dominated by large state-owned banks, which lend mostly to SOEs or large corporations with connections. It is not surprising that they have accumulated many nonperforming loans. Small and medium enterprises which could provide new dynamism to the economy struggle to obtain finance.

China's lack of capacity to innovate has also become a growing concern in recent years. Evolving from a manufacturing-based economy to an innovation powerhouse requires a holistic approach to the innovation ecosystem, including nurturing talent and technological readiness. It is a lot more than spending money on R&D, as China has been doing. It also requires an open society with freedom of speech and academic freedom, which is less and less the case in China today.

Despite the manifest need to give market forces a "decisive role" in the economy and to reignite the productivity genie, at this stage the Chinese government lacks the courage to do so. Little real reform has actually occurred, apart from stuttering reforms to financial markets. The greatest efforts have been employed on prestige projects, like having the RMB included in the IMF's Special Drawing Rights, rather than substantial projects.

What is holding China back?

Clearly the government is concerned about social stability risks due to job losses that might result from reform in light of growing labor and other social unrest. It is also struggling with local government and SOE vested interests which might lose from reform. Many SOE managers are also members of the Communist Party's Central Committee.

It also seems that the Chinese Communist Party is still in the midst of a power struggle on the reform agenda and other issues. Moreover, surrendering control of the economy to market forces is anathema to the "control-freak" nature of the Chinese Communist Party.

There is also a political agenda which is overriding economic imperatives. To preserve his political authority in the lead-up to the 19th National Congress of the Communist Party of China, held in the autumn of 2017,

President Xi could not risk an economic slowdown. The government is also attached to its goal of "building a moderately prosperous society in all respects and double the 2010 GDP and per capita personal income by 2020", and is already eyeing the 2021 celebrations of the centenary of the founding of the Communist Party. All of this means that the Chinese government is chasing economic growth at all costs by employing monetary and fiscal stimulus, and adding further to debt, rather than implementing much needed structural reform.

In addition to managing the complexity of Chinese politics, Xi Jinping is having to cope with the unpredictability of Donald Trump's politics. During the election campaign and before his inauguration, Donald Trump had much to say about China when it comes to trade, exchange rates, South China Sea, North Korea, climate change and so on. But the Chinese know very well that American presidents say one thing during election campaigns and other things once they are in office. While Xi Jinping has been working very hard to maintain stable relations, his honeymoon with Donald Trump was quickly over, as Trump became quickly frustrated at China's token efforts to control North Korea's nuclear and missile programs and launched an investigation into China's alleged theft of US intellectual property.

Despite China's economic (and political) travails, its enormous economic size does matter. As we have argued earlier, China is able to exert its market, financial and military power in many ways. For example, the magnet of China's large market makes many foreign enterprises and governments cave into many Chinese demands. Apple has removed apps from its China store that helped Internet users evade censorship, and has agreed to open a data center in China which may give Beijing access to troves of personal and industry secrets. And now that China is the leading trading partner of most Asian countries, the Chinese government routinely employs trade sanctions to express its displeasure at the actions of other Asian governments, as countries like Japan, Korea and the Philippines have experienced. China also froze political relations with Norway and blocked many business ties and joint research and academic relationships after the Nobel Peace Prize was awarded to Chinese dissident Liu Xiaobo in 2010. It took six years of quiet diplomacy in order to renormalize China–Norway ties.

Western governments now routinely "go soft" on criticizing China's human rights, out of fear of upsetting Beijing. China regularly uses its enormous foreign exchange reserves to buy subservience from Southeast

Asian countries concerning the South China Sea dispute. Beijing is also openly buying political influence in countries like Australia and the US. It has also been using its growing military strength to intimidate its Southeast Asian neighbors and to threaten India.

While it has been able to transform economic weight into economic, political and military power, China remains a fragile superpower which seems externally strong, but is internally weak.[44] The CCP's grip on power is dependent on its capacity to deliver a strong economy, at a time when the risks of financial crisis and stagnation are only rising. And rather than accelerating economic reform, Xi Jinping's administration is only ramping up repression and controls on freedom. China is also very weak in terms of soft power. No country aspires to the Chinese economic or political model. And China has extremely few friends, in contrast to its emerging rival, India.

## INDIA: A SLOW BURNER

India has never managed to achieve three decades of 10% annual economic growth rates like China has. But in all its long history India has never had a centralized, authoritarian regime like China has had for over 2000 years, which could provide strong political leadership.[45] India is an immensely diverse country, which is essentially a creation of the British Raj and the Indian railway system that it built. "No one person could change this country with 320 languages", once said Singapore's Lee Kuan Yew.[46] This diversity makes governance in India more complex than in China. But the Indian economy has performed very well these past 25 years, and the prospects for continued development may well be very good.

India is indeed a country with a great deal of potential. For example, Indians who have migrated to the US, and their descendants, earn on average $88,000 a year, compared with $66,000 for all Asian Americans, and $50,000 for Americans overall.[47] Indian success stories in the US include the CEOs of Microsoft (Satya Nadella), Google (Sundar Pichai) and Pepsi (Indra Nooyi). Indian companies like Infosys, Mahindra, Mittal, Reliance and Tata succeed famously on world markets. The Indian movie industry produces more films than any other country. And the Indian Premier League is the world's most lucrative and popular cricket tournament.

And yet, the Indian economy was for many years a chronic underperformer. During India's first four decades of independence, the economy chugged along at the "Hindu rate of growth"[48] of about 3.5% (or 1.3% in per capita terms) from the 1950s to the 1980s. Despite a vibrant democracy, India's economic policies drew more inspiration from the socialism of the USSR than the capitalism of East Asia or the West. This was typical of many countries at the time, which sought to achieve economic independence through inward-looking policies, once they had achieved political independence.

A financial crisis in the early 1990s triggered a wave of economic liberalization and reform. During the following 25 years, the Indian economy has averaged 6½% annual growth and is currently the world's fastest growing large economy with growth of around 7½%. India's GDP per capita more than tripled over this period, with the information technology sector playing a leading role.

Thanks to India's positive economic developments, the share of the population living in extreme poverty (less than $1.90 a day) has more than halved over the past decade to around 20%.[49] But this amounts to some 270 million people who are still suffering in "Incredible India". And despite this impressive achievement, almost 40% of the Indian population is caught between $1.90 and $3.10 a day in a situation of near poverty. India suffers from hunger more than most every other Asian country, even North Korea and Bangladesh.[50] The Indian government desperately needs to raise more taxes to provide basic services to its citizens—the OECD reports that less than 6% of Indians pay personal income taxes.[51]

India's GDP per capita remains less than half that of China, and about one-tenth of America's. India's ranking as the world's third biggest economy, as well as its status as an emerging power, is highly dependent on its enormous population. And like most countries which aspire to great power status, India is spending heavily on its military and space program. On the occasion of the launch of a rocket carrying satellites, Prime Minister Modi reportedly said it marked a "moment of immense joy and pride for India".

India has suffered from rising inequality like most Asian countries.[52] This has tempted Jean Drèze and Amartya Sen to observe that India looks "more and more like islands of California in a sea of sub-Saharan Africa".[53] And it is true that beyond the glitter of high-tech Bangalore, Bollywood and Indian cricket, India remains a rural country, with two-thirds of its population living in the countryside. But it is also undeniable that India has made immense progress. As someone who has visited the country in 1975, 1992 and 2014, I must say that India's progress is palpable.

In the 2014 national elections, the deeply corrupt and incompetent National Congress Party, the party of Nehru and Indira Gandhi, was soundly beaten by the Bharatiya Janata Party (BJP), under the leadership of Narendra Modi. This was the world's biggest exercise in electoral democracy and was widely applauded for its transparent, impartial and correct implementation. What is more, the transition of power from one party to the other went very smoothly. Indian governance may have its problems, notably widespread corruption, but its elections do work well. India's politics may seem chaotic compared with China's. But over the longer term, China's institutions may be more brittle and fragile, relying as they do on repression, censorship and propaganda.

Prime Minister Narendra Modi has been now leading the country for over four years. He promises so much, based on his successful pro-business leadership as chief minister of Gujarat state for over a decade. However, despite Modi's impressive reforms to date, India would still be a very difficult country in which to do business, according to the World Bank which ranks it 130th out 189 countries surveyed.[54] The OECD judges Indian policies to not be "competition friendly"; however, it does note a positive trend for barriers to entrepreneurship, and trade and investment.[55] There has been another positive trend in the World Economic Forum's Global Competitiveness Report where, after five years of decline, India has bounced back over the past two years to 39th place out of 138.[56] This is due to significant improvements initiated by Prime Minister Modi, whose pro-business, pro-growth and anti-corruption stance has improved the business community's sentiment toward the government.

India's human capital development is also hampered by one of the very worst education systems in Asia. By some estimates, half of the Indian population would be functionally illiterate. Even at the elite level, not one Indian university figures in the world top 200.[57] India spends next to nothing on public health. Improving human capital will be critical for taking advantage of the half a billion young Indians who will enter the labor force over the next decade. Already more than 30% of Indian youths aged 15–29 are not in employment, education or training, highlighting the immense challenges of reaping the demographic dividend of its youth bulge. Social discrimination is also rife in India, with a long list of victims like lower castes, religious minorities like Muslims and Christians, indigenous and tribal groups, and women.

A major element that has been lacking in India compared with East Asia has been the development of a strong manufacturing sector. India's manufacturing sector has been stuck at around 15% of GDP. The services sector, especially business process outsourcing and tourism, has been a key driver of the economy.

The East Asian model of urbanization and industrialization can be very effective for countries with large pools of lower-skilled labor. The model involves a structural transformation of the economy as low-productivity rural labor moves to urban areas to work in export-oriented factories. Today, industrialization could play an important role in India's development, since it faces the challenge of creating jobs for masses of semi-skilled young people entering the labor market, and transforming this demographic bulge into a dividend.

Fortunately, Prime Minister Narendra Modi's government is making efforts to develop its manufacturing sector. Major investments are being made in improving the country's logistics in areas like coastal shipping, highways and railways, which would help move products around. Inspired by the government's "Look East" policy, these efforts are being concentrated on the eastern side of the country, which is close to fast-growing Bangladesh and Southeast Asia. Special economic zones and economic corridors are also being developed.

The timing is right for India to become an industrial power, as China is now suffering from increasing wages, and investors like Japan are looking for new low-cost locations. This is where Prime Minister Modi's business-friendly policies are helpful. For example, the implementation of a national goods and services tax will help transform fragmented India into a common market. The government has also liberalized some policies for FDI, including through a "Make in India" initiative, with the result that flows of FDI surged to well over $30 billion in each of 2015 and 2016. Leading companies like Foxconn, Softbank, Microsoft and Huawei are all now investing in India. Korean companies in particular are very successful in India. "A growing share of this FDI comes from the Indian diaspora of over 30 million, the largest in the world, who Prime Minister Modi has been courting," said Kingsley Aikins, CEO of DiasporaMatters. "Looking ahead, India's 'diaspora capital' in terms of people, knowledge and finance will likely become a driving force for the Indian economy."

Overall, there are strong grounds to be optimistic about India's future, even if it remains an extremely long way behind the world's leading economies in terms of GDP per capita, and economic, business and technological sophistication. In particular, Narendra Modi and his BJP party remain very popular and could stay in power for some time, which should enable India to make serious progress in its ambitious reform program.

Over the course of the twenty-first century, India could well emerge as Asia's leading power. Already, India's economy is growing faster than China's, a trend which could continue, unless China gets serious about economic reform. Further, India's population will overtake China's in 2022 and could be some 50% higher by 2100, according to the UN.[58] And moreover, India has more friends among other Asian countries than does China.

In short, India is a slow burner compared with China, but it is moving decisively ahead.

## Indonesia's Oligarchy

When the corrupt, authoritarian regime of President Suharto crumbled under the weight of the 1997–1998 Asian financial crisis, Indonesia's future looked problematic. But it is now a democracy, which has achieved a solid economic performance, and which rapidly implemented a bold decentralization of government. However, the next phase of Indonesia's economic development could be rather challenging.

Indonesia's economy recovered quickly from the Asian financial crisis, thanks in part to reforms imposed by the International Monetary Fund. It then hitched its wings to the 2001–2010 commodity price boom, driven by rapid growth in China and India.[59] Indonesia is a commodity-rich country, and it benefited greatly from the threefold increase in prices for coal, crude palm oil and rubber, all of which it has in abundance.

Indonesia's economic growth rate has been in the 5–6% range since 2000.[60] It now has the world's eighth largest economy in purchasing power parity terms, thanks in large part to its population of 260 million, the world's fourth largest. Indonesia has achieved an impressive reduction in poverty, with the share of the population living under $3.10 a day falling from 85% in 1990 to 42% in 2012. But the middle class is miniscule with only 5% living on more than $10 a day. In 2013, some 36% of all children under the age of five (8.4 million) were stunted, a condition which delays motor development, impairs cognitive function, and results in lower IQ and poor school performance.[61] Inequality grew sharply during the commodity boom, as high-income households benefited much more than did low-income households. And GDP per capita remains only one-fifth of that of the US.

The Indonesian government squandered the sharp rise in public revenues during this boom period, with much of the windfall being consumed via fuel subsidies which benefited higher-income families disproportionately. At the same time, public investment in infrastructure lagged economic growth, with the result that Indonesia's terrible infrastructure deficit is now worse than ever, thereby cutting the potential for growing productivity.[62]

Overreliance on commodity exports, which account for over two-thirds of total, has also harmed Indonesia's longer-term development prospects. Manufactured exports have slipped back in importance, and Indonesia has experienced deindustrialization. Commodity-driven growth was also accompanied by further environmental degradation and rapid deforestation, along with illegal logging and fishing.

The Indonesian economy now stands at a critical juncture, as commodity prices have fallen back again since 2011, and its oil and gas production is in long-term structural decline. Indonesia has also been hit by China's economic slowdown.

The 2014 election victory of Indonesia's new president, Joko Widido ("Jokowi"), over ex-general Prabowo Subianto, and the smooth transition of power, was a testimony to the growing maturity of Indonesia's democracy.[63] But Jokowi faces a daunting agenda to keep the Indonesian economy on a path of solid growth.

Like India, Indonesia is a difficult country in which to do business, being ranked only 91st out of 190 countries surveyed by the World Bank, much worse than its neighbors Malaysia (23rd) and Thailand (46th).[64] Its policies toward inward FDI are very restrictive,[65] especially in the mining sector, and corruption is endemic. Symptoms of Indonesia's poor infrastructure are Jakarta's reputation for having the worst traffic in the world, and logistics bottlenecks which are preventing better integration into Asia's GVCs.

If only Indonesia could improve its business and investment climate, it has great opportunity to unleash the productive potential of the economy, and become an industrial power, especially in light of China's declining attractiveness as an investment destination. And also like India, Indonesia has a large youthful population entering the workforce over the coming years, who requires employment opportunities.

But to convert Indonesia's youth bulge into a demographic dividend will require a massive improvement in its education. Some 70% of Indonesian manufacturers indicate that it is very difficult to fill skilled positions. In this context, Indonesia was ranked near the bottom of the 72 countries surveyed in the OECD PISA education survey of 15-year-old students. Regrettably, Indonesia Corruption Watch reports that one-third of Indonesia's education budget is misappropriated, and some 20% of Indonesian teachers are absent from the classrooms every day.

President "Jokowi" made an impressive start to his presidency since he took office in October 2014. His decision to abolish most fuel subsidies was courageous, even if it was facilitated by the sharp fall in world oil prices. He is pushing hard to improve infrastructure. And he has launched a multitude of reform programs, though implementation is lagging greatly. But Jokowi faces very difficult political opposition in the parliament to advance his reform agenda.

However, Jokowi's greatest opponents are Indonesia's oligarchs, the vested interests of rich business and military elites. Indonesia is perhaps the classic case of an oligarchy—government of the "few", by the few and for the few, the very antithesis of the ideals of Abraham Lincoln. Indonesia's government has always been dominated by a small group who seek to distort government decision-making to favor or protect their financial and other interests—at the expense of the general population. I am reliably informed that nothing less than murder often occurs when an oligarch's privileged business position is threatened by an outsider.

Indonesia's oligarchy is reflected in the very high concentration of material wealth power, according to Jeffrey Winters.[66] The total wealth of Indonesia's 40 wealthiest citizens, $71.3 billion, is very much higher than those of Malaysia ($51.3 billion), Singapore ($45.7 billion) or Thailand ($36.5 billion), even though the GDPs per capita of these latter countries are much higher. Indeed, the combined wealth of this handful of Indonesian oligarchs equals some 10% of GDP. A majority of Indonesia's oligarchs live semi-permanently in Singapore, where much of their wealth is also stashed away.

Most of today's Indonesian oligarchs grew up under President Suharto, through the corruption, licenses and privileges of his regime. As a practitioner of "sultanistic oligarchy", Suharto limited their influence and kept his oligarchy under control. But with the demise of the Suharto regime in 1997, Indonesia's oligarchs proceeded to buy up the political system.

Indonesia's oligarchs now finance all the major political parties, and have large influence over all decision-making. Both candidates in

Indonesia's 2014 presidential elections had their election campaigns bankrolled by oligarchs, with the winner incurring immense post-election political debts. America's emerging oligarchy pales into insignificance with Indonesia's.

Indonesia has an immense policy agenda for it to continue a path of strong economic growth and poverty reduction, and to exploit the opportunities of the ASEAN Economic Community. Investments in infrastructure, education, health and social security all require public revenues for financing. But government spending represents a paltry 15% of GDP, and must be increased by raising more government revenues. But oligarchs and many others are reluctant to pay their taxes.

The Indonesian government's tax amnesty program to encourage Indonesians to bring back money stashed overseas is a promising initiative to cure the country of its tax cheats. But the results so far are a mere drop in the bucket of this massive problem.

Looking ahead, another factor which will likely weigh on Indonesia is the prospective Islamization of the nation's politics. The April 2017 election for the position of Jakarta governor pitted Basuki Tjahaja Purnama (known as "Ahok"), a Chinese Christian, against Anies Baswedan, a Muslim who won the election. The turbulent campaign featured mass rallies led by a hardline Islamist movement, which has strengthened in recent years in a country which had been long dominated by a moderate form of Islam (more than 80% of Indonesia's population professes Islam).

In a clear sign that religious pluralism and tolerance is now under threat in Indonesia, in May 2017 Ahok was sentenced to two years in prison for blasphemy. His crime was to say that Muslim clerics had used a Koranic verse to mislead voters by telling them that Muslims were not allowed to vote for a Christian. This mood will likely spill over to national politics, as the Jakarta governor election traditionally sets the tone for the country. Jokowi, Indonesia's President, was previously Jakarta's Governor. And politics in Indonesia and its neighbor the Philippines are now being destabilized by a growing presence of the Islamic State group (ISIS).

Indonesia has great potential to succeed in its development challenge. But for a country burdened by an oligarchic democracy, and many other political and social hurdles, it will be very difficult to realize this potential.

## Vietnam, the Next China?

Vietnam began its transition from central planning toward a market economy in the mid-1980s with reforms known as "Doi Moi" or "Renovation".[67] This was not a philosophical choice. With famines ravaging the country, and the loss of Cold War support from the former USSR, the government had to do something to get the country moving.

A long series of policy changes have included opening the economy to international trade and investment, and allowing private property rights and private enterprise. Reform is an ongoing process, with important milestones being a free trade agreement with the US in 2000, and membership of ASEAN in 2004, the World Trade Organization in 2007 and the TPP in 2015.

Vietnam also has an education system that delivers impressive results. The performance of 15-year-old Vietnamese students in mathematics, reading and science in the OECD's PISA study ranks 8th of the 70 countries covered, ahead of Australia (14th), the US (25th), and well ahead of its Southeast Asian neighbors of Thailand, Malaysia and Indonesia.[68]

Vietnam has thus been able to attract large flows of FDI. Vietnam's stock of FDI surged from $14 billion in 2000 to $103 billion in 2015,[69] representing some 53% of GDP. Investors have been attracted by Vietnam's strategic location near GVCs, its lower cost structure than China, and its political and economic stability. Japan, Singapore, Korea, China and Russia have been the leading investors in Vietnam.

These inflows of FDI have enabled Vietnam to join GVCs for products like garments, shoes and electronics. The FDI sector contributed 62% to exports in 2014, up from 47% in 2000, and some 18% of GDP in 2014, an increase from 13% over the same period. Trade has doubled to 160% of GDP over the past two decades, reflecting the active trade in parts and components that characterize GVCs.[70] But despite this excellent performance, Vietnam's exports are dominated by unsophisticated products with low domestic value added, and limited technological spillover from foreign to domestic enterprises.

These important developments have enabled Vietnam's economy to expand impressively, averaging 6–7% growth since the 1990s, with GDP per capita increasing fourfold to $6424. While this may still be only 40% of China's GDP per capita, it is a very impressive achievement from a late starter in Asia's development.

Vietnam's strong economic growth has resulted in a massive reduction in poverty. The share of its population living on less than $3.10 a day has fallen from 77% in 1992 to 14% in 2012. Vietnam's poverty reduction record was second only to that of China over this period. Vietnam's poverty is now highly concentrated among ethnic minorities, which account for 15% of the population and half of the nation's poor.

Like all middle-income countries, Vietnam now faces the challenge of taking its economy to the next level. This will require deeper and more challenging policy reforms. Vietnam is still ranked below Indonesia, Malaysia, the Philippines and Thailand when it comes to competitiveness,[71] rule of law[72] and corruption.[73]

Vietnam was to be perhaps the greatest beneficiary of the TPP. According to the World Bank, the TPP could have added as much as 8% to Vietnam's GDP, 17% to its real exports, and 12% to its capital stock.[74] Perhaps more importantly, the Vietnam implementation plan included commitments on the part of Vietnam to allow workers the autonomy to form and operate trade unions of their own choosing. Currently, all unions must be affiliated with the government-connected trade union confederation. It can only be hoped that the efforts currently underway to save the TPP by remaining 11 signatories will achieve success. But the TPP, without the US, would be a much less attractive proposition.

Corruption is reportedly rampant, starting at the top with the prime minister and his cronies, and is getting worse. One creative trick is buying jobs that provide opportunities for corruption. For example, a corporate board position can reportedly be had for $100,000; a national parks job brings in bribes when the incumbent turns a blind eye to illegal logging; and a job as a steward with Vietnam Airlines is said to cost about $25,000, but provide excellent opportunities for smuggling, including smuggling money outside the country for the elite.

More serious efforts are also required to reform the SOE sector. While their role has declined, they still account for one-third of GDP, half of exports and over a quarter of domestic government revenue. And as they benefit from access to cheap capital, close connections to government regulators and policymakers, weak corporate governance, and limited competition, they are much less efficient than the private sector.

SOEs control key industries of the economy, including electricity, petroleum and gas, mining and quarrying, the water supply, and banking. Reform has become urgent because a number of SOEs are showing signs of financial distress, while state-owned banks are accumulating significant amounts of nonperforming loans. But the government likes SOEs because they can implement the government's policies. And many SOE bosses like them in light of the opportunities for corruption.

In short, Vietnam is still very much in transition from a centrally planned to a market-based economy. And a much greater sense of urgency and leadership will be necessary for Vietnam to continue its very rapid economic development.

Despite the country's impressive economic development, its political development is still frozen. Vietnam remains a communist dictatorship, with the Communist Party of Vietnam (CPV) ruling the country since 1975.[75] It suppresses all forms of political dissent, using a broad array of repressive measures. The criminal justice system is controlled by the CPV. Freedom of expression, association and assembly are tightly controlled.

Like most authoritarian regimes in Asia, the CPV faces increasing challenges to maintain its grip on power. With prosperity and education, there are growing calls for democracy and greater freedoms, and also protests against corruption, especially by the younger generation in this very young country. The Internet and various forms of social media provide an effective vehicle for expression and protest. The government's reaction is to fight back with repression, including restrictions on Internet freedom, and punishment of dissident bloggers.

This political system not only has great costs in terms of political and human freedoms. Such restrictions on freedom also limit the capacity for innovation and productivity to become new drivers of economic growth, as do restrictions on academic freedom.

Overall, Vietnam's trajectory has many parallels with that of China. But with a population which is only 7% of China's, Vietnam could only ever be compared with a Chinese province like Guangdong. Vietnam does have the potential to match China's GDP per capita one day. Its people are well-educated, diligent and aspirational. Indeed, as former Singapore leader Lee Kuan Yew once remarked, "Vietnam is the most dynamic of all the ASEAN countries."

But a new wave of high economic growth of Chinese proportions would require leadership like that of Deng Xiaoping to open up and reform the economy more seriously, and leadership like that of Xi Jinping to root out the systemic corruption that is dragging the country down. Most regrettably, such leadership is not on the horizon.

## Concluding Comments

Asia's rapid economic development starting with Japan, continuing with Hong Kong, Korea, Singapore and Taiwan, followed by Southeast Asia, China and India, has been stunning. Yet no large Asian economy has caught up with world leaders like the US and Germany in terms of GDP per capita, and economic, business or technological sophistication. And there is no likelihood of that happening in the foreseeable future. Asia is suffering from stunted development. Asia's economic and political power derives from its very large population, rather than its level of economic development.

It is not surprising that Asia's stunning economic development should result in an equally stunning improvement in the lives of Asia's citizens. But while Asia has achieved a dramatic reduction in poverty, the region is a long way short from having a middle-class society, as we examine in the next chapter.

## Notes

1. CNBC (2015). Next largest retail market: Take a wild guess. Nyshka Chandran, 13 February 2015.
2. World Bank (1993). The East Asian Miracle: economic growth and public policy.
3. Buchanan, Ian (2012). Is regional economic integration enough? The search for 'Wave 3' growth. Asia Pathways, a blog of the Asian Development Bank Institute.
4. Akamatsu K. (1962). A historical pattern of economic growth in developing countries. Journal of Developing Economies, 1(1):3–25, March–August.
5. Asian Development Bank (2016). Asian Development Outlook 2016: Asia's Potential Growth. March 2016.
6. Acemoglu, Daron, and James A. Robinson (2012). Why Nations Fail: The Origins of Power, Prosperity, and Poverty.
7. Jain-Chandra, Sonali, Tidiane Kinda, Kalpana Kochhar, Shi Piao, and Johanna Schauer. Sharing the Growth Dividend: Analysis of Inequality in Asia. IMF Working Paper WP/16/48. March 2016.
8. PWC. The Long View: how will the global economic order change by 2050? February 2017.
9. SIPRI. SIPRI Fact Sheet. Trends in World Military Expenditure, 2016. April 2017.
10. Katz, Richard (1998). Japan: the system that soured. The Rise and Fall of the Japanese Economic Miracle.
11. Beeson, Mark. The rise and fall (?) of the developmental state: The vicissitudes and implications of East Asian interventionism.

12. Japan External Trade Organization (2015). JETRO White Paper and JETRO Global Trade and Investment Report.
13. OECD. FDI Regulatory Restrictiveness Index.
14. Abe, Shinzo (2013). Japan's New Growth Strategy: Bringing Rapid Reform to the Country.
15. US Department of State. Investment Climate Statement for Japan for 2016.
16. OECD (2017). Economic Survey of Japan 2017.
17. EF Indicator of efficiency in the English Language. Accessed 21 September 2016.
18. Palmisano, Samuel J. (2006). The Globally Integrated Enterprise. Foreign Affairs. May/June 2006.
19. Tonegawa, Susumu (2015). Only individual thinking can make big discoveries. Japan News, 8 January 2015.
20. OECD. Inequality. Accessed 22 September 2016.
21. OECD (2017). Economic Survey of Japan 2017.
22. IMF. Japan: 2017 Article IV Consultation-Press Release; Staff Report; and Statement by the Executive Director for Japan, 31 July 2017.
23. Tudor, Daniel (2012). Korea: The Impossible Country.
24. Transparency International. Corruption Perceptions Index 2016.
25. Forbes. The World's Most Valuable Brands 2017.
26. World Economic Forum. The Global Gender Gap Report 2016.
27. Ladies Professional Golf Association. Ranking: Top 100 Money List.
28. International Telecommunications Union. ICT Development Index 2016.
29. Witt, M.A. 'South Korea: Plutocratic State-Led Capitalism Reconfiguring'. In M.A. Witt & G. Redding (Eds.), The Oxford Handbook of Asian Business Systems, pp. 216–237. Oxford, Oxford University Press.
30. OECD. Indicators of Product Market Regulation.
31. US Department of State (2016). Investment Climate Statements. Korea.
32. Asian Corporate Governance Association. "CG Watch 2016—Ecosystems Matter". Presentation by: Jamie Allen, Secretary General, ACGA.
33. Asian Development Bank. Asian Development Outlook 2016.
34. OECD. Indicators of Product Market Regulation.
35. World Bank and Development Research Center of the State Council, the People's Republic of China (2013). China 2030: Building a Modern, Harmonious, and Creative Society.
36. OECD. Economic Survey of China 2017.
37. OECD. Economic Survey of China 2017.
38. IMF. People's Republic of China 2017 Article IV Consultation—Press Release; Staff Report; and Statement by the Executive Director for the People's Republic of China.
39. European Chamber of Commerce in China (2016). Overcapacity in China: An Impediment to the Party's Reform Agenda.

40. Economist Intelligence Unit (2017). China's supply-side structural reforms: Progress and outlook.
41. Forbes. The World's Most Valuable Brands. 2017 Ranking.
42. McKinsey Global Institute (2016). Meeting China's productivity challenge. August 2016.
43. World Economic Forum. The Global Competitiveness Report 2015–2016.
44. Shirk, Susan L. (2007). China: Fragile Superpower.
45. Fukuyama, Francis (2011). India vs. China. Carnegie Council for Ethics in International Affairs. Youtube clip.
46. Lee, Kuan Yew (2013). How will Lee Kuan Yew govern India? Singapore Now.
47. PewResearchCenter (2013). The Rise of Asian Americans.
48. Professor Rajkrishna, an Indian economist, coined the term "Hindu rate of growth" in 1978 to characterize the slow growth and to explain it against the backdrop of socialistic economic policies.
49. World Bank. Poverty & Equity data. The $1.90 poverty line may be more relevant to India than it is to other Asian countries.
50. International Food Policy Research Institute. Global Hunger Index 2015.
51. OECD. Economic Survey of India 2017.
52. Jain-Chandra, Sonali, Tidiane Kinda, Kalpana Kochhar, Shi Piao, and Johanna Schauer (2016). Sharing the Growth Dividend: Analysis of Inequality in Asia. IMF Working Paper. WP/16/48.
53. Drèze, Jean and Amartya Sen (2013). An Uncertain Glory: India and its Contradictions.
54. World Bank. Doing Business 2017.
55. OECD. Indicators of Product Market Regulation.
56. World Economic Forum. The Global Competitiveness Report 2016–2017.
57. Times Higher Education. The World University Rankings 2016–2017.
58. United Nations. World Population Prospects: key findings & advance tables. 2017 Revision.
59. World Bank. Indonesia: avoiding the trap. Development Policy Review 2014.
60. Asian Development Bank. Key Indicators for Asia and the Pacific 2016.
61. OECD. Economic Survey of Indonesia 2016.
62. OECD. Economic Survey of Indonesia 2015.
63. Ufen, Andreas (2014). Jokowi's Victory: The End of the New Order in Indonesia? Asia Policy Brief, August 2014. Bertelsmann Stiftung.
64. World Bank. 2017 Doing Business Report.
65. OECD. FDI Regulatory Restrictiveness Index.
66. Winters, Jeffrey A. (2016). Who will tame the oligarchs? Inside Indonesia. Edition 104. April–June 2011.

67. OECD. Agricultural Policies in Vietnam 2015.
68. OECD. Programme for International Student Assessment 2015 Results in Focus.
69. UNCTAD. World Investment Report 2016.
70. World Bank. Taking Stock reports on Vietnam.
71. World Economic Forum. The Global Competitiveness Report 2016–2017.
72. World Justice Project. Rule of Law Index 2016.
73. Transparency International. Corruption Perceptions Index 2016.
74. World Bank. Global Economic Prospects. January 2016.
75. Freedom House. Freedom in the World 2016.

**Open Access** This chapter is licensed under the terms of the Creative Commons Attribution 4.0 International License (http://creativecommons.org/licenses/by/4.0/), which permits use, sharing, adaptation, distribution, and reproduction in any medium or format, as long as you give appropriate credit to the original author(s) and the source, provide a link to the Creative Commons license and indicate if changes were made.

The images or other third party material in this chapter are included in the chapter's Creative Commons license, unless indicated otherwise in a credit line to the material. If material is not included in the chapter's Creative Commons license and your intended use is not permitted by statutory regulation or exceeds the permitted use, you will need to obtain permission directly from the copyright holder.

CHAPTER 3

# Asia's Mythical Middle-Class Society

"The explosion of Asia's middle class is stunning … The world has never seen anything like this before; it's probably one of the biggest seismic shifts in history," wrote Singapore's Kishore Mahbubani.[1]

It is true that Asian lives have improved enormously these past few decades. And yet, notwithstanding such hype, Asia's human and social development is just as stunted as the continent's economic development. Despite Asia's impressive poverty reduction, over one-third of Asian citizens still live in poverty, while only 15% have made it into the middle class. Fully one-half of Asians are living in an intermediate zone between poverty and the middle class, a zone of vulnerability and precarity.

And there are factors other than raw money which are also holding Asians back from joining the middle class: the vulnerability and precarity of informal or non-regular employment; deprivations like the lack of clean drinking water, inadequate health facilities and sanitation (i.e., clean, safe and hygienic toilets); the impact of Asia's all-too-frequent natural disasters; poor access to education and the Internet; and above all Asia's appalling human rights.

The arrival of a middle-class society would be a great achievement in terms of realizing an Asian Century. But at this stage, middle-class Asia is still a myth. Only a handful of Asian countries could reasonably claim to have middle-class societies. And as economic growth prospects for Asia have faded in recent years, the impending arrival of a middle-class society is also fading into the distance.

In this chapter, we examine the evidence for the rise of Asia's middle class. And we will conclude with a short section on Asia's super rich, a small group which is doing very well through Asia's rise, but is now suffering from some rich country problems like obesity and diabetes.

## Asia's Stunted Middle Class

There is no universal agreement on what middle class means. Economists think in terms of how much someone consumes or earns in income. Sociologists tend to reason in terms of education, occupation in a white-collar job or other social status.

In 2010, the Asian Development Bank (ADB) published a report which defined the middle class as those living in the range of $2–$20 a day.[2] The ADB concluded that the majority of Asia's middle class lived on $2–4 day, and were part of the "lower middle class". Many Chinese just laughed. No-one could live on $2 or even $4 day today in a Chinese city. Shanghai and Beijing are among the world's most expensive cities.

In another report, the OECD proposed a more realistic measure for the "global middle class", being consumption or income of $10–100 a day.[3] This is of course a much more meaningful measure of the middle class, and $10 a day is now increasingly accepted as the beginning of the middle class in emerging economies. At the same time, income or consumption of $10 a day would not be considered middle class in any advanced Western country. In other words, middle class has become a fuzzy concept, and must be interpreted with caution.

Using the $10 a day benchmark, some 650 million Asians could today be considered middle class. This sounds like a big number by any score. And it certainly sounds like a good market for businessmen wishing to hawk their wares. But this represents at best some 15% of Asia's population, based on World Bank statistics.[4] In short, it is far-fetched to talk about a middle-class Asia when only 15% of Asians could be considered middle class. As the Pew Centre has highlighted, a global middle class is still more a promise than reality.[5]

China, the country most talked about for its emerging middle class, only has 20% of its population living on more than $10 a day. And India and Indonesia, Asia's other two emerging giants, are even further away from having middle-class societies, with only 3% and 5%, respectively, of the population live on more than $10 a day. When you visit these countries you can experience the reality of middle-class life when you go shopping. For example, international companies are producing second-grade versions of their products, like clothes washing powder, to keep prices low for Chinese customers. Of course, this washing powder won't clean your clothes like you do back home. That's why friends of mine who live in Beijing carry back first-grade products from their European and American homes just so they can wash their clothes properly.

And while emerging Asian countries are struggling to achieve middle-class societies, advanced Asian countries like Japan and Korea are seeing their middle classes recede, as they are stalked by the new rich country problems of inequality and poverty. For example, Korea has seen its middle class decline from 75% of the population in 1990 to 67% in 2013 (with the middle class defined as those earning 50–150% of the median national disposable income, an appropriate measure for advanced countries).[6]

## MIDDLE CLASS IN MANILA

The life of my friend Edwardo gives us some insights into the lives of those on the cusp of the middle class in the Philippines. Edwardo is a taxi driver, who earns about $14 a day, while his wife earns small amounts by selling Tupperware and Avon products.

Edwardo has just become a grandfather at the age of 33. His 14-year-old daughter recently gave birth to a baby boy, fathered by her 16-year-old boyfriend, a fellow high school student. This is not an exceptional case. The Philippines has the highest rate of adolescent births in East Asia. The strong influence of the Catholic Church means that there is insufficient sex education and access to contraceptives.

The family of Edwardo shares a small apartment of one bedroom and one living room, which gets flooded out in the rainy season. Life is a constant struggle. Edwardo must provide for his family on a constant, daily basis. But his taxi earnings are not regular. Some days he earns more than $14, some days he earns less and some days he earns nothing at all after waiting for hours.

Financial management is thus key to Edwardo's survival. He is well trained for that thanks to his college degree in business studies (like many in developing Asia, he is vastly overqualified for his job). But at the moment, he is two months behind on paying his rent and three months behind on his electricity bills.

Edwardo is now contemplating emigration, the lifeblood of the Philippine economy and society. He has been exploring possibilities with migration agencies, but their fees are expensive, at least $2500. Then they sometimes rip off poor, naive migrants. And on top of the agency fees, there is the cost of the air ticket and pocket money to get started in a new country.

Edwardo is deeply worried. He doesn't know how he and his family can survive. Like many Filipinos, he hopes that God might help him.

## Escaping Extreme Poverty

While Asia has only made limited progress in achieving a middle-class society, it is certainly true that strong economic growth has enabled millions of Asians to escape the clutches of extreme poverty. Today, according to the World Bank, if you are living on less than $1.90 a day, you are living in "extreme poverty".[7] This means that you don't have enough income to cover the minimum costs of life's basic needs.

On this basis, extreme poverty fell from some 61% of the total population of East Asia and the Pacific (where China is by far the biggest economy) in 1990 to only 7% in 2012, and may have even fallen further to 4% by 2015, or 83 million persons. South Asia, dominated by India, saw a fall in extreme poverty from 51% of the total population in 1990 to 19% in 2012, and possibly further to 14% in 2015, or 231 million persons.

The World Bank, United Nations and others like to celebrate this extraordinary achievement. They feel that they are succeeding in the greatest challenge facing mankind, the "war against poverty". And while great progress has certainly been achieved, the $1.90 extreme poverty line is of very little relevance to Asia's developing and emerging economies. It was calculated by taking the average of the national poverty lines of the world's 15 poorest, mainly African, countries.[8] Only two Asian countries are included, Nepal and Tajikistan, while the great homes to Asian poverty, namely China, India and Indonesia, were not taken into account.

The World Bank has another, less well publicized, poverty line of $3.10 a day, which is much more relevant to most Asian developing countries. Some refer to this as a "moderate", rather than extreme, poverty line. On this basis, Asia's progress in poverty reduction is much less impressive. Indeed, some 22% of East Asians were living on less than $3.10 a day in 2012, triple the 7% based on $1.90 a day, while China's poverty rate jumps to 27% from 11%. And some 55% of South Asians were living on less than $3.10 a day, almost triple 19% based on $1.90 a day, as India's poverty rate rises to 58% from 21%. This means that in reality some 36% or 1.4 billion Asians are living in poverty.

This still represents very impressive progress in poverty reduction, but very much less than on the basis of $1.90. In either case, it is only the very beginning of living a decent life. If you are earning $1.90 or $3.10 a day, it simply means that you are unlikely to die from starvation from one day to the next. But it does not mean much more.

Indeed, the reality of Asian life is that most Asians who have escaped poverty are now caught between poverty and middle class (based on $10 day). Fully one-half of Asians are still living in a very vulnerable and precarious situation between $3.10 and $10 a day. At such low levels of income, people are at risk of falling back into poverty in the event of an earthquake, flood or other natural disaster, a sudden hike in food prices, or a personal/family problem like unemployment, or health problem.

## INEQUALITY HOLDS BACK ASIA'S POVERTY REDUCTION

The impressive reduction in Asian poverty could have been much greater had it not been for the rise in income inequality since 1990 in most of Asia, especially in Asia's population centers of China, Indonesia and India. This increasing inequality was a turnaround from the period before 1990 when economies like Hong Kong, Japan, Korea, Singapore and Taiwan were able to achieve "growth with equity". Income inequality, as measured by the "Gini coefficient", is now higher in Asia than in the rest of the world.

What has caused the increase in inequality? According to the International Monetary Fund (IMF), rapid technological change which requires high-skilled workers and displaces lower-skilled workers has been an important factor.[9] Rapid economic development has also favored urban areas rather than rural areas, giving rise to "spatial inequality". Unequal access to education has been another factor as richer towns offer better education than poorer towns do, and richer families can afford a better education for their children than poorer ones do.

But there are also other factors driving Asia's yawning inequality, most notably corruption. While petty corruption is widespread on the streets of many Asian countries, it is grand corruption that enables Asia's elites to fill their pockets at the expense of the general public. We will come back to this issue in greater detail in Chap. 9. And as Christopher Ng, Regional Secretary at UNI Global Union Asia Pacific, argues the proliferation of precarious, informal and irregular work is also a key driver of income inequality. We explore this later in this chapter.

There is much that governments can do to improve income inequality through government spending and redistribution. Moreover, it is important to improve the "equality of opportunity" to education, health and financial services which weigh on future inequality. And many governments, notably in China, are making the rights noises. But too little effort is actually being deployed. This is important, not only for enhancing the fight against poverty. Inequality can lower future investments in education and health, thereby compromising future economic prospects. It can also foster populism and weaken the support for pro-growth policies, as well as lead to social and political instability.

## Asia's Precariat

Asians living on $1.90 or $3.10 a day don't just suffer from a lack of money. They are also exposed to vulnerability and precarity because they are typically working in the "informal sector". The informal sector of the economy is composed of enterprises which are neither registered nor regulated, and whose workers have no contract or rights.[10] Minimum wage laws, collective bargaining, and health and safety standards are unheard of in the informal economy. Globalization can foster the informal economy, as multinational enterprises, notably in the garments industry, can outsource production to micro- and home-based operations to keep costs and prices low.

Some two-thirds of Asians have such low-quality jobs in the informal sector, a figure which has barely budged over the past two decades or more[11] (in comparison informal workers only account for about one-third of total in Latin America). The share of informal employment ranges from over 80% in Bangladesh and India, to 50–70% in countries like the Philippines, Thailand, China, Pakistan and Indonesia, and down to around 10% for Hong Kong and Singapore.

Workers in Asia's vast precarious, informal economy have been called the "precariat" by political scientist Guy Standing.[12] The precariat covers work in small factories, backyard mechanics, home-based producers, domestic servants, most agricultural workers, ambulant peddlers, street vendors and hawkers, casual construction workers and so on. "There are success stories about economic empowerment and entrepreneurship among the informals," writes Rene Ofreneo. "However, these are overwhelmed by the numerous sad stories about abuses, hardships and difficulties of worker survival in the harsh and unprotected world of the informals."

Migrants are also part of Asia's precariat. While most Asian low-skilled migrants travel outside the region, especially to the Middle East, there are large numbers of undocumented workers crossing Asia's porous borders, like the following corridors India–Bangladesh–Pakistan, China–Hong Kong, China–Indochina, Thailand–Myanmar, Indonesia–Malaysia and Malaysia–Singapore.

Most of these migrants cross borders without any legal papers or documents, and end up not only as unregistered, but also as highly vulnerable workers in the countries of destination. For example, stories abound of how migrants from Myanmar's Rohingya tribes are abused in Thailand and Bangladesh, and how Indonesian plantation workers suffer in Malaysia. Another group of the precariat is the large floating populations of internal migrants, especially in large economies like China and India. They flock to the industrial areas from the rural areas, picking up odd and casual jobs at pitifully low wages.

Most tragically, Asia accounts for 56% of the world's 21 million people who are made to work against their free will ("forced labor"), coerced by their recruiter or employer, for example, through violence or threats of violence, or by more subtle means such as accumulated debt, retention of identity papers or threats of denunciation to immigration authorities. Asia is also home to more working children than any other region in the world. An estimated 122 million Asian children aged 5–14 years are compelled to work for their survival. Millions are not enrolled in school at all. Although there has been progress in reducing child labor in many countries in the region, the problem persists.

It would be nice to think that economic development will lead to a reduction in Asia's precariat. But the reality is, as mentioned before, that there has been virtually no decline in emerging Asia's precariat population over these past two decades. Moreover, Japan has seen its widely admired system of life-time employment fritter away, and be gradually replaced by non-regular work contracts. Another disturbing trend is that each successive financial crisis, from the 1997 Asian Financial Crisis to the 2008 Global Financial Crisis, has seen a rise in precarious employment in Asia, and also in the US and other Western countries. Workers with regular jobs get laid off when crisis strikes, and are re-hired on irregular contracts when the economy recovers.

## Surviving on the Threshold of Poverty in Bangladesh

What is life like if you are surviving on $1.90 or even $3.10 a day in one of Asia's developing countries? Life involves a complex process of financial management, according to the authors of "Portfolios of the Poor".[13]

When you are living on such a low income, you spend most of your money on the basics, especially food. There is one big problem, though. Like the case of Edwardo, you are very unlikely to receive a steady check or payment from your boss. Since you are surely casually or part-time or self-employed in the informal sector, you make more on some days, less on others, and often get no income at all.

The government offers you very limited help, and when it does, the quality of assistance is apt to be low. Your greatest source of support is your family and community, though most often you'll have to rely on your own devices!

So how do the poor budget? In particular, how do they make sure that there is something to eat and drink each day? How do they deal with emergencies? How can they be sure that they can pay for the doctor and drugs when their children fall sick? How do they put together the funds for big ticket items like a home and furniture, education and marriage for their children, and some income for themselves when they are too old to work?

The evidence shows that for the poor, financial management is a fundamental and well-understood part of everyday life as they cope with incomes which are small, and often highly irregular and unpredictable. Indeed, even those living on less than 1 dollar a day per person rarely consume every penny of income as soon as it is earned.

Money management by the poor involves: storing savings at home, with others, and with banking institutions; joining savings clubs, savings-and-loan clubs and insurance clubs; and borrowing from neighbors, relatives, employers, moneylenders or financial institutions. At any one time, the average poor household has a fistful of financial relationships on the go.

The case of Hamid and Khadeja, a poor couple living in a Bangladeshi village, provides a window on financial management by the poor. When their first child was born, they moved to Dhaka, nation's capital, where they settled in a slum. After spells as a cycle-rickshaw driver and construction laborer and many days of unemployment, Hamid whose health was not good was taken on as a reserve driver of a motorized rickshaw. Khadeja stayed at home, earning a little from taking in sewing work. Home was one of a strip of small rooms with cement block walls and a tin roof, built by their landlord on illegally occupied land, with a toilet and kitchen space shared by the eight families that lived there.

They earned on average $70 a month, almost all by Hamid. One-fifth of the $70 was spent on rent (not always paid on time), and much of the rest went toward the most basic necessities of life—food and the means to prepare it. This put them among the poor people of Bangladesh, but not the very poorest.

Hamid and Khadeja are an unremarkable poor household. But they are very active money managers. They had built up reserves in six different instruments, ranging from $2 kept at home for minor day-to-day shortfalls to $30 sent for safe-keeping to Hamid's parents, $40 lent out to a relative, and $76 in a life insurance savings policy. In addition, Hamid always made sure he had $2 in his pocket to deal with anything that might befall him on the road.

Hamid and Khadeja are also borrowers, with a debt of $153 to a microfinance institution and interest-free private debts to family, neighbors, and Hamid's employer totaling $24. They owed money to the local grocery store and to their landlord. Khadeja was even acting as an informal banker, or "money-guard", holding $20 at home that belonged to two neighbors seeking a way to keep their money safe from their more spendthrift husbands and sons. Hamid himself also used a money-guard, storing $8 with his employer while waiting for an opportunity to send it down to the family home.

In addition to saving, borrowing and repaying money, Hamid and Khadeja, like nearly all poor and some not-so-poor households, also saved, borrowed and repaid in kind. Khadeja, sharing a crude kitchen with seven other wives, would often swap small amounts of rice or lentils or salt with her neighbors. She would keep a note of the quantities in her head, and so would her partners in these exchanges, to ensure that their transactions were fair over the long haul.

The case of Hamid and Khadeja shows that people with low and irregular incomes can, with some difficulty, cope and survive on $1.90 or $3.10 a day. But their financial management is a hazardous process which depends on the reliability, kindness, goodwill and norms of mutual obligation of their network of friends, family and colleagues. Fortunately, some microfinance institutions are now stepping into this space to provide financial services to the poor.

## Poverty in the Midst of Prosperity: The Case of Singapore

Any visitor to dazzling Singapore might be shocked to learn that a quarter of Singaporeans live in poverty, even though GDP per capita in the city state is the highest in Asia, and one of the highest in the world. And the poverty rate would be much higher if the situation of low-skilled migrants were included in analysis of the issue.

The life of Patricia, a Singaporean nurse, and her unemployed partner, Sham, illustrate the challenges of a life of poverty. Patricia works as a full-time nurse in a governmental hospital, and earns just S$1400 a month. She pays S$850 a month to rent a non-air-conditioned room in an apartment at Admiralty, in the north of Singapore, a 90-minute commute by public transport to her workplace.

Patricia's monthly rental does not entitle her to the use of her landlord's kitchen, so she and Sham must eat out for all their meals, often at McDonald's. Unfortunately, she cannot afford a small, two- bedroom condominium unit in the city center which would cost S$5000 or more. Life can be hard in the world's most expensive city.[14]

Singapore's poor can also be found selling packets of tissues outside food centers. Or spending the night on benches near their jobs to save the transport fare home—they are known as "sleepers". Or collecting empty soft drink cans out of trash bins.

Kishore Mahbubani, dean of the Lee Kuan Yew School at the National University of Singapore, wrote in 2001: "There are no homeless, destitute or starving people in Singapore. Poverty has been eradicated, not through an entitlements programme (there are virtually none) but through a unique partnership between the government, corporate citizens, self-help groups and voluntary initiatives".[15]

This comment is plainly misleading.

Inequality and poverty have indeed been deteriorating in Singapore, according to a study by the Lien Centre for Social Innovation and the Singapore Management University. The bottom 20% of Singapore residents saw their real median incomes fall by 8% from 1998 to 2010, while those in the top 20% increased by 27%. Singapore does not have a minimum wage. Thus the rate of inequality has risen dramatically, and is the second highest in Asia, after Hong Kong, and is one of the highest in the advanced world.

The consequence for Singapore's poverty situation is dramatic. Some 10–15% of Singapore's population are unable to meet their basic needs of food, clothing, shelter and other essential expenditures, with their monthly income below S$1250–1500. Most of these people include "working poor", unemployed poor households and poor retirees.

If the notion of basic needs is expanded to include in-school education, improving skills, and the purchase of goods like computers, Internet connection or mobile phones, about 25% of Singapore's population is living in poverty, below S$2500–3000 a month, sharply up over the previous decade. These expenditures are necessary to invest in human capital and create the possibility of social mobility or a life beyond continued basic subsistence for adults or children of the next generation.

It is hard to escape the conclusion that Singapore's poor, as well as its lower-skilled migrants, are there to suffer and serve Singapore's elite, which now counts 188,000 millionaires and 20 billionaires. Singapore has the highest concentration of millionaires per capita in the world.

Another sad reality is that most Singaporeans are not aware of the scale and depth of poverty in Singapore. And the Singapore government provides very much less assistance to the poor than do governments in other advanced countries. Thankfully, there are many civil society anti-poverty initiatives like "Singaporeans Against Poverty", launched by the Catholic group, Caritas.

### Japan's Two-Track Job Market and Vulnerability

It is not only Asia's poorer countries which are afflicted with vulnerability and low-quality jobs. Advanced countries like Japan and Korea are also suffering from similar problems. In Japan, the share of non-regular workers in the economy has almost doubled from 20% in 1994 to 38% in 2016.[16] The category of irregular workers includes fixed-term, part-time and dispatched workers, the latter being persons employed by temporary worker agencies who are sent to firms on a fixed-term basis. Over 50% of temporary and dispatch workers would prefer a regular job.

In the hypercompetitive world economy, companies are now resorting more and more to irregular workers who are easy-to-hire and easy-to-fire. The traditional Japanese system of life-time employment, seniority-based wages, firm-based training and regular job rotation, which served Japan so well during its high-growth period, is increasingly seen as inappropriate in the world of today.

Non-regular employees typically bear the brunt of the cyclical ups and downs in the economy. Japan's women are the biggest victims of non-regular employment, reflecting the discrimination from which women suffer in Japanese life. More than half of female employees have non-regular jobs, which means that they account for two-thirds of total non-regular employees. Non-regular work is frequent among youth and older workers; the latter are often re-employed at lower wages after they reach the occupational retirement age (typically 60) and until they reach the public pension age (65).

While non-regular employment may have much naive appeal to Japan's enterprises, it comes with great costs to the country's economy and society. Non-regular employees benefit much less from firm-based training, and once you are a non-regular employee, chances are you will be a non-regular employee for life. Non-regular employment is not a stepping stone to regular employment. In other words, the phenomenon of non-regular employment is creating an economic underclass, which is undermining the nation's long-term prosperity.

Non-regular employees systematically earn much lower incomes, about 40% less for equivalent jobs, and have much less access to social welfare like unemployment and health insurance even though they have precarious jobs. This is a key factor fracturing Japan's society, as its relative income poverty and inequality are now among the highest of the advanced OECD countries.[17] The lower income of non-regular workers is also discouraging marriage and hence reducing Japan's chronically low fertility rate, the main factor behind its dramatically aging population. It is not surprising that surveys have found that well-being and happiness level reported by non-regular workers is below that of regular workers and the self-employed.

Over the years, there have been many proposals to break down this dualism in the Japanese labor market (and society), such as by increasing social insurance coverage and upgrading training programs for non-regular workers and reducing effective protection for regular workers. But as with many of Japan's intractable policy debates, it's another case of all talk and little action. This rise in non-regular employment means that, as in Korea, increasing numbers of Japanese are also slipping out of the middle class.

## A Deeper Look at Poverty Reduction and Asia's Toilet Crisis

There is a lot more to poverty, vulnerability and the middle class than whether you are earning $1.90, $3.10 or $10 a day. Many Asians who earn such incomes may also suffer from other deprivations like no access to clean drinking water, clean and safe toilets, education for their children, basic healthcare facilities or personal security. Large countries like India, Indonesia and Pakistan have some of the worst records in these respects.

Can the citizens of these countries be happy with $1.90 a day or more in their pockets, if their wives die in childbirth, if their children die before they reach five years or if their children suffer from malnutrition?

The lesson is that Asia's rapid economic growth has been very effective at putting money in people's pockets. But Asian governments have been much less effective in providing their citizens with the basic social services that they need and deserve.

Perhaps one of the most egregious deprivations from which many Asians suffer is the lack of "improved sanitation" or, in plain English, clean, safe and hygienic toilets. Today, some 1.7 billion or 42% of the region's population still lack access to improved sanitation, according to the ADB.[18]

And while the region's toilet deficit was mainly a rural phenomenon, this problem is now becoming increasingly acute in urban areas, with tens of millions of people now migrating every year into slums and other infrastructure-poor urban areas.

Close to half of Asia's "toilet-poor" population lives in India. This country has nothing short of a "toilet crisis". In fact, many more Indians have access to a cell phone than to a toilet!

This emerging economic giant reportedly has the world's longest toilet queue, with some 775 million people without access to clean, safe and hygienic toilets.[19] China comes in runner up with 330 million people without toilets, while Indonesia is fourth-place (100 million), Pakistan sixth place (69 million) and Bangladesh seventh place (63 million).

If these 775 million Indians without toilets, more than 60% of the nation's population, were lined up in a queue, it would stretch from the earth to the moon and beyond. In percentage terms, the toilet situation in India is much worse than in virtually all other Asian countries. For example, in Cambodia 58% of the population is without toilets, in Nepal 54%, in Bangladesh and Indonesia 39%, the Philippines 26%, China 24% and Vietnam 22%.

Among those Indians that do have toilets, there are many millions who use homemade toilets, on a raised platform inside the house, which are not connected to a sewerage network or pit. So this human waste is then cleaned by poor Dalit women ("untouchables") who face horrific discrimination. India also wins the world prize for the most number of people practicing open defecation, with 173 million people relieving themselves behind bushes, in fields, by roadsides, or at some other unsavory and unsafe place in this beautiful country.

Lack of access to clean, safe and hygienic toilets is a big problem for many reasons. It can have dramatic effects on people's health through pollution of water supplies, which renders them unfit for drinking, irrigation and other purposes. About 80% of untreated sewage in India reportedly flows into rivers, lakes and ponds, and then often seeps underground thereby polluting drinking water sourced from groundwater.

Diarrhea is one major problem, which is caused by poor sanitation and hygiene practices and unsafe drinking water. It is a major cause of child malnutrition, disease and death. Nearly half of India's under-five children are stunted (too short for their age), with poor sanitation being a major underlying cause. More than 140,000 children younger than five years die each year in India from diarrhea. India also has high rates of maternal and newborn mortality linked to sepsis.

Open defecation also puts the safety of women and girls at risk. They are often subject to sexual harassment, physical assault and rape on the way to and from their defecation site.

Indian Prime Minister Narendra Modi announced in October 2014 his Swachh Bharat (Clean India) Mission. The objective is to deliver a toilet to every household and end open defecation by 2019, the 150th anniversary of Mahatma Gandhi's birth, and to educate people about the long-term health and economic benefits of using a toilet.

Some progress is being made, but the government's toilet construction is way behind schedule, and may take an extra ten years. But building toilets is the easy part. The waste management system across large parts of the country is a stinking mess. Most villages have no systems for disposal of drainage water, and urban areas cannot manage their waste.

But what is more disturbing is that, according to many reports, the new toilets are frequently not used. Many people consider toilets to be unclean, and prefer open defecation. They have been demolishing the new toilets or using them for other purposes.

Hindu tradition encourages defecation in the open, far from home, to avoid ritual impurity. So many people, notably in the Hindu-dominated Gangetic plains, today still show a preference for going in the open—even if they have latrines at home. Some Indians argue that open defecation is more wholesome, healthy and virtuous life. It is pleasurable, comfortable and convenient!

In short, the government must also tackle the cultural reasons for India's toilet crisis. Simply building the toilets won't be enough. Tackling India's toilet crisis requires a multifaceted strategy, with strong leadership. It requires an effective public education campaign, investment in sewerage systems as well as toilets, and cooperation between different levels of government in this vast country.

## A Deeper Look at Poverty Reduction and the Impact of Natural Disasters

Now what happens if you have your $1.90, $3.10 or even $10 a day in your pocket, but every couple of years it gets washed away in a flood, blown away in a typhoon or lost in an earthquake. Or what about if you have to use those few dollars to rebuild your life after a natural disaster because you have very few other assets to fall back on, no insurance, or because you receive insufficient help from your government or international donors.

Fortunately, the ADB has estimated for us the impact on Asian poverty from natural calamities like floods, landslides, tsunamis, earthquakes, droughts and storms.[20] When the vulnerability to such natural calamities is taken into account, over 400 million extra people were estimated to live in poverty in 2010, with more than half of them being in China, a country which is highly exposed to flooding. And since natural calamities are a growing phenomenon in Asia, this estimate of 400 million would only have increased since 2010. In short, natural disasters are yet another untold side of Asia's poverty.

It is hardly surprising that natural disasters should have such an impact on Asia's poverty and middle-class aspirations. The Asian continent is the most disaster prone in the world.[21] Indeed, after the US, China, India, the Philippines and Indonesia are the countries the most hit by natural disasters.[22] Active tectonic plate movements in the Pacific and Indian Oceans are a source of major earthquakes and tsunamis, while Indian and Pacific Oceans also regularly generate tropical cyclones and typhoons.

Over 2 million Asian people died from natural disasters between 1970 and 2014, some 57% of the global fatalities, with earthquakes and tsunamis being the main cause of deaths, according to the UN. The following mega disasters accounted for most natural disaster fatalities in recent years: the 2004 Indian Ocean tsunami (more than 200,000 deaths), Myanmar's 2008 Cyclone Nargis (140,000 deaths), Bangladesh's Cyclone Gorky in 1991 (140,000 deaths), China's 2008 earthquake (90,000 deaths), Pakistan's 2005 earthquake (75,000 deaths) and Japan's 2011 earthquake/tsunami (20,000 deaths).

What's more, some 6 million people from the region were affected by disasters over the same period, with floods and drought affecting the highest number of people. The economic cost from natural disasters over this 45-year period was over $1.15 trillion, with earthquakes, tsunamis, floods and storms being responsible for the lion's share. Indeed, the economic losses from natural disasters have been surging in recent years. And with climate change contributing increasingly to weather instability, the frequency of natural disasters will only increase.

Many organizations have flooded the world with recommendations for dealing with natural disasters. For example, the ADB recommends reducing population exposure to natural disasters, exploiting early warnings and strengthening resilience.[23] This is indeed wise advice. But it is much easier said than done.

In particular, the 2016 floods in China show how far behind the curve this emerging superpower is when comes to dealing with natural disasters at home. Hundreds were killed, more were missing and tens of millions affected, while vast areas of agricultural crops were destroyed. Chinese citizens complained of inadequate early warnings, illegal building in exposed areas, poor or non-existent drainage systems, government incompetence and cover-ups, and censorship of their social media reports.

While some officials have been fired, and the national government expressed sympathy, it is unclear whether serious efforts are being made to improve China's natural disaster risk management. Obfuscation and cover-up is the Chinese government natural response to any disaster. One of the most notorious cover-ups was regarding the 5335 students who died in the 2008 Sichuan earthquake due to the substandard construction that caused the collapse of more than 7000 classrooms in the region.

## Asia's Education Divide

A well-educated population is key to a middle-class society. And on this score, a good number of East Asian countries seem to have strong foundations for a middle-class society, based on OECD's latest Programme for International Student Assessment (PISA) survey, which evaluates the knowledge and skills of the world's 15-year-olds. But many questions are being asked about the real quality of these apparently successful Asian education systems. After all, Asia's elite are proud to see their kids to school in North America, Australia and the UK. And at the same time, there are just as many other Asian countries which have poor education systems.

PISA 2015 tested students in 72 countries on science, maths and reading. Students from Singapore came top in science, the principal focus of PISA 2015. The OECD reports that one in five Singaporean students masters the most advanced scientific problems and demonstrates that they can think like scientists. Six other Asian economies—Japan, Taiwan, Macao, Vietnam, Hong Kong and China (based on Beijing, Shanghai, Jiangsu and Guangdong)—make it into the top ten, along with Estonia, Finland and Canada, the only Western countries to do so.

Disturbingly, the OECD reports that only in Canada, Estonia, Finland, Hong Kong, Japan, Macao, Singapore and Vietnam do at least nine out of ten 15-year-old students master the basics that every student should know before leaving school. Germany and the US, which have two of the world's leading economies, are only ranked 16th and 25th, respectively. When it comes to mathematics, Singapore, Hong Kong, Macao, Taiwan and Japan were the five highest performers in PISA 2015, while Singapore, Hong Kong, Canada, Finland and Ireland topped reading.

How did these Asian countries do so well? According to the OECD, top performers, notably in Asia, place great emphasis on selecting and training teachers and prioritizing investment in teacher quality, not classroom sizes. They also set clear targets and give teachers autonomy in the classroom to achieve them. Children whose parents have high expectations perform better: they tend to try harder, have more confidence in their own ability and are more motivated to learn.

Others contend that the success of these Asian economies just reflects rote learning, memorization and immense drilling for tests. It is certainly true that students from these high-performing Asian countries are often sent to night school, a source of great psychological pressure.

The strong performance of China in three consecutive editions of PISA, together with the relatively poor US scores, has opened a lively debate on the relative merits of the two education systems. It is after all curious that Chinese families should be sending over 300,000 students to US schools. Even Chinese President Xi Jinping reportedly sent his daughter to Harvard.

Some Chinese leaders have made some relevant comments. Liu Jinghai, principal at a Shanghai Middle School, reportedly admitted that the much-feared college entrance exam—known as the gaokao—is all simply about memorization and rote learning. And at a conference in Beijing,[24] Cheng Siwei, Former Vice Chair, Standing Committee, Chinese National People's Congress, said that Chinese students are good at passing tests, but much less good at critical thinking and creativity. He argued that China has much to learn from the West in that regard.

However, the greatest problem in Chinese education may be the role of propaganda, censorship and ideology—things which do not affect the OECD study which does not focus on the social sciences and liberal arts. For example, the Great Leap Forward, the Cultural Revolution and the Tiananmen Square incident have been strictly taboo in studies of Chinese history. And since the 1989 Tiananmen Square incident, "patriotic education", which emphasizes China's victimhood at the hands of Western and Japanese colonial powers and the "century of humiliation" from the Opium Wars to the end of World War 2, has been a key element of Chinese education. The Chinese government has always considered education as an important means of ideological control.

Under the current leadership of President Xi Jinping, there has been a toughening in education policies as part of the government's efforts to stamp out dissent. The education minister Yuan Guiren has called for the banning of all foreign textbooks that promote Western values. President Xi has called on universities to improve their Marxist ideological and political work.

The relative academic freedom that most Chinese universities enjoyed is now under threat, as topics like press freedom, civil society, human rights and multi-party democracy constitutionalism are now "no speaks". Some Chinese professors who have criticized the Communist government have been fired or even jailed. Predictably, there has been a surge in Chinese applications to study at foreign universities.

Following the 2014 "Umbrella" protest movement, Chinese Communist Party control has now reached the Hong Kong education system, which had always enjoyed academic freedom. Professors who have been critical of the Beijing and Hong Kong governments are now being disciplined, and academic freedom is now also being eroded.

Turning back to the OECD's PISA study of 72 countries, you will find another group of Asian countries, namely Malaysia, Thailand and Indonesia well down in the bottom half of the list. These countries have a great deal of work to do before human capital can become a key driver of economic development and middle-class societies. As the OECD said in other reports, "half of Thai students in school are not acquiring the basic skills required for their own success and the country's continued development,"[25] and "Over 50% of Indonesian fifteen year olds do not master basic skills in reading and mathematics."[26]

Moreover, the absence of India in PISA 2015 is striking. In fact, two Indian states—Tamil Nadu and Himachal Pradesh—participated in PISA 2009. Although they are among the best-performing states in India, they were ranked in the bottom three participants, along with Kyrgyzstan, for all three criteria. But rather than using the PISA exercise as a useful tool for measuring, and tracking over time, the nation's education, the Indian government decided to blame the PISA test, which it considers to be unfair because it does not take account of India's sociocultural milieu.

Despite the government's reaction, these very low scores square with all other indicators which suggest that India has an appalling education system. An ADB 2010 study showed that Indian children had the lowest number of years schooling out of 12 leading countries from developing Asia. India's average number of years schooling (for the population aged 15 years and above) was 5.13 years in 2010.[27] This is well below the average for "Emerging Asia" (7.05 years), and even much further below the 11.0 years of developed countries. The results of this important ADB study would be even more damning if the ADB could have measured the quality of education, as well as the quantity.

## Asia's Digital Divide

Access to the Internet is increasingly seen as a human right and a mark of middle-class status. But less than half of Asians use the Internet.

The Internet is indeed the fundamental technology for modern life. It can provide citizens with education, entertainment, social connections, e-government services, awareness of world and local events, and transparency about the activities of government, business and society.

Thanks to the Internet, consumers can enjoy variety, and time and cost savings. And business benefits greatly from the Internet for global operations management, customer management, and analyzing and accessing new markets. Government can deliver and manage public services through the Internet, which can also facilitate policy analysis and implementation.

In short, the Internet is transforming the very nature of our economies and society, with profound impacts on GDP growth. But as with education, there are two distinct Asias when it comes to access to the Internet.

One Asia is that of the tech-savvy young population of Internauts who are developing and moving faster than the rest of the world, especially in Japan and Korea which have Internet penetration rates between 84% and 86%, like the US and Germany. But the overall reality is that more than half of Asia's 4 billion citizens still do not use the Internet, according to a McKinsey&Company.[28]

Some 85% of India's population of 1.3 billion do not use the Internet, despite all the hype of high-tech India. In China, the much vaunted emerging great power, 54% of the population of 1.4 billion are not online. And in Southeast Asia's leading country of Indonesia, 84% of its population are also not online. The situation is fairly similar in other populous Asian countries like Pakistan, Bangladesh, the Philippines, Myanmar, Vietnam and Thailand.

Not surprisingly, the offline population is disproportionately rural, low income, elderly, illiterate and female. And most tragically, in most countries religious and ethnic minorities are virtually excluded from the Internet—these groups are also not surprisingly virtually excluded from their country's political processes. Of Nepal's Madhesi group, only 1% are connected to the Internet, for China's Yi group the figure is 2%, Nepal's Muslims 2%, China's Bouyei 4%, India's Kashmiri Muslims 4%, the Philippines' Moro 5% and Indonesia's Papuans 9%.[29]

There is much more that governments could do to improve access to the Internet, like improving affordability, education, infrastructure, notably for mobile Internet coverage or network access, and electricity. For example, in India, nearly 1 billion people still cannot afford the cheapest mobile data plans. And literacy rates are particularly low in Bangladesh, India and Pakistan, especially for women.

Electrification is poor in many Asian countries. About 70% of the mobile connections in India and China are on 2G networks, with potentially limited mobile Internet capabilities. Any visitor to China can tell you how hellishly slow Internet speeds are, and that it is impossible to access Gmail in China.

With the exception of China, the majority of Internet content and services consumed in Asia's developing countries originates from outside the country. This means that foreign language capability, rare in many countries, is necessary to use the Internet.

While deep digital divide now exists between Asia and the advanced world, and between Asian countries, too many of Asia's non-democratic governments are imposing restrictions on freedom of the Internet. Only two Asian countries, Japan and the Philippines, are classified as having Internet freedom, out of the 15 Asian countries covered in a Freedom House report.[30] China was the worst abuser of Internet freedom in this report that surveyed 65 countries globally, representing 88% of the world's Internet user population. Other notorious cases in Asia were Vietnam, Pakistan, Thailand and Myanmar.

"Cyber sovereignty" is one of the high priorities of Chinese President Xi Jinping, as netizens are now prosecuted with "unprecedented" intensity for their offending content. There would be 84 netizens in Chinese jails as of September 2015, according to Reporters Without Borders. Xi has declared that the Internet has become the main battlefield for public opinion struggle. The Chinese Communist Party propaganda department and other agencies employ thousands of people to monitor, censor and manipulate content. China is also a major global source of cyberattacks.

Vietnam is another country classified as "not free", and is one of the world's worst jailers of bloggers. And since Thailand's military coup in 2014, harassment and arrests of Internet bloggers and users has skyrocketed.

## Asia's Appalling Human Rights

One of the hallmarks of a middle-class society should be the protection of human rights by sound legislation and their fair enforcement by the authorities. Nowhere in this world can you find a perfect situation for human rights, most notably in the US, that eternal preacher of human rights. Most regrettably, many people in positions of power will exploit this power by abusing the human rights of weaker people. And when it comes to human rights, Asia has never been a beacon.[31,32,33]

Asia has of course the notorious case of North Korea, the most repressive country in the region. A United Nations Commission of Inquiry in 2014 found that the North Korean regime practices extermination, murder, enslavement, torture, imprisonment, rape, forced abortions and other sexual violence. North Korea also has secret gulags for opponents of the regime.

As appalling as the case of North Korea might be, what is perhaps most disturbing is the lack of meaningful progress, and indeed the recent regression, in human rights in Asia's most dynamic economies. Political scientists imagine that human rights would improve in tandem with economic development and prosperity. In today's Asia, however, there are many grounds for disappointment.

It is true that Chinese citizens enjoy a much broader range of freedoms than they did just a few decades ago, especially under the regime of Mao Zedong. The Chinese can travel and study overseas, have relative freedom of movement within their country and have access to the Internet, despite its censorship. But this authoritarian state, which has always employed repression to maintain its grip on power, has only ramped up its repression under the regime of President Xi Jinping. Indeed, as China's economy and society have become more sophisticated, so have the instruments of human rights abuse and repression. Chinese citizens now talk about China becoming more and more like North Korea, a country they despise.

The most important policy initiative of President Xi has been his anti-corruption campaign. Rampant corruption on an industrial scale has been perhaps the greatest abuse of the Chinese Communist Party, and President Xi believes that this is a major threat to the Communist Party's rule. But as laudable as the anti-corruption campaign may seem, those accused and prosecuted are rarely being given a fair trial. Most observers believe that Xi is using the anti-corruption campaign as a ruse to eliminate his political enemies. At the same time, civil society groups that expose corruption are invariably put in jail and prosecuted themselves.

More generally, Xi has launched a widespread crackdown on lawyers, activists, journalists and civil society groups who are seen as a threat to the government. Torture of detainees remains widespread. The treatment of Nobel-prize winner Liu Xiaobo, who was denied potentially life-saving treatment, is testimony to how badly opponents of the regime can be treated. Forced confessions on the television, including by foreigners, are now increasingly common. While these confessions are seen as an obvious sham, they contribute to an atmosphere of fear of the Communist Party authorities. Censorship of the Internet and other media is intensifying, and journalists and others who are seen to be spreading rumors are punished.

Beijing has also been spreading its net beyond its borders in the search for threats to the Communist Party's grip on power. Five Hong Kong booksellers who were selling material critical of China were abducted to mainland China in 2015. This is just one example of the steady encroachment of the Communist Party on Hong Kong's freedoms, following the territory's "Umbrella Revolution" movement. The government successfully pressured Thailand to repatriate Chinese Uighur men back to China and also pressured Kenya to send some alleged Taiwanese criminals to China.

Freedom of religion is under even greater threat, with the campaign against Christianity intensifying through the removal of crosses from churches and the demolition of some churches in Zhejiang Province, the heartland of Chinese Christianity. Members of Falun Gong and other sects continue to be harassed and punished, while Tibetans and Uighurs continue to suffer from discrimination, repression, human rights abuses and restrictions on personal movement.

China's noxious attitude toward human rights is also evident at the UN Human Rights Council, as the pressure group Human Rights Watch has argued, where "China continues to act as a spoiler, blocking greater scrutiny of human rights situations in other countries, including Belarus, Iran, North Korea, Syria, and Ukraine."

But what is perhaps most disheartening about China's human rights situation is the relative silence on the matter by Western governments. They prefer to do profitable business with China, while only paying lip service to human rights.

Vietnam's trajectory is often compared with China's. And although it started its economic rise sometime after China, it has enjoyed similar rapid economic growth and poverty reduction, thanks to exports and foreign direct investment. But Vietnam is also similar to China in that human rights are not improving either. In the words of Human Rights Watch, Vietnam's human rights are "dismal".

The Vietnamese Communist government places great restrictions on freedom of speech, opinion, press, association and religion. The state has firm control over the media, the judiciary, and political and religious institutions. As in China, the government has been cracking down on independent writers, bloggers and rights activists seen as threatening to the ruling Communist Party.

Malaysia and Thailand are Asia's two great disappointments when it comes to human rights. Both have enjoyed great economic growth, achieved middle-income status and virtually eliminated extreme poverty. But both are now mired in middle-income traps and political crises, with human rights sadly deteriorating.

Malaysia's respect for human rights has been "plummeting", in the words of Human Rights Watch, as the crackdown on human rights defenders, activists, political opposition figures and journalists intensifies. And yet, Malaysian citizens have every reason to protest against the government. A government-owned investment fund, 1Malaysian Development Berhad (1MDB), whose board of advisors is chaired by Prime Minister Najib, has been severely tainted by a scandal involving allegations of massive corruption.

In February 2015, the Malaysian Federal Court upheld the conviction and five-year sentence of Anwar Ibrahim, a leading opposition figure, on sodomy charges. This "politically motivated prosecution and jailing" (in the words of the US State Department) is widely perceived as merely an attempt to weaken Malaysia's political opposition, at a time when the ruling United Malays National Organisation (UMNO) is progressively losing its grip on power. In October 2015, the United Nations Working Group on Arbitrary Detention determined that Anwar was being arbitrarily detained and demanded his immediate release and reinstatement of his political rights.

Thailand has never been a paragon of virtue for human rights. But things took a giant turn for the worse in May 2014, following a military coup. Thailand is now in the grip of deepening authoritarianism, as freedom of assembly, expression, association and the press are under assault. The lese majeste (insulting the monarchy) law is now subject to increasingly harsh and arbitrary enforcement.

Indians are proud of having the world's largest democracy, an active civil society, vibrant media and independent judiciary. But in many respects human rights are simply lousy in India, and they are not getting any better under the administration of Prime Minister Narendra Modi.

Muslims and Christians have been under attack from extreme right-wing Hindus, and the government has been doing very little in their defense. Indeed, leaders of the ruling Bharatiya Janata Party (BJP) have made inflammatory remarks against minorities. Many artists, writers and scientists have returned national honors in protest at the climate of growing intolerance. Minorities like Dalits and tribal groups are also subject to discrimination and violence. Violence against women, especially rape and murder, continues to run at epidemic proportions.

Freedom of expression by civil society groups and the media who criticize the government has also been under threat from authorities. Human rights defenders face arbitrary arrests and detentions. According to the US State Department, some of India's most significant human rights problems are "police and security force abuses, including extrajudicial killings, torture, and rape".

In Japan, extreme politeness, courtesy and kindness are the face of the country that most visitors see and appreciate so much. But there are other sides of Japan which are dark and sinister. This includes many shameful acts and practices which were highlighted by the United Nations Human Rights Committee (HRC) in 2014.[34]

For example, there is "widespread racist discourse against members of minority groups, such as Koreans, Chinese or Burakumin, inciting hatred and discrimination against them". Foreign trainees and technical interns are the subject of "a large number of reports of sexual abuse, labour-related deaths and conditions that could amount to forced labour". And "a large number of persons with mental disabilities are subject to involuntary hospitalization."

It is of course true that obnoxious behavior exists in all countries. But it is the role of the state to legislate against such behavior and to enforce that legislation. The state should promote attitudes of tolerance, respect and openness. It should not be complicit in abuses of human rights. Unfortunately, the HRC notes that the Japanese government has "not made any progress to establish a consolidated national human rights institution".

The HRC had stern comments to make about one of the great tragedies of modern times, the Fukushima Daiichi nuclear disaster. This is now widely regarded as a man-made disaster, not a natural disaster, as a Japanese parliamentary commission argued convincingly. The HRC is concerned that former residents have no choice but to return to highly contaminated areas because of "the high threshold of exposure level" that the government set in Fukushima, as well as the decision to cancel some of the evacuation areas.

The committee also expressed serious concern about the Japanese government's contradictory position regarding the sexual slavery practices against "comfort women" by the Japanese military during wartime, as well as a lack of effective remedies available to them as victims of past human rights violations.

As Asia's most mature democracy, and a country sitting in the midst of great economic and political power transitions, Japan should not treat the

HRC's report lightly. Its traditional approach of stonewalling is no longer viable. The HRC noted that many of its previous recommendations have not been implemented.

## HAPPINESS AND ASIA'S MIDDLE CLASS

As Asia aspires to realize a middle-class society, it is important for policy-makers to bear in mind that happiness and well-being are the most important measures of societal progress, not GDP alone. Disappointingly, most Asian countries score relatively poorly in the World Happiness Report[35] compared with North America, Western Europe and Latin America.[36]

Within Asia, Southeast Asia is doing better than East Asia, which is ahead of South Asia. And while happiness has improved in Southeast and East Asia over the past decade, it has declined in South Asia. Moreover, happiness in Asia is always not well correlated with GDP per capita. In other words, some advanced countries score poorly, while other less advanced countries do quite well.

Singapore is Asia's most happy country, but is ranked only 26th in the world. Then Thailand (32nd) and Malaysia (42nd) come in well ahead of the more prosperous Japan (51st), Korea (55th) and Hong Kong (71st). Other Southeast Asian countries are further down the list—the Philippines 72nd, Indonesia 81st and Vietnam 94th. While from South Asia, Pakistan ranks 80th, Bhutan 97th, Nepal 99th, Bangladesh 110th, Sri Lanka 120th and India 122nd. The case of China, ranked 79th, is particularly interesting. While China has enjoyed sharply growing per capita income over the past 25 years, happiness fell steadily from 1990 until about 2005, before since recovering to 1990 levels. Falling happiness is attributed to rising unemployment and fraying social safety nets.

Southeast Asia's positive edge was confirmed in a Gallup poll asking people if they experienced positive emotions the previous day, as Indonesia, the Philippines and Thailand come in at 12th, 13th and 14th in the world, way ahead of all other Asian countries.[37] Much further down the list are China (31st), Japan (60th), India (78th) and Korea (95th). In another initiative, the Gallup-Healthways global well-being index,[38] four Southeast Asian countries, Myanmar, Malaysia, the Philippines and Thailand, are ranked in the top 50, while Japan is 92nd, Korea 117th, Hong Kong 120th and China 127th.

In the OECD Better Life Index,[39] the Japanese and Koreans are less satisfied with their lives than the OECD average, with particularly low scores for work–life balance and self-reported health.

In short, money doesn't necessarily buy happiness. Southeast Asian countries like Indonesia, Malaysia, the Philippines, Singapore and Thailand perform much better than wealthier countries of Northeast Asia.

While happiness and well-being are important life objectives, they can also be important for the economy and society. Happy people with high well-being are healthier, more productive and creative, and more resilient in the face of crises and shocks. And happy members of society can contribute to a rich civil society. Countries like Australia, Canada, Denmark, Germany, Sweden and the US highlight the importance of happiness and well-being to all aspects of economic, social and political life.

Asian government, business and civil society leaders must pay much greater attention to happiness and well-being, and not just economic growth. Indeed, as Asian societies are now maturing, happiness and well-being can provide a new path to economic prosperity, as well as social stability and harmony.

## The Rise of Asia's Super Rich

While the majority of Asians have barely escaped the clutches of extreme poverty, a super-rich elite is also blossoming. We cannot resist saying a few words on them.

As a delightful introduction to this bizarre world, nothing beats Kevin Kwan's novel "Crazy Rich Asians".[40] It recounts the lives of three super-rich, pedigreed Chinese families. And the gossip, backbiting and scheming that occurs when the heir to one of the most massive fortunes in Asia brings home his American-born Chinese (ABC) girlfriend to the wedding of the season.

When Rachel Chu agrees to spend the summer in Singapore with her boyfriend, Nicholas Young, she envisions a humble family home, long drives to explore the island, and quality time with the man she might one day marry. What she doesn't know is that Nick's family home happens to look like a palace, and that she'll spend more time in private jets than cars. And with one of Asia's most eligible bachelors on her arm, Rachel might well have a target on her back.

Kwan introduces us to many of the super-rich stereotypes of the Asian century in this story of over-the-top consumerism, social excesses and jet-setting lives of the wealthiest and most snobbish families in Asia.

Here is a short sampling: Chuppies (Chinese yuppies); Hennessy-swirling, cigar-puffing fat-cat Asian tycoons; Hong Kong fashionista men; marriage-scheming mothers, aunts and in-laws; fortune-hunting "Taiwanese tornadoes"; Henwees (high-net worth individuals); bitchy shopaholic parties; penny-pinching old-money overseas Asians; spend-thrift new-money mainlander Chinese; and an Indian Singaporean who sends her saris back to New Delhi to be specially cleaned.

This is a story that reveals many of the social forces and tensions in Asia's rapidly changing society. Old money and new money. Overseas Chinese and Mainland Chinese. Generational divide between young Westernized Asians and their traditional parents. Snobbery attached to Asians who speak English with British rather than American accents. And more.

This is the world of at least some of Asia's super rich, the 412 Asian billionaires, who make up one-quarter of the world's 1694 billionaires.[41] Asia's leading super rich are China's Wang Jianlin (18th in the world), Hong Kong's Li Ka-shing (20th), Hong Kong's Lee Shau Kee (31st), China's Jack Ma (33rd) and India's Mukesh Ambani (36th).

Already China has 251 billionaires, placing it second on the global league table after the US, with India placed 6th and Hong Kong 8th. Even relatively poorer Asian countries like Indonesia, Malaysia, Thailand and the Philippines have their fair share of billionaires.

Even if Asia's super rich may not be a source of spiritual and cultural inspiration, they are certainly becoming drivers of the global economy, especially through their purchases of luxury products and international real estate, business and financial investments, and their children who attend international universities, sometimes showing off their Ferraris.

Indeed, China has been the engine of the global luxury goods market for a number of years now, especially for products, accessories and hard luxury items like watches and jewelry. Chinese consumers bought the largest portion of global luxury purchases (31%), followed by Americans (24%) and Europeans (18%), according to one survey.[42] Chinese shoppers spend far more abroad than in mainland China, which only accounts for 20% of their global purchases. In 2000, Japanese consumers accounted for more than one-quarter of global luxury purchases, but now they represent only 10%.

But as some Asians have become super rich, Asia has also become the center of rich country problems. For example, the world is in the midst of a diabetes epidemic, as this condition has risen astronomically these past three decades. More than 60% of the world's 382 million people who suffer from diabetes come from Asia.[43] Indeed, China has some 114 million adults with diabetes, and another 493 million with prediabetes, while India has 65 million with diabetes. And with obesity rising in Singapore, it is estimated that the city state will have half a million people with diabetes by 2020 and that this will rise to 1 million by 2050.

\* \* \*

Asia's rapid economic development has driven a dramatic improvement in Asian lives. But Asia is still suffering from stunted economic development, and the notion of middle-class Asia still remains a myth. In the following chapters, we examine the seven challenges that we believe are crucial for overcoming stunted economies and societies, and realizing an Asian century.

## Notes

1. Mahbubani, Kishore (2014). The Expanding Middle Class in Asia. Huffington Post, 26 March 2014.
2. Asian Development Bank (2010). Key Indicators for Asia and the Pacific 2010. Special chapter on "The Rise of Asia's Middle Class".
3. Kharas, Homi (2010). The Emerging Middle Class in Developing Countries. OECD Development Centre, Working Paper No. 285.
4. World Bank. Poverty & Equity Data. http://povertydata.worldbank.org/poverty/home/. Accessed 8 September 2016.
5. PewResearchCenter (2015). A Global Middle Class is More Promise than Reality.
6. Choi, Seong-keun, and Jun-hyup Lee (2015). Changes in the Quality of Life of Korea's Middle Class. Korea Focus.
7. World Bank and IMF (2015). Global Monitoring Report 2015/2016: Development Goals in an Era of Demographic Change.
8. These 15 countries are Chad, Ethiopia, The Gambia, Ghana, Guinea-Bissau, Malawi, Mali, Mozambique, Nepal, Niger, Rwanda, Sierra Leone, Tajikistan, Tanzania and Uganda.
9. Schauer, V., Kalpana Kochhar, Shi Piao, Sonali Jain-Chandra, Tidiane Kinda. Sharing the Growth Dividend: Analysis of Inequality in Asia. IMF Working Paper No. 16/48.
10. Ofreneo, Rene E. (2013). Asia and the Pacific: Advancing Decent Work Amidst Deepening Inequalities.

11. Asian Development Bank (2011). Key Indicators for Asia and the Pacific 2011. Special Chapter: Toward Higher Quality Employment in Asia.
12. Standing, Guy (2014). The Precariat: The New Dangerous Class.
13. Collins, Daryl, Jonathan Morduch, Stuart Rutherford, and Orlanda Rithven (2009). Portfolios of the Poor: How the World's Poor Live on $2 a Day.
14. Economist Intelligence Unit. Worldwide Cost of Living Report 2017.
15. Mahbubani, Kishore. Following Singapore's lead on the road of development. Earth Times, 15 January 2001.
16. OECD. Economic Survey of Japan 2017.
17. OECD. Inequality and Income Data.
18. DW (2014). Why sanitation in Asia requires more than just toilets. Interview with Jingmin Huang, Senior Urban Development Specialist, South Asia Department, Asian Development Bank.
19. WaterAid (2015). The State of the World's Toilets 2015.
20. Asian Development Bank (2014). Key Indicators for Asia and the Pacific 2014. Special Chapter: Poverty in Asia: A Deeper Look.
21. UNESCAP (2015). Overview of Natural Disasters and their Impacts in Asia and the Pacific, 1970–2014.
22. Centre for Research on the Epidemiology of Disasters, and United Nations Office for Disaster Risk Reduction (2015). The Human Cost of Weather Related Disasters 1995–2015.
23. Asian Development Bank. Development Asia, "Dealing with Disasters". January–March 2011.
24. 22nd Pacific Economic Cooperation Council General Meeting, Beijing, China, 10–11 September 2014.
25. OECD and UNESCO (2016). Education in Thailand—an OECD-UNESCO Perspective.
26. OECD (2015). Education in Indonesia—rising to the challenge.
27. Barro, R., and J.W. Lee. (2010). A New Data Set for Education Attainment in the World, 1950–2010. Working. ADB Economics Working Paper Series No. 216.
28. McKinsey&Co (2014). Offline and falling behind: Barriers to Internet adoption.
29. Bohannon, John (2016). Who is getting left behind in the Internet revolution. Science Magazine, 9 September 2016.
30. Freedom House. Freedom on the Net 2016.
31. Amnesty International Report 2015/16. The State of the World's Human Rights.
32. Human Rights Watch (2016). World Report 2016.
33. US Department of State (2015). Country Reports on Human Rights Practices for 2015.

34. United Nations Human Rights Committee (2014). Concluding observations on the sixth periodic report of Japan, 23 July 2014.
35. Helliwell, J., R. Layard, & J. Sachs. World Happiness Report 2017.
36. This report measures happiness based on six factors: GDP per capita, healthy years of life expectancy, social support (as measured by having someone to count on in times of trouble), trust (as measured by a perceived absence of corruption in government and business), perceived freedom to make life decisions, and generosity (as measured by recent donations).
37. Gallup (2014). People worldwide are reporting a lot of positive emotions, 21 May 2014.
38. Gallop-Healthways (2015). Country Well-Being Rankings.
39. OECD Better Life Index (accessed 13 September 2016).
40. Kwan, Kevin (2013). Crazy Rich Asians.
41. Forbes (2016). The World's Billionaires, 2016 Ranking.
42. Bain & Company (2015). Luxury Goods Worldwide Market Study. Fall-Winter 2015.
43. Nanditha, Arun, Ronald C.W. Ma, Ambady Ramachandran, Chamukuttan Snehalatha, Juliana C.N. Chan, Kee Seng Chia, Jonathan E. Shaw and Paul Z. Zimmet (2016). Diabetes in Asia and the Pacific: Implications for the Global Epidemic. Diabetes Care, 39 (9). American Diabetes Association.

**Open Access** This chapter is licensed under the terms of the Creative Commons Attribution 4.0 International License (http://creativecommons.org/licenses/by/4.0/), which permits use, sharing, adaptation, distribution, and reproduction in any medium or format, as long as you give appropriate credit to the original author(s) and the source, provide a link to the Creative Commons license and indicate if changes were made.

The images or other third party material in this chapter are included in the chapter's Creative Commons license, unless indicated otherwise in a credit line to the material. If material is not included in the chapter's Creative Commons license and your intended use is not permitted by statutory regulation or exceeds the permitted use, you will need to obtain permission directly from the copyright holder.

PART II

# Seven Challenges for an Asian Century

CHAPTER 4

# Getting Better Value Out of Global Value Chains

"Where do you think that your iPhone was made?" This is my favorite question to my economics students at Tokyo's Sophia University.

They all respond "China!" But the situation is much more complex than that, as Chinese professor Yuqing Xing has demonstrated.[1] The iPhone is assembled in China by Taiwanese companies Foxconn and Pegatron. But this assembly process accounts for less than 5% of the iPhone's manufacturing value added.

In reality, the iPhone is produced through a "global value chain" (GVC) which starts with its conception and design in California. High-tech components come from Japan, Korea, Germany, the US and elsewhere, with Japanese-made components contributing the biggest share. The iPhone is then assembled in China, while California manages the marketing and branding. One consequence of this supply "fragmentation" is that Apple directly employs only 63,000 of the more than 750,000 people globally involved in designing, selling, manufacturing and assembling its products.[2]

Many of us still harbor a nationalistic perception of how products are manufactured. But this does not make any sense in today's world of GVCs. Very few products are still made in one country. Most products are thus made "in the world", with different parts and components coming from different countries, and different production processes located in different countries. Overall, GVCs would account for some 80% of global trade, and they are much more developed in Asia than in other regions.[3]

© The Author(s) 2018
J. West, *Asian Century... on a Knife-edge*,
https://doi.org/10.1007/978-981-10-7182-9_4

A similar GVC story can be told for clothing, much of which today is manufactured in China, Bangladesh, Vietnam and Cambodia. For example, a jacket which is designed and sold in the US for $425, but manufactured in China, might have manufacturing costs representing only 9% of the total sales value.[4] US companies would account for much of the other 91%, through their intellectual property; services like retail, logistics and banking; and profits. In other words, products like jackets, which seem to be manufactured goods, are substantially packages of intangible, knowledge-based services. In fact, all manufactured goods embody large shares of services.

There are many other surprising examples of GVCs, some of which highlight the role of Japan in the engine room of today's GVCs. Japanese high-tech parts and components account for some 35% of the value of Boeing's 787 Dreamliner and 21% of the 777 widebody jets.[5] And as China is now celebrating the production of its first big passenger plane, the C919, which is in the testing stage, the reality is that many technologies, systems and parts are supplied by foreign companies, like the engines which come from a joint venture between America's General Electric and France's Safran.

While many Japanese manufacturers may have slipped off the global radar screen, they are indispensable linchpins in Asia's GVCs, as Japan accounts for 20–60% of the world's production of semiconductors, optical components, image sensors, microcontrollers, display drivers and silicon wafers.[6] And many of these parts and components are made by a new wave of small and medium Japanese companies ("hidden champions"), rather than big conglomerates.[7]

Even the explosives used by the Islamic State (IS) would be produced through a complex GVC. Conflict Armament Research (CAR) examined more than 700 components used by IS forces to manufacture improvised explosive devices (IEDs), identified their provenance and traced their chains of custody.[8] CAR identified 50 commercial entities and 20 countries involved in the GVC for components used by IS forces to construct IEDs. Turkey was the most important supplier, with 13 companies involved in the GVC supplying chemical precursors, containers, detonating cord, cables and wires.

India was the second most important supplier of components as seven Indian companies manufactured most of the detonators, detonating cord and safety fuses. Companies headquartered in Japan, Switzerland and the US manufactured the microcontrollers, signal relays and transistors used in the devices. The CAR report did not find any evidence that there were direct sales companies from these countries to the IS. Rather, there were sales to other companies, with the parts and components finding their way to the IS through subsequent transactions.

In sum, international trade and production of manufactured goods (even explosives) mainly take place through GVCs. Production is fragmented into different phases, which are located in different countries according to their comparative advantages. GVCs are usually driven by multinational enterprises (MNEs) through their business decisions, and a large share of international trade and investment now takes place within MNEs' networks of affiliates.

GVCs have been a major factor driving Asia's economic development. But to continue its rapid development, Asia must get better value out of the region's GVCs, and better manage their many risks and challenges, as we will discuss throughout this chapter.

GVCs are however a relatively new phenomenon, which took off during the 1980s and 1990s. When Japan was developing rapidly from the 1950s to the 1970s, the manufacturing landscape was fundamentally different. Most manufacturing activity took place under one factory roof, and in one country. So how did GVCs come about?

## Birth of GVCs

Politics played an initial role in the development of Asia's GVCs. In 1978, Chinese Vice Premier Deng Xiaoping visited Japan, the first-ever visit of a Chinese state leader.[9] Deng took Japan's bullet train ("shinkansen") from Tokyo to Osaka, and was stunned by Japan's technological development and modernity.

Deng visited a Panasonic TV factory in Osaka and queried the company founder Konosuke Matsushita, "Mr Matsushita, you are called the god of management in Japan. Would you be willing to help us advance the modernization of China?" The founder immediately responded, "We will do whatever we can to contribute to the modernization of China".[10]

Throughout the 1980s Matsushita transferred technology, trained Chinese workers and otherwise helped China modernize its industry through 150 separate projects. China learned how Matsushita made everything from electric irons to transformers and semiconductors. In return, Matsushita earned the Chinese government's goodwill and gained unparalleled expertise in manufacturing and selling in the Chinese market.

Panasonic's investment in China was just the beginning of the wave of Japanese investment in emerging Asia that was crucial to the establishment of the region's GVCs. Another impulse to the creation of GVCs occurred in 1985 when Western leaders pushed Japan to allow the yen to rise via the "Plaza Accord". As the higher yen adversely affected the competitiveness of exports, Japanese companies began relocating labor-intensive parts of their manufacturing industry elsewhere in Asia, especially to East and Southeast Asia.

Japanese companies now have some $360 billion worth of investments in Asia, with $110 billion in China and $50 billion in each of Singapore and Thailand. And as Hong Kong, Korea, Singapore and Taiwan climbed the development ladder, they also offshored large slabs of their labor-intensive manufacturing industry to Southeast Asia and China. Indeed, Japan's investments in China are now well exceeded by those of Taiwan and Hong Kong, with Hong Kong being by far the largest single source since China opened to foreign investment in the late 1970s. Today China might seem like an economic giant. But just a few decades ago, it was very much an economic pygmy compared with Hong Kong, Japan and Taiwan.

There were many other factors that combined to facilitate the development of GVCs. Seeing the success of export-oriented policies in Japan, Hong Kong, Korea, Singapore and Taiwan, Southeast Asian countries and China opened their markets to attract investment and stimulate trade. Governments offered great incentives like tariff free imports, and tax concessions, especially through special economic zones and export processing zones where loose policies with regard to labor rights and environmental standards were usually the norm. And China's membership in 2001 led to an acceleration of GVCs in the 2000s.

Declining transport costs also played a role, as it became less costly to ship components from one location to another. The falling cost of passenger aviation made it easier for managers and engineers to travel between locations. Chinese investors can easily afford a day-trip to visit their factories in Cambodia. Indeed, the close location of a large number of Asia economies of diverse levels of development and comparative advantages provided an opportunity to tie these economies together through GVCs.

Rapid progress in information technology has provided an essential tool for the coordination of what have become very complex GVCs. The challenge of managing Asia's GVCs is evident from the Apple's China

GVC which in 2015 included 198 companies and 759 subsidiaries, 336 (44.2%) of which were located in China.[11] It is no surprise that GVC management should be one of the most challenging and enriching jobs in Asia today.

So today, East and Southeast Asia is criss-crossed by a dense network of GVCs for a wide range of manufacturing products, notably electronics, automobiles, machinery and clothing. Each country specializes in tasks according to their comparative advantages. Hong Kong and Singapore tend to specialize in logistics and finance, and be home to corporate regional headquarters. Japan and Korea focus on branded product designs and high-tech components, and Malaysia and Thailand specialize in mid-range manufacturing. Thailand has become a regional manufacturing hub for the automobile industry in particular, being used by companies like Toyota, Mazda and Ford. China specializes in product assembly and lower-skilled manufacturing, although it is now graduating to higher value-added activities. Bangladesh and Cambodia are very active in clothing manufacture, while Indonesia and Mongolia are rich in natural resources.

This phenomenon has come to be known as "Factory Asia", and China is often referred to as the "Factory of the World". But since foreign investment in China's GVCs is still such as important motor of China's development, trade by MNEs still accounts for some 45% of China's total trade.[12] This may be down from the peak of 59% in 2005, as Chinese companies are becoming more active in international trade. However, MNEs remain a very important feature of China's GVCs and economy more generally. In a similar vein, the foreign value-added share in exports is above 30% in Singapore, Malaysia and Vietnam.[13]

East and Southeast Asian countries participating in GVCs have experienced very rapid economic growth, poverty reduction and rising incomes. GVCs have also been empowering for women, who dominate workforces in factories for garments and textiles, electronics and commercial horticulture. But not all Asian countries have managed to integrate into GVCs. Much of South Asia is missing the GVC boat, and being left behind, although India has been very active in the development of GVCs for IT-based business services, something we will discuss later.

All things considered, how useful are GVCs for countries wishing to get on a fast track to economic development?

## GVCs, A Fast Track to Development

The advent of GVCs can indeed offer a fast track to development. It is no longer necessary for one country to be capable of every phase in the production of, for example, an automobile or a television, as was the case when Japan and Korea were in the midst of their fast growth periods. Today, it is only necessary to perform one stage or task in the GVC to be able to hook onto new development opportunities. And small and medium enterprises have greater opportunities to participate in GVCs, by exporting just one part or component.

For example, the Chinese town of Qiaotou, once a mere farming village, has made its mark on Asia's GVCs by becoming the "button capital of the world". According to one estimate, Qiaotou's 700 family-run factories would produce over 60% of the world's clothing buttons, and 80% of the world's zippers, as it manufactures 15 billion buttons and 200 million meters of zippers a year. But Qiaotou is not the only example. China's industrial heartland is dotted with towns that specialize in all manner of things like socks, toothbrushes and cigarette lighters!

In a similar vein, Cambodia has hooked onto Asia's GVC for garment manufacture and export, and has thus joined the "Olympians of growth", according to the World Bank.[14] Following the UN-sponsored national elections in 1993, the Cambodian government opened up the economy to international trade and investment.[15] This enabled the country to attract enormous flows of foreign direct investment (FDI), coming mainly from China, Malaysia, South Korea, Taiwan, Vietnam and Japan. Cambodia's stock of inward FDI in Cambodia increased from $125m in 1993 to $14.8bn in 2015, an increase from 5% to 82% of the country's GDP. External factors like rising labor costs in China, the 2011 floods and political instability in Thailand, and the desire of Japanese investors to diversify their investment destinations have also driven inflows of FDI.

Cambodia's economy has grown at an annual rate of 7.7% over the past two decades, making it the world's sixth fastest growing economy, with exports contributing more than 50% to Cambodia's growth over the past decade. The garment sector accounts for three-quarters of merchandise exports, and has benefited from preferential access to US and EU markets, and relocation of production from China as the latter's wage costs have risen.

Thanks to a strong economy, the share of Cambodia's population living in extreme poverty (less than $1.90 a day) fell from 30% in 1994 to 2% in

2012 (those living in moderate poverty—less than $3.10 a day—fell from 67% to 22% over the same period).[16] And Cambodia's women, who account for 85% of the 600,000 employees in the garment sector, have benefited in particular from the sector's relatively higher wages. This is an astonishing achievement for a country that was torn apart by a horrifically genocidal war just a few decades ago that killed one-quarter of its population.

But Cambodia remains one of Asia's very poorest countries, with a GDP per capita of only $3483, well below its neighbors of Laos and Vietnam, and the lowest in Southeast Asia. And despite the undeniable benefits of hooking onto the GVC for garments, Cambodia faces the risk of getting stuck producing low value-added garments forever, unless it can upgrade its economy.

Cambodia faces daunting challenges in attracting higher quality FDI and in climbing the GVC to higher value-added activities. For one, its very successful garment sector is basically an enclave, with a few linkages to the rest of the economy. Domestic value added in the garment sector is low, with local workers undertaking merely "cut, sew and trim" functions. Higher value-added activities, like design, branding and marketing, are undertaken by MNEs like H&M, Inditex, Gap, Banana Republic, Nike, Levi, C&A, Puma, Old Navy, Adidas and Calvin Klein.

Most importantly, the country is still suffering from the lingering impact of the massive loss of skilled Cambodians and severe disruption to the country's education system suffered during the 1975 to 1979 Khmer Rouge period, when the country's educated elite was decimated.

"Cambodia's labour force is still characterised by low education and low skills. The average educational attainment of the labour force is currently at primary education level or even lower," says Shandre Thangavelu, a professor at Australia's University of Adelaide. "To continue to reap the benefits of FDI, it will be necessary to make major investments in school education, and technical and vocational training, as well as infrastructure and public institutions."[17]

Improving human capital is a long-term endeavor. But as Mr. Thangavelu says: "Without strong interventions to develop human capital, there is a high possibility of the economy becoming caught in a 'low-skill, low-wage' trap in the near future."[18]

Very poor governance is also holding the country back from realizing its great potential, as Cambodia is one of the world's most corrupt countries. It is ranked 156 out of the 176 countries in Transparency

International's Corruption Perceptions Index,[19] and 112 out of 113 countries in the World Justice Project's Rule of Law Index.[20] Cambodia's garment workers also suffer from widespread labor rights abuses like forced overtime, pregnancy discrimination, child labor and anti-union practices, as NGO Human Rights Watch has reported.[21] The Cambodian government makes little effort to enforce labor laws, while big Western apparel brands, whose garments are produced in Cambodia, turn a blind eye. Chinese-owned garment factories are reportedly among the worst offenders when it comes to labor rights abuses. Cambodia is also a hotspot for human trafficking, according to the US State Department.

The case of Cambodia shows that when a country is at the rock-bottom of the global development ladder, as Cambodia was, getting just a few things right (like its liberal trade and investment regime) can enable a country to join GVCs and stimulate rapid growth, and poverty reduction. But the case of Cambodia also shows that to continue developing, and extracting greater value out of GVCs, it is necessary to improve human capital, the quality of governance and infrastructure. Cambodia's developmental journey has barely begun.

## Hooking on to GVCs

All Asian countries, including Cambodia, could do much more to exploit the possibilities of GVCs by attracting more and better-quality foreign investment.

Since GVC participation by low- and middle-income countries is mainly driven by investment from MNEs, it is critical to foster an investment-friendly ecosystem. This means good transport, logistics and other infrastructure, human capital, open trade and investment policies, intellectual property protection, minimal red tape especially for customs procedures and strong institutions.

But the narrative is all too often the same in Asia. A small group of countries are world leaders, while the rest trail off into the distance. For example, only Singapore, Hong Kong and Japan make it into the world top 20 in the World Bank's Logistics Performance Index,[22] while only the same three countries and Taiwan score a top 20 ranking World Economic Forum's Global Competitiveness Index,[23] and the same three countries and Korea are classed in the top 20 of the World Justice Project's Rule of Law index.[24] Outside of North East Asia, other Asian countries score poorly in the OECD's PISA study, which assesses the education performance of 15 year old students.[25]

At the same time, China, India, Indonesia, Myanmar, the Philippines and, to a lesser extent, Malaysia have simply enormous barriers to foreign investment, which greatly restrict their capacity to participate in Asia's GVCs. While Japan may have low formal barriers to foreign investment, this unique country's business and social practices have proved a virtual insurmountable barrier to investors.

This means that Japan, which has done so much to create GVCs in other Asian countries, has virtually no GVC footprint at home. Japan's economy is losing so much through its inability to attract GVC investments at home. Indeed, it is a vast outlier compared with other advanced countries like the US, Germany, UK and France, which are enormous overseas investors, but which also receive large inward flows of investment. In Japan's case, the stock of inward foreign investment is less than 15% of its stock of outward investment.[26]

Asia is in desperate need of a new boost to its GVC-driven development, and trade and investment liberalization offers one path forward. But the arrival of Donald Trump in the presidency of the US, and his withdrawal of America from the Trans-Pacific Partnership (TPP) will only undermine the prospects for trade and investment liberalization in Asia.

## Asian Trade and Investment Liberalization

Opening economies to international trade and investment has played a key role in the development of Asia's GVCs. Some countries have unilaterally opened their economies. For example, Hong Kong and Singapore have the world's most open economies in contrast to most of their trading partners. This is one reason why they are Asia's most advanced economies. China and indeed most Asian economies have made partial openings of their economies through special economic zones. They can be an effective way of attracting international business and starting liberalization, but such zones also result in unbalanced, distorted economies.

Countries like China have liberalized their trade and investment as they joined the World Trade Organization (China joined in 2001), while longer-term members of the WTO/GATT have opened markets during multilateral trade deals like the Uruguay Round. And India, Indonesia, Korea and Thailand liberalized trade and investment in response to financial crises, often under pressure from the IMF.

Regional integration has also played a role. The Southeast Asian countries of ASEAN signed an ASEAN Free Trade Area agreement (AFTA) in 1992, and this is now being transformed into an "ASEAN Economic Community". The AFTA was also enhanced through a series of separate FTAs between ASEAN and six other regional countries, namely China, Japan, Korea, Australia, India and New Zealand. For its part, Taiwan has been virtually shut out of most Asian FTAs because of pressure from China, although Taiwan does have an FTA with Singapore, New Zealand, and in 2010 it did sign the Economic Cooperation Framework Agreement with China. Taiwan is also pursuing a possible FTA with India.

Despite the apparent great success of Asia's trade and investment policies, most Asian countries have relatively closed economies, according to the OECD's FDI Regulatory Restrictiveness Index. Indeed, only Cambodia and Japan score better than the average for the advanced OECD countries. And the Philippines, Myanmar, China, Indonesia and India are highly closed to foreign investment, the key driver of GVCs.

In other words, there is much work that Asia needs to do to open its economies to trade and investment, and make the most of GVCs. In recent years, two separate sets of multilateral trade talks have offered the hope of a new wave of trade and liberalization in Asia, namely the TPP and the Regional Comprehensive Economic Partnership (RCEP).

## Trans-Pacific Partnership

The TPP negotiations were successfully concluded on 6 October 2015, but the US Congress never ratified the deal. And then in January 2017, to the dismay of the US business community, US President Trump withdrew the US from the TPP. This was after all a trade agreement designed by the US business community, for the benefit of the US business community, pushed onto allies and partners, and then rejected by a business man president. Above all, the TPP was an important geopolitical initiative that would have enabled the US to set high standards for trade, investment and GVCs in twenty-first century Asia, something that no other country could do.

On the presidential campaign trail Trump declared the TPP "another disaster done and pushed by special interests who want to rape our country". No trade and investment deal is perfect. They are the product of compromises between participating governments. But this is a great pity. The TPP was very much the right agreement for today's world of GVCs where companies from "headquarter economies" like the US, Japan and Korea create and design products, and then outsource the labor-intensive stages of manufacturing to "factory economies" like Southeast Asia or China.

The TPP went beyond mere trade liberalization and sought to establish a more seamless environment for trade and investment. It dealt with issues like services, electronic commerce, telecommunications, competition policy, state-owned enterprises (SOEs), intellectual property, government procurement, and transparency and anti-corruption. The concerns of US workers and environmental activists were also taken on board in labor and environment chapters. Vietnam, Malaysia and Brunei made important commitments regarding freedom of association for trade unions, forced labor and human trafficking.

The TPP was economically very important. Its signatories were Australia, Brunei, Canada, Chile, Japan, Malaysia, Mexico, Peru, New Zealand, Singapore, the US and Vietnam, which account for 40% of the world economy and one-quarter of world trade. The absence of China is often alleged to be a deliberate geopolitical ploy by the US. In reality, China was invited to join the TPP trade talks, but declined. And China would have immense political difficulties signing up to the TPP's chapters for labor rights and SOEs. While all countries including the US stood to gain substantially from the TPP, countries like Vietnam, Malaysia and Japan stood to gain the most through their promised market opening.

The great value of the TPP is evident in the efforts of governments from Japan, Australia, Singapore and others to try to convince the Trump administration to reconsider its objection to the TPP. The 11 remaining members of the TPP are now discussing the possibility of proceeding with the TPP without the US. It is far from clear that all 11 would be willing to proceed without the prospect of improved access to the large and lucrative US market. It is also far from clear that they will all be willing to sign up to the labor rights, SOE and environmental chapters without US pressure.

## Trump Trade Policy

During the US presidential election campaign and before his inauguration, Donald Trump had much to say about US trade and investment with Asia. He accused China of raping the US. He threatened to label China a currency manipulator, to levy an import tariff of 45% on American imports from China and to penalize companies that locate manufacturing investments in China rather than the US. But Trump's rhetoric on trade policy has been evolving and softening from these defiantly protectionist messages. He is now emphasizing his support for both free and fair trade.

According to the President's 2017 Trade Policy Agenda, America has not benefited from its trade deals over the past couple of decades due to the lack of reciprocity in trading relations. He complains that many countries have high trade barriers, while their companies can export freely to the US. Indeed, there is a widespread consensus that China has been flouting world trade rules, stealing US intellectual property, conducting state-sponsored industrial espionage, buying up US companies while keeping its own markets closed, and discriminating against American companies based in China. In a retreat from a practice from the Cold War, the Trade Policy Agenda indicates that US will no longer turn a blind eye to unfair trade practices that disadvantage Americans for "putative geopolitical advantage", something which make Japan and Korea shudder.

The US' trade deficit is the lightning rod for Donald Trump. Indeed, the US has had a trade deficit since 1975, and today has the world's largest trade deficit, some $763 billion in 2016. The US' trade deficit with China of $347 billion represents almost half, with Japan ($69 billion) and Korea ($28 billion) being among the other leading contributors.

Trump would now like US trade policy to focus on bilateral rather than multilateral deals. Through bilateral trade diplomacy an aggressive hegemon like the US can extract maximum benefits from its relatively weaker partners, and can also unilaterally sanction any partner that causes it displeasure, without having to bother with international dispute settlement mechanisms and the rule of law. Trump clearly has China, Japan and Korea in his sights. The new Trade Policy Agenda highlighted the tripling of the US' trade deficit with China since it joined the WTO, and the doubling of its trade deficit with Korea following their free trade agreement.

On the occasion of their summit meeting in February 2017, Trump and Japanese Prime Minister Shinzo Abe agreed to establish a new framework for economic dialogue, which is expected to lead to a bilateral free trade agreement. And when Trump met Chinese President Xi Jinping in April 2017, trade was also top of the agenda. Xi was very keen to avoid a trade war with its biggest trading partner as the two sides agreed to a rushed 100-day negotiation over some of their thorniest trade and investment disputes. But very little was achieved through this 100-day deal. And at their June 2017 summit, President Trump told

Korean President Moon Jae-in that the US intended to renegotiate their free trade agreement.

While the US Treasury has backed off from Trump's claims of Chinese currency manipulation, it did establish a "Monitoring List" of major trading partners that merit close attention to their currency practices, which includes four Asian economies, namely China, Japan, Korea and Taiwan.[27] Despite some softening in Trump's trade rhetoric, there remains a strongly protectionist undercurrent, as Trump's overriding trade policy goals are reducing the US' bilateral trade deficits (notably with China, Japan and Korea), and bringing back manufacturing jobs to America. And Trump's launching in August 2017 of an investigation into China's alleged theft of US intellectual property has deeply troubled the Chinese government, and raised the specter of a possible trade war between China and the US. Trump has also threatened to disregard World Trade Organization dispute settlement rulings. While Trump is promising to shake up trade relations with Asia, China is actively seeking to foster trade within Eurasia through its Belt and Road Initiative.

With America's retreat from the TPP, many commentators have argued that China will take over the lead of trade liberalization in Asia, notably through the RCEP. Nothing could be further from the truth!

## Regional Comprehensive Economic Partnership

The RCEP is a negotiation which seeks to create one single FTA between the ten ASEAN member states (Brunei Darussalam, Cambodia, Indonesia, Lao PDR, Malaysia, Myanmar, Philippines, Singapore, Thailand, Vietnam) and those six countries which already have FTAs with ASEAN—Australia, China, India, Japan, Korea and New Zealand—the "Plus-6 countries". The RCEP were launched in in November 2012, with the goal of completing the deal by end 2015.

On paper, the RCEP looks like a huge deal. It involves half the world's population. The participating countries account for 30% of global GDP and about a quarter of world exports and foreign investment. It could thus become the world's biggest trading bloc. The RCEP promises to create one agreement building on the complex "noodle bowl" of agreements between ASEAN and the Plus-6 countries, and result in "significant improvements" over the existing agreements. The RCEP will also require agreements between those Plus-6 countries that don't already have agreements.

But the RCEP is proving much more difficult than envisaged. Rationalizing into one agreement the complex "noodle bowl" of agreements between ASEAN and the Plus-6 countries is in fact very challenging, as many of these agreements are quite different from each other, having been negotiated at different points in time. Filling in the gaps between the Plus-6 agreements is also proving arduous, especially in light of the need for FTAs between China and India, China and Japan, and Korea and Japan, countries which have testy relations. And the RCEP is ultimately not very ambitious. Its main focus is on merchandise trade barriers, rather than issues like services, investment, intellectual property and competition policy which are key to GVCs.

The reality is that the RCEP negotiation may never be concluded. And if it is, it will not result in any significant market opening. In fact, apart from Singapore and Hong Kong, Asian economies have never been thrilled about open markets for trade and investment. They are mainly concerned with serving the interests of their entrenched business elites. This is a great pity as Asia desperately needs much more open markets to continue its development.

In the press the RCEP was often billed as a China-led negotiation, which excludes the US, and which seeks to rival the US-led TPP, even though officially it is an ASEAN-led deal. But from all reports, the RCEP negotiations are suffering from a lack of strong leadership. Some countries like India and Indonesia are not enthusiastic at all about RCEP, and China shows no visible signs of wishing to further open its markets. The negotiating deadline of end-2015 was initially extended to 2016, and now there is the mere hope that it will be finalized in 2017. Perhaps the best indicator of the value of the RCEP is that US business is not interested in it at all.

In sum, Asia is in desperate need of a new wave of trade and investment liberalization to dynamize its GVCs as a motor of development. But the US' abandonment of the TPP and adoption of a bilateral rather than multilateral approach means a great loss of leadership in trade and investment liberalization, and we can expect trade relationships between the US and Asia's leading countries to be fractious. While many assume that China will be able to step into the empty gap left by the US, there is no evidence whatsoever of Chinese leadership in trade and investment diplomacy. Like Japan and Korea before it, China practices mercantilism, as promotes exports and protects its domestic market from imports.

## Climbing GVCs

A major development challenge for Asia's emerging economies is to increase their share of the value added in their GVC exports through functions such as high-tech componentry, product design and branding. As the examples of the iPhone and the jacket at the beginning of this chapter highlight, all too often Asia's emerging economies contribute only a minor share to their GVC exports, even if they have been increasing their value added since 2008.[28] And perhaps the ultimate challenge is to become corporate leaders of GVCs, rather than just following the lead of MNEs from advanced countries, which direct most of the GVCs in Asia today.

How can a country climb up the GVC and become a GVC leader? The bottom line is that Asia's emerging economies need to develop their economic, business and technological sophistication.

The very act of participating in GVCs facilitates knowledge and technology transfers. Local people who work in MNEs gain valuable experience and exposure to global best practices. Local companies who have supply contracts with multinationals also learn to comply with the global product standards. In other words, GVCs provide an opportunity for learning by doing, as knowledge can flow along GVCs and lay the foundation for them to make a high value-added contribution to GVCs.

But experience shows that such passive upgrading may not take you a long way up the GVC. As in the case of Cambodia, all too often GVC activities can be an enclave that has very few linkages to the local economy. And for its part, Apple has been reluctant to involve many Chinese companies in its GVC as suppliers of key components or as major assemblers of Apple products.[29] The majority of Apple's suppliers, even many of those located in China itself, are foreign companies, principally from US, Japan, Taiwan and Korea. Apple's choice of supplier companies reflects their ability to deliver the highest quality in good time and at the negotiated price. This may reflect questions of trust related to business culture, as protection of intellectual property is notoriously weak in China.

At the same time, it is also true that China is in the midst of an impressive process of technology catch-up. China has developed a strong niche in high-speed trains building on technology transfer from Japan. And e-commerce giant Alibaba has been an amazing success story. But many other successful Chinese companies, like Huawei, Xiaomi, Lenovo and ZTE, remain basically "copycat companies" which are now tackling the lower ends of markets occupied by advanced countries.

Today, there is no government making greater efforts to climb Asia's GVCs and get better value for its economy than China's. It is keenly aware that its position as a low-cost producer is now being challenged by countries like Cambodia, India, Indonesia and Vietnam, while there is a yawning gap between China's manufacturing capacities and those of Germany, Japan and the US, despite some isolated success stories.

It is also relevant that countries like Malaysia and Thailand, which have been successful participants in GVCs, have never managed to break out and become industrial and technological leaders themselves. Technology is also seen as a security issue by the Chinese government. It craves to have indigenous information technology and to not be dependent on American and other Western companies.

At this stage, China's manufacturing industry is facing four major challenges—insufficient innovation, weakness in core technologies, excess energy consumption and severe pollution. This is why the Chinese government launched a "Made in China 2025" initiative which seeks to upgrade China from a manufacturing giant into a manufacturing power, building on earlier such initiatives.

While delivering the 2015 Annual Government Work Report, Chinese Premier Li Keqiang said, "We will implement the 'Made in China 2025' strategy, seek innovation-driven development, apply smart technologies, strengthen foundations, pursue green development and redouble our efforts to upgrade China from a manufacturer of quantity to one of quality".[30] The ultimate goal is to become the world's leading manufacturer by 2049, the hundredth anniversary of the foundation of the People's Republic of China.

## China's Efforts to Climb GVCs

China has thus been pursuing various activities to acquire knowledge and technology to improve the sophistication of its economy, such as investing in domestic R&D, investing in foreign companies to acquire their technology, promoting "innovation mercantilism", practicing industrial espionage and fostering entrepreneurship—all of which can play an important role in China's GVC participation.

## China's R&D

China has been ramping up its spending on R&D dramatically, with R&D averaging 20% annual growth between 2003 and 2013.[31] China accounts now for about 20% of global spending on R&D, not too far behind the US' 27%. China will likely overtake the US in the coming years, and become the world's leading R&D nation. Indeed, China's new 5-year plan promises that by 2020, R&D investment will account for 2.5% of gross domestic product, compared with 2.05% in 2014 (US spending on R&D represents 2.7% of GDP).[32]

Many questions are raised about the quality of China's R&D spending which tends to favor large companies and high-profile prestige projects, rather than dynamic small companies and projects that would have more of an impact on the lives of Chinese citizens. But China is unquestionably on the road to becoming a science and technology powerhouse. China and India now together produce almost half of the world's new undergraduate science and engineering (S&E) degrees, the EU 12% and the US 9%. The US, however, still produces more S&E doctoral degrees than China and India and remains the leader in S&E higher education, as well as the destination of choice for international students.

## China "Innovation Mercantilism"

China has long practiced "innovation mercantilism", a strategy that embraces a new kind of protectionist trade policy, to improve domestic innovation capacity and technology—even though it regularly contravenes its commitments under its membership of the WTO.[33] This involves many things like subsidies and access to finance to keep production artificially cheap. This underpins its massive excess capacity across a wide range of industries. Although it is less of a problem today, for a long time China manipulated its exchange rate to enhance the competitiveness of its export and import-competing sectors.

China also uses the power of its market size to force MNEs to transfer technology to Chinese companies, to push them to go into joint ventures with Chinese companies, and to coerce require them into establishing research centers into China. For example, Apple has been coerced into establishing R&D centers in China. And in order to open motor vehicle factories in China, Ford had to enter into a joint venture with Chinese automobile producer Chang'an Motors. It was also required to open an

R&D laboratory employing at least 150 Chinese engineers. Forced technology transfer was also how China became a leader in the high-speed train sector.

China has many restrictions on market access, such as for its semiconductor market. The "Made in China 2025" initiative is targeting "40 per cent self-sufficiency in semiconductors by 2020, rising to 70 per cent by 2025". This would reduce Chinese imports of US semiconductors by half in 10 years and ultimately eliminate them entirely within 20 years.

The Chinese government introduced "indigenous innovation" policies explicitly designed to discriminate against foreign-owned companies in its enormous government procurement market. It has introduced security and industry rules, especially requirements for "secure and controllable" equipment, which effectively exclude foreign technology products.[34]

### *China's Outward FDI*

Over recent years, China has become a major outward investor, with flows averaging $120 billion a year over the past three years.[35] A number of years ago, it was mainly investing in energy, natural resources and agricultural properties in Australia, Africa and Latin America. But now China's investment is now increasingly targeting Western companies with technology, know-how and brands to enable it to climb further up the GVC.

Both the US and Europe have been receiving large inflows of Chinese investment. Some of the most important recent investments in the US have been Haier's acquisition of GE's appliances unit, Wanda's purchase of Legendary Entertainment, the acquisition of Omnivision Technologies by a Chinese consortium and, in the automotive sector, Ningbo Joyson's acquisition of Key Safety Systems.[36]

In Europe, Tencent bought Finland's Supercell, Beijing Enterprises bought Germany's EEW Energy from Waste operation, and ChemChina acquired Switzerland's Syngenta, Italy's Pirelli and Germany's KraussMaffei Group. Fosun bought Germany's Hauck & Aufhäuser Privatbank, Dalian Wanda acquired Britain's yacht maker Sunseeker and Haitong bought Spain's Banco Espirito Santo's investment banking business.[37]

China has also reportedly been hiring German and Japanese industrial experts. And companies like Huawei, ZTE, Lenovo and Xiaomi have been buying patents through licensing deals and acquisitions.

But China's accelerating purchases of Western companies is giving rise to many concerns by Western governments, and may not be a sustainable strategy, even though the accumulated stock of Chinese investment remains modest for the moment. Among these many concerns are: the potential loss of core technologies and the impact that may have on the local economy; the lack of transparency of some Chinese investors; and the perceived political risks of accepting investments from state-owned companies with close links to the Chinese Communist Party. Other concerns are that China's own market remains relatively closed to foreign investors, and no foreign company would be allowed to buy critical infrastructure or core technologies in China.

More recently, the Chinese government has become concerned about the quality of some of its companies' investments, especially at a time when it is concerned about controlling capital outflows. So in 2017, it began clamping down on some overseas investments by Chinese companies.

### China's Industrial Espionage

China did not invent industrial espionage, but it has certainly mastered the art. And intellectual property theft, especially from the US has been reportedly rampant, and has been called the "great brain robbery".[38] Keith Alexander, former director of the US National Security Agency, once said the loss of industrial information and intellectual property through cyber espionage constitutes the "greatest transfer of wealth in history".[39] The US Commission on the Theft of American Intellectual Property estimates that the annual cost to the US economy continues to exceed $225 billion in counterfeit goods, pirated software and theft of trade secrets and could be as high as $600 billion, and that China remains the world's principal IP infringer.[40] And Microsoft estimates that 95% of the copies of Microsoft's Office software in China are pirated, and at least 80% of China's government computers use versions of the Microsoft Windows operating systems that were illegally copied or otherwise not purchased.

In 2015, US President Obama and Chinese President Xi agreed that the US and Chinese governments would not conduct cyberattacks to steal intellectual property for economic gain from each other. Reports suggest that there may have been a subsequent fall in such espionage, although there is always a risk that implementation of this agreement could fall foul of future tensions in US/China relations. But even if there were a sudden stop to industrial espionage, China would already have stolen a big march in its development through its acquisition of technologies in the areas of

IT, renewable and nuclear energy, biotechnology, telecommunications, agriculture and so on.

## Entrepreneurship in China

Chinese Premier, Li Keqiang is also promoting "mass entrepreneurship" (along with innovation) as a new engine of China's economic development. This is a very good initiative. Since the Chinese government started removing the shackles of central planning and state ownership, entrepreneurship has been a key driver of the Chinese economy. Chinese entrepreneurs range from families that open up a small restaurant, shop or factory to people like Jack Ma of Alibaba, Ma Huateng (Pony Ma) of Tencent or Lei Jun of Xiaomi.

Jack Ma is the symbol of the swashbuckling Chinese entrepreneur. He admits with almost great pride that Harvard University rejected his application ten times, and that his job application at Kentucky Fried Chicken was also rejected. And yet as the founder of e-commerce behemoth Alibaba, he is now the world's eighth richest man in tech with a net worth of $29 billion.

Despite the great success of Jack Ma and others, budding entrepreneurs have faced many great challenges in China. Better education for entrepreneurship is needed. China's typical rote learning education is not very useful for stimulating the animal spirits of budding entrepreneurs. Weak rule of law, rampant corruption and heavy state bureaucracy are further drags on entrepreneurial ambitions. And access to finance, a break on entrepreneurs everywhere, is even more of a challenge in China where so much finance from state-owned banks is channeled to SOEs, based on cozy connections.

Under the leadership of Premier Li Keqiang, the Chinese government is making radical changes to improve the climate for young entrepreneurs, and according to all the signs, entrepreneurship is booming in China, especially in the IT space. But needless to say, Rome wasn't built in a day.

All things considered, China's efforts to get better value out of Asia's GVCs are very impressive, and will no doubt help climb further up the GVC. But China's approach is basically a top-down, centrally-controlled brand of "techno-nationalism". Japan and Korea have also implemented similar policies in earlier years. This enabled them to climb fair way up the GVC, but their progress became stunted.

The real lesson of the world's innovation leaders like Switzerland, Sweden, the UK and the US[41] is that other ingredients are necessary. Open economies are necessary to boost competition as well as cooperation between different companies and countries. Open societies are required to allow academic freedom, freedom of speech and thought, and a dynamic competition of ideas. And open politics and the rule of law are necessary to keep governments clean and honest, and so that bad ones can be thrown out of office. China and much of Asia are a very long way short of these ideals, and will never maximize the value of their participation in GVCs until they embrace and practice them.

## Asia's Weak Participation in GVCs for Services

Asia's GVC successes, such as they are, have been mainly in the manufacturing sector. In contrast, the services sector in most of Asia's emerging economies is bogged down in traditional services with low productivity. Heavy government regulations that protect incumbent players are the main factor holding back the development of high-value modern services like information and communication technology, finance, logistics, professional business services and transport.[42] And together with barriers to trade in services, this is preventing most Asian countries from participating in GVCs for services. In China, India and Indonesia such barriers are often two to three times higher than in the advanced OECD countries. World-class service sectors cannot be developed if they are isolated from best international practice and world-class inputs.[43]

Shortages of highly skilled workers (notably accountants, business managers, engineers, lawyers, medical doctors, scientists and software specialists) and inadequate infrastructure are also preventing Asia from developing modern services sectors and joining services GVCs. Even Japan[44] and Korea,[45] two of Asia's leading economies, have weak services sectors, with services productivity just half that of their manufacturing sectors. In Asia, only Singapore and Hong Kong have dynamic services sectors.

Asia will never fully climb the development ladder and GVCs until it takes its services sector more seriously. You cannot succeed with lop-sided development that sees fully one half or more of the economy limping along. In much of developing Asia, labor productivity in the services sector is less than 20% that of advanced economies, while it languishes at around 10% in China and India. This is also holding back manufacturing sectors where services provide critical inputs.

There is, however, one area where India and the Philippines are enjoying great success, and that is in GVCs for business process outsourcing (BPO). Advances and diffusion of information technology have facilitated the outsourcing of business services, especially those which are routine, and which are electronically deliverable and don't require face-to-face contact with customers. The BPO sector began with call centers, and then extended to telemarketing, accounting, paralegal, human resources, software development, medical transcription and so on.

India and the Philippines, more than any other Asian countries, have been able to seize the opportunities of the BPO sector thanks to several factors—good English language skills, low-wage costs and tech-savvy youth. For some time, India was the BPO front runner. But according to market reports, the Philippines has leapt ahead to become Asia's call center leader, with India losing a great chunk of its business to the Philippines. Citibank, Safeway, Chevron and Aetna are just a few of the international corporations to have BPO operations in the Philippines.

The Philippine government has also provided greater support to the BPO sector than the Indian government. Most BPO offices are designated as special economic zones, with benefits like tax holidays, duty-free import of capital equipment, simplified import and export procedures, and freedom to employ foreign nationals. The passage of the Data Privacy Act has also put in place international data privacy standards, which are beneficial especially for the multitude of sensitive information like banking and insurance details handled by the BPO sector.

Call centers and associated BPO services now employ more than one million Filipinos, an increase of ten times over the past decade. The BPO sector is now the country's fastest growing sector and brings in $24 billion in revenues in 2015, not far behind the $27 billion the country earned from migrants' remittances. However, the majority of these revenues come from voice call centers, as opposed to more technical IT outsourcing where India still retains an edge.

Overall, the BPO sector now makes up 6% of the Philippines' GDP. But it has tended to be an economic enclave, with very little interaction with the rest of the economy.[46] It is neither a large buyer nor provider of inputs to other sectors of the economy, and its main impacts have been through the retail and real estate sectors.

Could BPO activities become a key driver of economic development in India and the Philippines, as manufacturing has been in countries like Japan, Korea and China?

Most regrettably, the BPO sector seems unlikely to become a key driver of economic development, despite the sector's many benefits. It is no development panacea. The BPO sector only offers employment to the relatively well educated, and not to the vast swathe of lower-skilled people who need jobs. Only 2% of the Philippine workforce is employed in the BPO sector. Both India and the Philippines need a manufacturing renaissance to offer employment to the lower-skilled.

There is also much that both the Philippines and India could do to get better value out of the GVC for BPO activities. This means stronger investments in human capital and infrastructure, and further opening of the economy to foster higher value-added activities like animation, software development, game development, engineering design and knowledge process outsourcing research activities.

## Risks and Challenges of GVC-Based Development

While Asia needs to do much more to get better value out of GVCs, the region also needs to better manage some of the risks and challenges from staking their development strategies on GVCs.

Many East Asian countries, especially China, had placed their bets strongly on GVCs as a key and reliable driver of economic development. They had even biased their development strategies in favor of GVCs by creating special economic zones and export processing zones, which gave special treatment to MNEs which invested in them. Such special treatment can take the form of duty-free imports, tax holidays, soft regulations for labor and environment, access to cheap land and other resources, and exemption on limits on foreign ownership.

But while these special economic zones encouraged participation in GVCs, they were a form of unbalanced development that indirectly discriminated against the domestic economy. They also overly exposed these East Asian economies to the vagaries of international markets, most notably in the context of the 2008 Lehman shock, and ensuing the global financial crisis and "great trade collapse". The recession in the US and Europe saw international trade fall five times more than global GDP from 2008 to 2009. And ever since there has been protracted sluggish growth in advanced markets and growing protectionism.[47]

The global financial crisis has thus highlighted the need for "rebalancing" growth and fostering new sources of growth in the domestic economy. Hence, the new mantra in China has become the need to rebalance its economy away from export- and investment-led growth toward a model based on domestic consumption and the services sector.

This is easier said than done for many reasons. It is not easy to just close up export factories and switch investment and above all workers to the domestic economy. Then there are many vested interests—many of whom are high-ranking Communist Party officials—who oppose the difficult adjustments. And the holy grail of a consumption-led economy is becoming elusive as China's labor share of GDP has been declining, as China's has experienced the greatest increase in income inequality in Asia, and as citizens save in preparation for the country's rapid population aging.

China's rebalancing agenda has become even more acute as it colliding with the effect of rising labor costs, which undermine its competitiveness, and an associated trend of "reshoring" of previously offshored manufacturing activities back to the US and other advanced markets. Chinese wages have been increasing strongly, as its pool of "surplus labor" is becoming exhausted, thereby reducing its attractiveness as low-cost destination, an issue that we will explore in great depth in the next chapter.

"Reshoring" or "insourcing" of production back to high-cost destinations like the US, Europe and Japan is being driven by several factors. While Asia's wage costs have been rising, the US has also regained competitiveness thanks to post-crisis restructuring and lower US domestic energy prices. Rapid technological changes, like robotics, 3D printing, artificial intelligence and the Internet of things, are making advanced countries more attractive business destinations. Indeed, John Lee of the Hudson Institute has argued that robotics and 3D printing might even kill the Asian Century, and that Asia's newly emerging economies will need a changed model from the "export manufacturing" that drove development in Japan, Korea and Taiwan.[48]

Some observers also argue that offshoring to Asia had become a fad, with many companies being seduced by low labor costs and not taking account all of the hidden costs. For example, outsourcing puts you at a time-disadvantage in getting products to market. Another lesson is that the co-location of manufacturing and R&D can exploit the obvious synergies. Insourcing also makes it easier to protect intellectual property, a big issue especially in China. And since President Xi Jinping came to office, many foreign companies have experienced increasing costs and frictions of doing business in China, as they are harassed over issues like monopoly pricing and corruption.

Maintaining adequate quality control is also critical for keeping GVCs competitive. China has been littered with many scandals regarding the quality of food and other products in recent years—to such a point that Chinese citizens often travel abroad, especially to Hong Kong, to buy safer internationally branded food products. The tales from Paul Midler's "Poorly Made in China" highlight the difficulty of product quality in China.

Political and social instability can also present risks to the benefits of GVCs. Political tensions in recent years between China and Japan led to physical attacks on Japanese products and production facilities. They adversely affected demand for Japanese products by Chinese consumers. This is one reason why Japanese business has been turning away from China toward the Southeast Asian economies (ASEAN) and India. The economic costs of China's foreign policy posture toward Japan have become evident to the Chinese leadership and have been one factor behind the calming down of tensions. With an increasingly wobbly economy at home, China cannot afford to scare away good Japanese investment.

And lastly, we cannot talk about politics and GVCs without mentioning Donald Trump's posture toward outsourcing to China and his desire to bring manufacturing back to the US. Trump has been pressuring companies to bring manufacturing back to America, and he claims that "Since my election, Ford, Fiat-Chrysler, General Motors, Sprint, Softbank, Lockheed, Intel, Walmart, and many others, have announced that they will invest billions of dollars in the United States and will create tens of thousands of new American jobs."[49] Whether these investment plans are due to pressure from Trump or not is difficult to assess. But Trump is certainly offering incentives which may encourage investors to change their plans.

## THE QUEST FOR SOCIALLY RESPONSIBLE GVCs

Socially responsible GVCs, with socially responsible business practices, are essential for decent middle-class societies. But the widespread occurrence of labor rights and other human rights abuses in Asia's GVCs highlights how far Asia is from this aspiration.

How can such abuses happen in countries that seem to have made much such economic and social progress? In some cases, there are no appropriate laws and regulations in place. And more often where laws and regulations do exist, they are not effectively enforced. All too often, these abuses take place in special economic zones which are very light on laws and regulations, and where foreign investors are pretty free to do whatever they want.

In this section, we will review three illustrative cases—working conditions at Apple's China-based subcontractors, forced labor in Malaysia's electronics industry and the tragic collapse of Rana Plaza in Bangladesh.

Jobs at the factories of Apple's China-based subcontractors, Foxconn and Pegatron, are very much sought after because they usually pay quite well by Chinese standards. But in recent years, there has been a series of horror stories about the sweatshop working conditions.

The horror stories include forced excessive working hours (over 60 hours a week); paltry wages; living in crowded dormitories; exorbitant obligatory payments for living expenses; exposure to toxic chemicals; coercion of students to work as interns; child labor; and substantial use of "dispatch workers", who have employment contracts with an agency, but not directly with the factory, meaning that they are deprived of benefits and protections.

It is perhaps not totally surprising that in 2010 there was a spate of 14 suicides at Foxconn's factories. Foxconn responded by increasing wages, installing suicide-prevention netting, conducting prayer sessions with Buddhist monks and asking employees to sign no-suicide pledges. For its part, Apple also responded swiftly by establishing a Code of Conduct for its suppliers, conducting factory audits, pressuring its assemblers to improve working conditions and preparing an annual Apple Supplier Responsibility Progress Report.

In Apple's 2016 Report, Chief Operating Officer, Jeff Williams, said "At Apple, we are deeply committed to making sure everyone in our supply chain is treated with the dignity and respect they deserve".[50] Apple's report presents an impressive story of Apple's efforts across its supply chain. But scratching through the details of the report, you will find that there was only a 66% compliance with Apple's standards of excellence for "wages, benefits and contracts". There were also relatively low compliance rates for health and safety permission (55%), emergency prevention, preparedness and response (63%) and occupational health safety and hazard prevention (66%).

In other words, despite Apple's hype, all is not yet well across Apple's GVC. Indeed, an investigator from China Labor Watch, an activist group, was hired at Pegatron as a production line worker. He reported that the awful working and living conditions that Pegatron workers faced in 2015 were generally no better than those witnessed in 2013.[51] Young production workers toil six days a week in 12-hour shifts. But each day they are only paid for 10 and a half hours, not counting 15 minutes of unpaid meetings. The mandatory overtime shift runs from 5.30 pm until 8.00 pm. Seventy-one percent of the pay stubs collected in October 2015 showed average workweeks that exceeded Apple's self-imposed 60-hour limit.

After their long shifts, workers took a 30-minute shuttle bus back to their dormitories where up to 14 people were crammed into a room. Mold grew pervasively along the walls. Bed bugs had spread throughout the dormitory, and many workers were covered in red bug bites.

It is understandable that workers' wages should be low in a relatively poor country like China. But as Apple says itself, workers in its GVC deserve to be treated with the dignity and respect. Despite the protestations of Apple CEO Tim Cook and other Apple senior management, Apple still has a long way to go to achieve this objective.

Malaysia is one of Asia's very most successful countries. From 1990 to 2016, its GDP per capita quadrupled to $28,000, and it has virtually eliminated poverty. Participation in Asia's GVCs, especially for electronics, has been one of the secrets of the Malaysian success story. The electronics sector, which accounts for one-third of Malaysia exports, is mainly driven by investment from MNEs from the US, Japan, Europe, Taiwan and Korea, which usually operate in special economic zones.

But Malaysia's success has ridden substantially on the back of large numbers of vulnerable migrants who are victims of "forced labor", as documented by the non-profit organization, Verite.[52] Some 32% of foreign workers surveyed by Verite were assessed to be victims of forced labor, while another 46% of all workers were deemed to be on the threshold of forced labor.

One in five workers in the study were deceived about their wages, hours, overtime requirements or pay, provisions regarding termination of employment, or the nature or degree of difficulty or danger of their jobs. Virtually all foreign workers interviewed reported that their passports were held by their employer or their broker/agent, something which is against the law in Malaysia.

Many foreign workers are in a state of virtual bondage, as they are tied to their employers and jobs through their work permits, which require the sponsorship of a particular employer. Almost half reported experiencing harassment from immigration officials, police or volunteer citizen security corps—oftentimes they were subject to financial extortion from these groups.

There was hope that Malaysia's participation in the TPP would help improve the situation. It had committed to significant legal and institutional reforms in the areas of forced labor and freedom of association. It had also committed to fully implement the recently passed amendments to the anti-trafficking law to allow trafficking victims to travel, work and reside outside government facilities, including while under protection orders. Even though the TPP discussions are still continuing, without the US in the TPP there will be much less pressure on Malaysia to work for socially responsible GVCs, even if the TPP talks succeed with the remaining 11 members.

The Malaysian government has the aspiration to climb Asia's GVCs, and move its semiconductor industry beyond basic operations such as assembly, testing and packaging to higher value-added activities. But Malaysia will never achieve its ambition of reaching high-income status, while ever it bases its development strategy on low-wage, low-skilled factory jobs performed by vulnerable and abused foreign workers.

Bangladesh is one of Asia's very poorest countries, with an annual GDP per capita of merely $3600. Its population of 163 million is densely packed into this small country which is often afflicted by natural disasters. In many ways, Bangladesh seems a country with little hope. It is one of the world's most corrupt countries according to Transparency International, ranked 145th out of 176 on its Corruption Perceptions Index.[53] It suffers from chronically poor competitiveness according to the World Economic Forum, which places it 106 out of 138 on its Global Competitiveness Index.[54]

And yet, seemingly against the odds, things have been improving in this country, born a little more than four decades ago following the Bangladesh Liberation War. Economic growth has averaged more than 5% since 1990. The share of the population living in extreme poverty has fallen sharply, from 44% in 1990 to 19% in 2010 (based on the $3.10 poverty line, poverty fell from 82% to 57% over the same period). Since 1990, life expectancy has leapt by ten years to 70, while infant, child and maternal mortality rates have improved dramatically.

One key factor in Bangladesh's improved conditions, especially for women, has been its success in hooking onto GVCs as an exporter of "ready-made garments" (RMGs), thanks in large part to its free access to the EU market. RMGs account for over 80% of Bangladesh's total exports, and more than 10% of GDP. The industry employs some 4.2 million people, of whom about 80% are women. It thus contributed greatly to the empowerment of women in this very traditional society. It also indirectly supports as many as 40 million Bangladeshis, about 25% of the population. Bangladesh's clothing industry is only second to China's in size.

But the dark side of Bangladesh's participation in garment GVCs was brought to the attention of the whole world in April 2013, when Rana Plaza, a building housing several RMG factories, collapsed killing 1138 workers, mainly young women, and left more than 2000 injured. It was one of the worst industrial accidents in history, and came close on the heels of the Bangladesh's Tazreen factory fire of November 2012, in which 112 people died.

Who was responsible for this tragic disaster? In the words of Philip Jennings, General Secretary, UNI Global Union, a trade union group, "Many were complicit: the international brands that turned a blind eye to glaring problems in the factories where their garments were made; the factory owners who knowingly put their workers at risk in order to keep costs low; and the Bangladeshi authorities who made no effort to enforce their own health and safety laws".[55]

The many red faces were pressured into responding. A Sustainability Compact was thus forged, committing the Government of Bangladesh, in cooperation with the EU, the US, the International Labour Organization (ILO) and the private sector to bring about the necessary changes in the garment sector. But overall, responses and reactions have been "too little, too late".

It took more than three years for murder charges to be brought against those responsible for the building collapse. The Rana Plaza Donors Trust Fund was established by the ILO in January 2014 in order to collect voluntary contributions to finance the compensation awards. But it took until June 2015 for companies to make sufficient payments to meet the target of $30 million.

On the third anniversary of this tragedy, the EU noted the "tangible progress on the ground", but insisted that "essential reforms—not least as regards the effective respect of trade union rights and promotion of genuine social dialogue—are still needed to ensure a better future for Bangladeshi garment industry workers ... The EU sees still an urgent need to swiftly investigate and prosecute all acts of anti-union discrimination, including in export zones."[56]

On the same occasion, Human Rights Watch noted that "Garment workers face daunting challenges to unionisation, and remain at risk of interference and threats by factories three years after the Rana Plaza building collapse".[57] As Phil Robertson of Human Rights Watch said, "Let's remember that none of the factories operating in Rana Plaza had trade unions ... If their workers had more of a voice, they might have been able to resist managers who ordered them to work in the doomed building a day after large cracks appeared in it."

These issues have given rise to a lively debate on the extent and nature of corporate social responsibility of the brands that sourced their products from Bangladesh, notably Benetton, Bonmarche, the Children's Place, El Corte Ingles, Gap, H&M, Joe Fresh, Monsoon Accessorize, Mango, Matalan, Primark and Walmart. OECD Secretary-General, Angel Gurria, argues that "global businesses must look beyond the bottom line and "go responsible" ... they must act responsibly through their supply chains."[58] But the reluctance of much of the business sector to play the game responsibly is evident in the comments of Winand Quaedvlieg, chair of the investment committee of the Business and Industry Advisory Committee to OECD, "an over-extensive interpretation of responsibilities along the supply chain would be counterproductive".[59]

\* \* \*

Asia's participation in GVCs has provided a fast track to development. GVCs have also been substantially staffed by workers who have migrated from the countryside to the city. But while urbanization also has great potential to drive Asia's development, Asia is not making the most of urbanization's potential, as we analyze in the next chapter.

## Notes

1. Xing, Yuqing and Neal Detert (2010). How the iPhone Widens the United States Trade Deficit with the People's Republic of China. Asian Development Bank Institute Working Paper Series. No. 257. December 2010.
2. United Nations Development Programme. Human Development Report 2015. Work for Human Development.
3. OECD, WTO, World Bank (2014). Global Value Chains: Challenges, Opportunities, and Implications for Policy.

4. World Trade Organization, Fung Global Institute and Temasek Foundation Centre for Trade and Negotiations (2013). Global Value Chains in a Changing World.
5. Bloomberg. Boeing Hands 21% of 777X Components to Japanese Suppliers, 12 June 2014.
6. OECD (2013). Interconnected Economies. Benefiting from Global Value Chains.
7. Lippert, Stefan (2014). Japan's 'hidden champions'. Beacon Reports, 20 October 2014.
8. Conflict Armament Research (2016). Tracing the supply of components used in Islamic State IEDs.
9. Vogel, Ezra F. (2013). Deng Xiaoping and the Transformation of China.
10. Konosuke Matsushita Today in History October 28. Panasonic website. Accessed 4 October 2016.
11. Grimes, Seamus, & Yutao Sun (2016). China's evolving role in Apple's global value chain. Area Development and Policy. Volume 1, 2016—Issue 1.
12. Chinese Ministry of Commerce. Invest in China. Public Information Services website. Accessed 5 October 2016.
13. World Bank. Global Economic Prospects 2016. Potential Macroeconomic Implications of the Trans-Pacific Partnership.
14. World Bank (2014). Cambodia Economic Update, October 2014.
15. West, John (2016). Will Cambodia's skills shortfall derail its stellar economic growth? FDI Intelligence, 23 February 2016.
16. World Bank. Poverty & Equity Data.
17. West, John (2016). Will Cambodia's skills shortfall derail its stellar economic growth? FDI Intelligence, 23 February 2016.
18. UNDP (2014). Human Capital Dynamics and Industrial Transition in Cambodia.
19. Transparency International. Corruption Perceptions Index 2016.
20. World Justice Project. Rule of Law Index 2016.
21. Human Rights Watch (2015). "Work Faster or Get Out", 11 March 2015.
22. World Bank. Logistics Performance Index 2016.
23. World Economic Forum. The Global Competitiveness Report 2016–2017.
24. World Justice Project. Rule of Law Index 2015.
25. OECD. PISA 2015 Results.
26. West, John. Are Abenomics arrows off target when it comes to reviving Japanese FDI? FDI Intelligence, 12 June 2014.
27. US Treasury, Treasury Releases Report on Foreign Exchange Policies of Major Trading Partners of the United States, 14 April 2017.
28. OECD. Key Indicators for Asia and the Pacific 2016.

29. Grimes, Seamus, and Yutao Sun (2016). China's evolving role in Apple's global value chain. Area Development and Policy. Volume 1, 2016—Issue 1.
30. South China Morning Post. Made in China 2025: How Beijing is revamping its manufacturing sector, 9 June 2015.
31. American Institute of Physics. Report: U.S. Global Lead in R&D at Risk as China Rises, 1 February 2016.
32. McLaughlin, Kathleen. Science is a major plank in China's new spending plan. Science Magazine, 7 March 2016.
33. Atkinson, Robert D. Enough is Enough: Confronting Chinese Innovation Mercantilism. Information Technology & Innovation Foundation, 28 February 2012.
34. Cory, Nigel. The Worst Innovation Mercantilist Policies of 2015. Information Technology & Innovation Foundation. January 2016.
35. UNCTAD. World Investment Report 2016.
36. Hanemann, Thilo and Cassie Gao. Chinese FDI in the US: Tripling Down on America. Rhodium Group, 22 July 2016.
37. Hanemann, Thilo and Mikko Huotari. A New Record Year for Chinese Outbound Investment in Europe. Mercator Institute for China Studies and Rhodium Group, February 2016.
38. Schindler, John R. (2016). The Unpleasant Truth About Chinese Espionage. Observer, 22 April 2016.
39. Rogin, Josh (2012). NSA Chief: Cybercrime constitutes the "greatest transfer of wealth in history". Foreign Policy, 9 July 2012.
40. The Commission on the Theft of American Intellectual Property (2017). Update to the Report on The Theft of American Intellectual Property: Reassessments of the Challenge and United States Policy.
41. Global Innovation Index 2016.
42. Asian Development Bank. Asian Development Outlook 2012 Update: Services and Asia's Future Growth.
43. OECD. Services Trade Restrictiveness Index.
44. OECD. Economic Survey of Japan. April 2015.
45. OECD. Economic Survey of Korea. May 2016.
46. Asian Development Bank. An Analysis of the Philippine Business Process Outsourcing Industry. March 2007.
47. Global Trade Alert.
48. Lee, John. Will robots kill the Asian Century? National Interest, 22 April 2015.
49. President Donald J. Trump's address to a Joint Session of Congress, 28 February 2017.
50. Apple. Supplier Responsibility 2016 Progress Report.

51. China Labor Watch (2015). Something's Not Right Here: Poor Working Conditions Persist at Apple Supplier Pegatron.
52. Verité. Forced Labor in the Production of Electronic Goods in Malaysia: A Comprehensive Study of Scope and Characteristics, 17 September 2014.
53. Transparency International. Corruption Perceptions Index 2016.
54. World Economic Forum. Global Competitiveness Index 2016–2017.
55. Jennings, Philip. Rebuilding Bangladesh and the global supply chain. OECD Observer No. 299 Q2, 2014.
56. European Commission. Statement by Commissioners Malmström, Thyssen and Mimica on the 3rd anniversary of the Rana Plaza tragedy, 22 April 2016.
57. Human Rights Watch. Bangladesh: Garment Workers' Union Rights Bleak, 21 April 2016.
58. Angel Gurría. Building an inclusive, resilient and responsible world. OECD Observer No. 299 Q2, 2014.
59. Quaedvlieg, Winand. Defining clear roles. OECD Observer No. 299 Q2, 2014.

**Open Access** This chapter is licensed under the terms of the Creative Commons Attribution 4.0 International License (http://creativecommons.org/licenses/by/4.0/), which permits use, sharing, adaptation, distribution, and reproduction in any medium or format, as long as you give appropriate credit to the original author(s) and the source, provide a link to the Creative Commons license and indicate if changes were made.

The images or other third party material in this chapter are included in the chapter's Creative Commons license, unless indicated otherwise in a credit line to the material. If material is not included in the chapter's Creative Commons license and your intended use is not permitted by statutory regulation or exceeds the permitted use, you will need to obtain permission directly from the copyright holder.

CHAPTER 5

# Making the Most of Urbanization's Potential

There are many good reasons for people to leave the country for city life ("urbanization"), as millions of Asians are doing today: job opportunities, availability of services, bright lights and excitement, or an escape from constraining social and cultural traditions in rural villages. Some people are also pushed into urbanization as they flee hunger and poverty, conflicts, natural disasters and environmental crises like desertification. There is, however, one common denominator—all these people are seeking a better life, and usually urbanization can satisfy that wish.

Interestingly, there are growing numbers of reports of the joy that young Indian girls experience when leaving the strictures of rural life—with its obligation of arranged marriages and subservience to a male-dominated traditional society—to work in a factory in the city. It may be difficult for Westerners to think of work in a factory, earning $100 a month, with the opportunity to meet both boys and girls who are not from your own village or family, as a sort of emancipation. But it certainly seems to be, even if the distant family still holds great sway.

My friend Ashok left his home in a small village in the northern Indian state of Himachal Pradesh for New Delhi for quite different reasons. He came to Delhi to earn enough money to send his two daughters to a private school because India's public education system is so lousy. He wants them to have the education that he wishes that he could have had. And so with an average income of $10 a day, he is able to support the lives of his wife and daughters in their village. But Ashok does not want to stay in Delhi, despite all its opportunities, because he misses his family dearly. His dream is to save up enough money to buy a business or farm back in his home village.

And so it is that Asia is in the midst of the fastest tide of urbanization that the world has ever seen. Asia's urban population has jumped from 27% of the total population in 1980 to 48% in 2015, while over the same period China's urban population skyrocketed from 19% to 56%, India's increased from 23% to 33% and Indonesia's increased from 22% to 54%.[1] Despite these mind-boggling statistics, we are little more than half way through Asia's potential urbanization process. For example, Asia's urban population of 48% of total compares with 94% for Japan and 89% for Australia. According to the UN, 64% of Asia's population could live in urban areas by 2050, with urbanites accounting for 76% of total in China, 50% in India and 71% in Indonesia.

This means that Asia's transition from having 10% of its population living in urban areas to 50% (in 2025) will take only 95 years.[2] This compares with 210 years in the case of Latin America, 150 years in Europe and 105 years in North America. China made this urban transition in just 61 years! Overall, from 1980 to 2010, Asia added more than 1 billion people to its cities, with a further billion set to become city dwellers by 2040.

Asia leads the world for megacities, meaning cities with populations over 10 million. Eight of the world's ten biggest megacities are in Asia—Tokyo, Shanghai, Jakarta, Seoul, Beijing, Guangzhou, Karachi and Delhi (New York City and Mexico City are the only non-Asian cities in the top ten). But while Asia's megacities capture the headlines, most urbanites actually live in second- or third-tier cities and towns. Asia is also home to eight of the world's most densely populated cities—Mumbai, Kolkata, Karachi, Shenzhen, Seoul, Taipei, Chennai and Shanghai. Such high density makes their populations highly vulnerable to natural disasters.

While Asia's new urbanites have their personal motivations for moving to towns and cities, urbanization can bring many great benefits to the whole economy. As people move from the countryside to the city, they also usually move from a very low-productivity job on a farm to a much higher-productivity job in a factory or construction or the urban services sector. There are also many great efficiencies arising from business and life being on a much larger scale (economies of scale). And there are also economies of agglomeration to be harvested as different businesses and workers cluster together creating networks for knowledge-sharing and cooperation, as well as boosting competition.

It is more cost effective for governments to provide public services in big cities than in villages. City governments also usually have much more resources for public services like education—for example, the quality of public education in China's cities is very much better in its cities than in the countryside. Urbanites are usually faster adopters of new technologies, in part because information technology infrastructure is better developed in cities. And most significantly, cities can also become hubs of creativity and innovation, thanks to the co-location of companies, universities, research institutes, and cultural and sporting activities, which attract creative workers and create an environment which is propitious for innovation.

Despite all these potential benefits of urbanization, Asia's model of urbanization is flawed in many respects. In China, migrants from rural areas are denied access to social services. In all emerging Asian economies, too many people leave rural poverty only to live in urban slums with poor infrastructure, while most of Asia's cities are environmental disasters. In the case of Asia's advanced countries, very few cities offer an "ecosystem" which fosters innovation-driven development. In other words, there is much that can be done by Asian governments to make the most of urbanization's potential.

## INSIGHTS FROM SIR W. ARTHUR LEWIS

In 1979, Sir W. Arthur Lewis, from the small Caribbean island of St Lucia, was awarded the Nobel Prize in Economics for his simple, but profound, insights into economic transformation. Lewis paints a picture of a "dualist economy" which has an advanced capitalist sector, but also a "subsistence" non-capitalist backward sector.[3]

"Surplus labor", with very low productivity in the subsistence sector, migrates to the capitalist sector, attracted by higher wages. This enables the capitalist sector to grow, and make profits which fuel continued investment. Initially workers' wages do not increase. The demand for labor by the capitalist sector is satisfied by a continued flow of surplus labor from the subsistence sector. And economic activity and wages in the subsistence sector are not affected because the surplus labor had only very low productivity.

But comes a day, predictably, when the surplus labor becomes exhausted. Labor shortages are felt in both the capitalist and subsistence sectors. And wages begin to rise. This moment is known as the "Lewis turning point".

This is a very critical point in an economy's development process. It is the moment where businesses can no longer rely on cheap labor alone for their competitiveness. They need smart labor. Investment in human capital, technology and research become necessary to drive development forward, especially as cheap labor activities migrate to lower-cost countries. Asian countries like Japan, Hong Kong, Korea, Singapore and Taiwan navigated their Lewis turning points successfully to become high-income, knowledge-based economies, notwithstanding their current challenges. By contrast, Malaysia and Thailand have become bogged down as middle-income economies, as they have not adjusted to the challenges of this phase of their development.

Many analysts argue that China reached the Lewis turning point around 2010.[4] Certainly Chinese wages have increased dramatically, with an average annual growth rate of 15% in dollar-terms between 2000 and 2012, and with continuing increases expected through to the year 2020 at least.[5] And China has been losing investments to lower cost countries like Vietnam, Bangladesh and Cambodia. There have even been reports that some iPhones will be assembled in India, starting from 2017. China's many initiatives to climb global value chains (GVCs) which we discussed in the previous chapter are critical for enabling China to graduate successfully from its Lewis turning point. If China does not navigate this stage successfully, it could fall into a "middle-income trap" and see its development severely stunted. Indeed, as we have discussed in earlier chapters, China's reform momentum may have run out of steam, and its future progress is very much in question.

Transition through the Lewis turning point is challenging for other reasons. The current generation of rural migrants in China's factories is different from the first waves of migrants. They are better educated, more aware of their rights, and more willing to protest. So, not only have Chinese workers been demanding high wages, they have also been demanding better working conditions and the right to form trade unions. More recently, wage increases have slowed a little due to the sluggish world economy, and there have been growing numbers of factory closures, layoffs, restructurings, relocations and pay cuts. All these factors have combined to provoke a massive wave of labor unrest in China.

## Labor Unrest in China

China is in the midst of a big wave of labor unrest and could well become the "epicenter of global labor unrest".[6] According to the China Labor Bulletin, a Hong Kong-based advocacy group, there were over 2700 strikes and protests in 2015, more than double the previous year.[7] Labor unrest can take many forms, such as strikes, suicide threats, holding corporate executives hostage and threatening to reveal a company's dirty laundry. Such unrest has also been facilitated by social media and grassroots activist groups.

The main factors driving this new wave of labor unrest are unpaid wages, severance payments and other benefits like pension contributions. The fact that some local governments habitually fail to enforce labor laws doesn't help. In addition, younger workers have higher expectations and are no longer willing to tolerate the abuse and exploitation their parents had to endure. High profile industrial disasters, like the 2015 explosion at a Tianjin chemicals warehouse, are also motivating labor unrest.

In the face of this labor unrest, the Chinese government is caught between the devil and the deep-blue sea. It has been pressuring companies to pay workers unpaid salaries and other benefits. It has also been offering financial assistance to companies to retain workers. But it has also fearful of labor unrest turning against the government, in the context of more general social unrest. It has thus been clamping down aggressively on protesting workers, imprisoning activist groups and dismantling grass-roots labor rights groups. China would be one of the world's worst countries for workers, according to the International Trade Union Confederation.[8]

A recent appalling example of repression, in March 2015, was the case of a group of eight construction workers who were arrested for staging a protest over unpaid wages in the city of Langzhong in Sichuan province.[9] They were found guilty of "obstructing official business", and sentenced to six to eight months in jail, with the court holding a public sentencing to humiliate them. The employers who did not pay their wages got off scot-free.

Today's labor unrest highlights the fragile state of China's social contract. The public has accepted the Chinese Communist Party's (CCP) monopoly on political power because it had guaranteed economic growth, full employment and improved living conditions. So today's labor unrest, and social instability more generally, is spooking the CCP, as it clings to power.

The CCP has every reason to be spooked. Labor unrest could increase further in China in the coming years, as the country needs massive restructuring of its economy to return to a high-growth path. Inefficient, debt-ridden "zombie" state-owned enterprises need to be brought to heel, which will require massive layoffs (up to six million according to some estimates). As will the shift from a manufacturing-export colossus to modern service-oriented economy. Quite obviously factory workers cannot be transformed into management consultants overnight. It is not surprising that the government is now becoming cautious about the necessary restructuring of zombie companies, since it will lead to structural unemployment. At the same time, delaying these necessary reforms would also compromise further growth prospects.

How the Chinese government manages the labor unrest in the years ahead may well determine the survival of the Communist regime. Its current knee-jerk reaction toward repression is not the most effective way. It needs to let steam out of the social pressure cooker. One thing that it should certainly do is to allow workers to form free trade unions, as they provide a means of dialogue between labor and management, which could ease labor unrest. But as part of President Xi Jinping's clampdown on all voices of dissent, clandestine labor rights organizations are also suffering from renewed repression. Chinese legal trade unions must be affiliated with the official All-China Federation of Trade Unions which is merely a stooge of the Communist Party, which typically supports management over workers. The government should also bolster social security nets, rather than increasing its public security budget for even more repression.

In addition to having very poor labor rights, China's rural migrants suffer from great discrimination in their life in China's cities, through the household registration system, known as the "hukou" system in Chinese.

## China's Urban Apartheid

When the new Communist government assumed power in 1949, after its victory in China's civil war, it decided to prevent the movement of rural citizens to the city through a household registration (hukou) system. Each Chinese citizen had either a "rural" or "urban" hukou, which was basically an internal passport system. This was a divisive system that created two classes of citizenship. Urban citizens worked in the industrial sector and had access to social welfare and full citizenship. Peasants were confined to farms where they grew food for urban workers, but for the rest, they had to fend for themselves.

As Professor Chan Kam Wing said, "These measures effectively circumscribed the peasantry's economic, social and political opportunities and rights, creating a massive pool of super-low-cost rural labor tied to land of very little market value—essentially a de facto underclass."[10]

But when China opened up to the global economy in the 1980s and 1990s, there was a great need for low-skilled manual labor to work in factories, construction and low-end services. So the Chinese government lifted restrictions on internal migration for rural labor who then became the backbone of China's manufacturing GVCs. But these rural migrants did not become eligible for regular urban welfare benefits like access to schools, health-care, pensions or public housing.

Rural migrant labor, while living and working in the city, retained their rural hukou, and became an urban underclass, de facto foreigners in their own country. They are often referred to as China's "floating population". Even their children who were born and grew up in the city retain a rural hukou. Thus, a city's population is now divided into local and outside populations. In short, it is a system of urban, social apartheid.

China's floating population has risen exponentially since the early 1980s when it was only 20–30 million. By 2000, it was 130 million, after which it leapt to 250 million in 2014 (more than 10 million of whom are college graduates). By the year 2020, they could be close to 300 million.

This means that China's apparently impressive urbanization needs to be interpreted carefully, since the floating population makes up a growing of urban residents. While some 56% of the Chinese population may live in urban areas, only 37% do so with urban hukous (not far ahead of India's urbanization rate of 33%). China's floating population now represents some 19% of China's total population, a share that has been continuously rising. In manufacturing hubs like Shenzhen and Dongguan, rural migrants represent some 70–80% of the city's population, while about 40% of Shanghai's population are rural migrants.

Many urban, middle-class Chinese are very happy with the hukou system. They like having rural migrants to work as maids and nannies. And they appreciate having a low-cost working class to work in factories, building construction, restaurants and massage parlors. But they also object to the idea of sharing their privileged access to public social services with peasants. Indeed, according to some surveys, large numbers of China's city dwellers look down on rural migrants and would never want to live next to them. At the same time, some rural migrants would prefer to keep their rural hukou because they fear losing the plot of land in their village.

The hukou system imposes great costs on the Chinese economy, despite the country's ambition of becoming a global economic power. It traps rural migrants in low value-added activities and near-poverty, by preventing them and their families from improving their human capital and benefiting from basic social services. The social costs are also large. Families are split up. There are some 61 million children "left-behind" in their villages, usually staying with their grandparents. They typically receive a poor education in country schools, with enormous class sizes and very few computers. There have been cases of child suicides, and reportedly widespread psychological problems.

The hukou system is also a major factor driving China's yawning inequality. And rural migrants are treated like second-class citizens, as they suffer from disenfranchisement, marginalization and vulnerability. Large numbers of rural migrants live in factory dormitories, construction sites and slum conditions in "villages-in-city". And many suffer from wage arrears and other abuses at the hands of their employers. In short, they are at the very bottom of the GVC.

Over the years, there has been talk of reform of the hukou system, but little action. Most recently, in 2014, the Chinese government announced an ambitious urbanization blueprint to increase China's urbanization rate to 60% in 2020 (from 54% in 2014), with plans to grant 100 million urban hukous to rural migrants during the period to 2020.

Priority for urban hukous will be given to those with stable work and the well-educated, only exacerbating China's inequality. Further, the government also announced a full opening for migration (with hukous) to towns and small cities, an orderly opening in medium-sized cities, while maintaining strict control in very large cities. But this is not expected to improve the lot of rural migrants, most of whom are attracted by the very large cities which offer the most job opportunities, and have by far the best infrastructure.

Overall, under these reforms the share of the floating population would only decline a couple of percentage points by 2020, and it would take three to four decades at least to fully dismantle China's hukou system, if ever. Interestingly, some argue that the government really wants to maintain the hukou system, because it also operates as a system of social control. For example, the Shanghai government has been trying to control real estate prices by imposing restrictions on the capacity of residents without a Shanghai hukou to purchase real estate.

The cost of offering social services to rural migrants is usually cited as a reason for not reforming the hukou system, especially by local governments which would foot the bill for providing public services. But such concerns about the cost of hukou reform are totally ingenuous. The Chinese government has plenty of money for building high-speed trains, creating new institutions like the Asian Infrastructure Investment Bank, and establishing military installations in the South China Sea, but at the same time claims that it does not have enough money for the country's rural migrants.

The slow pace of hukou reform will not only pose great costs on the Chinese economy. It also runs great risks for the Communist Party. Labor and other social unrest is invariably perpetrated by rural migrants, especially the new generation of migrants which is more aware of their rights.

All things considered the hukou system is a relic from a bygone era of history, which has now gotten out of control. It should be abolished as soon as practicable to enable all Chinese citizens to make the most of urbanization's potential. Professor Chan Kam Wing has made ambitious, but realistic, proposals for gradually eliminating China's hukou problem over the period through to 2030.[11] But it does not seem that Beijing is reading them.

While the hukou system is fairly unique to China, most of Asia's emerging countries have disenfranchised underclasses who suffer from urban poverty in slums.

## URBAN POVERTY AND SLUMS

It should not be surprising that Asia's poverty rates are much lower in urban areas than in rural areas given the availability of employment and public services in cities and towns. Indeed, urbanization has been one of the principal drivers of economic development and poverty reduction in Asia. But urban poverty is still a major problem, especially in India and other South Asian countries.[12] And as Asia's urbanization proceeds, Asia's poverty is becoming increasingly urban in nature.

While urban poverty is in some ways similar to rural poverty, a life in urban poverty can also be fundamentally different and profoundly insidious. Very often the urban poor lack the familiar social and community networks of rural areas, they can be victims of crime and violence, exposed to pollution, and be at a greater risk of HIV/AIDS. Slums are the urban face of poverty, and emerge when cities do not provide basic services and jobs for their citizens, and do not plan and regulate urban development.

Although we all have some sense of what a slum is, UN Habitat has come up with a helpful definition—"a slum household is a group of individuals living under the same roof in an urban area who lack one or more of the following: 1. Durable housing of a permanent nature that protects against extreme climate conditions. 2. Sufficient living space which means not more than three people sharing the same room. 3. Easy access to safe water in sufficient amounts at an affordable price. 4. Access to adequate sanitation in the form of a private or public toilet shared by a reasonable number of people. 5. Security of tenure that prevents forced evictions."[13]

Asia's slum population has declined significantly as a proportion of total urban population over the past decades—from 49% of the total urban population in 1990 to 30% in 2009—in tandem with the reduction in poverty in the region.[14] But as Asia's urban population has grown, the actual number of people—over 500 million—living in slums has not declined over this 20-year period. Even in Asia's great success stories, slum population remains very high, with China's at 29% of the total urban population, and India's and Indonesia's at 29% and 23% respectively. The slum situation is horrendous in countries like Bangladesh (62%), Nepal (58%), Pakistan (47%) and the Philippines (41%). And many more live in slum-like conditions in areas which are not officially designated as slums.

Asia is increasingly suffering from an "urban divide" as the rich live in well-serviced, gated communities, while the poor live in slums or poor neighborhoods, either in the inner-city or the edge of the city. Poverty leads many Asian slum populations to settle in areas greatly exposed to natural hazards. For example, Metro Manila, one of the world's most densely populated city, with its 13 million inhabitants, is often a victim of typhoons, floods and earthquakes, with its slum population being the most affected. And fires in Manila's slums are also a regular occurrence, with a fire tearing through Navotas in early 2017, leaving 15,000 homeless.

Asia's urban divide is just one manifestation of Asia's divided societies. And the enormous disparities between in wealth, services and opportunities can be a source of social frustrations and political tensions. Fragile democracies and authoritarian regimes should beware of restive urban populations.

Asia's future is being threatened by unplanned urbanization. But there is much that governments can do to tackle these issues and make the most of urbanization's potential—rapid economic growth alone cannot solve urbanization's challenges. It is critical to provide infrastructure and public services in tandem with the growth of urban populations, an issue that we will explore in one of the following sections. Urban planning is also necessary, rather than just allowing the uncontrolled settlement of any land, irrespective of whether it is a high-risk location. And an effective system of land tenure must be established. Many slum dwellers are merely squatters with no title for the land.

But too many local governments are ineffective and/or corrupt. The building collapses and factory fires that are ever too frequent, especially in Bangladesh and India, are just one manifestation of this. Usually, as in the case of Rana Plaza, they are due to building owners flouting building, safety and fire regulations, often with the complicity of local authorities.

In the next section, we will have a look at life inside Dharavi, India's most famous slum, before digging in deeper to Asia's infrastructure deficits, focusing on Indonesia's capital of Jakarta.

## Dharavi, India's Most Famous Slum

Asia has many large slums, like Manila's Tondo, Jakarta's Kelurahan Penjaringan, Dhaka's Korail, Karachi's Orangi Town, Baotou's Beiliang in China, Osaka's Kamagasaki, Seoul's Guryong Village and Hong Kong's rooftop slums. But Mumbai's Dharavi may be the most famous, thanks in part to the film it inspired, "Slumdog Millionaire".

Tragically, India is tainted by having the world's biggest slum population. And according to one estimate, over 60% of the population of Mumbai lives in slums. Some even refer to Mumbai as the global slum capital. And yet, it is India's capital of finance, business and cinema capital. This is India, with the best and worst of everything.

Slums, like all human settlements, are a world of the own, and a world to discover for the curious at heart, as we will see in Dharavi. Obviously, there is the squalor. And there is no shortage of that at Dharavi. Although there are no hard data, most of Dharavi's slum dwellers reportedly survive on a $1–2 a day. There are about one million people living within 1 square mile (almost 3 square kilometers), making it perhaps the most densely populated area on planet earth.

The entire residential area lacks any sort of infrastructure such as roads, public conveniences and toilets. With an average of 1 toilet per 500, most residents use alleys or the local river as a toilet, even though the river is also a source of Dharavi's fresh water. Children play in open sewers, while dead rats line the alleyways, and live ones run up and down.

The slum has severe public health problems, with a long history of epidemics and other disasters. While India's life expectancy is 67 years, the average life span in Dharavi is less than 60. Virtually all housing has been constructed illegally, and is extremely crowded and small. Up to five people sleep in each tiny bedroom.

But Dharavi is not only squalor. There are also important businesses there with leather, textiles, pottery, jewelry and steel being the most important industries, along with a large recycling business.[15] There are reportedly some 300 bakeries. And with "slum tourism" a recent fad, Dharavi is now receiving a rising number of visitors. According to one estimate, Dharavi would have a billion-dollar economy, with over 15,000 factories, which export products all over the world.

Dharavi's business is illegal, untaxed and unregulated. Needless to say, the work environment is extremely hazardous and unsafe, resulting in fatalities and disease. Toxic sludge flows down alleyways. And child labor is widespread—many of Dharavi's kids start school, but few of them finish.

Dharavi is also a hub of creativity, which was highlighted in a mobile museum, the "Design Museum Dharavi", conceived by two Amsterdam-based artists. In addition there is the Dharavi Biennale, "Alley Galli Biennale", which showcases installation and performance art. And Dharavimarket.com has been established as an ecommerce marketplace for leather product manufacturers, potters, shoe makers, jewelers and various accessory makers who want to sell their wares on domestic and international markets.

Dharavi also has a vibrant society. Since all activities involve sharing cramped spaces, life is a continuous social affair. As many urban planners say, Dharavi has a very strong sense of community, its residents seem happy, and the crime rate is very low—although one should not romanticize too much about life in Dharavi.

There are three main communities—Hindu (60%), Muslim (33%) and Christian (6%)—each living in its own district, with temples, mosques and churches. Badi Masjid, a mosque, is the slum's oldest religious structure. Dharavi residents come from all parts of India, not only the local Maharashtra state.

Dharavi has a long history.[16] The area was a mangrove swamp inhabited by Koli fishermen. Then the slum was established in 1882 during the British colonial era, and grew due to the expulsion of factories and residents in downtown Mumbai by the colonial government. Some 60% of Dharavi's families have lived in the slum for more than 60 years.

There have long been plans to redevelop Dharavi. It is located on prime building land, and would be worth millions to developers. But resistance is great from its inhabitants and activists. Offers of compensation for the locals have been inadequate. And many residents like Dharavi's very cheap and affordable housing, with rents as low as $3 a month. Mumbai is one of the world's most expensive cities. The slum is also conveniently located smack in the middle between Mumbai's two main suburban rail lines, the Western and Central Railways.

It is tempting for city governments to succumb to the temptation of such development projects. But history shows that they are invariably a heartless failure. Former slum residents usually get packed up into characterless apartment blocks. All sense of community is lost. And industries like pottery and recycling disappear.

It would be much more human to provide slum residents with adequate infrastructure, and titles to the property they occupy, and then help them clean up the slum. De-slumification might then occur naturally in tandem with economic development, and obviate the need for simply demolishing whole communities. But Indian cities are still grossly underprepared to deliver a high quality of life that is sustainable in the long term. In a recent survey, Mumbai scored an appalling 4.2 on a scale of 1–10 (New York scored 9.70), but it was still the second highest ranking of the assessed 21 Indian cities, with Chandigarh bringing up the rear with 2.[17]

Appalling infrastructure may be the bane of life in Mumbai and indeed much of "Incredible India". But when it comes to infrastructure deficits, India is far from alone in Asia. The Asian Development Bank estimates that Asia's infrastructure needs amount to $1.7 trillion a year, including the effect of climate change mitigation and adaptation costs, if the region is to maintain growth momentum.[18] And with Asia's urban population growing rapidly, an ever-increasing share of these infrastructure needs is to be found in urban centers. And yet, ironically, Asian cities like Hong Kong, Singapore, Tokyo and Seoul have some of the world's best infrastructure, something that make visitors from Australia and North America feel rightly jealous. This is yet another manifestation of the "Asian divide".

In the following section, we look at Indonesia's infrastructure crisis which is also inhibiting poverty reduction and economic growth, and is breeding dangerous slums in its major cities.

## INDONESIA'S INFRASTRUCTURE CRISIS

Jakarta and other Indonesian cities are feeling the pinch of the nation's infrastructure crisis at many different points. Indeed, under-investment in the nation's infrastructure, chiefly transportation, would have lopped more than one percentage point a year off Indonesia's potential economic growth over the past decade, thereby robbing the country of further poverty reduction and prosperity growth.[19]

Although traffic is notoriously bad in many Asian cities, Indonesia's capital city of Jakarta's traffic is regularly rated as among very worst traffic in the world.[20] Other Indonesian transportation infrastructure is also totally inadequate, notably rail networks, seaports and airports. This is of course a great inconvenience to Indonesian citizens. But it also has severe adverse effects on domestic business and foreign investment. Indeed, Indonesia's logistics costs, at around 24% of GDP, are very much higher than neighbors like Malaysia and Thailand.[21] A telling example of Indonesia's logistics problems is that it is cheaper to import oranges from China than from the Indonesian island of Kalimantan.

The 34 million Indonesians who still live in urban slums also suffer from an acute infrastructure deficit,[22] especially for things like water, sanitation, electricity and Internet access.[23] Some 80% of Indonesians lack access to piped water, and 98% of the population doesn't have access to sewerage systems. This means that, taking account of all the population's deprivations, Indonesia's poverty would be higher than based on income measures of poverty.

Many Indonesian regions suffer electricity blackouts and brownouts, with power demand outstripping supply. Indonesia may be on the brink of a power crisis, despite the country's abundance of energy resources. Some 47% of the country's primary schools lack access to electricity, effectively excluding their students from e-learning. Indonesia has only around 1.2 fixed broadband connections per 100 persons, as compared with 8.4 in Malaysia and 5.0 in Vietnam.

How did Indonesia get into its infrastructure crisis? Indonesia's infrastructure investment collapsed during the 1997/1998 Asian financial crisis, and has not fully recovered since. Infrastructure spending averaged less than 2–3% of GDP over the 2000–2014 period, compared with 6% during Soeharto era before the financial crisis. In sharp contrast, China and Indonesia's neighbors have been investing 7% or more of GDP in infrastructure.

There are several factors which have kept infrastructure spending low, notably low and falling government revenues, heavy public spending on subsidies and entitlements, and a 3% cap on the budget deficit, which has limited government financing for infrastructure. It is also the product of ineffectual government under the previous President, Susilo Bambang Yudhoyono, who did not manage to get many projects got off the ground. In short, Indonesia's infrastructure spending is way below the level that is needed to cope with continuing rapid urbanization.[24] It is also below the level need to sustain a respectable economic growth rate of 6–7% of GDP.

The present government of President Joko Widodo has made infrastructure investment one of its highest priorities, while the new Indonesian National Medium Term Development Plan (2015–2019) devotes significant attention to infrastructure. And there has been an acceleration in the launch of projects. However, despite these good intentions, Indonesia faces many challenges in addressing its infrastructure crisis, which will take many years, if not decades, to solve. The government doesn't have the wherewithal to finance the country's infrastructure needs. And not even the finances of the World Bank, Asian Development Bank or the much-publicized Asian Infrastructure Investment Bank would be sufficient. Although there is much talk about the potential of public–private partnerships, the best thing that Indonesia could do is to make better efforts at improving tax collection and tackle the widespread tax cheating of the country's elites.[25]

But despite the urgency of the situation, the government bureaucracy has been slow to move into action, in part due to weaknesses of institutional capacity. Inefficient state-owned enterprises dominate the infrastructure scene. And to attract private sector interest requires a robust pipeline of bankable projects. But Indonesia suffers from issues of project preparation quality, regulatory clarity, legal certainty and corruption. One of the biggest bottlenecks is land acquisition as local people refuse to sell their land or only do so at very high prices.

For Indonesia to make the most of its rapid urbanization, it needs to make very much more serious efforts to improve the state of its urban infrastructure. Otherwise, urbanization will lead to growing urban poverty, squalor and slums, with even greater risk of social instability, crime and violence. Too many Asian cities are also becoming environmental disasters.

## Asia's Urban Environmental Disaster

A few years back, the Asian Development Bank bravely made a case for "green urbanization" in Asia.[26] And there certainly are some reasons why urbanization can be good for the environment. Urbanization brings higher productivity thanks to economies of scale and agglomeration, thereby reducing the economy's ecological footprint. As development proceeds, lower-pollution services take over from manufacturing as key driver of the economy. And compact urban-living reduces energy consumption, a major source of pollution.

Environmental-friendly infrastructure and public services are more affordable for urban governments, than in dispersed rural communities. Experience also shows that urbanization can foster innovation, including for green technologies. And as urbanization drives economic development, emerging middle-class populations will pressure governments, even in authoritarian China, to manage the environment better. Middle-class families are very rightly worried about the health of their children.

Many economists believe there to be an "environmental Kuznets' curve" (the original curve by economist Simon Kuznets pertained to inequality). This means that while the early stages of economic development see a deterioration in the urban environment, over time, urbanization and development become positive forces for the environment.

When you visit cities like Singapore and Tokyo, it is easy to be convinced of an environmental Kuznets' curve operating in Asia. But most Asian countries are not at all in this situation. Urbanization and development are creating great stresses for the environment, and vulnerabilities to climate change and natural disasters are only getting worse. Indeed, much of Asia is still very much on the bad side of the Kuznets' curve. And it will take very many years, if ever, for most Asian cities to see the good side of the Kuznets' curve.

Most Asian cities now have simply terrible pollution problems. As Asia's rural residents rush to live in cities, they buy cheap cars, take high-polluting public transport and work in dirty factories. Traffic-related congestion costs in Asia are estimated to amount to 5% of GDP. Many Asians still cook their food and heat their habitations with small fires, the major source of air pollution. And if they have access to electricity, it comes from small-scale diesel electricity generators or coal plants. And the weak, incompetent and often corrupt governments who allow more than 500 million Asians to keep living in slums contribute to pollution by not providing clean toilets, and leaving trash to rot, rather than collecting it.

It is not surprising that the environment of most Asian cities is simply appalling and even life-threatening for many. Out of the world's 3.3 million premature deaths due to air pollution, 1.4 million occur in China, followed by India with 645,000 and Pakistan with 110,000. By 2050, there could be 6.6 million such premature deaths every year worldwide.[27] Asia tops the world when it comes to all the indicators of polluted cities. According to the World Health Organization (WHO), some 62 Asian cities figure in the list of the world's 100 most polluted cities by "particulate matter concentration", with the top ten including Delhi, Patna, Gwalior, Raipur, Ahmedabad and Lucknow from India; and Karachi, Peshawar and Rawalpindi from Pakistan.[28]

On an average day, the residents of Delhi breathe air fouled by fine particles at a concentration of 153 µg/m$^3$. This has damaged the lung function of half the city's 4.4 million children so severely that they will never fully recover. Delhi's score is close to three times the Beijing mean and 15 times the WHO guideline of 10 µg/m$^3$. Beijing, with its notorious air quality, only ranks 76th on the world list. China's air pollution may seem not so bad compared with other countries because some Chinese cities allegedly manipulate air pollution data to comply with the air quality standards.

But this WHO index only measures one of the many forms of pollution. There are many other Asian cities which suffer from other forms of pollution. In Linfen, China, the air is constantly soiled with burning coal. Also in China, a lot of lead ends up in the soil and water in Tianying, and ultimately in the bloodstream of children, because of a lack of regulation of lead production in China. In Sukinda, India, studies show that the drinking water includes more than double the international standard of Hexavalent Chromium. And in Vapi, India, groundwater has been found to contain mercury levels almost 100 times higher than the WHO's recommended amount.

Climate change is another factor adversely affecting urban life. Indeed, Asia has some 15 of the world's top 20 cities ranked in terms of population exposed to coastal flooding for the period 2010/2070, due to the effects of both climate change and socio-economic change.[29] And it is the urban poor who face the greatest risk from such natural disasters because they tend to live in areas which are most prone to disasters, and have the least assets for protecting themselves. The cities are Kolkata, Mumbai, Dhaka, Guangzhou, Ho Chi Minh City, Shanghai, Bangkok, Yangon, Haiphong, Tianjin, Khulna, Ningbo, Chittagong, Tokyo and Jakarta. In terms of numbers, over 300 million Asian urbanites were at risk of coastal flooding in 2010, a figure which could rise to 410 million by 2025.[30] In 2010, about 250 million people were vulnerable to inland flooding, which could also rise to about 350 million by 2025.

The prospects for climate change, and thus Asia's urban environment, have only become worse since the election of US President Donald Trump. He has withdrawn the US from the Paris Climate Change Agreement, rolled back Obama-era clean energy regulations, proposed slashing the budget of the US Environmental Protection Agency (EPA) and appointed as EPA Administrator Scott Pruitt, who is a staunch opponent of the work of the Agency.

While many Asian cities will be adversely affected by global warming, they are also part of the problem in that they emit a disproportionate amount of greenhouse gases due to the concentration of economic activities in urban areas. But there is also much that Asian governments could do to turn around their urban environmental disaster, and make the most of urbanization's potential for Asia's development.

Since energy consumption is one of the biggest sources of pollution, it is critical to improve energy efficiency by eliminating energy subsidies, taxing pollution using the polluter-pays principle, promoting the use of renewable energy and smart electricity grids. And environmental regulations and standards should be elaborated and above all enforced. Slum conditions can be improved by providing basic services, and granting land titles to slum dwellers. And rather than passively letting urbanization happen, governments should create satellite cities linked by high-speed public transport, and incorporate environmental priorities into city planning.

Given the exposure of Asian cities to the adverse effects of climate change, they also have a stake in working toward solutions. This means implementing carbon taxes and/or cap-and-trade schemes and implementing the Paris Agreement on Climate Change. Already, three of the world's top five carbon-emitting nations are in Asia, viz., China, India and Japan. And looking ahead, Asian cities are poised to contribute more than half the rise in global greenhouse gas emissions over the next 20 years, if no action is taken. Urban infrastructure will also need to be able to cope with Asia's increasingly frequent natural disasters, notably by building in safe areas, investing in drainage infrastructure and climate forecasting technology, and improving housing affordability for the poor.

With Asia's continuing rapid development, its environmental challenges and vulnerability to climate change and natural disasters will only get worse, in the absence of decisive action. Indeed, GVCs in Southeast Asia are likely to experience significant falls in productivity over the next 30 years due to rising temperatures and extreme heat stress impacting labor forces.[31]

As a late-comer to urbanization, Asia has much to learn from other countries' experiences and mistakes. With political will and leadership, it could solve Asia's urban environmental disaster. Most regrettably, however, except for a few cases, Asia's urban environmental crisis seems to be getting only worse, not better. Another area where Asian governments could do a lot better is in providing ecosystems that foster innovative cities.

## Urbanization and Asia's Innovation Imperative

Economies like Singapore, Hong Kong, Japan, Korea and Taiwan have long reached the point where innovation should be a principal motor of economic growth. They have passed through the "copycat" stage of development, where much progress up the development ladder can be made by absorbing technology, knowledge and lessons from more advanced countries. And now that China has passed the Lewis turning point, it must also focus more on the innovation imperative.

Urbanization is key to innovation—meaning "new" or "significantly improved" products, processes, marketing or organizations—because cities are the human hubs where most innovation takes place. More than 80% of the populations of these five Asian economies now live in urban centers.

How can we ignite the innovation genie? Innovation analysts highlight the necessity of developing an "ecosystem" that fosters innovation. There is not one magic bullet. The OECD emphasizes things like knowledge and skills to generate new ideas and technologies, bring them to the market and implement them in the workplace; an open and competitive business environment; public investment in research; government incentives for business investment; and open access and participation in the digital economy.[32]

A Melbourne-based organization "2thinknow" has a different approach, as it emphasizes three preconditions for innovation, namely cultural assets, human infrastructure and networked markets.[33] Cultural assets include arts, culture, sports, music, environment, parks and spaces—they inspire new ideas. Human infrastructure means universities and businesses which help with the development of ideas. And networked markets through physical trade or digital communication enable the sharing of ideas with the rest of the world.

Our take is that a melting pot of artists, academics and investors, men and women, young and old and of different ethnic and cultural backgrounds, provides a potent force for generating and realizing new ideas. It also helps if there is an environment which tolerates or even encourages differences, rather than conformity, promotes risk taking and does not instantly punish making mistakes.

How do Asia's leading cities stack up in terms of the innovation imperative? This is an impossible question to answer accurately and thoroughly. But let's have a look at a few indicators.

Universities are key for innovation. They produce our brightest minds, they are the cradle of much fundamental research, and many of the best ones work in partnership both with the business sector and internationally. Asian cities have some excellent universities, and they are certainly getting better. But overall they are not yet in the same league as Western universities like Oxford University, California Institute of Technology, Stanford University, University of Cambridge, Massachusetts Institute of Technology and Harvard University.[34]

According to the Times Higher Education, the highest ranked Asian university in 2016–2017 is National University of Singapore which comes in 24th. Other Asian universities drift off further down the top 100 list, namely Peking University, 29th; Tsinghua University, 35th; University of Tokyo, 39th; University of Hong Kong, 43rd; Hong Kong University of Science and Technology, 49th; Nanyang Technological University, 54th; Seoul National University, 72nd; Chinese University of Hong Kong, 76th; Korean Advanced Institute of Science and Technology, 89th; and Kyoto University, 91st.

And only seven Asian "think tanks" have been rated in the top 50 of Think Tanks Worldwide.[35] These are Japan Institute of International Affairs, Asian Development Bank Institute, China Institutes of Contemporary International Relations, Chinese Academy of Social Sciences, Korea Institute for International Economic Policy, China Institute of International Studies and Korea Development Institute.

The livability of our cities is key to attracting the "creative class", including from overseas, who typically drive the innovation process. So how "livable" are Asian cities? Singapore is the most livable Asian city, based on Mercer's assessment of the political, economic, socio-cultural and natural environment, education, health and other public services.[36] But it only ranks 26th in the world, well behind many cities from Europe, Canada and Australasia, though ahead of 28th placed San Francisco, America's highest ranked city. You then have to slide further down the list to 44th place to find Tokyo, which is followed by Kobe (46th), Yokohama (49th), Osaka (58th), Nagoya (62nd), Hong Kong (70th), Seoul (73rd), Taipei (84th), Kuala Lumpur (86th), Busan (91st) and Taichung (100th). The highest ranked Chinese city is Shanghai at 101st, the top Indian city is Hyderabad at 139th, while Manila and Jakarta make it at 136th and 142nd respectively!

The low ranking for the livability of many Asian cities is hardly surprising in light of the horrendous pollution, the congestion and insecurity that many have, not to mention their restrictions on social and political freedom. And as my friend Asit Biswas has argued, the truly great cities have a soul.[37] This is where high-tech, squeaky-clean cities like Singapore or Korea's Songdo miss the boat. And this is why we love San Francisco and New Orleans.

An open competitive economy is also crucial for fostering innovation. And Asia's leading economies are doing pretty well on that score, according to the World Economic Forum's Global Competitiveness Index.[38] Singapore (2nd), Japan (8th), Hong Kong (9th) and Taiwan (14th) all rank in the world's top 20 nations. Just a bit further down the list are Malaysia (25th), Korea (26th), China (28th), Thailand (34th) and India (39th).

An open society and political system are crucial for the innovation imperative. Innovators need to be able to think the unthinkable, say the unsayable and do the undoable. Japan and Korea are regarded as free and open societies by most observers like Freedom House, even if there has been backsliding under the regimes of Japan's Prime Minister Shinzo Abe, and Korea's former President Park Geun-hye.[39] Taiwan also has an open and free society, and a vibrant democracy, but the island's freedom is constantly and increasingly undermined by interference from Beijing.

The situation is much less promising in Asia's innovation-oriented economies. Freedom House ranks Hong Kong as only "partly free", with things only getting worse due to recent restrictions on freedom of the press and freedom of assembly due to Beijing's nefarious influence over Hong Kong. Singapore is "partly free" case with the "soft authoritarian" regime maintaining restrictions over freedom of speech, Internet and assembly. Such freedoms are very much worse in the "unfree China", and have only been deteriorating under the leadership of President Xi Jinping.

All things considered, Asian cities and countries are laggards in the global innovation race. Only seven Asian cities make it into the world's top 50 as estimated by the "global innovation agency", 2thinknow.[40] These cities are Tokyo, Singapore, Seoul, Beijing, Shanghai, Hong Kong and Osaka.

Over the years, there has been much analysis and speculation on the limitations of the Asian model, a few of which we will conclude with here.

Widespread government controls and regulations in many Asian societies stifle freedom of thought and action. Economies are dominated by established big business with collusive links to government, which protects their dominant positions. Most small and medium enterprises tend to be subcontractors for large enterprises, rather than startups and independent drivers of innovation. And financial systems are dominated by banks which service mainly large enterprises—risk capital for innovative startups is all too scarce.

Education systems tend to emphasize rote learning and memorization rather than critical thinking. All too often academics are locked away in prestigious ivory towers, rather than working in partnership with business. Societies are usually male-dominated, hierarchical, conservative and conformist, rather than risk taking. And migrants tend to be marginalized, rather than providing the power of diversity. This means that innovation in Asia rarely involves disruptive, major breakthroughs, and tends to be "incremental innovation" which adapts and perfects innovations coming from elsewhere.

Most Asian governments are very conscious of their innovation imperative. Some even speak of the desire to create a new Steve Jobs or Bill Gates. But they are also uncomfortable with the free and open societies which provide the fertile soil that allowed such innovation leaders to flourish. Success stories like Chinese artist Ai Weiwei, SoftBank's Masayoshi Son or even Grameen Bank's Muhammad Yunus are too often seen as threats rather than social assets. As the old saying goes, if you want to make an omelet, you have to break some eggs. In this context, many Asian countries need to take new approaches in governing their urban economies and societies, if they are to make the most of urbanization's potential for innovation.

## Asia's Best City: Singapore Versus Hong Kong

As Asia's leaders in terms of GDP per capita, and the region's only truly cosmopolitan cities, Singapore and Hong Kong have long vied for the crown of Asia's best city. But Singapore has crept well ahead of Hong Kong, a trend that is bound to continue, in light of China's persistent interference and mismanagement of Hong Kong.

However you measure it, Singapore has an edge on Hong Kong. Its GDP per capita is higher, despite Hong Kong having a locational advantage, sitting right next to fast-growing China. The Lion City is also ahead of Hong Kong when it comes to education, according to the OECD. Singapore is an easier place to do business, reports the World Bank, and is also ahead of Hong Kong in terms of competitiveness, with the World Economic Forum noting that "The challenge for Hong Kong is to evolve from one of the world's foremost financial hubs to become an innovative powerhouse". Innovation is one of the weakest aspects of Hong Kong's performance and the business community consistently cites the capacity to innovate as their biggest concern. Most other analyses of innovation capacity also put Singapore ahead of Hong Kong.

When it comes to the quality of governance, Singapore again maintains its edge in Transparency International's Corruption Perceptions Index, and the World Justice Project's rule of law index. And Hong Kong topped the list of 23 advanced countries in the Economist "crony-capitalism index". In other words, it has the worst cronyism of all the economies surveyed, while Singapore is further down the list at 5th. Despite Hong Kong's free market pretensions, its domestic economy is in reality dominated by cartels, monopolies and oligopolies. The tycoons control everything from supermarkets to drugstores, electricity supply to ports and buses, and construction. This pushes prices up and quality down, and results in low environmental standards. In other words, Hong Kong politicians and businessmen have their hands deep in each other's pockets.

The social and political context in Hong Kong has been changing dramatically, in response to two main factors. Student-led protests, under the banners of "Occupy Central" and the "Umbrella Movement", seeking greater social justice and democracy have unsettled both Beijing's and Hong Kong's leaders. Beijing has been more openly asserting its influence over Hong Kong, often in defiance of Hong Kong's constitution, the "Basic Law", since Xi Jinping has been China's President.

There are very many examples of Beijing's interference. Academic freedom and university autonomy are now increasingly compromised in Hong Kong. Publishers of books critical of Beijing have been abducted to the mainland. In a speech on the occasion of the twentieth anniversary of the handover of Hong Kong to China, Chinese President Xi Jinping made clear that Beijing is the boss of Hong Kong. Xi warned that "any attempt to endanger China's sovereignty and security, challenge the power of the central government" or to "use Hong Kong to carry out infiltration and sabotage against the mainland is an act that crosses the red line and is absolutely impermissible."

In sum, Hong Kong's fading freedom, together with China's growing interference and mismanagement of Hong Kong, is gradually undermining the island's uniqueness relative to other Chinese cities, and especially relative to Singapore.

Nevertheless, citizens from both Singapore and Hong Kong have many reasons to be cheerful. Their economies are very prosperous, and well-managed, and their societies are among the safest in the world. And while both can pride themselves as gastronomic hubs, Hong Kong wins hands down, with 6 Michelin three-starred restaurants, whereas Singapore only has one!

But citizens from both also have reasons to be frustrated. The gap between rich and poor is enormous, with Hong Kong having the highest inequality in the advanced world, just ahead of Singapore. Beyond the manifest glitz and bling of both cities, lurks poverty for too many citizens, as well as slave-like conditions for the low-skilled migrants who keep these economies ticking over. And Singapore is the world's most expensive city, with Hong Kong just a sliver behind at number two, according to one survey.[41]

All things considered, it is thus not surprising that Singapore should score much better than Hong Kong on international league tables like the World Happiness Report,[42] where Singapore ranks a respectable 26th, while Hong Kong is languishing at 71st out of the 155 countries covered.

Another report, by Civic Exchange, a Hong Kong-based think tank, suggests that Hong Kongers are miserable compared with residents from Singapore and Shanghai.[43] Some two-thirds of Hong Kongers believe that their city has become a worse or much worse place in which to live since they started living there, and that it is not a good place to raise children. Only about one-tenth of Shanghai and Singapore residents have the same feelings about their cities. And it's young Hong Kongers who are most likely to say that their city has become worse, with 79% in the 18–29 age cohort saying so. Hong Kongers' main concerns are housing, quality of government, education and environmental protection.

What future for Asia's leading cities? As Hong Kong is increasingly swallowed up into China's world, its competitive edge vis-à-vis cities like Shanghai, in terms of rule of law, freedom of the press and good governance, will gradually diminish. It will continue to play an important role, but one that is less unique than in the past. Hong Kong is now little more than a Chinese economic dependency, reliant on China for its commerce and tourists, with very little economic independence. And political tensions will continue to rise, as Hong Kong's youth population become even more frustrated with Beijing's influence over Hong Kong, and push for greater freedom and even independence.

Singapore is a very different case. The government is resolutely committed to managing the economy as best it can, in Singapore's interest, and promoting a Singaporean identity. It maintains very good relations with both the US and China, and is able to balance relations with these super-powers, and remain staunchly independent. Singapore also has a unique broader Asian role, with excellent links, not only with China but also with Southeast Asia and India. As a Singapore-based journalist once said to me: "Singapore is the only truly Asian city in the region. All the other big Asian cities are more national in focus."

\* \* \*

GVCs and urbanization have provided immense opportunities for Asian economies and their citizens. But as we discuss in the next chapter, too many Asians are prevented from accessing opportunity because of discrimination, prejudice and persecution.

## Notes

1. United Nations. World Urbanization Prospects, the 2014 revision.
2. Asian Development Bank (2012). Key Indicators for Asia and the Pacific 2012. Special Chapter: Green Urbanisation in Asia.
3. Lewis, W.A. (1954). Economic Development with Unlimited Supplies of Labour. The Manchester School. May.

4. Cai, Fang and Meiyan Wang. Labour Market Changes, Labour Disputes and Social Cohesion in China. OECD Development Centre. Working Paper 307.
5. Economist Intelligence Unit (2014). Still making it: an analysis of manufacturing labour costs in China.
6. Friedman, Eli. China in Revolt. Jacobin.
7. China Labor Bulletin. Strikes and protests by China's workers soar to record heights in 2015, 7 January 2016.
8. International Trade Union Confederation. The 2015 ITUC Global Rights Index. The World's Worst Countries for Workers.
9. Wall Street Journal. Chinese City Publicly Shames Migrant Workers Who Protested Unpaid Wages, 18 March 2016.
10. Chan, Kam Wing. "The Household Registration System and Migrant Labor in China: Notes on a Debate". Population and Development Review 36(2): 357–364 (June 2010).
11. Kam Wing Chan. "Achieving Comprehensive Hukou Reform in China". Paulson Policy Memorandum. Paulson Institute. December 2014.
12. Mathur, Om Prakash (2014). Urban Poverty in Asia. Asian Development Bank.
13. UN Habitat. State of the World's Cities 2006/2007.
14. UNESCAP. Statistical Yearbook for Asia and the Pacific 2014.
15. Kevin McCloud: Slumming It. Australian Broadcasting Commission, 13 December 2015.
16. National Geographic. Dharavi: Mumbai's Shadow City. May 2007.
17. Janaagraha Centre for Citizenship and Democracy, and Jana Urban Space Foundation. Annual Survey of India's City-Systems 2015.
18. Asian Development Bank (2017). Meeting Asia's Infrastructure Needs.
19. World Bank (2014). Indonesia: Avoiding the Trap.
20. Castrol. Castrol Magnatec Stop-Start Index.
21. World Bank. Logistics Performance Indicator. Global Rankings 2016.
22. Indonesia-Investments. Poverty in Indonesia: Around 34.4 Million Indonesians Live in Slums, 3 October 2014.
23. Department of Foreign Affairs and Trade. Australian Government. Indonesia Infrastructure Program (2016–2026) Investment Concept (Revised) November 2015.
24. Tabor, Steven A. Constraints to Indonesia's Economic Growth. Asian Development Bank Papers on Indonesia, No. 10, December 2015. Asian Development Bank.
25. IMF. Developing Economies' Untapped Revenues. IMF Survey, 17 June 2016.
26. Asian Development Bank. Key Indicators for Asia and the Pacific 2012. Special Chapter: Green Urbanization in Asia.

27. Max Planck Institute for Chemistry. More deaths due to air pollution: Air pollution could claim 6.6 million lives by 2050, 16 September 2015.
28. WHO Global Urban Ambient Air Pollution Database (update 2016).
29. Christian Aid. Act Now or Pay Later: Protecting a billion people in climate-threatened coastal cities. May 2016.
30. Asian Development Bank. Key Indicators for Asia and the Pacific 2012. Special Chapter: Green Urbanization in Asia.
31. Verisk Maplecroft. Heat stress threatens to cut labour productivity in SE Asia by up to 25% within 30 years, 28 October 2015.
32. OECD. (2015). OECD Innovation Strategy—an agenda for policy action.
33. 2thinknow. Innovation Cities Index 2016–2017.
34. Times Higher Education. World University Rankings 2016–2017.
35. University of Pennsylvania. 2016 Global Go to Think Tank Index Report.
36. Mercer. (2016). Quality of Living Rankings.
37. Biswas, Asit K. Smart Cities? The truly great have soul. Asian Century Institute, 26 March 2014.
38. World Economic Forum. The Global Competitiveness Report 2016–2017.
39. Freedom House. Freedom in the World 2016.
40. 2thinknow. Innovation Cities™ Index 2016–2017.
41. The Economist Intelligence Unit. Worldwide Cost of Living 2017.
42. World Happiness Report 2017.
43. Lai, Carine, and Michael E. DeGolyer. Asian Urban-Wellbeing Indicators Comparative Report: Hong Kong, Singapore, Shanghai (2016 First Report). Civic Exchange. June 2016.

**Open Access** This chapter is licensed under the terms of the Creative Commons Attribution 4.0 International License (http://creativecommons.org/licenses/by/4.0/), which permits use, sharing, adaptation, distribution, and reproduction in any medium or format, as long as you give appropriate credit to the original author(s) and the source, provide a link to the Creative Commons license and indicate if changes were made.

The images or other third party material in this chapter are included in the chapter's Creative Commons license, unless indicated otherwise in a credit line to the material. If material is not included in the chapter's Creative Commons license and your intended use is not permitted by statutory regulation or exceeds the permitted use, you will need to obtain permission directly from the copyright holder.

CHAPTER 6

# Giving All Asians a Chance!

"I'm proud to be gay, and I consider being gay among the greatest gifts God has given me," said Tim Cook, CEO of Apple, in an essay published by *Bloomberg Businessweek*.[1] "Part of social progress is understanding that a person is not defined only by one's sexuality, race, or gender ... The company that I am so fortunate to lead has long advocated for human rights and equality for all."

The "coming-out" of Tim Cook is emblematic of the wave of openness and tolerance, and embrace of diversity that is occurring in many Western countries today. True, discrimination, prejudice and persecution of some groups of citizens still exist and may never be fully beaten. But through my own life I have witnessed a sea change in attitudes. It is ironical that on the very same day that Cook's essay was published, Singapore's Court of Appeal upheld the country's ban on gay sex.

Indeed, while many Asian countries have made progress over the past few decades, social inclusion remains a distant ideal, as testified by the experiences of the lesbian, gay, bisexual and transgender (LGBT) community, women, ethnic and religious minorities and lower castes which we explore in this chapter. Insufficient efforts to give all Asians a better chance in life will continue to cost Asia dearly in terms of both its economic development and its quest to create decent middle-class societies.

## LGBT Rights in Asia

LGBT communities may suffer from some of the most egregious discrimination in Asia. According to a 2014 Gallup poll, most Asian countries are not LGBT friendly, and things may have since gotten worse.[2] The best performing Asian countries are the Philippines and Taiwan, where 58% and 39% of respondents, respectively, consider their home city or area to be LGBT friendly (indeed, in May 2017, Taiwan's top court ruled that gay couples will be allowed to marry). Scores were less than 30% for Japan, India, Myanmar, Thailand and Vietnam, below 20% for Bangladesh, Korea and China, and 10% or below for Malaysia, Mongolia, Sri Lanka, Indonesia and Pakistan.

Indonesia is an interesting case. Unlike its neighbors Malaysia and Singapore, it does not have national laws that punish homosexuality, although there has reportedly been a proliferation of homophobic bylaws at the local/provincial level. Nor does it have laws that protect the LGBT community from discrimination and harassment. Traditionally, Indonesia's LGBT community has lived in relative peace, in large part by keeping a low profile. They need to do so. A 2013 report by the Pew Research Center showed that over 93% of Indonesians believe that homosexuality should not be accepted[3] (other Asian countries with high non-acceptance rates were Pakistan, Malaysia, China and South Korea). And according to a report by a local NGO, "Arus Pelangi" (Indonesian for Rainbow Currents), over 89% of LGBT people have been victims of "psychological, physical, sexual, economic and cultural abuses".

Against this background, a wave of homophobia has been sweeping through Indonesia, and threatens to undermine its economic and social progress. "Beginning in January 2016, however, a series of anti-LGBT public comments by government officials grew into a cascade of threats and vitriol against LGBT Indonesians by state commissions, militant Islamists, and mainstream religious organizations", reports Human Rights Watch.[4] In response to media pressure to comment on Indonesia's homophobia, Indonesian President Joko Widodo has claimed that there is no discrimination against anyone in Indonesia. But he repeatedly qualifies such comments by noting that Indonesia is the world's largest Muslim nation and that LGBT rights are not consistent with its religious and social norms.

The regression in LGBT rights in Indonesia runs directly against the positive revolution in LGBT rights that is sweeping through the Western world. In the same 2014 Gallup poll, some 69% or more of respondents from 14 Western countries indicated that their city or area is a good place to live for gay or lesbian people. And LGBT rights are increasingly accepted as fundamental human rights, and promoted as such by the United Nations (UN), the US foreign aid agency (USAID) and NGOs like Human Rights Watch—all of which are active in Indonesia.

In addition to being fundamental human rights, LGBT rights also make good economic sense. As Cook said, Apple is a "company that loves creativity and innovation and knows it can only flourish when you embrace people's differences." It is not surprising that Apple should be ranked the most innovative company.[5]

Indonesia, Singapore, China and other Asian countries dream of having homegrown companies like Apple. But until they embrace diversity, and fight against discrimination, prejudice and persecution of LGBT and other social groups, the dream of building successful innovative companies will remain a pious hope.

Is there any glimmer of hope for LGBT rights in Indonesia and other Asian countries? Sakdiyah Ma'ruf is a female Indonesian stand-up comedian who tackles many taboos in Islamic culture in her comedy routines, and who reminds us of the power of educated youth in fostering a more open-minded and tolerant future. We can only hope for social progress thanks to generational change through Asia's millennials.

Under the Obama administration, USAID also worked to bolster basic LGBT rights across the continent through its "Being LGBT in Asia" initiative. Between 2012 and 2014, USAID and the United Nations Development Programme implemented a landmark review and analysis of LGBT circumstances across 18 Asian countries. It found that Asia's LGBT people suffer not only from unsupportive policies and laws but also from high levels of stigma and discrimination, affecting every aspect of LGBT people's lives from families and the workplace to law enforcement, the media and health and education services.

Key objectives of "Being LGBT in Asia" include working with LGBT civil society to engage with country level institutions to advocate for LGBT protective laws and policies, and supporting community empowerment and mobilization activities. The initiative also supports multi-stakeholder dialogues on LGBT rights, promoting advocacy frameworks to address discrimination and assist in legal challenges. It's not difficult to imagine that this very important initiative could be one of the victims of President Trump's proposed slashing of the USAID budget, along with the agency's active work in the promotion of gender equality and advancing the status of women and girls in Asia.

\* \* \*

As we explored in earlier chapters, there is much to admire in Asia's economic development, even if most countries remain underachievers. But there is much less to admire when it comes to the region's social development, especially for women's rights and access to opportunity. Asia's leading economies are way down the list in the World Economic Forum's Global Gender Gap Index which examines the gap between men and women in four fundamental categories—economic participation and opportunity, educational attainment, health and survival, and political empowerment.[6]

Singapore may have the highest GDP per capita in Asia, and one of the very highest in the world. But it only ranks 55th out of the 144 countries surveyed in the Global Gender Gap Index. Japan and Korea have long been leading Asian economies, but the relative status of women is near the bottom of Asia's list, with rankings of 111th and 116th. And while Asia's three giants of China, India and Indonesia may be ahead of Japan and Korea, they are still wallowing at ranks 87, 88 and 99, respectively, in the Global Gender Gap Index. Asia's best performers are the Philippines, which comes at 7th, and Laos at 43rd.

In the following sections, we explore a few of the very many ways in which Asian women are prevented from contributing to Asia's economic and social development.

## The Many Trials of Womanhood in Japan

It would be easy to imagine that the lot of Japanese women is finally beginning to change. In July 2016, Tokyo elected its first woman mayor, Madame Yuriko Koike, who beat a male candidate supported by Japan's ruling right-wing government. In September 2016, Japan's opposition Democratic Party of Japan elected its first woman leader, Madame Renho Murata (who has since resigned from that position). And "womenomics" has been at the center of the Japanese government's Abenomics program.

But overall the lives of most Japanese women are changing ever so slowly, if at all. As the OECD reports, women's wages are much lower than men's, with the gender wage gap being the third highest among the OECD group of advanced countries.[7] And as Japanese Prime Minister Shinzo Abe once said, "Japan's corporate culture, by contrast, is still one of pinstripes and button-downs. After all, the female labour force in Japan is the most under-utilised resource. Japan must become a place where women shine".

For all Mr. Abe's ambitions for women to play a much greater role in business and government, progress has been glacial. Women still only hold 2% of seats on boards of directors in Japan, compared with 36% in Norway, around 30% in France and Finland and about 20% in Canada and the US. And women only filled 3% of managerial positions in the national government in 2014.

There are many factors that conspire to restrict the opportunity of Japanese women to succeed in business, government and politics.[8] Japan's gender discrimination raises its ugly head around the moment of childbirth, when the majority of women leave their careers and stop working. Japanese corporate life with its long hours, late drinking sessions with colleagues and forced transfers to other regions or countries is not readily compatible with family life.

The macho-sexist attitude of Japanese corporate life is enforced by Japanese men who can make work environment insufferable for professional Japanese women. Maternity harassment, or "matahara" in Japanese, is a growing problem in Japan. A recent government study showed that 20% of full-time working women are bullied, fired or pressured into quitting by their employers once they become pregnant, while nearly half of temporary workers suffer from matahara. The only recourse that these women have is to take their bosses to court, which most do not want to do. So the usual scenario is for Japanese women to only return to the workforce after they have raised their children. But when they do so, the majority are only able to find relatively low-paid non-regular jobs.

The plight of Japanese women imposes many costs on the Japanese economy. Japan desperately needs more workers, as its poor demographics mean that the nation's workforce has been declining for over 20 years, and now the total population is declining. The organization of the Tokyo Olympic Games in 2020 is also increasing the demand for workers. At the same time, Japan still has a cultural aversion toward substantial increases in immigration.

Improving the opportunity for Japanese women to work is an ideal response to this predicament. Indeed, the OECD has estimated if female participation in the workforce were to converge to the same rate as men by the year 2030, the country's GDP could be almost 20% higher. Indeed, the impact might well be higher since young Japanese women are on average better educated than young Japanese men. In 2013, 67% of Japanese women aged 25–34 years had a tertiary degree compared with just 56% of men. And Japanese women have the world's highest life expectancy at 87 years (compared with 81 year for men).

There is so much that the Japanese government could do, but isn't doing, to improve the opportunity of Japanese women to pursue a career. Fundamentally, it is a matter of creating an environment that enables women to easily combine a family life with a working life. Japan's draconian immigration laws should be relaxed to enable families to hire care workers from countries like the Philippines. The government needs to substantially boost its investment in childcare and after-care facilities. Japan spends only about one-third as much as Sweden and the UK, as a share of GDP, on such facilities. And Japan's tax system should also be amended to eliminate the disincentive for women to work.

There is also much that the business sector could do. Japan's crazy work culture is in desperate need of modernization. Japanese companies should wake up to the fact that militaristic work practices may have been effective in the country's recovery from World War 2, but that today Japan has much lower productivity than most other advanced countries. Japanese companies could boost their productivity by adopting more flexible working practices, and installing childcare facilities to help their female workers. Japanese companies should also wake up to the fact that more gender diversity in their workforces can be a strength, and managers should be given diversity targets to achieve.

If Japanese men also had a more sane working life, they could do much more at home to support the lives of their working wives. The typical Japanese man doesn't do anything at home other than eating and sleeping. They spend less than one hour per day of household chores and childcare—compared with 3+ hours for Swedish and German fathers and 2.5 hours for Americans.

There are many womenomics naysayers, and one of their standard arguments is that Japan's already low birth rate would fall even lower if more Japanese women had careers. This is wrong. Today, many women are virtually forced to choose between a working life and a family life. However, the international evidence shows that countries which have family-friendly working environments—countries like Sweden, Denmark, the Netherlands, and the UK—tend to have both higher female labor force participation and higher fertility rates.

There is much pessimism about the prospects for womenomics in Japan. You can still meet many Japanese men who are convinced that Japanese women do not want to work, that they prefer a life at home, going to coffee shops with their girlfriends and package tours to Europe. Akira Matsumoto, Chairman and CEO of Calbee, advises women to be more aggressive in upending "vested interests" rooted in power, money and status — traditionally the domain of men—"Men's mindset won't change. ...If you wait to see change, it will probably take another 300 years".

But having spent a lot of time in Japan, on-and-off for eight years, it seems to me that attitudes may be changing in the millennial generation. Japanese boys seem much less macho than their fathers, while Japanese girls are becoming more assertive. Female entrepreneurship also seems to be a burgeoning new trend. Ambitious women who can see the limited prospects of upward mobility in a traditional Japanese company are sometimes more willing to try starting up their own business. And if Japan does succeed in attracting more foreign investment into its market, foreign companies will surely start hiring many of Japan's talented women. In other words, the future may not be so bleak, even if change will come slowly.

## THE PLIGHT OF SOUTH ASIA'S WOMEN

As dismaying as the situation of Japanese (and also Korean) women might be, the plight of many women in poorer Asian countries, especially in South Asia, is nothing short of tragic, as we will discuss in the next few sections. East Asia has now moved well ahead of South Asia, as the subcontinent now has more in common with Sub-Saharan Africa for things like nutrition, health, education and economic and political participation when it comes to gender equality, depriving the region of a significant source of human potential.

Half of South Asian women still cannot read. In South Asia, women are also much more vulnerable to poverty, sexual and other violence, and HIV/AIDS. Overall, the UN's Gender Development Index for South Asia is now the lowest of all the world's regions. Perhaps the most important thing holding South Asian women back is conservative traditional values in male-dominated societies that deprive them of both the necessary security and opportunities to lead fulfilling lives.

In the following sections, we look in detail at the issues of Asia's missing women, forced child marriage in Asia and Pakistan's dishonorable honor-killing epidemic.

## Asia's Missing Women

Perhaps the greatest opportunity that too many Asian women are deprived of is the right to life. From the 1990s, prenatal gender selection has resulted in a sharp decline in the proportion of girls being born, especially in China and India. This has given rise to the phenomenon of Asia's "missing women", which was first identified by Nobel Prize-winning economist Amartya Sen,[9] and represents a manifest violation of women's human rights.

There are three main reasons for the phenomenon of Asia's missing women.[10] First, in Confucian and patriarchal cultures, families have a preference for sons over daughters, because sons inherit the family name and assets, and they look after parents as they age. This is very important in countries with very weak social welfare systems. And in India, girls are seen as a bad investment because of the dowry that their marriage will require.

Then, the ability to exercise this preference for a son has been facilitated by the spread of ultrasound technology and the availability of abortion in the private healthcare system. And the general decline in fertility rates, in tandem with economic development and rising education, has heightened the need for prenatal gender selection. When family sizes were large, there was always a high likelihood of having at least one son. But as family sizes declined dramatically, there is a much greater risk of not having a son among the one or two children in the family. In this regard, China's one-child policy no doubt played in gender birth selection.

Sex ratios at birth are estimated by the UN to be 118 boys for every hundred girls in China, and 111 in each of India and Vietnam. This compares with the standard biological level of around 105 male births for every 100 female births. It is thus estimated that the world would have 117 million missing women, with 57% being attributable to China and 30% to India. According to a study by Mara Hvistendahl, the figure could be as high as 163 million.[11]

Please don't think that it is poor and illiterate families who are the main cause of Asia's missing children. On the contrary, it is the urban and educated middle classes who are leading the way in having smaller families and have the financial wherewithal to make prenatal gender selection. And for those girls who are lucky enough to be born, life is not always rosy. Many suffer from discrimination in their access to healthcare, nutrition and education.

Looking ahead, it is possible, as in the case of Korea, that with economic and social development over time, Chinese and Indian families become more gender neutral in their birth preferences. But there is also a risk of a continued deterioration in gender birth ratios, as gender birth imbalances have not yet spread across the entire country in China and India.

One dramatic consequence of Asia's missing women is the increasing number of Asian men who will be unable to find a wife and have a family (surplus men are known as "bare branches" in China). According to the UN, after the year 2030, the number of single men looking for a wife in China and India could exceed the available unmarried women by 50–60% for several decades. And the men most adversely affected will likely be those who are underprivileged in terms of income and education. In other words, unequal opportunity for marriage is becoming another feature of an increasingly unequal Asia.

The potential socio-economic consequences of the rise in involuntary bachelorhood are enormous, with the likelihood of mental health problems, increased crime, violence and drug abuse. There is also evidence of abduction and trafficking of women for marriage, with Vietnamese girls often being victims of kidnapping for marriage in China. Marriage migration is also a growing trend in East Asia, but this only transfers the missing women problem from one country to another.

Governments need to implement stronger policies to prevent prenatal gender selection, and campaign against traditional patriarchal value systems. But change will only come slowly, and the impact of the past decades of prenatal gender selection will continue also for decades to come.

## Forced Child Marriage in South Asia

If a South Asian girl is lucky enough to survive prenatal gender selection, and be born, the next problem that she could face is being forced into a marriage while she is still a child.

"In South Asia, young girls are a burden, especially for poor families", an Indian colleague once explained to me. "They are just an expense item—a mouth to feed, a person to educate. And when times get tough, like when a natural disaster strikes, poor families feel obliged to look after young boys first. Since the cost of a dowry is much lower for young girls, many families marry off their young daughters as soon as they can."

There are also social pressures for girls to marry as soon as they reach puberty. Many families see early marriage as a means of protecting their daughter from possible abduction, and sexual violence.[12] There are also reports from Malaysia where men accused of rape seek to marry their alleged (usually very young) victims in order to avoid prosecution, since rape within marriage is not a crime.

Child marriage, defined by the UN as marriage under the age of 18, is endemic in South Asia.[13] Despite laws against child marriage, some 66% of girls from Bangladesh get married before the age of 18, while 47% of Indian and 41% of Nepalese girls do so.[14] What's even worse, 29% of Bangladeshi girls get married before they reach the age of 15. And despite Asia's rapid economic progress, there has only been a slight decrease in the prevalence of child marriage these past three decades.

The effects of child marriage can be catastrophic for the poor girls involved. Many abandon school and become pregnant, bringing an abrupt end to their education and childhood. They are more likely to die during pregnancy and childbirth than women in their twenties. Their children are more likely to be stillborn or die during their first month of life. Child brides are also more vulnerable to domestic violence and HIV/AIDS.

These South Asian governments have been making commitments to seriously tackle the issue of forced child marriage, including through a UN Girl Summit in 2014. But progress has been slow. There is much push back from conservative forces in these male-dominated societies.

## PAKISTAN'S DISHONORABLE HONOR-KILLING EPIDEMIC

While forced child marriages are a tragedy for young girls in South Asia, those girls who stand up for themselves and refuse such marriages, or allegedly bring dishonor on their families in other ways, expose themselves to the risk of being murdered in so-called honor killings. The year 2016 saw an epidemic of honor killings in Pakistan, with the murder of Pakistani social media star, Qandeel Baloch, by her brother being only the most talked about.

Indeed, it seemed like every week that a new case of an honor killing hit the international media. One Pakistani man reportedly killed his two sisters the evening before their weddings because they had chosen their own husbands, rather than settling for arranged marriages According to another report, a Pakistani mother-of-three and a 21-year-old man were tortured and hanged from a tree after reportedly having an affair. Similarly, a British-Pakistani beautician was allegedly killed by her ex-husband as her father held her down, while visiting relatives in her ancestral village in northern Punjab. Another Pakistani man said "I am not ashamed what I have done" after he slit his second wife's throat, 15 years after murdering first wife.

What exactly are honor killings? The most typical example occurs when someone (usually a young woman) is deemed to have brought dishonor on a family by marrying a person of lower status or caste, by refusing to enter into an arranged marriage, having sex outside of marriage, being a rape victim or even dressing inappropriately.

In these circumstances, the family leaders might get together, and decide that it is necessary to murder the offending person(s) in order to restore the honor of the family. A family member is usually appointed to commit the murder. This is sometimes a young person, who would be subject to lesser punishment than an adult. Another frequent scenario is when one person takes it upon themselves to undertake the honor killing to the shock and horror of other family members.

There have been all too many headline cases in recent times. Another example, in 2014, was that of Farzana Parveen, who was three months pregnant, and was stoned to death in the front of the courthouse of Lahore (Pakistan's most cultured city) by family members angry that she had married without their permission.

Honor killing is against the law in most countries. But all too often, the police turn a blind eye, considering this to be a matter for the family. Punishment could be lightened or waived, if the victim's family forgives the murderer. In the year 2000, the UN estimated that there were about 5000 honor killings in the world annually, with 1000 taking place in each of Pakistan and India. And there is a growing number of cases in Western countries like the US, UK, Canada and Australia, in tandem with the increasing numbers of migrants from these regions. The real figure for world honor killings may be closer to 20,000, according to Amy Logan, President of the US National Committee for UN Women. Large numbers go unreported, or are falsely reported as suicides.

There is every reason to expect that these figures are growing. As economic development and urbanization proceed, young women are better educated and have aspirations for a more independent and freer life. In countries like Bangladesh, where clothing and textile manufacture is a growth industry, many women are the principal breadwinner, something which can be a big "ego-shock" in male-dominated societies. Overall, there is a growing gap between the traditional attitudes of parents, and those of younger women, in South Asia and the Middle East.

The numbers of deaths from honor killings may seem small for highly populous countries like Pakistan and India. And indeed they are when compared with the numbers of people who die in these countries from car accidents or from air or water pollution. But the other side of the tragedy is that of the millions of women who live their life in fear, who forego marrying the person they love, who accept forced arranged marriages or who are subject to other abominable acts like acid-throwing attacks. Aspiring economic powerhouses like India and Pakistan will never succeed or achieve their potential, while ever archaic medieval practices like honor killings remain part of the social landscape.

Thankfully, the film, "A Girl in the River: The Price of Forgiveness",[15] directed by Pakistani woman filmmaker Sharmeen Obaid-Chinoy, won the 2016 Oscar for the best documentary short subject, and attracted global attention to this problem. It really is a must-see. The girl in the river, Saba, was shot in the face and thrown into a river by her father and uncle, after she married for love and not through an arranged marriage. Miraculously, Saba survived. Saba was then pressured to forgive her father and uncle to restore peace to her village. Saba's father remained unrepentant. "Everyone says I am more respected. They say I am an honourable man. They say what I did was right," he said. "I have other daughters. Since this incident, each daughter has received proposals because I am called an honourable man."

After he saw the film, Pakistan Prime Minister Nawaz Sharif, announced that his government was "in the process of legislating to stop such brutal and inhumane acts in the name of honor". Then following the murder of Qandeel Baloch, the Pakistani Parliament finally revised its laws to stiffen the punishment for honor killings, as well as for rape. But of course there are loopholes that will allow killers to get off light and may be even escape punishment altogether.

What will it take for Pakistan to seriously tackle this heinous crime against women?

Fundamentally, it will require a revolution in the misogynist mind-sets of Pakistani men. But this will be difficult. Some Pakistani politicians and religious leaders criticized Obaid-Chinoy for bringing dishonor on Pakistan through her film! Right-wing political groups and Muslim clerics have strongly resisted attempts to provide legislative protection against honor killings. Tribal leaders and family members exert immense pressure to stay quiet. As in the film, survivors of attempted honor killings are forced to forgive their aggressors. And murder is condoned in Pakistani society.

Pakistani women have a massively uphill battle in their quest for a decent life. Pakistan is an extremely backward country in many respects. It is ranked the second worst country among the 144 countries surveyed in the World Economic Forum's Global Gender Gap Report.[16] Pakistan ranks just ahead of the unsavory case of Yemen, and just behind Syria. Pakistan would also be one of the world's worst countries for rule of law, according to the World Justice Project. And the Fragile States Index has put Pakistan on "high alert".

Most regrettably, this is the state of Pakistan. In many ways, it is the direct descendant of the great Mughal civilization, and yet today it is one of the very least civilized countries on the planet!

* * *

Following our discussion of some of the very many ways in which Asia's women are not given a fair chance to contribute to the economy or society, we will take up the case of Asia's indigenous peoples and ethnic minorities who are similarly disadvantaged.

## Asia's Indigenous Peoples

Asia's indigenous peoples are another segment of the region's citizens who are deprived of the opportunity of contributing fully to the economy and society. According to the International Work Group for Indigenous Affairs (IWGIA), there are some 260 million indigenous peoples in Asia, three-quarters of the world's total.[17] This makes Asia the most culturally diverse region in the world.

"Asian indigenous peoples face problems such as denial of self-determination, the loss of control over their land and natural resources, discrimination and marginalization, heavy assimilation pressure and violent repression by state security forces", reports the IWGIA. In other words, they suffer from a profound lack of empowerment. The average poverty rate of Asia's indigenous peoples is three times higher than the Asian average. And education, health and other social conditions are also much worse.

While rapid economic growth has lifted millions of Asians out of poverty, most indigenous peoples have benefited little from this economic growth. Specific policy interventions will be required to improve the lives of indigenous peoples. In particular, it is necessary to fight against discrimination, prejudice and persecution even if the experiences of the US, Canada, Australia and New Zealand highlight how very difficult it can be to bring indigenous peoples into the mainstream of the economy and society.

Who are Asia's indigenous peoples? Where do they live? As the IWGIA documents, indigenous peoples live in most Asian countries, for example:

- Myanmar has over 100 different ethnic groups, with Burmans making up an estimated 68% of the country's 53 million people. The other ethnic nationalities include the Shan, Karen, Rakhine, Karenni, Chin, Kachin and Mon. These indigenous groups suffered greatly from the oppressive policies of the former Burman-dominated military regimes. As the country has moved toward democracy, political prisoners have been released, and the government has engaged in ceasefire and peace talks with ethnic armed groups. However, many critical issues remain unresolved, most notably regarding the Muslim Rohingya in Arakan State, who are known as the world's most persecuted people. They have been victims of terrible state-sponsored human rights abuses for a number of years, which is not abating. The human tragedy of the Rohingya reached a head in 2015 with a human smuggling crisis, and again in 2017 as thousands of Rohingya fled to Bangladesh to escape violence from the military (we take up this issue in greater detail in Chap. 9).
- In India, 461 ethnic groups are recognized as Scheduled Tribes, "Adivasis", who are considered to be India's indigenous peoples. With an estimated population of 84.3 million, they comprise 8.2% of the total population. There are, however, many more ethnic groups that should qualify for Scheduled Tribe status but which are not officially recognized.
- Japan has two main indigenous peoples, the Ainu and the Okinawans. The Ainu mainly live in Japan's northern island of Hokkaido, although many have migrated to Japan's urban centers for work and to escape discrimination on Hokkaido. According to government surveys, Ainu population in Hokkaido would be 16,786, although Ainu observers estimate those of Ainu ancestry to be between 100

and 300,000. The Okinawans, which number over one million, live in Japan's southern islands of Okinawa.
- The Philippine national population of over 100 million includes an indigenous population of between 10% and 20%. They generally suffer from a lack of access to education and other basic social services, and few opportunities to participate in economic or political life. Since their lands are rich in minerals, forests and rivers, they are vulnerable to land grabbing and other "development aggression".
- Vietnam's 53 recognized ethnic groups, beyond the Kinh majority, account for around 14% of the country's total population of 90 million. While Vietnam has achieved a spectacular decline in its poverty, among its ethnic minorities poverty remains very high.

The sad reality is that Asia's authoritarian regimes and fragile democracies usually see indigenous peoples as at best a nuisance, and all too often as a threat to their fragile grip on power. This is in sharp contrast to Western countries like the US, Canada, Australia and New Zealand, with important indigenous populations, which are often motivated by a sense of historical guilty conscious, and moral rectitude to help their indigenous populations.

In this context, we will look in a little more detail at the cases of Indonesia's West Papuans, China's Tibetans and China's Uyghurs in the following sections.

## Indonesia's West Papuans

Indonesia's West Papuans and China's Tibetans share similar fates in that their hopes for independent nationhood were dashed by greedy big brothers.

In many ways, Indonesia is defined by its immense ethnic diversity. Its population of 260 million includes some 50–70 million indigenous peoples, from 1128 officially recognized ethnic groups. And while the population of West Papua may only be around 3 ½ million, this people has endured a tragic history.

West Papuans, who are the neighbors and ethnic brothers and sisters of Papua New Guinea, have virtually no common cultural links with the rest of Indonesia. West Papuans are mainly Christian and Melanesian, while Indonesians are principally Muslim and of Malay race. The only thing that tied them together was their common colonial history, as both were part of the Dutch East Indies.

Immediately following the end of World War 2, Indonesia became an independent nation, while West Papua remained a Dutch colony. The vast majority of West Papuans wanted independence for their land, and in principle West Papua was being prepared for independence. But it became entangled in Cold War political machinations involving the US, the Netherlands, Indonesia and the UN. Then, following a sham referendum in 1969, in which little more than 1000 Papuans were allowed to vote (out of a population of around 800,000), West Papuan became part of Indonesia. The Indonesian government since has turned it into two separate provinces, namely, Papua and Papua Barat, in order to weaken it politically.

Since being folded into Indonesia, West Papua has been a veritable battleground. It has been basically occupied by Indonesia military and security forces who have waged a struggle against the West Papuan pro-independence movement, the Free West Papua group. Some 500,000 West Papuans have been allegedly killed by Indonesian security forces, with many more raped, tortured or imprisoned. Some have called it a "slow motion genocide". Some West Papuans are now refugees in Papua New Guinea, or working as virtual slaves in mines or forests. A strong undercurrent in the relationship is the attitude of arrogance and derision of Indonesians who consider West Papuans to be primitive natives.

Also at stake have been West Papua's immense rich natural resources, especially copper, gold and timber. Some of the worst human rights abuses take place in the vicinity of major resources developments, which pay for protection from the Indonesian military forces. Abuses include land-grabs by Indonesian and international business groups, denial of land rights and severe environmental degradation. And many international companies are in a virtual race to destroy West Papua's tropical forests.

The Grasberg Mine—the world's largest gold mine and second largest copper mine—has been a major sore point. This is owned by the American mining giant, Freeport-McMoRan. The rights to this mine were established between the US and Indonesia four years before West Papua even became Indonesian. Some argue that this project motivated US government support for Indonesia's takeover of West Papua. There has been much criticism of the severe environmental damage caused by its waste deposits.

By the same token, the Indonesian government has also been paying off West Papuan elites to keep them onside. Migration to West Papua from elsewhere in Indonesia has been very substantial such that West Papuans are now becoming a minority in their own land. Indonesia's actions and policies in West Papua have been facilitated by its closest neighbor, Australia, which has turned a blind eye, as it does not wish to disturb the important relationship.

Despite West Papua's immense resources, and being host to Indonesia's largest taxpayer, Freeport-McMoRan, West Papuans suffer from high poverty, poor healthcare and education, high infant and maternal mortality, and a high incidence of HIV/Aids. They also suffer from stringent restrictions on freedom of expression and assembly.

Governments like that of Indonesia usually hope that a problem like West Papua would fade away in time. They hope that restrictions on access to West Papua imposed on foreign journalists and rights monitors will keep it out of the news. But it hasn't. In 2015, West Papua was granted observer status in the Melanesian Spearhead Group (MSG), a sub-regional coalition composed of Fiji, the Solomon Islands, Vanuatu, Papua New Guinea and New Caledonia's Front de Liberation Nationale Kanak et Socialiste (FLNKS). West Papua will now sit on the inside of the organization alongside Indonesia. This is hoped to be an historic step toward addressing the human rights atrocities committed by the Indonesian army. The MSG was founded in 1986 to promote and strengthen trade, promote Melanesian cultures, further the economic growth of its members, sustainable development, good governance and security.

There was great hope that Indonesia's President Jokowi would turn a new page in human rights in West Papua, and he has indeed released some political prisoners, and granted access to West Papua for foreign journalists. But there is virtually no likelihood of a sea change under his presidency.

## China's Tibetans

For its part, China is also a multi-ethnic country, and all ethnic groups are considered equal before the law. Besides the Han Chinese majority, the government recognizes 55 ethnic minority peoples within its borders, who number 114 million persons, or 8.5% of the country's total population. The government has made great efforts to improve the lives of China's indigenous peoples, in the areas of education and health. They were also allowed to have two or three children, and were thus exempt from the one-child policy. But certain groups like Tibetans and the Uighurs still suffer terrible human rights abuses.

Tibet has indeed lived through a turbulent history. There were times when it was ruled by the Mongols and Chinese, together with times when it was independent, such as through much of the first half of the twentieth century. But through all this Tibet developed and maintained a distinctive religion, culture and way of life. At the same time, economic development was minimal, and most Tibetans were desperately poor.

In 1950, following the Communist Party's victory in the Chinese Civil War, the Chinese military invaded Tibet to assert what it claimed to be centuries-old sovereignty. The Chinese government considers Tibet to be an important strategic buffer between China and India. It is also interested in Tibet's vast natural resources. Following a failed anti-Chinese uprising in 1959, the Dalai Lama fled Tibet for India where he set a government-in-exile, which has ever since been a strain on Indo-Chinese relations. Most Tibetans consider Tibet to be under occupation by a foreign power.

The Dalai Lama has been a voice for Tibetans on the international stage, and the Tibetan question has been a symbol of the tortured relations between China and the West. Human rights supporters and activists have an idealistic and almost romantic sympathy toward Tibet. This was most manifest in the Dalai Lama being awarded the Nobel Peace Prize in 1989. For its part, the Chinese government reacts with hysteria when senior Western political and other personalities meet with the Dalai Lama. So most Western governments and businesses now cave into Chinese economic and political power and ignore the Dalai Lama.

China has poured literally billions of dollars of investment into Tibet. This has developed Tibet's transport, power and other infrastructure, and boosted the economy, which today is growing faster than the rest of the Chinese economy. High-speed rail links have fostered a booming tourist industry. China's state-owned enterprises have also been instructed to invest in Tibet. At the same time, there has been a large wave of immigration into Tibet of Han Chinese. It is a common assessment that these Chinese immigrants have benefited much more than the local Tibetans from this economic development, and that all the massive subsidies from Beijing have done little to promote private sector development.

But the Chinese government has also combined political repression with its economic development policies, with the Dalai Lama being a favorite target of Chinese government vitriol. The Chinese government has aggressively suppressed Tibetan political opposition and Tibetan identity. Most of Tibet's monasteries were destroyed during the Cultural Revolution. Some 1.2 million Tibetans would have been killed under Chinese rule, according to the Dalai Lama, who accuses China's government of "cultural genocide". In more recent times, there was a wave of unrest in 2008, and there has been a wave of self-immolations by Tibetans opposed to Chinese rule. And under President Xi Jinping, political repression of peaceful dissent has increased in Tibet, as it has elsewhere in China.

In order to solve the current Tibet issue, the Dalai Lama has proposed the "Middle-Way Approach" through a non-violent and negotiated solution. He is not seeking independence for Tibet. Rather he is seeking to achieve a genuine autonomy for all Tibetans living in the three traditional provinces of Tibet within the framework of the People's Republic of China. According to the Dalai Lama, this approach "safeguards the vital interests of all concerned parties—for Tibetans: the protection and preservation of their culture, religion and national identity; for the Chinese: the security and territorial integrity of the motherland; and for neighbors and other third parties: peaceful borders and international relations."[18]

China simply rejects the Dalai Lama's Middle-Way Approach, and is clearly waiting for the 82-year-old Dalai Lama to die, hoping that this will see the end of the Tibet issue. But this may well be a miscalculation. When the Dalai Lama passes, the Chinese government will lose a voice of reason and moderation, and will likely get entangled in disputes and conflicts as it tries to control the nomination of the next Dalai Lama.

## Dire Situation of China's Uighurs

The sentencing of Chinese Uighur scholar Ilham Tohti to life imprisonment in 2014 highlights the dire situation of this poor Muslim community. It is also a harsh reminder that China is still an empire, not a nation—an empire that employs repression and violence to control peoples within its imperial borders, and which hinders their ability to contribute to both society and the economy.

The Uighurs are a Sunni Muslim people of ten million people, of which eight million live in the vast Xinjiang region in western China, which borders five Muslim countries. They are ethnically and culturally much closer to Central Asia than to China. The region's economy was traditionally based on agriculture and trade, with towns like Kashgar being part of the famed Silk Road. The Xinjiang region was brought under Chinese imperial administration through the Xing Dynasty conquests of 1745. But the region was left largely to its own devices. Following the fall of the Xing Dynasty in 1904, Xinjiang enjoyed a few brief periods of independence.

Following the 1949 Communist Party victory in the Chinese Civil War, the new People's Republic of China reasserted control over Xinjiang. According to the Chinese government, Xinjiang has been an inseparable part of the Chinese nation for over 2000 years, since the days of the Western Han Dynasty. The Uighurs are officially recognized by the Chinese government as one of the country's 55 ethnic minorities. Back in 1949, Han Chinese only accounted for 7% of Xinjiang's population. But internal migration, especially since the 1990s, has dramatically increased the Han population to over 8 million (and may be a lot more, if Chinese police and military are fully counted), such that the Uighurs now find themselves a minority in their own province.

The Chinese government has actively developed the Xinjiang's vast mineral and oil deposits. Xinjiang accounts for 28% of China's natural gas reserves, and gas output increased sixfold between 2000 and 2012, while oil production rose by half. Some 60% of Xinjiang's GDP is now derived from petroleum. Most job opportunities are given to Han Chinese. Many job advertisements indicate that only Han Chinese or native Mandarin speakers will be considered. Uighurs are frozen out of government positions, the region's booming oil and gas industry, and many other industries because of the perceived risk of terrorism. Uighur unemployment is very high. Education favors Mandarin over Uighur. And very few local Chinese speak the Uighur language.

Poverty is high among the Uighur population. Some Uighur farmland has reportedly been confiscated for development. Their culture is also under threat through restrictions on religious practices, including bans on the observance of Ramadan, and rules that discourage women from wearing headscarves and young men from growing beards. It is difficult for Uighurs to get passports. They are routinely denied access to hotels. Heavily armed police are positioned throughout Uighur neighborhoods. There is a vast web of government informers, and Internet and cellphone surveillance. Uighurs are second-class citizens in Xinjiang.

Ethnic tension has been fueled by economic disparities, cultural repression, and the fundamental lack of trust between the Uighurs and the Chinese government. This has given rise to movements for greater autonomy and independence, as well as incidents of terrorism.

Separatist groups rose in importance after the collapse of the Soviet Union, and the independence of Muslim states in Central Asia, with street protests in the 1990s, and again in the lead-up to the Beijing Olympic Games. In more recent times, there has been an escalation of violence. In 2009, there was large-scale rioting in the regional capital of Urumqi, with 200 people being killed, most of them Han Chinese. In 2012, six Uighurs reportedly tried to hijack an internal flight. In 2013, Uighurs were allegedly behind a car explosion in Tiananmen Square. In 2014, two cars crashed into an Urumqi market.

China blames the conflict on independence-seeking separatists, terrorists and the spread of radical Islam. The government believes acts of terrorism are organized by jihadists outside of China. China has used the post-9/11 war on terror to paint the Uighurs as terrorists. Authorities have stepped up campaign against terrorism, and tightened up security. Most observers believe that the Chinese authorities exaggerate the threat posed by the Uighurs, even if a small minority is radicalized.

Uighur groups claim that their discontent is a response to religious oppression and economic marginalization. Many prominent Uighurs have been imprisoned or sought asylum abroad. As China responds to its fears of fundamentalism and radicalization, it appears to be actually provoking troubles. "The entire Uighur ethnicity feels asphyxiated, having become suspect as sympathetic to extremism," said Nicholas Bequelin of Human Rights Watch. "Xinjiang is trapped in a vicious cycle of increased repression that only leads to more violence."

It was against this background that Ilham Tohti, an economics professor at Beijing's Minzu University, was arrested and eventually sentenced to life imprisonment for separatism in September 2014. Ilham has long spoken critically of the Chinese government's policies toward the Uighurs. The Chinese court found that Ilham had "bewitched and coerced young ethnic students" into writing separatist tracts for Uighur Online, a website he founded in 2006. The court found that he had "encouraged his fellow Uighurs to use violence" and that he had "internationalized" the Uighur issue by giving interviews to foreign media. The court also demanded the seizure of all his assets. Ilham has become yet another victim of Xi Jinping's broader crackdown on activists, intellectual and lawyers.

The verdict is "a sign of further tightening of civil liberties that has been going", said Maya Wang of Human Rights Watch. "It does not bode well for the already tense relationship between Han and Uighurs in Xinjiang". Ironically, Ilham is a voice of moderation who wants better treatment for Uighurs and more autonomy for Xinjiang, rather than independence. Many see the life sentence as an act of repression itself. It is much worse than sentences to be handed out to other dissidents for similar activities.

The sentence will make this previously little-known lawyer, who represented hardly any threat to the Communist Party, an international symbol for human rights activists just like Liu Xiaobo, who was awarded the 2010 Nobel Peace Prize. Dissident writer Wang Lixiing said that the Chinese government has made him a "Uighur Mandela". Overall, the approach of the Chinese government to the Uighurs has been denial of self-determination or greater autonomy, taking control of their land and natural resources, discrimination and marginalization, heavy assimilation pressures and violent repression by state security forces.

History shows that such an approach is not only unjust, it is doomed to failure. China should employ policies of inclusive development, whereby Uighurs are given autonomy to manage their affairs within China, and have the opportunity to develop their own natural resources and the freedom to practice their own culture. Openness and dialogue, rather than repression, is necessary to achieve reconciliation between the Uighurs and the Chinese government. This would require wise leadership on both sides. It is ironical that Ilham, the man who has been imprisoned for life, is a very effective and moderate leader who may have been able to help facilitate a peaceful reconciliation between the Uighurs and the Chinese. But eliminating a voice of moderation makes it easier for the Chinese government to paint a negative image of all Uighurs.

## SRI LANKA NEEDS NATIONAL RECONCILIATION

Sri Lanka, a teardrop-shaped tropical island, would seem to have everything going for it. Delicious tea. Fragrant cinnamon and other spices. Precious gemstones. Abundant rubber. And wonderful beaches and hill country. It truly is the "great and beautiful island". Over 90% of its population is literate, and its life expectancy of 74 years is eight years higher than India's.

It is thus not surprising that Sri Lanka's GDP per capita of $12,300 in 2016 should be about double that of India, while only 15% of its population live on less than $3.10 a day, compared with close to 60% for India. But Sri Lanka could have been even much further ahead had it not suffered from a three-decade-long civil war, which pitted the island's minority

Tamil population (around 12% of total) against the majority Sinhalese (74%).

How could this predominantly Buddhist and Hindu nation descend into the horrific violence that ravaged the country?

In the eyes of the Buddhist-Sinhalese population, the Hindu-Tamils received favorable treatment by the British colonial administration, which ruled the country from 1802 to 1948. And so, following independence, the new Sinhalese-dominated government, propelled by Buddhist nationalistic fervor, implemented policies that favored the Sinhalese majority and discriminated against the Tamil minority. For example, in 1956 the "Sinhala Only Act" replaced English with Sinhala as the only official language of the country. This meant that it was very difficult for Sri Lankan Tamils to work in the civil service. Until then, 60% of civil service workers were Tamils.

Frustration, resentment and disenfranchisement of the Tamil population led to disintegrating communal relations. Periodic tensions and conflicts escalated into a full-blown civil war from 1983 to 2009, with the Liberation Tigers of Tamil Elam "Tamil Tigers" opposing Sri Lanka's national army. Despite several international attempts at peace negotiations, the conflict only came to end when former "strong-man" President Mahinda Rajapaksa launched a decisive attack by the Sri Lankan Army, which destroyed the Tamil leadership and recaptured their lands in 2009.

According to one estimate, the total economic cost of the war was $200 billion, about 5 times the GDP of Sri Lanka in 2009. At least 100,000 people died in the bloody conflict. A report by a UN-appointed panel of experts concluded that as many as 40,000 people, mainly civilians, were killed in the final weeks of the war.[19] Buoyed by the final victory, which was very popular among much of the Sinhalese population, President Mahinda Rajapaksa's regime descended into authoritarianism, nepotism, corruption, and restrictions on freedom of the press and expression. Rajapaksa's government rejected calls by the UN and major countries to seriously investigate human rights abuses during the war. Ostracized by Western countries, Rajapaksa turned to China, which became the country's biggest investor and second-largest trading partner.

To the surprise of most observers, and to his great dismay, Rajapaksa was defeated in the presidential election of January 2015 by Maithripala Sirisena, who had defected from Rajapaksa's government. Sirisena now leads a national unity government, with support from all of Sri Lanka's ethnic groups. But Rajapaksa, still a popular figure among Buddhist nationalists, remains ever present as he has returned as a member of parliament.

Under President Sirisena, Sri Lanka has come a long way in terms of improving human rights. And the Sri Lankan government has adopted an open and cooperative approach to the UN's human rights concerns, in sharp contrast to the hostile attitude under Rajapaksa. However, a September 2015 UN report concludes that there are reasonable grounds to believe that gross violations of international human rights law, serious violations of international humanitarian law and international crimes were committed by all parties in the conflict, notably unlawful killings, arbitrary arrest and detention, abductions, enforced disappearances, torture, rape and other forms of sexual violence, recruitment of children and their use in hostilities, and more.[20]

Thus, the UN High Commissioner for Human Rights has recommended the establishment of a "hybrid special court", integrating international judges, prosecutors, lawyers and investigators, to try war crimes and crimes against humanity allegedly committed by all parties to the armed conflict. The UN believes that State's criminal justice system is not yet ready or equipped to do so alone.

The Sri Lankan government has committed to setting up "National Consultations on transitional justice" to investigate the atrocities committed during the conflict. But it has been very slow in honoring this commitment, and is staunchly resisting international participation. Many members of Sri Lanka's ethnic Sinhalese majority do not want foreigners to get involved in prosecuting such cases. The same nationalism that underpinned the long conflict is also undermining national reconciliation. Indeed, many Sinhalese are unrepentant, as they proudly tell you that theirs is the first country in the world to eliminate terrorism at home.

Since the cessation of the conflict, the Sri Lankan economy has enjoyed a "peace dividend", with the economy growing in the 6–7% range. But the Sri Lankan economy could be doing so much better. The civil war left deep unresolved scars and fractures on Sri Lankan society, which are also undermining the country's further economic development. As the UN High Commissioner for Human Rights has said, there is much that the government could do to promote social cohesion and reconciliation.

Rebuilding trust in the state and between communities will be necessary since large parts of the country have been physically, politically, socially and economically separated from each other for much of the past three decades. Further, the military is still holding much land that it seized, and this should be returned to its rightful owners. This would enable communities of displaced people to return home. But according to a report by the Oakland Institute, the military has engaged in large-scale property development, running luxury tourist resorts and business ventures on land seized from local populations.[21] This raises serious questions about the government's seriousness regarding national reconciliation.

The size of the military force in the North and the East should be reduced to a level that is less intrusive and intimidating. As the Oakland Institute also reports, some six years after the end of the war, the traditional Tamil homeland is still under heavy military occupation by at least 160,000 mostly Sinhalese soldiers, one for every six Tamil civilians. And as the International Truth and Justice Project–Sri Lanka has documented in its report on torture, sexual violence, arbitrary detention and more during the 2009–2015 period, ethnic Tamils continue to face grave and comprehensive challenges in post-war Sri Lanka.[22] The report highlights the comprehensive, wide-ranging and pernicious nature of Sri Lanka's state security apparatus, which continues to operate with impunity. The country's state security apparatus does not seem to have changed its ways since Sirisena assumed the presidency.

In the words of UN High Commissioner for Human Rights Prince Zeid Ra'ad Al Hussein, "Sri Lanka must confront and defeat the demons of its past. It must create institutions that work, and ensure accountability. It must seize the great opportunity it currently has to provide all its people with truth, justice, security and prosperity."[23]

The Sri Lankan government has indeed a daunting agenda before it. But the stakes are high, and achieving success is imperative. We could, for example, imagine a prosperous and peaceful Sri Lanka becoming the Singapore of South Asia one day in the future. However, continued disgruntlement by the country's Tamil minority could feed future instability, and drag the country down again. President Sirisena will need to demonstrate great political will and courage than he has done to date to chart the country on a path of stability and security.

## INDIA'S CASTE SYSTEM IS STILL ALIVE AND WELL

"I can sweep your living room, Ma'am, but I cannot sweep your garden. Someone from another (lower) caste must do that".

This fragment of a conversation between an Indian maid and her Western employer reveals many things. Despite some waning in India's caste system, it is still alive and well, even in a big city like New Delhi. The caste system is more complex than the simple four groups presented in introductions to Indian society. And it continues to divide society, restricting opportunity for large numbers of Indian citizens and preventing the nation from realizing its full human potential.

Academics are still debating the origin of India's caste system. All societies are of course shaped by social stratification, and that was more marked before modernization. India's caste system has now endured longer than most others, and seems more rigid. Some argue that it became more rigid under British colonial rule, with the British appointing only upper-caste members to its colonial government.

The caste system is typically classified into four castes, namely, Brahmins (priests), Kshatriyas (warriors), Vaishyas (merchants) and Shudras (artisans). Dalits or untouchables were excluded from this classification. In reality, there are thousands of sub-castes. And even within the Dalit, who account for over 200 million of India's total population 1.3 billion, there are reportedly more than 900 sub-castes.

The term Dalit means in Hindu "ground", "suppressed", "crushed" or "broken to pieces". Traditionally, Dalits have worked in "impure" occupations involving leatherwork, butchering, removal of rubbish, animal carcasses, and cleaning streets, latrines and sewers. Hence, there is an argument for separating them from other castes. While upper castes were happy to employ Dalit for these tasks, even today some Dalits are keen to keep their monopoly over these occupations.

Discrimination against lower castes is illegal under India's constitution. And since 1950, the government has implemented a number of affirmative action initiatives to improve socio-economic conditions, such as college entry quotas and job reservations. There certainly has been much progress in the situation of Dalits, especially in the urban environment. Some Dalit success stories include Ram Nath Kovind who was elected as India's 14th president in July 2017. Kovind is the second Dalit to become Indian president, after K. R. Narayanan who held office from 1997 to 2002. In addition, K. G. Balakrishnan was Chief Justice, Mayawati Kumari was Chief Minister of Uttar Pradesh and Meira Kumar was the first female speaker of the Indian parliament.

Today, Dalits are doing much better than before in terms of education, health and poverty. Inter-caste marriage is also increasing, though limited in this country where arranged marriages are still all too common. Despite these positive trends, Dalit poverty is twice the national average and discrimination on the ground remains endemic, especially in rural areas where most Indians live. In parts of India, Dalit communities are still denied access to community water sources, denied service by barbers, served tea in separate cups, barred from entering shops, excluded from temples and prevented from taking part in community religious and ceremonial functions. Not surprisingly, most people of low-caste background remain low in the social order today, and most of those from the higher castes are still top of the social pecking order today.

In 2007, the UN found that "de facto segregation of Dalits persists" and highlighted systematic abuse against Dalits including torture and extrajudicial killings, an "alarming" extent of sexual violence against Dalit women, and caste discrimination in post-tsunami relief.[24] It called for effective measures to implement laws on discrimination and affirmative action, and sought proper protection for Dalits and tribal communities against acts of "discrimination and violence." Human Rights Watch reports that Dalits endure segregation in housing, schools and access to public services.[25] They are denied access to land, forced to work in degrading conditions and routinely abused at the hands of the police and upper-caste community members who enjoy the state's protection.

Manmohan Singh became the first sitting Indian prime minister to openly acknowledge the parallel between the practice of "untouchability" and the crime of apartheid. Singh described "untouchability" as a "blot on humanity," adding that "even after 60 years of constitutional and legal protection and state support, there is still social discrimination against Dalits in many parts of our country."

Human Rights Watch documents how Indian schools persistently discriminate against Dalit, tribal and Muslim children, denying them their right to education.[26] Four years after an ambitious education law went into effect in India guaranteeing free schooling to every child ages 6–14, almost every child is enrolled, yet nearly half are likely to drop out before completing their elementary education because of caste or other forms of discrimination at school.

Another Human Rights Watch report from 2014 documents the coercive nature of "manual scavenging."[27] Across India, "manual scavengers" collect human excrement on a daily basis, and carry it away in cane baskets for disposal, despite long-standing legislation and government policy to end manual scavenging. More than 1.3 million Dalits—mostly women— clear human waste from dry pit latrines, while men do the more physically demanding cleaning of sewers and septic tanks. The report describes the barriers people face in leaving manual scavenging, including threats of violence and eviction from local residents but also threats, harassment and unlawful withholding of wages by local officials.

In many ways, the next phase of the Asian Century could well belong to India, which will become Asia's most populous country in 2022, and is the world's fastest-growing large economy. But for India to realize its great potential, it will be necessary to address very seriously its discrimination, prejudice and persecution of lower castes, women, indigenous people and also religious minorities, especially Muslims.

Before we complete our quick overview of India's caste system, please don't think that it is the only country with an untouchable class. Japan has a similar outcast group, the Burakumin, who are at the bottom of the Japanese social ladder. Like in India, the Burakumin worked in occupations like executioners, undertakers, workers in slaughterhouses, butchers or tanners. Japan's Burakumin can still be subject to discrimination especially in the context of marriages, for which background searches are often made. A high-profile case of discrimination was that of Hiromu Nonaka, a Chief Cabinet Secretary, a natural candidate for prime minister in the 1990s, who was reportedly sidelined because of his Burakumin origin.

\* \* \*

Discrimination, prejudice and persecution are some of the social ills that are holding back Asia's economic and social development. In the next chapter, we will explore another social issue, the demographic dilemmas that afflicting both Asia's rapidly aging societies and those with large youth bulges entering labor market.

## Notes

1. Bloomberg. Tim Cook Speaks Up, 30 October 2014.
2. Gallup. Nearly 3 in 10 Worldwide See Their Areas as Good for Gays. Justin McCarthy, 27 August 2014.
3. PewResearchCenter. The Global Divide on Homosexuality, 4 June 2013.
4. Human Rights Watch. "These Political Games Ruin Our Lives". Indonesia's LGBT Community Under Threat, 10 August 2016.
5. Boston Consulting Group. The Most Innovative Companies 2016. January 2017.

6. World Economic Forum. The Global Gender Gap Report 2016.
7. OECD. Economic Survey of Japan 2015.
8. Goldman Sachs. Womenomics 4.0: Time to Walk the Talk.
9. Sen, Amartya. More Than 100 Million Women Are Missing. New York Review of Books, 20 December 1990.
10. United Nations Population Fund (2012). Sex Imbalances at Birth: Current trends, consequences and policy implications.
11. Hvistendahl, Mara. Unnatural Selection: Choosing Boys Over Girls, and the Consequences of a World Full of Men, 2011.
12. Human Rights Watch. "Our Time to Sing and Play". Child Marriage in Nepal, 7 September 2016.
13. UNICEF. Child protection from violence, exploitation and abuse. Child marriage.
14. International Center for Research on Women. Child Marriage Facts and Figures.
15. A Girl in the River: The Price of Forgiveness (2015). Director: Sharmeen Obaid-Chinoy. Stars: Asad Jamal, Sabaç.
16. World Economic Forum. Global Gender Gap Report 2016.
17. International Work Group for Indigenous Affairs. The Indigenous World 2016.
18. His Holiness's Middle Way Approach For Resolving the Issue of Tibet. Website of His Holiness The Fourteenth Dalai Lama of Tibet.
19. UN (2011). Report of the Secretary-General's Panel of Experts on Accountability in Sri Lanka.
20. United Nations High Commissioner for Human Rights (2015). Comprehensive report of the Office of the United Nations High Commissioner for Human Rights on Sri Lanka.
21. Oakland Institute (2015). The Long Shadow of War: The Struggle for Justice in Postwar Sri Lanka.
22. International Truth and Justice Project (2016). Silenced: Survivors of Torture and Sexual Violence.
23. UN High Commission for Human Rights. Statement by UN High Commissioner for Human Rights, Zeid Ra'ad Al Hussein, at the end of his mission to Sri Lanka, 9 February 2016.
24. UN (2007). Report of the Committee on the Elimination of Racial Discrimination.
25. Human Rights Watch (2007). India: 'Hidden Apartheid' of Discrimination Against Dalits.
26. Human Rights Watch (2014). India: Marginalized Children Denied Education.
27. Human Rights Watch (2014). India: Caste Forced to Clean Human Waste.

**Open Access** This chapter is licensed under the terms of the Creative Commons Attribution 4.0 International License (http://creativecommons.org/licenses/by/4.0/), which permits use, sharing, adaptation, distribution, and reproduction in any medium or format, as long as you give appropriate credit to the original author(s) and the source, provide a link to the Creative Commons license and indicate if changes were made.

The images or other third party material in this chapter are included in the chapter's Creative Commons license, unless indicated otherwise in a credit line to the material. If material is not included in the chapter's Creative Commons license and your intended use is not permitted by statutory regulation or exceeds the permitted use, you will need to obtain permission directly from the copyright holder.

CHAPTER 7

# Solving Asia's Demographic Dilemmas

Japan has a new breed of modern young women, the "parasaito", according to Michael Zielenziger.[1] These women choose career over marriage and family, despite Japan's endemic gender discrimination in the workplace. They live with their parents well into their twenties and thirties, and their favorite pastimes are shopping, traveling abroad and living for the moment. He refers to this as the "womb strike".

Fundamental changes have also swept through Japanese society. Until the 1970s, marriages were often arranged. For example, in Japanese companies and government ministries, one of the responsibilities of a senior ("sempai") was to find a wife for his junior ("kohai"). As recently as 1982, three in ten marriages were arranged. With modernization, there has been a decline in matchmaking, which means that young Japanese may have more difficulty meeting each other. The dramatic rise in non-regular employment is also changing the nature of working relationships in Japan.

Social relations in Japan would also be affected by its "homosocial society" says Zielenziger. Social life for most Japanese men involves drinking with other male colleagues. You only have to walk the streets of Tokyo to see salarymen drinking and eating together. At the same time, fancy restaurants and tea salons are full of well-dressed ladies gossiping together. This is why the Japanese government has been increasing its sponsorship of spouse-hunting events ("konkatsu") to encourage more people to marry and lift the nation's fertility rate.

© The Author(s) 2018
J. West, *Asian Century... on a Knife-edge*,
https://doi.org/10.1007/978-981-10-7182-9_7

Then there are more than half a million young Japanese who you don't see, the social recluses (or "hikikomori") who avoid contact with the outside world and rarely leave the house. According to a Japanese cabinet survey, there would be 541,000 young Japanese aged between 15 and 39 leading such lives, who have not left their homes or interacted with others for at least six months.[2] The hikikomori are typically men, rather than women, who suffer from anxiety or depression due to the shame associated with an experience of failure in life or the high expectations that society placed on them. They typically spend their days playing computer games and reading manga (Japanese comic books).

These socio-psychological factors would be some of the causes of the drop in Japan's fertility rate from 2.1 children per woman in 1974 to around 1.4 today, which is driving the aging of Japanese society and the decline in its population, thereby threatening the nation's prosperity (a fertility rate of 2.1 is necessary to maintain a country's population size and is called the "replacement rate").

China's fertility rate, which fell from around 2.7 children per woman in the 1980s to around 1.7 today, has also been affected by socio-psychological factors, in particular China's "leftover women" ("sheng nu" in Mandarin).[3] As everywhere, Chinese women are now much better educated and more career oriented than in the past. One consequence is that one in five Chinese women in the 25–29 age group would still be unmarried today in China. But even though China suffers from a shortage of women, as discussed in the previous chapter, the vast majority of Chinese men believe that women should be married by the age of 27. And what's more China's notoriously macho men prefer to "marry down" in terms of age and educational attainment. In practical terms, this means that that A-quality guys will look for B-quality women, B-quality guys look for C-quality women and C-quality men look for D-quality women.

The net result of all of this is that China's best educated and most successful women find themselves unmarried (and so are China's least privileged men). And like Japan's parasaito girls, China's leftover women are not necessarily unhappy about that. While they are typically not against marriage, they also have other aspirations like career and travel. The main problem that China's leftover women have to deal with is the pressure from family, friends and even state-run media. In typical Chinese communist style, the national media seeks to stigmatize and bully leftover women into getting married and starting a family. After all, A-quality women are critical to China's future. As in Japan, some Chinese local governments are now in the business of organizing matchmaking events for leftover women.

But there is another demographic reality in Asia. Countries like India and Pakistan, where child marriage is still widespread and female education weak, have fertility rates of 2.5 and 3.3 children per woman, respectively. These fertility rates may be around half those of 50 years ago, but they are still sufficient to keep their populations young and growing. According to the UN, the population of India will overtake China's in 2022, to become the world's most populous country.[4]

The Philippines is another country whose fertility rate is still relatively high at 3.1 children per woman. In this country where the Catholic Church still casts a strong influence over sex education, the availability of contraception and attitudes toward family planning, teenage pregnancies are the highest in Asia according to the UN.[5] One in ten young Filipino women—between 15 and 19 years of age—is already a mother, a figure that has not declined over the past two decades, bucking the trend in the rest of Asia where teenage pregnancy has declined.

This demographic diversity in Asia between the low-birth and high-birth countries creates a great opportunity for mutually beneficial migration which we will explore later in this chapter. However, the sad reality is that demographic-deficit countries like Japan and Korea are not opening up sufficiently to this great opportunity, while demographic-surplus countries, like India and the Philippines, are facing immense challenges handling the colossal youth bulges entering their labor markets. Only Hong Kong and Singapore are seriously opening the gates to immigration, although only skilled migrants are treated decently in these economies.

But before we explore the issue of mutually beneficial migration, we must examine Asia's demographic transitions, and the manifold challenges of population bulges and population aging. Demographic dilemmas represent one of the greatest risks to the Asian Century.

## Asia's Demographic Transitions

East Asia's most advanced economies—Japan, Korea, Taiwan, Hong Kong, Singapore, China and Thailand—are in the midst of rapid population aging.[6] In contrast to the others, China and Thailand will become "old" before they become rich. Another group of Asian economies, notably Bangladesh, India, Indonesia and the Philippines, have massive youth bulges now entering the jobs market. In this section, we will review demographic transitions sweeping Asian societies.

For much of human history, both birth and death rates were very high, such that populations only grew very slowly. But since economic development started taking off in Asia, the region has been experiencing major demographic transitions, meaning the transition from a high mortality and fertility pattern to a low mortality and fertility one, following the trend of Western countries in earlier times. The first demographic transition typically starts as mortality rates fall, especially for infants and children thanks to improved hygiene and nutrition as the economy develops. This leads to steep increases in the population, as the share of young and dependent people grows.

When this large group of youth advances into working age, this is the moment to reap the potential a "demographic dividend", as youthful and energetic workforces can drive their economies up the development ladder (the second demographic transition). This effect can be enhanced by a decline in fertility rates, due to the influence of urbanization, better education for women, improvement in women's rights and prosperity. This will reduce the numbers of dependent youth, and mean that a very large share of the population is of working age.

Economies like Japan, Korea, Taiwan, Hong Kong, Singapore and China have all benefited greatly from demographic dividends. Some economists argue that one-quarter or even one-third of their rapid economic growth was due to their demographic dividends. But their demographic dividends were not only due to large youth bulges. They also occurred thanks to their youth being well educated, and their strongly growing economies which created sufficient job opportunities. Economies like Bangladesh, India, Indonesia and the Philippines are at this very point now. But all the signs are that they will struggle to benefit as much from a demographic dividend due to their relatively poorer education systems, and also the incapacity of their economies to generate enough job opportunities.

When this demographic bulge advances into retirement age, we are in the midst of the third demographic transition, whose effect is enhanced by increased life expectancy thanks to improved access to health care and healthy lifestyles. Population aging, the rising share of senior citizens in the population, can act as a tax on the economy, as senior citizens are much less likely to work. As Japan, Korea, Taiwan, Hong Kong, Singapore and China are now all discovering, population aging can be very expensive for the public purse, or the purse of the extended family, because of the cost retirement income, and health and aged care expenses.

Lastly there is a fourth demographic transition which has surprised most demographers. That is where fertility rates fall and remain below the replacement rate of 2.1 children per woman, with the result that populations ultimately decline. Japan has led the world in this context, with its population falling from 128 million in 2010 to 127 million in 2016, and predicted to fall to 109 million by 2050 and further to 85 million by 2100,[7] with some estimating that before the year 4000 that we would see the end of the Japanese race. But Japan is not the only one to face the prospect of long-term population decline. A number of other countries are in a similar situation, especially many countries from East Europe (including the Ukraine and Bulgaria), and Central and Western Europe (such as Germany, Greece, Hungary and Italy), along with Puerto Rico in the Caribbean.

In the next section, we will explore India's demographic destiny and the challenge it faces in realizing a demographic dividend, before then moving onto the other end of Asia's demographic transitions, with the region's fading fertility and China's two-child policy.

## India's Demographic Destiny

India, along with countries like Bangladesh, Indonesia and the Philippines, is in the midst of a major demographic transition. Life expectancy has leapt from just 41 years in 1960 to 68 in 2015 thanks notably to improvements in infant mortality. And while its fertility has fallen dramatically from almost 6 children per woman in 1960 to 2.4 in 2015, it still remains well above the replacement rate of 2.1.

The net result is that India's population has boomed from 450 million in 1960 to some 1.3 billion today. Looking ahead, India's population is set to overtake China's by the year 2022 according to the UN, as we mentioned above. And by the year 2100, India's population could be 1.5 billion, some 50% higher than China's. Not only will India's population be bigger than China's, it will be very much younger for much of this period. For example, the median age of India's population in 2030 will be only 31, while China's will be 43.

If population is power, then we should be looking more at India rather than China.

The stark contrast between the demographic destinies of China and India is very much with us today. China's workforce started declining in 2012, while India's is in the midst of a dramatic expansion. India will see an expansion in its working-age population of 300 million between 2010 and 2040, representing one-quarter of the world population increase for this age group. But can India reap a large demographic dividend thanks to this large, youthful and energetic labor force? After all, Asia's successful tiger economies like Japan, Korea, Taiwan and China benefited greatly from demographic dividends.

There are grounds for optimism, based on India's experience over the past few decades. India's youthful demography would have contributed a substantial fraction to India's growth acceleration since the 1980s according to the IMF.[8] And a demographic dividend could add 2 percentage points to India's annual economic growth rates over the coming three decades. But the prospects for achieving this also seem daunting. Demography is not just a question of quantity. It is also a question of quality. And the quality of India's human capital is one of the poorest in Asia, despite the brilliance of the country's elite.

Only three-quarters of the population are literate according to official statistics. And according to deeper analysis by Indian economist Santosh Mehrotra, only half the nation's population would be "functionally literate".[9] Such an estimate is hardly surprising in light of India's deep poverty, malnutrition, bad health conditions and poor education system. For those 300 million additions to the Indian jobs market to find work, they will also need practical skills. But India has one of the lowest proportions of trained youth in the world. What's more, many of this youth cohort will be Dalits. India will not reap the full benefits of its demographic dividend while ever caste discrimination remains as it is.

India needs to improve its education system at every level. What is most critical is to create an effective Vocational Education Training (VET) system which would cater to the vast majority of India's young population.[10] But VET has received very limited funding, is of poor quality, and involves little industry collaboration. The result is that just 2% of the Indian workforce has skills training in formal vocational education. And only another 2 ½% have received any informal vocational training at all.

The need for VET is perhaps the greatest for rural workers who are flowing into cities in search of opportunity in the construction, manufacturing and service sectors. Without any vocational training, these workers end up in the informal sector, working in low-paid jobs and joining the ranks of urban poverty. Even today, India's economy is being held back by a large skills deficit. Its jobs market suffers from shortages of skilled labor, while unemployment and underemployment are also widespread.

Training is only one side of the jobs equation. India also needs business investment to drive industrialization. As dazzling as India's IT and business process outsourcing might be, the sector only employs three million people. Realistically most Indians could not find a place in this sector. Only more serious industrialization could provide sufficient jobs for its growing workforce.

With China now suffering from rising wage costs and a weak demography, India has a window of opportunity to become a manufacturing powerhouse. And India has been attracting large flows of foreign investment thanks in part to the policy reforms of Prime Minister Narendra Modi's government. But India will need to maintain the reform momentum, as it is also competing with countries like Vietnam, Cambodia and the Philippines to attract investment. If India's leaders are unable to tackle the country's chronic problems, the country will not only miss out on a big opportunity. Its demographic opportunity could turn into a demographic time bomb. Social unrest in recent years in Arab countries and elsewhere shows the social and political risks of large populations of unemployed and frustrated youth.

And while India and some other countries face the challenge of managing large youthful populations, Japan has led East Asia's development in terms of its fading fertility. How did Asia's most developed economies end up in such a quandary?

## East Asia's Fading Fertility

Japan has led the world into the fourth demographic transition where fertility rates below the replacement rate ultimately result in a falling, as well as an aging, population. Today, it's easy to forget that Japan's fertility rate, which is 1.4 children per woman, was over 4 children per woman during the 1930–1950 period.

Japan's experience is not unique in terms of having fertility below the replacement rate. Germany's fertility rate fell below 2.1 in 1971, and today is lower than that of Japan, as is also the case for countries like Greece, Italy, Spain, Portugal and Poland. In sharp contrast, Australia, France, the UK and the US still have fertility rates close to 2. Neither is

Japan unique in East Asia where Hong Kong, Korea, Macao, Singapore and Taiwan all have fertility rates below Japan.

What are the main factors behind East Asia's collapsing fertility? This is a strange trend according to evolutionary biologists. Normally natural selection produces individuals who are good at converting their resources into lots of fertile descendants.

Fertility rates have fallen dramatically the world over reflecting changes in values and the status of women, education, industrialization, urbanization and the advent of contraception. As we discussed above, a major reason why Japan's fertility rate has fallen so low is that as Japanese women have become more educated, they are also more interested in working, but the Japanese work environment is not very compatible with raising a family. In this context, the declining rate of marriage in Japan is also often attributed to the reluctance of educated Japanese girls to assume all the traditional responsibilities of a Japanese wife, namely raising the family, looking after the husband, running the household and tending to in-laws.

It is also reported that the phenomenon of "hypergamy" is common, where educated Japanese girls will only marry men of equal or higher education or income status to themselves. Hypergamy is becoming increasingly difficult to practice since Japanese girls now achieve, on average, better education results than boys. And the growing prevalence of precarious, non-regular work situations provides a great disincentive for having a family. Only 27% of men in their thirties with non-regular jobs are married, compared with 66% of men the same age with permanent jobs, according to government statistics.[11] And even when they marry, Japanese girls now tend to do so at higher age which affects their reproductive behavior.

Some social commentators argue that Japan is suffering from a "celibacy syndrome" or "sekkusu shinai shokogun". A survey in 2011 found that 61% of unmarried men and 49% of women aged 18–34 were not in any kind of romantic relationship, a rise of almost 10% from five years earlier.[12] Another study found that one-third of people under 30 had never dated at all.

Many of the same factors, notably the incompatibility of work and family life, are relevant to East Asia's other low-birth countries. Korean women seem to have much in common with their Japanese counterparts. They are less and less interested in marriage, with a recent government survey revealing that only 46% of Korean young women being interested in marriage, in contrast to 63% for young Korean men.

Soaring housing costs are another factor pushing down fertility in the small, tropical and highly urbanized Chinese-speaking islands of Hong Kong, Macau, Singapore and Taiwan. And like Japan, despite being Asia's most developed economies, these "Chinese islands" are suffering from yawning income inequality and growing poverty in the midst of prosperity, which are having an adverse effect on marriage and fertility.

The cost of education is a deterrent to child birth in some East Asian countries, none more than Korea. The country's national obsession with achieving high grades means that vast amounts of money are spent on private education, especially for after-school tuition. Around three-quarters of Korean students undertake after-school education in private schools called hagwons, and many students have private tutors as well.[13] It is not surprising that education fees should be cited as the most serious obstacle to having children in a survey undertaken by the Hyundai Research Institute.

One factor preventing fertility rates from falling even further in countries like Korea is the growing "marriage migration", with China, Vietnam and the Philippines being the top sources for Korea's migrant brides. The birth rate among immigrant mothers is higher than that of native Korean women reports Katharine Moon from the Brooking Institution.[14]

What should East Asian governments and societies do about their chronically low fertility rates? Japan's population is already declining, and population decline is on the horizon for Korea, Taiwan and China. This is having dramatic effects on the economy, society, politics and even international relations. All East Asian governments have provided various financial and other incentives to attempt to revive fertility rates. The Japanese and Singaporean governments have even had policies to encourage "dating and mating". But none of these policies have had much effect.

At the heart of East Asia's fading fertility phenomenon is rapid progress in the economy and education of women which has not been matched by commensurate changes in policies and attitudes in the workplace, the family and society at large. We need to have societies which enable us to combine both a work life and a family life. As we discussed in the previous chapter, this means major changes in government policy, corporate/work culture and family life.

A longer term perspective on population decline is also warranted. Of course it seems frightening at first blush, as it evokes images of the possible extinction of the human species. But what we may be seeing is only a partial reversal in the world's population explosion these past two–three centuries.[15] And there are many benefits that could occur. A lower population could ease the immense pressures on the global environment and resources like food, energy and clean water that are resulting from the combination of a large population and high economic growth. In a world with a lower population, workers' wages may be higher as they become a relatively scarce resource.

But the process of adjusting to a lower population will be bumpy and difficult. Villages, towns and even cities might disappear. Japan already has a burgeoning ghost-town problem. There will also be a transitional period of super-aging societies, where small numbers of youth must support large numbers of seniors. And countries with declining populations may lose political power and feel strategically vulnerable.

We cannot leave the issue of Asia's fading fertility without looking at perhaps the most horrific experiment in social engineering the world has ever seen, China's one-child policy which is now being transformed into a "two-child policy".

## China's "Two-Child Policy"

In 2015, when the Chinese government announced its decision to transform its one-child policy into a two-child policy, there was much celebration in the media. With its rapidly aging population, and declining working-age population, demographers and economists had long argued that the one-child policy, whatever its initial merits, was no longer useful to China. But closer scrutiny suggests that the effect of the policy on China's fertility rate may only have been modest, despite the associated horrors of the policy. And that the benefits of a two-child policy may also be modest.

How did China get itself into this "demographic pickle"? China's great leader Deng Xiaoping is revered for his role in opening the Chinese economy to the world. But under his watch, the Chinese government also did some appalling things, like the Tiananmen Square massacre and implementing China's infamous one-child policy.

Population has long been an issue in China. Chairman Mao once famously said "The more people there are, the stronger we are."[16] But Deng and his experts thought differently, even though China's fertility rate had already fallen from 5.8 children per woman in 1970 to 2.8 in 1980 thanks to softer efforts to encourage fewer births. So in 1980, they implemented China's infamous one-child policy.

Like everything in China, the one-child policy was never implemented uniformly across the nation. Single women are still not allowed to have a child outside of wedlock. Against that, many people have long been allowed to have two children, such as ethnic minorities like the Tibetans and Uighurs, rural residents whose first child was a girl and couples where both parents are only children. This means that the strongest population growth has occurred among groups with the worst access to education and health services—not a good sign for China's economic future.

In short, the one-child policy mainly applied to urban dwellers. But even here there were always inequities. Families who violated the one-child policy law were subject to fines ("social maintenance fees"), which the wealthy could usually afford to pay despite their arbitrary method of calculation. Another way around the system has been "birth tourism" whereby pregnant Chinese women travel to Hong Kong or the US (Saipan is the closest US territory to China, and Chinese citizens do not require a visa to travel there).

Since poor people could not afford to pay fines or travel overseas to give birth, they were all too often subject to horrendous forced abortions, sterilization, contraception and other draconian acts by the family planning agency. According to one estimate, there have been 336 million abortions, 196 million sterilizations and 403 million intrauterine devices inserted since 1971 in China.[17] There are also many stories of "hidden children" (some 13 million were recorded as lacking birth registration in the 2010 census), transferring excess children to childless couples, infanticide and about 100,000 adoptions by Western families. The Ministry administering the one-child policy behaves like a spy and police organization, with a system of paid informants, "womb police". Human rights lawyers who defend victims of the one-child policy suffer abuses, the most prominent case being the blind lawyer, Chen Guangcheng, who escaped prison to the US.

There is much debate about the real impact of the one-child policy. Official experts claim that it has reduced China's population (today around 1.4 billion), by some 400 million.[18] It is more likely that it only reduced China's population by about 100 million, a decimal point in such a large country. As Nobel Prize-winning economist Amartya Sen has argued, China's fertility rate would likely have continued its downward trend in tandem with economic development, urbanization and education.[19] Most other East Asian countries have lower fertility rates than China's 1.7 children per woman—even Thailand's is lower rate at 1.4. As we discussed in the previous chapter, the one-child policy may have contributed to China's prenatal gender selection in favor of boys. One of the many social implications of the one-child policy is the "little emperor syndrome" of spoilt one-child brats who are found to be "significantly less trusting, less trustworthy, more risk-averse, less competitive, more pessimistic, and less conscientious individuals" than previous generations.[20]

The Chinese government's decision to transform its one-child policy into a two-child policy is a positive step. But it is a case of too little/too late. Many Chinese urban-dwelling women now would prefer to have just one child. In fact, the evidence to date shows only a small rise in fertility thanks to the two-child policy. Moreover, Chinese women will still have unfair restrictions on their reproductive freedom. And China's dastardly family planning agency will still have too much power over Chinese citizens. There have already been reports of its draconian enforcement of the two-child policy.

Indeed, one factor holding back more significant reform of population policy was the powerful family planning bureaucracy which employs 500,000 full-time and 6 million part-time workers.[21] It collected over $3 billion in fines each year, with over $300 billion collected since 1980. With the new two-child policy, it is still in business! Some commentators like Reggie Littlejohn of Women's Rights Without Frontiers have argued that the one-child policy is a system of social control, masquerading as population control.[22] And that whether it is a one-child or two-child policy, it is still a system of social control, which the rich can avoid by paying fines, while the poor must obey.

China is in desperate need of sensible population policies to adjust to its aging population, already falling working-age population, and the prospect of a declining population (its population is projected to peak at 1.4 billion in 2030, before falling to 1.0 billion in 2100). But this means widespread reforms, not just family planning, to address its demographic challenges.

In the following sections, we will discuss some of the economic and social policy implications of population aging.

## Economic Costs of Asia's Aging Populations

Population aging started to bite hard on the Japanese economy from 1995, when its working-age population (15–64) began falling. With less and less available workers, labor flipped being a positive to a negative force for the economy. Less workers also means lower national saving rates. So

Japan's annual "potential" economic growth rate fell sharply from over 3% in the early 1990s, and has been hovering in the 0–1% range over the past 15 years.[23] The Organisation for Economic Cooperation and Development (OECD) currently estimates Japan's potential economic growth rate at ½% a year. And with Japan's stubborn reluctance to undertake structural reform, there has been no productivity improvement to offset the effect of falling labor supplies. Indeed, population aging would have exacerbated Japan's productivity weakness, as history shows that much innovation emanates from younger workers.

In other words, Japan's population aging, and above all the country's failure to respond effectively to the challenge, is making the country relatively poorer. Looking ahead, Japan's growth potential faces continued downward pressure from population aging. The working-age population is already falling by more than one million per year and could decline by nearly 40% by 2050.

As in many things, Korea is following Japanese trends. Korea's working-age population is set to peak in 2016, at 37 million before declining steadily to 33 million in 2030, and perhaps to 22 million in 2060 (total population decline is also on the cards, starting in 2030).[24] Korea can also expect that its declining working-age population will drag down potential economic growth.

When Japan was struck by declining working-age population, it was already a very prosperous country, with GDP per capita within shooting distance of the US. And while it remains a moderately prosperous country, it has been slowly slipping down the OECD pecking order in terms of GDP per capita. For its part, Korea will be hit by a declining working-age population at an earlier stage than Japan. Today, its GDP per capita is only about half that of the US, and it declining workforce could see it fall slowly further and further behind the US.

But the impact of China's population on the economy is likely to be very much more dramatic. Already in 2012, China's working-age population began its inexorable decline, with a combined decline of 10 million over the 2012–2014 period. Some estimate that China's working-age population could decline by 1 1/2% a year over the coming decades, representing big cumulative whack. But China is being hit by its demographic drama at a much earlier point in its economic catch-up, when its GDP per capita is only 26% of that of the US.

Thailand is a curious case where the working-age population is also expected to start falling after 2017.[25] The country is set to become the "old man" of East Asia, with its senior population (aged 65 and over) projected to increase from 8.9% in 2010 to 19.5% in 2030. Thailand is being hit by an aging population at around the same stage of development as China.

In other words, in contrast to the cases of Japan and Korea, China and Thailand are becoming old before they become rich. What to do? The reforms that we discussed in earlier chapters—getting better value out of global value chains, making the most of urbanization's potential, and giving all Asians a chance—would all go a long way toward improving productivity and better exploiting Asia's potential in order to maintain prosperity in aging societies. In this context, the Japanese government has accepted very little of the advice offered from organizations like the OECD and the IMF, or even from Japan's own distinguished like Masahiro Kawai or Naohiro Yashiro. And at this stage, Korea, China and Thailand seem to following Japan's path of inaction.

There is also much that could be done to offer greater work opportunities to Japan's seniors, who have the world's highest life expectancy. After all, much of the challenge of aging comes from failure of things like retirement ages to keep pace with rising life expectancy. But in the context of Japan's rigid seniority-based wage system, Japanese companies have a retirement age of 60. True many workers are then rehired on irregular contracts at a much lower salary. But a much more flexible labor market would allow seniors to continue their career much later, making important contributions to the economy and society. Korean companies also have a rigid labor market with seniority-based pay, which means that seniors are pushed to retire at a low age. And similarly in China, the retirement age for men is 60, while that of women is only 50. Plans are reportedly afoot to gradually lift China's retirement age in the coming years. And none too soon! Fast-aging Asian countries also need migrants, an issue that we will take up at the end of this chapter.

The experience of Japan, with over two decades of stagnation under its belt, should be salutary to not only China, Korea and Thailand but also Japan itself. Undertaking structural reform to lift productivity is always important, but even more so in an aging society, where productivity improvements can compensate for effects of a declining workforce. But postponing bitter medicine seems easy in the short term. Vested interests supporting the status quo are always difficult to tackle, be they in a democracy or an authoritarian regime. Unless the Japanese, Korean, Chinese and Thai governments seriously tackle the challenge of aging populations, their countries will likely wither away. Asia's demographic dilemmas may be the greatest threat to the realization of an Asian Century.

In the next section, we will examine some of the social policy implications of Asia's aging populations, notably retirement incomes and health expenses. In later sections, we will explore migration, one part of the solution to rapidly aging populations.

## Social Policy Challenges of Asia's Aging Populations

It's not so long ago that the social policy challenges of aging populations were a non-issue in much of Asia. For one thing, life expectancy was much lower than it is today, and senior citizens made up a very much smaller share of the population.

And only back in 1990, some two-thirds of Asians lived in rural communities, where extended families typically supported their elders. Today, only one-half of Asians live in rural areas, and this figure is rapidly declining as people move to cities in search of more opportunities. As urbanization proceeds, traditional families and communities are breaking down, and being replaced by the nuclear family. While urban migrants send financial remittances to their families in rural areas, over time the Confucian sense of family responsibility is fading, as lifestyles become more individualistic and Westernized. And as fertility rates decline, and family sizes become smaller, supporting one's family can be an enormous burden, especially if you come from a one-child family. Today, a single child can find him or herself with the weighty burden of caring for two parents and four grandparents, the 4-2-1 problem! The Chinese government has responded with a law which requires adult children to visit and care for their aging parents.

All Asian governments are now faced with the responsibility of providing at least some social security, in the form of pensions and health care, to their senior citizens. As poverty declines and prosperity grows, senior citizens have growing expectations. And as education and access to information improves, governments must also take into account public opinion, and govern on the basis of a social contract, even in the case of authoritarian regimes which are scared of social instability. All this means responding to the expectations of senior citizens for a better slice of the rapidly growing economic pie.

So all Asian countries are in the midst of establishing systems of social security which can provide government-financed pensions and health care.²⁶ Each Asian country will need to develop their own social security systems for their senior citizens in their own historical, political and social contexts. This is a challenging enterprise, as it involves a much greater role of the state than in the past. Revenues must be raised to finance such social security. Systems must be designed which are fiscally sustainable, and which are fair and equitable.

Despite the very rapid progress made, social security systems are still very underdeveloped in Asia and play a much smaller role than in advanced Western countries. Government spending on social protection and health only represents 5% of GDP compared with over 20% in the mature advanced economies. While only 22% of Asia's population above the legal retirement age receive pensions against more than 80% for advanced economies.²⁷ For its part, China has been quick to develop public pension systems, but these mainly apply to urban rather than rural residents. And in the hyper-wealthy Hong Kong and Singapore, public pensions are virtually non-existent. Asian countries have many lessons to draw on from the experience of other countries, especially in Europe and the US. But closer to home the examples of Korea and Japan, two of Asia's most advanced countries, highlight some of the potential pitfalls.

## Korea's Shameful Demographic Drama

Over the past half century, Korea has had the fastest-growing economy among the advanced OECD countries. But looking ahead, the OECD projects that population aging in Korea will also be the fastest in the OECD area.²⁸ Already, Korea's life expectancy has skyrocketed from only 53 years in 1960 to 82 in 2015, while its fertility rate has fallen over the same period over 6 to 1.2 children per woman. This means that Korea's seniors (aged 65 and over) could jump from 11% of the total population in 2010 to 37% in 2050, the second highest among the OECD countries. According to one estimate, if this trend continues, Koreans could be extinct by the year 2750.

The great shame of Korea's demographic trends is that the generation that created the country's economic miracle is now suffering, and is unable to enjoy the benefits that they so richly deserve. The OECD reports that in 2013 some 50% of the population aged 65 and over lived in relative poverty, more than three times greater than poverty rate for the nation as a whole. This is in sharp contrast to the OECD area as a whole where relative poverty for the elderly is about the same as for the overall population.

What's worse is that some 30% of the elderly population are estimated by the Korean government to be living in "absolute poverty", meaning that their income is below the minimum cost of living. Most of those living in poverty today were reportedly comfortable and prosperous in their careers, and have since fallen on hard times through the tumultuous changes transforming Korea.

Many elderly persons had assumed that their children would provide for them in the traditional Confucian manner. But over the past 15 years, the percentage of children who think they should look after their parents has shrunk from 90% to 37%, according to government polls, even though their parents may have invested greatly in their education.[29] Confucian filial piety is now a waning phenomenon. Perhaps the Korean government should follow China in establishing "Confucius laws" which require children to visit or provide for their elderly parents.

So increasing numbers of elderly Koreans are now turning to Christian charity, as they line up outside churches for handouts of cash or food. And violent crime by Korea's elderly is also rising sharply, according Korean police statistics. This is put down to poverty, illness and loneliness. With three-quarters of Korea's elderly poor now living alone, this is hardly surprising. Increasing poverty among the elderly has contributed to a more than doubling of suicide among this group over the past decade—from 35 per 100,000 persons in 2000 to 82 in 2010. The suicide rate among the Korean elderly is the highest in the OECD area, with the suicide rate of elderly men being double that of women.[30]

In short, the high poverty rate for Korea's elderly population is a major and urgent social problem, which will only get worse in the decades ahead unless something is done. Successive governments have been slow to create an old-age income support system that is necessary in a modern society. The current system provides only paltry benefits to the country's elderly, and is totally inadequate for dealing with the elderly poverty. The new Basic Pension is useful, but not sufficient. The old-age income support system needs a complete overhaul, including increasing taxes, to deal with not only today's challenges, but also to prepare for the country's prospective "silver future".

The Global AgeWatch Index, which ranks countries by how well their older populations are faring, puts Korea at the lowly position of 60th out of the 96 countries covered, way behind Japan at 8th and even the Philippines at 50th and China at 52nd.[31] If Korea does not get its act together, its inability to manage the challenges of its aging population will result in not only a broken society but also a broken economy. This would be a sad ending to the "miracle on the Han River".

We will now turn to the case of Japan where social welfare for the elderly, though not particularly generous, has driven Japan's national government debt to world record levels.

## Japan's Silver Democracy

Japan's gross public debt has skyrocketed from 70% of GDP in 1992 to 220% in 2016 following 22 years of budget deficits, reports the OECD. And the main driver has been the doubling as a share of GDP of public social spending, most of which goes on pensions, long-term care and health for senior citizens.[32] Social spending now accounts for more than half of Japan's general government spending. Looking ahead, unless something is done, Japan's public debt could be heading over 600% of GDP by 2060!

Some say that this is no big deal. Some 90% of public debt is held by Japanese institutions, and with low interest rates, the servicing of this debt is not such a great burden. But the OECD is quite rightly worried that at some point markets could lose confidence in Japan. Interest rates could shoot up, adding further to the budget deficit and debt. Although loyalty is a prized Japanese virtue, it may not last forever among Japanese investors. This could lead to capital flight.

Japan desperately needs a serious "plan" to bring its debt under control which should include bringing public social spending under greater control. Lifting the retirement age (currently 65 for men and 63 for women) for receiving public pensions would be a great help. This should be no great burden since Japan still has the world's highest life expectancy at 81 for men and 87 for women. There is also much that could be done to cut back on public health expenditure. Japanese seniors spend enormous amounts of time in expensive hospitals, but often for long-term care rather than medical attention. It is a waste of money to use expensive hospitals as hostels for seniors who are looking for sociable company. And the cost of pharmaceuticals could also be cut back by greater use of generics, for example.

While it is scandalous that Japan's seniors should be bankrupting the country, it is even more scandalous that the working population should be financing this highway robbery. After all, Japan's seniors are the wealthiest segment of Japan's population. This is a case of "intergenerational injustice", one generation (Japan's seniors) ripping off another generation (Japan's working-age population), while Japan's working-age population has been suffering from growing poverty and inequality.

Japan is an "intergenerationally unjust" country, ranking the second worst after the US among 29 advanced OECD countries, according to a study by Germany's Bertelsmann Stiftung, that looks at its environmental, economic-fiscal and social aspects.[33] The study assesses unfair burdens of policy outcomes and their legacies for future generations, and examines the extent to which current socio-economic policies reflect a bias toward today's older generation.

Not surprisingly, Japan ranks the worst of all 29 countries for its public debt. Each Japanese child (between 0 and 14 years old) bore a crushing $794,000 in public debt in 2011. The burden of Japanese children is more than 2 ½ times that of Italy and Greece, the next two worst cases. Japan also scores poorly for other criteria like the strong bias of public social spending toward the elderly, and child poverty which restricts future economic and social opportunities.

In other words, Japan has been maintaining its wealth and prosperity at the expense of its children and succeeding generations. How could a country like Japan which, to outside Western eyes, seems to have such a cohesive society, be one of the world's worst countries when it comes to socio-economic justice between generations?

Japan's intergenerational injustice is a product of the country's "silver democracy" or gerontocracy.[34] In other words, Japan's large senior population has a large and dominant voice over the nation's politics. The share of Japanese voters over 60 years old has more than doubled to 44% over the past three decades, while the share of voters in their twenties has fallen from 20% to 13% since 1980.[35] This effect is magnified in rural areas, which have smaller population sizes and are dominated by senior citizens. And lastly, senior citizens, who know very well their interests, also have a much higher voting turnout than younger citizens.

In short, this means that it would be electoral suicide for any government to propose a substantial cutting of benefits for seniors, especially if more benefits were to be allocated to the working-age population suffering from poverty and inequality. Many ideas have been put forward to address these issues. Political leaders could appeal to youth to become more involved in politics. The education system could seek to promote greater political literacy among youth. Leaders could undertake a campaign to better inform seniors of the issues at stake, and appeal to their reason and altruism. Electoral boundaries could be redrawn more fairly to reduce the influence of seniors in rural districts. Voting rights could be allocated to parents by the number of their children.

But advancing any of these ideas would take great political leadership, something for which Japan is not well known. It is difficult to see Prime Minister Shinzo Abe investing himself in such a campaign, when he is fully occupied by security issues and Abenomics. The other fundamental problem is that any changes to Japan's silver democracy would require the agreement of the country's seniors, something which is unlikely in Confucian Japan where seniors take themselves very seriously!

We will now turn to the issue of immigration in Japan and Korea which could help these countries solve their demographic dilemmas.

## Japan's Immigration Imperative

Immigration has become a topic of lively debate in Japan over the past couple of decades, especially since its working-age population began declining in 1995. And Japan's foreign-born population has indeed increased from about 1% of the total population in 1990 to 2% today. But Japan has the lowest foreign-born population, as a share of the total, of all the advanced OECD countries except for Mexico. It has always been averse to immigration due to the notions of cultural uniqueness and homogeneity that pervade Japanese thinking.

Japan's immigration policies remain highly restrictive for lower skilled migration. And while Japan is very welcoming, in policy terms, to highly skilled migration, the country has had difficulty attracting such migrants. Many of them choose Hong Kong or Singapore instead. Japan ranked a mere 48th out of 60 countries for its "attractiveness to foreign-born highly skilled professionals" in a survey by Switzerland's International Institute for Management Development.[36]

The most dynamic response to Japan's immigration imperative has been an internship program which ostensibly gives people from developing countries the opportunity to learn skills they could bring back home. According to the Japanese government, there were close to 200,000 interns in Japan at end-2015, an increase of about 15% over the previous year, with China, Vietnam and the Philippines being the biggest sources. But as the US government has observed, this program "has effectively become a guest-worker program" as many interns are "placed in jobs that do not teach or develop technical skills", and "some of these workers continued to experience conditions of forced labor."[37] Japan's labor ministry has also found that abuses such as the failure to pay adequate overtime and subjecting workers to unsafe conditions are rampant in this program.[38]

With the continued decline in Japan's working-age population, the country is now beset with labor shortages which are adversely affecting economic growth, as the IMF has argued.[39] According to a study by Daiwa Institute of Research, there would be labor shortages in the 340,000–660,000 range during FY 2015 and FY 2016, which are cumulatively cutting GDP by some 2%.

According to a survey by the Manpower Group, 81% of Japanese firms are having difficulties in filling jobs in 2014. This is the highest of all the countries surveyed. Japan's labor shortages are most pronounced in construction, health care, home service and long-term care, as well as restaurants. This presents a particular challenge for the reconstruction following the 2011 triple disaster (earthquake, tsunami and nuclear meltdown), and also with regard to preparing for the 2020 Olympic Games.

The corporate sector and some commentators have been arguing for greater openness to immigration. The government's "Abenomics" program also includes a policy to increase the utilization of foreign workers. The government has implemented some measures for highly skilled foreign professionals and for lengthening the stay of internship migrants from three to five years. But these responses remain very modest.

Looking ahead, there is little end in sight to Japan's labor-shortage problems. Under one scenario, the Japanese government is projecting the labor force to shrink from 66.3 million in 2010 to 56.8 million in 2030, with economic growth remaining near zero. The Japanese government needs to abandon its ad hoc, reactive approach to immigration. It should develop a comprehensive immigration policy as an integral part of the country's medium term growth strategy.

Taking this step is all the more important as immigration is an important complement to other policy issues. This applies nowhere more than on Abe's signature policy issue—"womenomics". As we mentioned earlier, enhancing women's participation in the economy is constrained by restrictions on immigration of home service and care workers. That makes it difficult for Japanese women to combine work and family life.

Entrepreneurship and innovation are two other areas where Japanese performance has been relatively weak. According to the Global Entrepreneurship Monitor (GEM), Japan's entrepreneurial activity has been very low since GEM started collecting data in 1999. In 2014, Japan ranked second lowest among the more than 100 countries surveyed (coming just before Surinam). Many studies have shown that well-managed immigration can be a powerful source of entrepreneurship and innovation. Where would Silicon Valley be without its immigrants?

Prime Minister Shinzo Abe's ambitious target of doubling the stock of foreign direct investment into Japan from the woefully low 4% of GDP could also be facilitated by greater openness to immigration. Many immigrants arrive with a stock of assets for investment, and can also be useful workers for international companies requiring bilingual staff. And at a time when Japan is seeking to court more diplomatic friends in the Asian region, in the context of geopolitical rivalries, one important friendship gesture would be greater openness to immigration.

Given its concern about the cultural suitability of potential migrants, Japan should also make greater efforts to facilitate the integration of its international students into the economy following their graduation. After a few years study, they are usually at ease with the Japanese language and cultural customs. But less than 10% of Japan's international students currently seek working visas. Targeting international students as potential immigrants might also improve the attractiveness of Japan as an international education destination.

Japan could also enhance its position as a responsible stakeholder in the international community by reforming its closed-door refugee policy. Few nations are as financially generous as Japan in financing international relief efforts for persons displaced by war, civil strife and natural disasters. Japan is the fourth-largest donor to the UN High Commission for Refugees, with a grant of $182 million in 2014. Conversely, few nations are as miserly as Japan in providing physical asylum to refugees. In 2016, the Immigration Bureau only approved 28 of the 10,901 applications (0.26% of total) for refugee status.[40]

Is it realistic to think of Japan opening up to immigration as a potential source of economic revitalization?

After all, Prime Minister Shinzo Abe and many parts of his government remain steadfastly against having an immigration policy, citing the social problems experienced in Europe with large-scale immigration. Against that, some government ministers like Shigeru Ishiba and Taro Kono have recently spoken out in favor of increased immigration.[41] And a recent survey shows that Japanese public opinion may be changing, as 51% of Japanese respondents said they support Japan accepting foreigners who want to settle, while 34% were opposed to expanding immigration.[42]

Without more serious efforts to address the challenges of its aging population, there is a risk of Japan simply withering away under the weight of poor demographics and the burden of massive public debt and increasing its vulnerability to the growing fragility of its regional security environment. A well-designed immigration strategy could make an important contribution to Japan's future.

## Toward a Multicultural Korea

Unlike its neighbor Japan, Korea has accepted a dramatic increase in immigrants. In 1990, Korea had only 50,000 foreign residents, representing just 0.1% of the population. By end-2016, this number had leapt to 2.1 million or 4% of the total population. By the year 2020, foreigners could constitute about 5% of the total Korean population, and 10% by the year 2020, according to Brookings' Katherine Moon.[43] According to a report by the Korea Economic Research Institute, Korea might need up to 15 million migrants by the year 2060.[44] But in contrast to the past, Korea will also need to attract highly skilled and educated foreign workers, as do Hong Kong and Singapore, in order to maintain its economic dynamism.

Who make up Korea's foreign population, and by what means did they arrive in Korea? Korea's foreign population covers students, white-collar workers, migrant workers in agriculture, low-end industries and service jobs, undocumented workers and foreign brides. Migrants from China, usually ethnic Koreans, are the most important group, accounting for around 40% of total. There is also a growing number of North Korean defectors, with some 30,000 reportedly living in the South today.

There have been several programs facilitating the arrival of Korea's migrants.[45] In the early 1990s, there was the Industrial Trainee System. Then from the 2000s, the Employment Permit System (EPS) has permitted the entry of migrants from Southeast and Central Asia to work in labor-shortage industries like agriculture and stockbreeding, fishery, construction and manufacturing. Many of Korea's farming villages are now highly dependent on foreign labor. The EPS is in reality a guest-worker program, with little hope of nationalization, which only allows migrants to work for a limited number of years. EPS guest-workers are not allowed to bring family members and are only allowed to change jobs with the consent of their employer, leaving many trapped and highly vulnerable to abuse.

Marriage migration constitutes another avenue for migration to Korea. This enables a range of Korean men, such as agricultural workers, the urban poor or lower-middle-class bachelors or divorces, to find wives. Most foreign brides come from China (Korean ethnics), the Philippines, Thailand and Vietnam. Marriage migration is one of the very few paths to Korean naturalization. Marriage migration has become necessary because less and less Korean girls are now interested in marriage. Only 46% of Korean girls are interested in marriage, compared with 63% for Korean males, according to a recent survey. In more recent years, there has been an influx of professional expats, foreign teachers and international students. Some students are reportedly attracted by Korea's vibrant pop culture scene.

Today, there are over 820,000 people (including 300,000 foreign spouses) belonging to multicultural families in Korea, a figure which has more than doubled over the past eight years, reports Katherine Moon. Children born with at least one Korean parent are automatically granted Korean citizenship. In rural areas, about 40% of new marriages per year are between a Korean male and a foreign-born female. And for the Korean nation as a whole, some 10% of marriages are multicultural.

Despite these new trends toward a multicultural Korea, "New Koreans" suffer from discrimination by the larger society, and from economic insecurity and socio-cultural marginalization. Korean businesses are free to refuse to serve foreigners, something which is not uncommon. Korean identity has long been based on notions of racial and ethnic purity. To put it bluntly, racism is a big problem in Korea, despite reports of Koreans becoming somewhat more accepting of foreigners.

The impact of discrimination is particularly disturbing for children of mixed marriages, very many of whom suffer greatly and do poorly at school. Many multiracial children have difficulty speaking Korean, because their mothers lack fluency. Over time, this could become a major problem unless addressed, as the immigrant mothers have a very much higher birth rate than natives. Other problems are domestic abuse of migrant wives by their Korean family members and labor or marriage brokers. This is creating diplomatic issues with countries like Vietnam. There have been some limited positive developments. In 2012, Jasmin Barcunay Lee, a Philippines-born immigrant, was the first naturalized Korea to win a seat in the National Assembly. Over the years, the government has implemented a number of policies to facilitate the economic and social integration of migrants. It even promotes the idea of Korea becoming a multicultural society. And foreign residents were given voting rights in 2006, the first Asian country to do so.

The Korean government has however been taken to task by the UN for not having comprehensive anti-discrimination laws, and for the country's racism and xenophobia.[46]

"As Korean society becomes more exposed to foreigners and migrant workers living in the country, it is important to continue addressing the issue of racism, xenophobia and discrimination," said Mr. Ruteere, UN Special Rapporteur on racism. Mr. Ruteere noted that comprehensive anti-discrimination legislation would allow the appropriate institutions to play a more significant role in receiving complaints from victims, investigate and issue relevant recommendations for the government to follow up.

He encouraged the South Korean authorities to fight racism and discrimination through better education, as well as ensuring that the media is sensitive and conscious of the responsibility to avoid racist and xenophobic stereotypes and that perpetrators are punished where appropriate. He also called on the government to improve legislation on employment in order to offer a better protection to migrant workers and their families, and encouraged the authorities to ratify the International Convention on the Protection of the Rights of All Migrant Workers and Members of Their Families.

One of the most egregious examples of migrants' rights abuses in Asia is that of the exploitation and forced labor of migrant agricultural workers in South Korea, as reported by Amnesty International.[47] Listen to the voice of NT, a 35-year-old woman from Cambodia, who was working at a fruit and vegetable farm in South Jeolla province. "I was supposed to have a day off every other Saturday. But from April to June I worked every day without rest from 3am to 7pm. Otherwise rest days were given arbitrarily by the boss, who didn't want me to be free on Saturdays, because he didn't want me befriending other Cambodians. He was probably afraid that others would find out about my long work hours."

Agricultural migrant workers in Korea typically enter under the EPS. Their labor is important to the survival of farms throughout the country. Despite this, a significant number of employers exploit migrant agricultural workers who endure excessive working hours, underpayment, discrimination and poor living conditions. Many are also denied a weekly paid rest day and annual leave. Severe restrictions on migrants' ability to change jobs prevent many from escaping exploitative conditions. In addition, the Labor Standards Act excludes agricultural workers from legal protections covering working hour, breaks and weekly rest days.

Amnesty's report reveals how the majority of migrants interviewed were trafficked for exploitation and were working in conditions of forced labor. Most were coerced into working under conditions to which they did not agree, most commonly through threats and violence. Amnesty also highlights shortcomings in the redress mechanisms, finding that many people who sought help from the authorities were actively discouraged from taking complaints forward. Consequently, many unscrupulous employers have been allowed to exploit migrant agricultural workers with virtual impunity. Until the rights of these migrants are protected in practice, the EPS will continue to be synonymous with a system of labor exploitation, argues Amnesty International.

Amnesty's findings are supported by evidence compiled by the National Human Rights Commission of Korea. Concerns about the treatment of migrants under Korea's EPS have also been raised by a number of UN bodies, but the Korean government has consistently failed to implement their recommendations. Korea has not ratified a number of relevant international conventions, namely: the UN Protocol to Prevent, Suppress and Punish Trafficking in Persons, Especially Women and Children; and the ILO Conventions on Forced or Compulsory Labour, and Abolition of Forced Labour.

When compared with cosseted Japan, Korea's opening to immigration to help address its demographic drama is very impressive. But the Korean government and many Korean citizens do not treat their migrants as human beings, with human rights. They treat them more as a technical solution to a demographic and economic problem. Now that Korea has been a member of the OECD for some 20 years, it is high time that Korea adhered to the values of this organization, notably respect for human rights and pluralist democracy. Much more serious efforts to promote an open and inclusive multicultural society would not only provide great benefits in terms of social cohesion and stability. It would also foster a more creative and dynamic economy.

\* \* \*

Asia's politics are being buffeted by its demographic dilemmas and a vast array of other factors. As we explore in the next chapter, fixing Asia's flawed politics will be crucial in Asia's quest for economic development and middle-class societies.

## NOTES

1. Zielenziger, Michael (2007). Shutting Out the Sun: How Japan Created its Own Lost Generation.
2. The Japan Times. Japan home to 541,000 young recluses, survey finds, 7 September 2016.
3. BBC. China's 'leftover women', unmarried at 27, 21 February 2013.
4. UN. 2015 Revision of World Population Prospects.
5. UNFPA, UNESCO and WHO 2015. Sexual and Reproductive Health of Young People in Asia and the Pacific. A review of issues, policies and programmes. Bangkok: UNFPA.
6. ADB. Asian Development Outlook 2011 Update. Preparing for Demographic Transition.
7. UN. World Population Prospects. 2017 Revision.
8. Aiyar, Shekhar and Ashoka Mody. The Demographic Dividend: Evidence from the Indian States. IMF Working Paper. WP/11/38.
9. Mehrotra, Santosh, Ravi Raman, Neha Kumra, Kalaiyarasan, Daniela Röß. Vocational Education and Training Reform in India: Business Needs in India and Lessons to be Learned from Germany. Working Paper. Bertelsmann Stiftung.
10. German President visits Bertelsmann Stiftung conference on creating vocational education system in India, 10 February 2014.
11. Wall Street Journal. Why Japan's Economy Is Laboring, 8 April 2016.
12. The Guardian. Why have young people in Japan stopped having sex?, 20 October 2013.
13. BBC. South Korea's schools: Long days, high results, 2 December 2013.
14. Moon, Katharine H.S. South Korea's demographic changes and their political impact. Brookings, 26 October 2015.
15. Friedman, George. Population Decline and the Great Economic Reversal. Geopolitical Weekly, 17 February 2015. Stratfor.
16. Hayoun, Massoud. Understanding China's One-Child Policy. The National Interest, 15 August 2012.
17. Financial Times. Data reveal scale of China abortions, 16 March 2013.
18. Chang, Gordon G. Shrinking China: A Demographic Crisis. World Affairs, May/June 2015.
19. Sen, Amartya. Women's Progress Outdid China's One-Child Policy. New York Times, 2 November 2015.
20. Cameron, Lisa, Nisvan Erkal, Lata Gangadharan, and Xin Meng. Effects of China's One Child Policy on its children. Science Daily, 10 January 2013.

21. Wall Street Journal. China to Move Slowly on One-Child Law Reform, 17 November 2013.
22. Morse, Anne Roback. Police Brutality Happens Every Day in China. Population Research Institute, 6 May 2015.
23. OECD. Economic Survey of Japan 2017.
24. Wall Street Journal. South Korea May Need Up to 15 Million Immigrants, Study Says, 15 December 2014.
25. Guilford, Gwynn. Thailand's joining Japan and Korea as one of the "old men" of Asia. Quartz, 23 August 2013.
26. ADB. Pension Systems in East and Southeast Asia. Edited by Donghyun Park, 2012.
27. Jain-Chandra, Sonali, Kalpana Kochhar and Tidiane Kinda. Reducing Inequality in Asia: Sharing the Growth Dividend. IMF Blog, 24 May 2016.
28. OECD. Economic Survey of Korea 2014.
29. Korea Joongang Daily. Only piety is no longer enough, 6 July 2015.
30. The Economist. Elderly suicides in South Korea—Poor spirits, 7 December 2013.
31. helpage.org. Global AgeWatch Index 2015.
32. OECD. Economic Survey of Japan 2017.
33. Bertelsmann Stiftung (2013). Intergenerational justice in aging societies. A Cross-national Comparison of 29 OECD Countries.
34. Yashiro, Naohiro. How to overcome the Silver Democracy in Japan? Presentation to Brookings Conference, 3 December 2014.
35. Harney, Alexandra. Japan's Silver Democracy: The Costs of Letting the Elderly Rule Politics. Foreign Affairs, 18 July 2013.
36. Kodama, Takashi. Japan's Immigration Problem. Daiwa Institute of Research, 29 May 2015.
37. US Department of State. Trafficking in Persons Report 2016.
38. Nikkei Asian Review. Abuses rampant in foreign trainee program, Japan labor ministry finds, 18 August 2016.
39. Ganelli, Giovanni, and Naoko Miake. Foreign Help Wanted: Easing Japan's Labour Shortages. IMF Working Paper. WP/15/181.
40. nippon.com. Japan's Closed-Door Refugee Policy, 19 May 2015.
41. The Japan Times. Government weighs immigration to maintain population, boost workforce, 6 January 2016.
42. Asahi Shimbun. 51% of Japanese support immigration, double from 2010 survey, 18 April 2015.
43. Moon, Katharine H.S. South Korea's demographic changes and their political impact. Brookings, 26 October 2016.
44. The Korea Times. Why Korea must be more open to immigration, 20 March 2015.

45. Oh, Jung-Eun, Dong Kwan Kang, Julia Jiwon Shin, Sang-lim Lee, Seung Bok Lee, and Kiseon Chung. Migration Profile of the Republic of Korea. International Organisation of Migration. IOM MRTC Research Report Series No. 2011-01.
46. UN News Centre. Republic of Korea: UN rights experts urges adoption of anti-discrimination law, 9 October 2014.
47. Amnesty International. South Korea: End rampant abuse of migrant farm workers, 19 October 2014.

**Open Access** This chapter is licensed under the terms of the Creative Commons Attribution 4.0 International License (http://creativecommons.org/licenses/by/4.0/), which permits use, sharing, adaptation, distribution, and reproduction in any medium or format, as long as you give appropriate credit to the original author(s) and the source, provide a link to the Creative Commons license and indicate if changes were made.

The images or other third party material in this chapter are included in the chapter's Creative Commons license, unless indicated otherwise in a credit line to the material. If material is not included in the chapter's Creative Commons license and your intended use is not permitted by statutory regulation or exceeds the permitted use, you will need to obtain permission directly from the copyright holder.

CHAPTER 8

# Fixing Asia's Flawed Politics

"The Communist Party are the lawmakers, but they do not follow the law, nor respect the constitution," once said Chinese dissident artist Ai Weiwei.[1] "The problem is that the Party does not trust people, and is afraid of their power ... The Party wants to take control of everything, even in areas it is incapable of dealing with." And yet today the Chinese Communist Party (CCP) now seems more firmly in control of China than ever.

## Asia's Democracy Deficit

Democracy has very shallow roots and many enemies in Asia, and not only in China. Indeed, not one Asian country would have a "full democracy", according to the Economist Intelligence Unit (EIU).[2] Asia's most democratic countries—Japan, Korea, India and Taiwan—are classified as "flawed democracies". And not one Asian country would have a "good situation" when it comes to freedom of the press, according to Reporters Without Borders, a media watchdog.[3] The freest press in Asia would be in Taiwan, which was ranked only 45th in the world out of the 180 countries covered, and placed in the "satisfactory situation" category.

In sum, mature democracy is struggling to take hold in Asia, which is compromising the lives and freedoms of Asia's citizens, and imposing great costs on the economy as well.

The parlous state of democracy in Asia is perhaps not totally surprising, as the region was traditionally governed by communist autocracies, military dictatorships and paternalistic strong-men. And overcoming the past is never easy. But political scientists are right to be disappointed with the state of democracy in Asia. There has been a long series of modernization theorists starting with Seymour Martin Lipset,[4] who have predicted that economic development together with rising middle classes, education and urbanization would foster democratization.[5] And the successful transformation of Korea and Taiwan from authoritarian regimes into democracies raised hopes that other Asian countries would follow suit.

Many have also thought that encouragement from the international community, especially from "democracy evangelists" like the US, would motivate countries to democratize. Indeed, as emerging economies climb the development ladder, they can be attracted to becoming respected members of the international community. In the case of Korea, joining the Organisation of Economic Co-operation and Development (OECD) was a great "badge of honor", as the OECD is the group of rich, developed countries which stands for the principles of market economy, pluralist democracy and respect of human rights.[6]

More recently, many analysts have also thought that the advent of the Internet could fuel democratization. The Internet and social media are providing citizens in many non-democratic countries with unprecedented access to information and with effective tools for social mobilization. Indeed, Asia's youth elite is typically tech-savvy, highly connected through social media, educated overseas, international in outlook, self-confident, and as I have seen through teaching many Asian students, they are all too aware of the moral bankruptcy of many of their own leaders.

But democracy is struggling to take root in many Asian countries where the preconditions should be ripe for democracy. And democracy is not maturing as countries climb the economic development ladder. Traditional elites are engaged in a strong rearguard action in their defense of authoritarian or single party regimes.[7]

The poverty of democracy in Asia is clearly evident from the EIU's Democracy Index 2016 which surveys 167 countries. Asian countries find themselves in the flawed democracies, hybrid regimes or authoritarian categories, rather than the full democracy category where most Western countries are placed. This index recognizes that there is more to democracy than holding elections ("electoral democracy"). And so it should. Asia is replete with countries that administer shonky elections, and have weak institutions and rule of law. In addition to the electoral process and pluralism, the EIU index takes into account other factors like the functioning of government, political participation, political culture and civil liberties.

To help understand the state of region's politics, we would like to propose the following classification of Asian countries:

- Japan and Korea, Asia's most democratic countries, which are ranked 20th and 24th respectively by the EIU, are oligarchic democracies where big business has a large influence over policy-making through collusive relationships with government.
- Hong Kong, Malaysia and Singapore (ranked 68th, 65th and 70th) are pro-business economies which have very open markets, and are much more globalized than Korea or Japan. But these countries also have very much weaker democratic foundations than either Korea or Japan.
- Policy-making in Taiwan (33rd), Hong Kong (68th), Cambodia (112th) and Laos (151st) is subject, either willingly or unwillingly, to substantial influence from Communist China which is seeking to establish a system of client states in its neighborhood. In recent times, Sri Lanka and Myanmar have made some efforts to escape the tight clutches of Beijing.
- Asia has a large number of weak and fragile democracies which are riddled with corruption and burdened by ineffective states, namely India 32nd, Indonesia 48th, Philippines 50th, Mongolia 61st, Sri Lanka 66th, Bangladesh 84th, Nepal 102nd and Myanmar 113th.
- The military has long played an important role in Asian politics, especially in three countries where the military still plays an outsized role as it controls civil governments—Thailand (100th), Pakistan (111th) and Myanmar (113th).
- Lastly, there are three staunchly authoritarian Asian countries—Vietnam (131st), China (136th) and North Korea (167th). While there are some forces pushing for more transparency, accountability, rule of law and even democracy, these authoritarian regimes remain firmly in control with virtually no immediate threat to their viability.

## What's Holding Back Asia's Democratization?

There are many factors which are responsible for the parlous state of democracy in Asia. For example, many in Asia's middle and upper classes are not great supporters of democracy, as they have been substantial beneficiaries of Asia's rapid economic development, and rising inequality. Rather, they are supporters of the status quo, and often fear the possible impact of allowing the whole population to have a say in their nation's politics. They often look upon poorer, rural populations as uneducated country bumpkins, who represent a potential threat to their privileged position.

Some members of Asia's middle and upper classes (especially from China) want democracy and freedom, but achieve this by opting out and migrating to countries like the US, Canada, Australia and New Zealand. Recent years have seen large flows of Asian migration to these countries,[8] together with massive investments in real estate and illicit financial outflows.

The Internet and social media have proved to be two-edged swords in the quest for democracy. While they have greatly improved access to information, many Asian governments have responded by imposing censorship controls on the Internet (like China's great firewall), by disseminating propaganda through the Internet, and by using the Internet for surveillance of its citizens. The Internet and social media are now a dynamic battleground where activists are working to get around government controls and where both activists and governments are competing to get their messages out.

Desperate elites can also go to enormous lengths to hold onto power, as in case of Malaysia with its repeated prosecution of opposition leader Anwar Ibrahim. While the ruling party, the Barisan Nasional (BN), always wins national elections, its majorities have been declining. So in recent years, it has been involved in a dirty and violent struggle to hang on to power through "intimidation, electoral fraud and gerrymandering", according to Joshua Kurlantzick.[9]

Western democracy is painted in a bad light in many authoritarian countries, especially in China, with the British referendum to leave the EU (Brexit) and the election of Donald Trump to the presidency of the US, being cited as evidence of the shortcomings of Western democracy. In response to the US State Department's annual reports on human rights across the world,[10] the Chinese government issues its own report where it castigates the state of human rights in the US. In China's 2016 report,[11] it said "Wielding 'the baton of human rights,' it [the US] pointed fingers and cast blame on the human rights situation in many countries while paying no attention to its own terrible human rights problems." It added "With the gunshots lingering in people's ears behind the Statue of Liberty, worsening racial discrimination and the election farce dominated by money politics, the self-proclaimed human rights defender has exposed its human rights 'myth' with its own deeds."

Most Western governments and business now widely accept and tolerate China's one-party rule and all the human rights abuses that go with it. The attraction of China's big market and growing political power mean that most criticism of China is very softly done. Some companies are even willing to adapt their products to meet China's non-democratic concerns. Reports that Facebook has worked on special software so it could potentially accommodate censorship demands in China are particularly disturbing.

There was a time when most political scientists believed that China's growing integration into the world economy would foster a convergence of social and political culture with the West. If anything, the reverse has happened whereby Western dependence on Chinese markets, and political cooperation for issues like North Korea and climate change has eased external pressure on China's one-party system. And China has been able to use other countries' dependence on its market to impose economic sanctions on them to express its displeasure at their actions, as Japan, Korea and the Philippines have discovered.

Populism is another political force that is leaving its mark in Asia, not only in the US and Europe, and not always to the benefit of democracy. It should be hardly surprising that political leaders are appealing to the popular masses by criticizing traditional elites, with President Duterte of the Philippines being the prime example (Thailand's Thaksin Shinawatra was an earlier case). Duterte promised and is now practicing an illiberal form of democracy through his murderous war on drugs and crime where human rights abuses and disrespect for the rule of law are the order of the day.

Against this background, we will examine in greater detail several cases of Asia's flawed politics in the following sections: will China democratize, oligarchic democracy in Korea and Japan, the Philippines' gyrating populism and military politics in Myanmar and Thailand. In the final sections, we will explore the debate about whether authoritarian regimes like China's are more efficient than messy democracies like India's, and the economic benefits of democracy.

## WILL CHINA DEMOCRATIZE?

There is perhaps no issue that irritates the Chinese leadership more than America's obsession about whether, when and how China will become a democracy. It seems natural for America that democracy will be China's final political destination, and that single party rule by the CCP is just a transitional situation. It is perhaps part of the American mindset that we should all ultimately become like them. But the Communist Party believes that it should be in power forever, and is working toward that end.

It is easy for Western observers to underestimate the power and strength of the Chinese state. Indeed, China was the first country in the world to create a modern state—almost 2300 years ago and some 1700–1800 years before Europe—as political scientist Francis Fukuyama has argued.[12] But it is also true that China has never had the rule of law, by which the country's highest political authority should also obey the law. Even today, the Communist Party is a law unto itself, and China's judiciary is highly politicized and corrupt. "Constitutionalism" is a taboo subject in China.

Nor have China's rulers ever been subject to "downward accountability" to the country's citizens through democratic elections. This situation was facilitated by the feudal nature of Chinese society through much of its history when the vast majority of Chinese citizens were poor farmers living in rural areas. Dramatic economic and social changes have totally transformed China's political context, as Chinese citizens are now better educated, more prosperous and urbanized, and they have breathed the fresh air of economic freedom and opportunity. The challenge for China's government has thus been how to adapt single party rule to this new context.

Just a decade after Deng Xiaoping began opening the economy, the CCP was shaken to its bones by the near-death experience of the 1989 Tiananmen Square student protests. Now more than 25 years after, the CCP still shudders on the anniversary of the "June Fourth Incident". It clamps down on social and other media, and the movement of activists, and it exerts a maximum of repression of any possible commemoration or even discussion of the event.

China's rehabilitation following this horrendous massacre took a few years. Deng Xiaoping's "southern tour" of 1992, when he relaunched China's economic reforms, marked the next phase in China's economic, social and political development. The post-Tiananmen phase of China's development proceeded on the basis of a "social contract". The implicit deal was that the Chinese population would accept the authoritarian rule of the CCP because it was very successful in engineering economic growth, the key to poverty reduction and prosperity.

This became the basis of the CCP's legitimacy, "performance legitimacy". And it also earned the admiration of many Western and other observers who were impressed with the Chinese government's capacity to make big decisions, and implement large projects like the Three Gorges Dam in the face of large opposition and environmental destruction. Quashing human rights seemed to be a worthwhile price to pay for economic efficiency, especially when compared with the inefficiency of India's chaotic democracy.

Following the Tiananmen Square incident, the CCP further bolstered its role as the legitimate representative of the Chinese civilization and people with a highly nationalistic discourse. One lesson that the Chinese leadership drew from the Tiananmen Square incident was that the Communist Party needed to make greater efforts to promote nationalism to improve support for the Party. Students and citizens were taught how the Communist Party was leading China's recovery from its "century of humiliation" (from the opium wars to the end of the civil war in 1949).

National victimhood has thus become a key narrative. But victimhood has morphed into resentment and the desire for revenge which is evident in much of its international behavior from cyber-hacking to claiming sovereignty over the distant South China Sea. China is now not only in the midst of an economic recovery, but also the restoration of national pride, and the CCP is leading this battle.

The post-Tiananmen period has seen a great expansion in economic and personal freedoms. Many young Chinese have been allowed to study overseas, especially to the US. More recently, the numbers of Chinese traveling overseas as tourists have grown to the point whereby China has the world's highest number of international tourists, with Japan becoming a very popular destination. Chinese citizens also enjoyed increasing access to information and participation in social media thanks to the Internet. Indeed, during the regime of President Hu Jintao and Premier Wen Jiabao (2002–2012), it seemed that China has loosening up its political controls. Premier Wen even made some encouraging speeches on China's need for political reform.

But toward the end of the Hu/Wen regime, and especially under the current President Xi Jinping, political freedoms have moved backward, repression has intensified and China has become more assertive in its relations with both its neighbors and the West. China is in the midst of a "great leap backward" according to James Fallows.[13] "The country has become repressive in a way that it has not been since the Cultural Revolution," writes Fallows.

Increased repression is evident everywhere—be it in tighter controls over the Internet; instructions to the media that it must "serve the Party"; warnings by the Chinese leadership that dissent will not be tolerated; stiffer curbs on freedom of expression, association, assembly and religion; prosecution and jailing of lawyers and civil society leaders; extraterritorial actions against perceived enemies of the regime such as the abduction of booksellers from Hong Kong; and discrimination against foreign enterprises and all things foreign. Chinese leaders now explicitly reject the universality of human rights, seeing them as "foreign infiltration".[14] And the Chinese military's assertiveness vis-à-vis neighbors has greatly eroded trust, increased tensions and seen many countries turn to the US for support.

What is behind this great leap backward? Factors driving repression include the global financial crisis which highlighted the fragility of China's export-oriented economic model, public disgust at the Communist Party corruption and rising inequality, the appalling local environment, shudders at the sight of the Arab Spring and rising social unrest. According to one estimate, the number of public protests in 2010 was of the order of 180,000 and 230,000.[15] And while external assertiveness can be used to camouflage domestic fragilities, the Chinese leadership also interpreted the global financial crisis as a clear sign of the decline of the West, and the success of the 2008 Beijing Olympics as symbolic of Chinese ascendancy. They also saw US President Obama's diplomacy-first approach to foreign relations as a sign of weak leadership it could take advantage of.

Xi Jinping's ascension to the presidency of China and head of the Communist Party in late 2012/early 2013 was also marred by factional infighting and a murderous scandal involving his nemesis, Bo Xilai, who was prosecuted and now lives in jail. Xi thus began his presidency with a CCP more divided between factions and clans than since Tiananmen Square. In his first five-year term at the helm of China, Xi Jinping has focused almost entirely on fighting corruption which he believes is a live-or-death issue for the Communist Party.

Xi's anti-corruption campaign has been vast, implicating thousands of both flies (low-level bureaucrats) and tigers. Although Xi's anti-corruption drive has merely scratched the surface, he has exposed a complex system of patronage which holds the CCP together. The anti-corruption campaign has equally been a strategy for eliminating Xi's political enemies and rivals to "consolidate power". And in doing so, Xi has accumulated more power than any Chinese leader since Deng Xiaoping and perhaps since Mao Zedong—although many locals think that a comparison with Russia's Putin might be more apt. At the same time, the deeper that the anti-corruption campaign digs, the more enemies Xi makes. President Xi has also launched his own propaganda campaign in the form of the "Chinese Dream", which Xi has described as the "great rejuvenation of the Chinese people ... improvement of people's livelihoods, prosperity, construction of a better society and a strengthened military".

Analysts have been predicting the possible demise of the CCP or the impending democratization of China for many years. In 2001, Gordon Chang predicted the "coming collapse of China".[16] In 2013, Minxin Pei argued that China's GDP per capita was already well into the "zone of democratic transition", and above those of Korea and Taiwan on the eve of their democratic transitions.[17] Minxin Pei has also argued that President Xi's war on corruption could hasten the CCP's fall.[18] And in 2016, David Shambaugh argued "the Chinese Leninist system [is] once again in a state of atrophy and inexorable decline ... Hard Authoritarianism is a recipe for economic stagnation, social instability, and the political decline of the Chinese Communist Party." Unless there is a return to Soft Authoritarianism, which is unlikely, "secular stagnation will continue, the reforms will continue to stall, and the CCP will gradually lose its grip on power".[19] There is much that the CCP could do to return China to "Soft Authoritarianism" or even transfer it into a "Semi-Democracy" like Singapore, without even necessarily giving up its monopoly on power. But this does not seem to be on the cards.

For its part, the CCP is openly worried that the stability of the Party will be undermined by Western ideas and "universal values" like constitutional democracy, human rights, media independence and transparency, which it regards as being responsible for the "color revolutions" in Eastern Europe and the Middle East. It is also worried about the large flows of outward migration by China's elites, as well as massive capital flight. And yet, despite all the doomsdayers, there are also many who believe that the CCP will hang on to power for at least the foreseeable future. They argue that much of the middle class, which has benefited from China's economic miracle, still support the CCP, and most certainly fear the consequences of instability. Further, over 85 million people are members of the CCP, who are important stakeholders in the existing system. The CCP "co-opts" into the Party members of social elites, like academics, professionals and entrepreneurs. This is a way to neutralize social groups who are normally forces for democratization.

China's internal security service and the People's Liberation Army are arguably strong enough to keep things under control. A massive domestic security budget (more than the military budget) is employed to maintain social stability. And China reportedly has an "Internet police force" of some 2 million, who are constantly monitoring, censoring and spreading propaganda on the Internet. Most certainly, President Xi is firmly intent on holding onto power, and has no intention implementing any democratic reforms. Xi has analyzed the demise of the Soviet Union, and concluded that, in contrast to Gorbachev, the CCP must stand firm. Any political reform is about the CCP reforming itself, not reform of the political system.

What does the future hold for China? Only time will tell. But as David Shambaugh said, we should not expect developments in China to be linear—"Sharp changes of course have occurred with some regularity throughout China's history." In the short term, we can expect President Xi to tighten even more his grip on power. He will be anointed for second five-year term at the 19th National Congress of the Communist Party of China in October 2017, when he will also stack the Politburo Standing Committee with loyalists. Policy will be geared to achieving the goal of "building a moderately prosperous society in all respects and double the 2010 GDP and per capita personal income by 2020". And Xi will invest great political energy and capital in the 2021 celebrations of the centenary of the founding of the Communist Party.

## Korea's Corrupt Democracy

The 2017 impeachment of Korean President, Park Geun-hye, and prosecution of Lee Jae-yong, the head of Samsung, highlight Korea's deep corruption. But they are also testimony to the strength of Korea's democratic institutions.

Korea experienced a horribly authoritarian period in the 1960s and 1970s under President Park Chung-hee, the father of the impeached Korean president. But Korea's political space was always contested—especially by two individuals who became president in the 1990s, Kim Young-sam, and Kim Dae-jung. And protests by Korea's well-educated students were also a recurrent feature.

In 1987, in the midst of widespread student and trade union protests, designated presidential successor Roh Tae-woo made the historic decision to hold elections, which he won. Korea's democratic transition was confirmed by the election in 1992 of President Kim Young-sam from the center-right-wing Democratic Liberal Party. This transition was most significant in that Kim, a democratic activist, succeeded Roh, who was a former army general, closely linked to Korea's authoritarian past.

The 1997 election of President Kim Dae-jung from the center-left-wing party, National Congress for New Politics, demonstrated the capacity of Korea's new democracy to accept the alternance of power between right- and left-wing presidents. Kim Dae-jung had survived years in jail and several assassination attempts, and is often referred to as "Asia's Mandela".[20] The growing maturity of Korea's democracy was demonstrated by the election of another center-left president, Roh Moo-hyun, in 2002, followed by two right-wing presidents, Lee Myung-bak (elected 2007) and Park Geun-hye (elected 2012). As Freedom House has observed, "Political pluralism is robust [in Korea], with multiple parties competing for power and succeeding one another in government."[21]

Korea's transformation from an authoritarian regime to a democracy represents one of Asia's greatest post-war achievements. In the space of a generation, Korea moved from being a recipient of foreign aid to being a member of the OECD, the club of advanced democracies and aid donors. As former OECD Secretary General Donald J. Johnston said, "Korea has set an example for other emerging market economies to follow."[22]

But Korea's democracy is still very much tainted by the country's authoritarian past. Freedom of the press is greatly compromised, and getting worse, according to Reporters Without Borders, which ranked Korea only 70th in the world in 2016 (out of the 180 countries surveyed), ten places lower than in 2015.[23] The Park government did not entertain criticism, and threatened media independence. Public debate about relations with North Korea is taboo. Korea's spy agency has now admitted that, in the lead-up to the 2012 presidential elections won by Park Geun-hye, it had cyber-teams spreading pro-government opinions and suppressing anti-government views.

And most troubling, as of March 2016, 74 trade unionists including the President of the Korean Confederation of Trade Unions (KCTU) were in prison. Five hundred and four other KCTU members were charged with "obstruction of traffic" in relation to a demonstration held in 2015. When Korea joined the OECD in 1996, it committed to reform its labor law to bring in line with the standards of the International Labour Organisation (ILO). Yet, basic labor rights, including the right to organize and to bargain collectively, are not observed in today's Korea, according to Trade Union Advisory Committee (TUAC) to the OECD. State interference in trade union activities remains the norm.

"Regrettably, twenty years after its accession, Korea is still far from having built a system of industrial relations based on ILO standards that can manage conflict, reduce inequality and ensure social progress. In the past three years, repression against unions and the criminalisation of their activities appear to have returned," said John Evans, TUAC General Secretary.[24]

Corruption is also endemic in the highest levels of Korean political and business life. Indeed, all of Korea's democratically elected presidents or their families have been implicated in corruption scandals. For example, at a time of corruption scandals involving his family, Roh Moo-hyun committed suicide in May 2009. And President Kim Dae-jung's historic peace summit in June 2000 with North Korean leader, Kim Jong Il, was also tainted by suicide. Hyundai's Chairman Chung Mong Hun took his life while he was facing criminal charges for his part in a deal to allegedly pay a bribe of $500 million to Kim Jong Il for participating in the summit.

Even by Korean standards, the corruption scandal that brought down the presidency of Park Geun-hye in 2016–2017 was bizarre. President Park's close friend Choi Soon-sil, a "Rasputin-esque" figure and daughter of a shadowy cult figure, extorted at least $70 million dollars from Korea's chaebols for two of her foundations—allegedly in collusion with Park. Samsung, the veritable symbol of Korea, was also dragged into this scandal. In August 2017, its head, Lee Jae-yong, was sentenced to five years in prison for bribery and embezzlement charges. Samsung allegedly gave $38 million to Choi in return for favors, notably government support for a merger of two Samsung affiliates in 2015 that helped Lee inherit corporate control from his incapacitated father.

President Park's scandal is even murkier. She was seemingly possessed by Choi who is alleged to have dictated or influenced all manner of official and personal decisions taken by Park. Choi would have had access to confidential documents and information of the president. The scandal was allegedly broken by Choi's "toyboy" who apparently fell out with her. Choi has been charged with abuse of authority, coercion and fraud.[25]

As this scandal became public from October 2016, there were massive protests against President Park every Saturday evening in Seoul for two months. On 9 December 2016, the National Assembly passed a motion recommending impeachment of Park. Korea's leadership was put in the hands of an Acting President, Hwang Kyo-ahn. Then on 10 March 2017, the Constitutional Court unanimously upheld the impeachment. Park has lost her presidential immunity and is now being prosecuted in a criminal trial.

In May 2017, Mr. Moon Jae-in, head of the left-of-center Democratic Party, won Korea's presidential election. Like liberal presidents before him, Moon would like to reopen dialogue and cooperation with North Korea, in conjunction with tough sanctions. Although this puts him at variance with Donald Trump, Trump's tough talk seems increasingly empty, as virtually all he is doing is begging China to solve his North Korea problem.

As a liberal, President Moon will likely be more conciliatory with China, to the displeasure of the US, and also tougher with Japan, again to the displeasure of the US, which has been encouraging its two Asian allies to improve cooperation with each other. At the moment, relations with China are tense, as China is objecting to the US' installation of the Terminal High Altitude Area Defense (THAAD) system, ostensibly to protect Korea from missiles from the North. China is concerned that it will enable the US to spy into its territory, and imposed economic sanctions on Korea.

As Korean leaders including Park have proposed in the past, President Moon will need to break the cozy ties between the chaebol and the government, which are at the heart of Korea's big corruption problem. One heartening point that we can draw from President Park's corruption scandal is that Korea's democratic institutions have functioned well, with Park having to face up to the will of the people and the rule of law. They give hope that Korea could reform its democracy and come out stronger in the end. The widespread protests are also perhaps evidence that Korean citizens are democratic at heart, something we cannot yet say about Japan.

## Japan's Oligarchic Democracy

Japan's oligarchic democracy has much in common with Korea's, but it also has important differences. In its long history as a nation, Japan had virtually never been a democracy, apart from a modest experience in the 1910s and 1920s at the time of emperor Taisho ("Taisho democracy").[26] Authoritarian, fascist, feudal and/or military regimes were the norm. After Japan surrendered in defeat at the end of World War 2 some 70 years ago, the US post-war occupation regime under General Douglas MacArthur instituted democracy in Japan. Unlike France, Korea and many other cases, the Japanese people did not fight for their democracy. This may be why Japan has been a virtual one-party state for much of the post-war period, with the right-wing Liberal Democratic Party (LDP) holding nominal power.

Nevertheless, political power has been substantially exercised by Japan's powerful bureaucracy, which managed the "iron triangle" of bureaucrats, business and politicians, that engineered Japan's miraculous recovery from the ashes of military defeat. Today, we may marvel at Japan's excellent infrastructure as testimony to the great efficiency of the iron triangle. But public investment in infrastructure also served other roles, notably financing Japan's electoral system through kickbacks from construction companies to politicians, and buying public support for LDP politicians. And Japan's international corporate success stories like Toyota grew up behind walls of protection against international competition, which enhanced their support for the iron triangle system. While gerrymandering of rural political constituencies, and large financial support for Japan's farmers, further bolstered support for the LDP.

The credibility of LDP-led government gradually eroded over the years, as a result of a series of outrageous corruption and other scandals, and its inability to respond effectively to the bursting of Japan's bubble economy in the early 1990s. In 2009, the LDP was swept from power in a landslide electoral victory by the left-wing Democratic Party of Japan (DPJ), which won 64% of the parliamentary seats. This change of power raised many hopes that Japan had finally become a true democracy. But the DPJ's tenure was a great disappointment. It was characterized by inexperience, incompetence, conflict with the bureaucracy which then undermined the government, and conflict/misunderstandings with the US concerning its military bases in Japan, which are still home to some 50,000 troops.

Perhaps the greatest blunder of the DPJ government was the purchase of the Senkaku Islands from their private owner. As the sovereignty of these islands is still disputed with China, this act provoked an outsized reaction from the Chinese government, which continues to this day. The poor response to the March 2011 triple crisis of earthquake, tsunami and nuclear disaster was further evidence of the systemic weakness of Japan's system of governance. As the Fukushima Nuclear Accident Independent Investigation Commission concluded, the nuclear crisis was not a natural disaster, "…this was a disaster "Made in Japan". Its fundamental causes are to be found in the ingrained conventions of Japanese culture: our reflexive obedience, our reluctance to question authority, our devotion to 'sticking with the program', our groupism and our insularity."[27] The inadequate regulation and supervision of Tokyo Electric Power Company (TEPCO), another major cause of the disaster, also highlighted the role of the nuclear iron triangle ("nuclear village"), where business and political interests were ganging up against citizens' interests. TEPCO is, for example, a large donor to the LDP and other organizations.

In the space of three years, the DPJ had three leaders, which meant that there was very little policy continuity and very little was achieved. And so it was that LDP was swept back into power in December 2012, under the leadership of Prime Minister Shinzo Abe. But this was not a real victory for the LDP. It was a rejection of the DPJ. The promise of democracy, raised by the 2009 DPJ victory, has faded in the distance. The DPJ was decimated in the 2012 election and is now a spent force as it won a mere 12% of the parliamentary seats. The LDP, and its junior coalition partner, the "Komeito" Party (a Buddhist party), now govern without any effective opposition. As in much of the post-war period, Japanese political competition mainly takes place behind closed doors between the different factions within the LDP, a similar situation to the one-party rule in Communist China. And for the moment, the hyperactive Mr. Abe has been able to ward off opposition from rival faction leaders.

Although Mr. Abe's principal mandate is to revive the economy through Abenomics, he has in fact spent much more energy on other issues, for which there is much less public support.[28] Abe has pushed through a change in Japan's post-war pacifist security policy in the area of "collective self-defense", by reinterpreting Article 9 of the Constitution to the horror of most legal scholars. This would enable the Japanese military to come to the defense of allies, notably the US. Abe's dream is to revise Japan's pacifist constitution by which the "Japanese people forever renounce war as a sovereign right of the nation and the threat or use of force as means of settling international disputes" and that military forces "will never be maintained".

Today, Japan's democracy is bedeviled by many factors—some old and some more recent. Japan has reverted to being a virtual one-party state dominated by the LDP and its leader, Shinzo Abe. Japan's national political opposition may never have been weaker than it is today. Japan has never had a truly free and independent media, and this continues to be the case. The press clubs ("kisha clubs") that each government ministry operates foster unhealthily cozy relations between journalists and government officials, which inhibit critical reporting. The national broadcaster, NHK, is now clearly under the government's thumb. NHK journalists have quietly told me they are not allowed to criticize the government. Some commentators have suggested that NHK behaves like a national broadcaster in Communist China. And like Korea, Japan continues to be plagued by high level corruption in the political and business spheres, even though at the street level, the Japanese people are perhaps the world's most honest.

Japan's oligarchic democracy is very costly to the country in many ways. Japan's lost decades since the 1990s financial crisis are the direct result of vested interests blocking the necessary structural reforms, and of sluggishness in responding to the unfolding demographic drama. The government is reluctant to hold open discussions on national security issues, with most important decisions being pushed through behind closed doors. And decisions on questions like the future of nuclear energy are often taken in defiance of public opinion.

Only the Japanese people can make Japan a real democracy by becoming more politically active and assertive. But their society leaves them ill-equipped to do so for many reasons. For example, Japan's deeply entrenched culture of social hierarchy means that there is insufficient questioning of authority. Its education system is based on rote learning and memorization, rather than critical thinking and analytical skills, leaving youth insufficiently capable of analyzing the world around them. Fervent nationalism and an exaggerated sense of cultural uniqueness inhibit the capacity of Japanese citizens to draw lessons from the experiences of other countries. And Japan's conformist and conservative society is sustained by what Yoshio Sugimoto calls a system of "friendly authoritarianism".[29] "Japanese society has various forms of regimentation that are designed to standardize the thought patterns and attitudes of the Japanese and make them toe the line in everyday life," according to Sugimoto.

## Philippines' Populist Temptation

The Philippines' modern political history is tainted with populism and turbulence. And yet, in the 1950s, the Philippines was one of Asia's most promising young democracies. But the country's leadership fell into the clutches of President Ferdinand Marcos from 1965 to 1986, who hijacked its fragile democracy and instituted martial law for a decade. Marcos and his cronies wreaked havoc on the Philippine economy, just at the time that Asia's miracle economies were taking off. During Marcos' term, national debt grew from $2 billion to almost $30 billion, which Filipinos are still repaying to this very day. Marcos his family and cronies amassed an estimated $10 billion. Human rights abuses were widespread, as opposition figures were murdered and tortured. The Philippines thus became the sick-man of Asia.

The populist People Power Revolution of 1986 restored democracy. Then in 1998, Joseph Estrada, a former actor, was elected President, as a man of the people, with the largest vote margin in Philippine history. But charges of corruption saw his political demise in another extra-constitutional People Power movement in 2001.

Since the restoration of democracy, the Philippine economy has slowly been clawing its way back. The economy improved greatly during the presidency of Benigno Aquino (2010–2016), when it has been one of the world's fastest growing economies, with an annual growth rate of close to 6%. Key drivers of the economy were migrants' remittances and the business process outsourcing sector. The Philippines also experienced a welcome boom in foreign direct investment.[30] Aquino won plaudits from the international community for tackling corruption, and improving governance. For example, the Philippines was rewarded by the major international credit rating agencies—Moody's, Standard & Poor's, Fitch and the Japan Credit Rating Agency—with upgrades in its sovereign credit ratings to "investment grade".

But Filipinos remained rightly frustrated, particularly when comparing their country with its neighbors like Malaysia and Thailand which are way ahead in terms of GDP per capita and poverty reduction. Lack of opportunity has pushed many talented Filipinos to find work overseas, all too often in jobs well below their skill level and in dangerous countries in the Middle East—10% of the population lives overseas. The appalling state of the Philippines' infrastructure is evident as soon as you arrive at Manila airport, and then make your way, at a crawling speed through traffic jams, to your hotel.

And the Philippines is quite simply a very dangerous country.[31] Violent crime is a significant problem, especially theft, physical assault, robbery, pickpocketing, confidence schemes, acquaintance scams and credit card fraud. Carjacking, kidnappings, robberies and violent assaults also occur sporadically. Victims of kidnapping can be beheaded, if their family doesn't pay a ransom. Terrorist attacks can occur at anytime, anywhere in the Philippines, including in Manila. Drug abuse and trafficking have been major problems in the Philippines, especially the reported usage of "shabu", the street name of methamphetamine.

The regrettable reality is that the Philippines is neither a mature nor an effective democracy, and has never had a strong and effective state or leadership. The EDSA People Power Revolution of 1986 only returned to power the old Philippine oligarchy which is mainly interested in its protecting privileges. As Philippine political scientist Richard Heydarian has argued, the Philippines' dysfunctional democracy is dominated by the country's oligarchic elites.[32] "The vast majority of legislators (70 percent) hail from political dynasties, dwarfing even comparable Latin American countries like Mexico (40 percent) and Argentina (10 percent)," said Heydarian. And the Philippines' elites have also been milking the economy dry in recent years, as Heydarian notes—"76% of newly-generated wealth was swallowed by the 40 richest families, the worst kind of growth concentration in Asia."

It is perhaps not surprising that the Philippine people should have voted populist firebrand Rodrigo Duterte as their new president in 2016. Like Donald Trump, this man of the people, with his tough-talking style, seems much more authentic and entertaining than the representatives of the establishment. In this feudalistic nation, with an uncaring elite and disenfranchised masses, personalities have always mattered more than policies in national politics. Duterte, also known by sobriquets like "Duterte Harry" and "the Punisher", promised to tackle head on the country's chronic problems of drugs, criminality and corruption. As Mayor of Davao City on the southern island of Mindanao for over 20 years, Duterte brought peace and security to this city, in the Philippines' most violent and unstable region. However, Duterte also admitted to having links to Davao death squads which conducted extrajudicial killings of over 1000 alleged drug traffickers, criminals, gang members and other lawless elements.

Since assuming the presidency, Duterte has launched his war against drugs with a vengeance inviting citizens and vigilante groups to kill criminals. Various reports suggest that over 8000 people have been killed, and many more thousands have turned themselves in. As the US, Europe, the UN and others criticized his manifest abuses of human rights, Duterte merely responded with threats and insults. He has also been pursuing a more "independent" foreign policy, by forging closer relations with China and Russia, and reducing the country's longstanding reliance on the US.

While Duterte is losing friends in the international community, he is very popular at home, where people can already feel an improvement in the local security environment. Families and friends of innocent victims do not, as yet, seem to pose a threat to his popularity, as most of those killed come from poor and powerless backgrounds. Overall, Philippine citizens have been willing to trade some of their hard-won human rights and freedoms for the promise of greater security from a brutal crackdown on crime, drugs and corruption in this dangerous country. Filipinos have succumbed to "authoritarian nostalgia", as they look back to the mythical good old days of strong leadership under President Marcos.

As impressive as Duterte's war on drugs and criminality may seem, it is deeply flawed in many ways. Most victims of the violent crackdown have been small-time drug users and sellers, with big drug lords, many of whom come from China, escaping scot-free. There have also been many innocent victims. And the Philippines does not have enough facilities to treat drug users, nor even sufficient jail space to house more criminals. It may be just a matter of time before Filipinos decide that wholesale murder is not a solution to the nation's drug problem.

There is another war, a more important one, that the Philippines needs to win, and that is the war against poverty, which is a major root cause of the Philippines' drug problem. Duterte does have some constructive proposals, like boosting infrastructure spending. But progress has been slow.

More recently, the fragility of the Philippine state has been exposed by the infiltration of Islamic State (ISIS) ideology into the southern island of Mindanao, and the capture of the southern city of Marawi by Islamic extremists. While Islamic terrorism has long been a problem in the southern Philippines, many observers, including Australia's foreign minister Julie Bishop, are now concerned that ISIS might seek to declare a caliphate in the southern Philippines, and that Southeast Asia could become the new battleground against ISIS.

There are also grave concerns that Duterte's new love affair with China, and use of Chinese loans to finance much-needed infrastructure, could lead to a substantial rise in the country's debt, and an erosion in national sovereignty, as potential debt bondage could leave the country vulnerable to Chinese geopolitical interests. Thailand is another country that has been vulnerable to populism and political instability. But its government has been more effective in promoting economic development.

## Thailand, the Land of a Thousand Coups

Thailand's politics have long been dominated by the military and the monarchy, which have ensured that the economy serves the direct interests of the Bangkok elites (the monarchy, military, the judiciary, the senior civil service and business leaders). Governments have typically been kept weak and vulnerable, and regularly deposed by the military.

The "land of smiles" has nevertheless enjoyed great success over the past few decades. Thailand's GDP per capita leapt from $4300 in 1990 to $16,900 in 2016. The country ranks 34th in the World Economic Forum's Global Competitiveness Index. And extreme poverty has been virtually eliminated. Keys to Thailand's success have been its ability to attract large flows of foreign direct investment, especially from Japan, and international tourists—despite periodic bouts of instability. And thanks to its "locational advantage", it has been able to attract many corporate regional headquarters. Thailand's success is particularly outstanding compared with its neighbor, the Philippines.

Despite Thailand's relative success, it has fallen into a "middle-income trap". Like the cases of several Latin American countries before it, there seems little prospect of Thailand achieving high-income status. There are many reasons for this. Thailand's education system is poor, as reflected in its low ranking in the OECD's PISA education program.[33] It has not been able to take advantage of its participation in global value chains to graduate to higher value added activities. Vietnam, Myanmar and Indonesia have recently emerged as strong competitors for Thailand. And it now has a very rapidly aging population, and the economy increasingly relies on poorly educated migrants.

Moreover, Thailand has a terribly polarized society. Income inequality is high. One of the most striking aspects of inequality is the large gaps between the poor, rural north and northeast regions, and the Bangkok area. And political instability has also been dragging the country down. It was against this background that in 2001 Thaksin Shinawatra was elected Thailand's Prime Minister, as a "champion of the poor", much to the displeasure of the Bangkok elites. Thaksin himself is not however poor. He is an extremely rich telecommunications tycoon.

Thaksin implemented pro-poor policies for infrastructure, education, public health, debt relief and microfinance. Most agree that these policies bettered the lives of poor rural north and northeastern communities. Moreover, Thaksin proved to be a politician who honored his promises to the poor, who still support his party strongly today. Critics of Thaksin's pro-poor policies describe them as "populist" or even vote-buying. But there was more to Thaksin than inclusive growth. Aggressive efforts to tackle the drug trade involved brutal, extrajudicial violence, and very many deaths. High-handed policies in Thailand's deep south helped fan a violent separatist insurgency. And Thaksin was seen as being extremely corrupt, even by Thai standards, for example, by exploiting government contracts. In short, Thaksin proved to be a divisive, polarizing figure, who pitted himself against the traditional Thai elite.

Thaksin was ousted in a bloodless military coup in 2006. He was convicted of corruption, and now lives in exile in Dubai. His proxy party was re-elected in 2007. But defections led to a change of government in 2009. The Democrat Party, led by Abhisit Vejjajiva, ruled from 2009 to 2011. However, in 2011 it lost an election to Thaksin's sister Yingluck Shinawatra and her Phue Thai Party. The reign of Yingluck was also marked by controversy such as accusations of behind-the-scenes interference by Thaksin, abuse of power in government appointments, and a flawed and corrupted rice scheme that created a national financial disaster, with estimated losses of $15 billion.

A major catalyst for further social unrest was a foolishly provocative attempt by Yingluck to pass an Amnesty Act that would have allowed Thaksin to return to Thailand without having to face a two-year jail sentence for corruption. Yingluck was removed from power in May 2014 by the constitutional court, rather than through the democratic electoral process. The military then took over in a coup, by one count the 20th coup since 1932. One of the reasons given for the coup was the violent civil unrest that had erupted between the supporters of the two main political factions: the "yellow shirts" (representing the establishment) and the "red shirts" (Thaksin and pro-democracy faction). There were rumors that royal palace members helped foment these street protests.

But the military's 2014 coup had a much bigger agenda. First, the military was determined to eliminate the Shinawatra family and the red-shirt movement from Thai political life ("de-Thaksinification"). It sees majoritarian democracy as an existential threat to its dominance of Thai political life, since the Bangkok elite does not have the numbers to win a democratic election. Indeed, Shinawatra-affiliated parties have won all elections since 2001. Yingluck was impeached in 2015 and banned from political life for five years. The military has substantially eliminated the red-shirt movement. The lese-majesty law (defaming, insulting or threatening the monarchy) is being freely used to curb political dissent and eliminate opposition figures. The military government is imposing widespread restrictions on freedom of speech, press and assembly, and there many reports of human rights abuses. In August 2016, the military government pushed a new constitution through a bogus referendum which tightens military rule in Thailand. In 2017, Yingluck was prosecuted for her flawed and corrupted rice scheme, but escaped the country before the judgment was handed down.

Human rights and civil rights activists, journalists and academics are in particular subject to great restrictions. For example, outspoken academic Pavin Chachavalpongpun, a Thai political scientist based in Japan, received an arrest warrant, had his passport revoked and had to apply for refugee status in Japan. His family has been intimidated, and the military government unsuccessfully asked the Japanese government to extradite him (and other similar cases) to Thailand.

Second and most importantly, the military wanted to be in control of Thailand during the succession of Thai monarch, Bhumibol Adulyadej, who died in October 2016. The King was loved and revered by most Thai people and had been a key to national stability, intervening periodically as a national conciliator in Thai politics, with the support of the military. The major problem for Thailand's royal succession was that the Crown Prince, Maha Vajiralongkorn, could never be like the semi-godlike figure of King Bhumibol. The Crown Prince is widely regarded as a playboy, with little interest in the royal court. He has not been liked by the Thai people or the military.

Thailand needs to establish a genuine majoritarian democracy, based on the rule of law, to ensure long-term political stability, and to return the country to a path of sustainable economic growth. Economic growth has been poor these past few years, averaging only around 3% per annum. But successful majoritarian democracy requires several challenging conditions. The military should return to the barracks, and no longer intervene in national politics. Military intervention in politics is now only exacerbating Thailand's polarized society. The monarchy should also retreat from national politics.

Above all, national reconciliation and a new social contract are necessary. The Bangkok elite must recognize that the world has changed. They must learn to compromise, share the spoils of economic growth and find a new political consensus. Thanks to Thaksin, the poor from Thailand's north and northeast have tasted the benefits of inclusive growth, and many are willing to fight on for social justice. Further, Thailand now has a growing democracy movement thanks to its emerging middle class and better educated population, which has access to the Internet and social media, a broader political awareness and desire for political participation.

In other words, Thailand needs a new democratically elected government which governs on behalf of the whole nation, based on a new deal which is seen to be a fair deal by all major groups of society. But looking ahead, democracy's prospects in Thailand are dim. Duncan McCargo of the University of Leeds once summed up the situation neatly when he said "I've never really been more pessimistic than I am at the moment."[34]

## MILITARY HANGS ON IN MYANMAR

The poor people of Myanmar have lived through a tragic history since the country's independence from the UK in 1948. A young democracy was snuffed out by a military takeover in 1960, ushering in a regime which virtually closed the country to the rest of the world. This country of immense natural resources, which had been the world's biggest rice exporter, descended into corruption and cronyism, with much of the population living in squalid poverty and suffering from appalling human rights abuses. The economy was run by the military and its cronies, which plundered natural resources like oil and gas, jade and tropical timber, as well as trafficking in narcotics.

Civil war began at independence between the country's Bamar Buddhist ethnic majority, led by the army, and the dozens of ethnic minorities living in Myanmar's mountainous borderlands. Ethnic minorities make up one-third of the country's population. Control of Myanmar's abundant natural resources is at the heart of the conflict. The military regime virtually destroyed the country's economy, infrastructure, institutions and society.

Following student protests in 1988, the military government decided to hold elections in 1990. But it then annulled the results when the National League for Democracy (NLD) won, under the leadership of Madame Aung San Suu Kyi. She is the daughter of General Aung San, leader of Myanmar's fight for independence from Britain. The government imprisoned NLD leaders and activists. Aung San Suu Kyi would spend 15 of the next 20 years under house arrest. She was thus unable to receive the Nobel Peace Prize that she was awarded in 1991. The US and the EU began imposing heavy trade and financial sanctions on Myanmar.

In 1989, the military regime changed the name of country from Burma to Myanmar.

In 2003, the military government outlined a seven-step roadmap to "disciplined democracy", by which the army would still retain much power. And then in 2008, it drafted a new constitution, which it had approved by a sham referendum. This is a very special constitution, through which the military is able to keep its very strong grip on national power. The army is reserved 25% of the parliamentary seats. And to change the constitution requires the votes of more than 75% of members of parliament.

The army also has the control over three powerful ministries, namely, defense, border affairs and home affairs. It nominates one of the two vice-presidents. And then there is the National Defense and Security Council which is the most powerful body in Myanmar, and can overrule the government. It has 11 members, six of whom come from the military. The military is so fearful of the popularity of Aung San Suu Kyi that it drafted a clause in the constitution that prevents her from becoming president. The clause bars anyone with a foreign spouse or children from occupying this position.

Myanmar's military dictatorship surprised the world by holding elections in 2010. These elections were however boycotted by the NLD and were won decisively by the Union Solidarity and Development Party (USDP), the main military-backed political party. The military government was thus replaced by a new military-backed civilian government led by President Thein Sein, a former military officer. Although the elections were dismissed as a sham by the international community, they paved the way for gradual political and economic reforms, and opening up of the country.

One week after the elections, Aung San Suu Kyi was released from house arrest, and agreed to cooperate with the government. And responding to public opinion, in 2011 the President suspended construction of a controversial Chinese funded hydroelectric dam. Reforms included the release of many political and other prisoners, and child soldiers. Freedom of association for trade unions was authorized, media censorship was relaxed, and ceasefire agreements were signed with eight major non-state ethnic groups, even though conflicts continue with groups like the Kachin, Shan and Wa.

Economic reforms included liberalization of foreign investment, privatization of state-owned enterprises, anti-corruption measures and exchange rate reform. Thanks to the opening up of the telecommunications sector, virtually everyone can now have a smartphone and Internet access. But most of the benefits of reforms have gone to urban centers like Yangon. The military and their cronies have benefited greatly from privatization and infrastructure contracts. Rural Myanmar, where some 70% of the population lives and where poverty is endemic, has been forgotten. Indeed, farmers have suffered from rising prices and land grabbing. The gap between rich and poor in Myanmar is massive.

In 2012, the NLD members, including Aung San Suu Kyi, won 43 out 45 seats in landmark parliamentary by-elections. In the same year, Barack Obama became the first US president to visit Myanmar, following a visit by Secretary of State Hillary Clinton the previous year. The US and the EU began easing many sanctions. But also in 2012, there was a wave of atrocious human rights abuses, allegedly with government complicity, against the Rohingya, a Muslim minority in the Rakhine state. More than 100,000 Rohingya became displaced people, living in refugee camps, and very many also became victims of human smuggling and trafficking, an issue we look at in Chap. 8. Most regrettably, Aung San Suu Kyi was silent on this issue, fearing a backlash from the extreme Buddhist nationalists. In 2017, the Rohingya were again victims of cruel violence from the Myanmar military. In the words of UN human rights chief Zeid Raad Al Hussein, this "seems a textbook example of ethnic cleansing". More than 600,000 Rohingya fled to Bangladesh.

In November 2015, general elections were held. The NLD won landslide majorities in both houses of parliament, with about 80% of the votes cast. According to most observers, Myanmar's elections were a resounding success, free and relatively fair. Over 6000 parliamentary candidates from 93 political parties contested the elections (but Muslim candidates were excluded from NLD lists). The outgoing president handed over power peacefully. And the head of the army, Min Aung Hlaing, supported the country's transition. Mr. Htin Kyaw, a long-term confidante of Aung San Suu Kyi, was appointed president. The army refused Miss Suu Kyi's lobbying to change the constitution to allow her to become president. She was thus appointed minister of the prime minister's office and foreign minister, as well as "state counselor", a position which she has indicated will be "above the president".

The hybrid civilian-military nature of the new government was highlighted by the remarks of army head Mr. Min Aung Hlaing at a parade on 27 March 2016 when he reminded Myanmar's citizens that the army "ensure[s] the stability of the country" and "has to be present in a leading role in national politics." Thant Myint-U, an historian from Myanmar, summed up the situation neatly when he said this "was not an election of a government. It was an election for a spot in a shared government with the army."

What motivated Myanmar's surprising political changes? There has been much debate and speculation about the reasons for Myanmar's surprising political changes. It seems clear that sanctions imposed by the US, EU and other countries on Myanmar's military regime had little impact. If anything, the sanctions may have hardened the resolve of the regime. As Joshua Kurlantzick and many others have argued, Myanmar's "new openness may stem from leaders' fear that they had grown too dependent on Beijing."[35] Myanmar "was becoming virtually a Chinese client state, with Beijing offering a rich source of trade, aid, investment, and diplomatic cover for Myanmar's military regime". Democratization was the only way of resuscitating relations with the US and the EU, and thus breaking the hold of China's suffocating embrace. "China sort of looks at the country as a province of China, in their sphere of influence", said Priscilla Clapp, a former US chief of mission in Myanmar.[36]

Another factor is that Myanmar's highly unpopular military rulers may have judged that a gradual reform process could enable them to retain their ill-gotten gains, and position of economic and political dominance, and avoid the risks of a more violent popular upheaval that several Middle East countries experienced during the Arab Spring. In this regard, Myanmar's military has been brilliantly successful. It has greatly improved public support. It has achieved an end to many sanctions and its pariah status. At the same time, the military has maintained its dominant control of the country, and has been benefiting greatly from the opening of the economy. This has been called by some as "democracy on a leash". Nevertheless, Myanmar and the lives of many of its citizens have changed immeasurably these past few years.

An optimistic scenario for Myanmar would be that continued economic development and an emerging middle class would eventually lead pressures for full democracy. A great risk for the country, however, will be the transition to a post Aung San Suu Kyi era. She is 70 years old, and despite her saintly aura, she is far from immortal. Myanmar's new politicians have no experience whatsoever in governing, and are not well placed to succeed her. (In point of fact, Aung San Suu Kyi herself has no experience in governing.) Thus, another realistic scenario is that Myanmar descends into political instability following her eventual passing, and that the military reasserts great control over the country. And it is still not clear that Myanmar's government and military will be able to achieve durable peace with the countries many armed ethnic groups.

Myanmar's new government faces immense challenges as the military dictatorship has left the country in a deplorable state. Despite rapid economic growth over the past decade or so, Myanmar's GDP per capita is still one of the very lowest in Asia. It has the highest poverty rate in Southeast Asia. The country's infrastructure and overall competitiveness would be among the worst in the world, and it is still one of the very most difficult countries in which to do business.

Economic wealth and power are concentrated among the army elite and their cronies. Myanmar would be one of the world's very most corrupt countries, and is one of the weakest countries when it comes to the rule of law. Myanmar is also a major center in Asia's narcotic trade, being an important source of opium and exporter of heroin, second only to Afghanistan. And since the mid-1990s, it has also become a regional source for amphetamine-type stimulants.

In short, the government faces the daunting task of trying to manage three systemic transitions—from conflict toward peace, authoritarianism toward democracy and closed economy toward an open economy. Even in the most optimistic of scenarios, it would take several decades for Myanmar to even catch up with its Southeast Asian neighbors.

The greatest challenge that the government faces is that of working with the military, which still retains great power, and is not accountable to any civilian authority. Unfortunately, a very large share of the government budget is spent on the military, at a time when it is necessary to invest massively in education, health and infrastructure. Recalibrating Myanmar's relationship with China will also be essential. While Myanmar had become overly dependent on China, cooperation with China has holds great promise for the economy, given their shared border, and Myanmar's rich endowment of natural resources, low-cost labor and access to the Indian Ocean. And with the Trump administration distracted elsewhere, China is seizing the opportunity to rebuild good relations with the Myanmar government, especially through the peace process with ethnic minorities. Lastly, great patience will be necessary, together with managing high expectations of a public who have suffered repression and lack of opportunity for over six decades.

## Naïve Appeal of Authoritarian Government

As we have argued in this chapter, democracy has very shallow roots and many enemies in Asia. But does it really matter? After all, authoritarian states like China and Singapore, as well as Korea and Taiwan before they democratized, have achieved much superior economic development than chaotic democracies like India and the Philippines. Could a "good dictatorship" a much more effective path to prosperity than democracy?

It is true that Asia has seen some "good dictators" who have been able to rush their countries up the development ladder by enlightened leadership. But a key element of their leadership has also been expanding economic freedom, such that they are often less authoritarian than they are portrayed. Also they made efforts to share the benefits of development with their citizens through education, health and other social policies. The most notable examples are Singapore's Lee Kuan Yew, China's Deng Xiaoping, Korea's Park Chung-hee, Taiwan's Chiang Kai-shek and Malaysia's Mohamad Mahathir.

But Asia has also had more than its fair share of bad dictators notably China's Mao Zedong, the military generals in Myanmar and Pakistan, and the Kim family in North Korea. And once bad dictators are in power, it can be very difficult to remove them and they can do immense damage along the way. Even after the horrors of the Great Leap Forward and the Cultural Revolution, our Chinese friends had to await the death of Mao to be rid of his murderous regime. Despite widespread agreement on Mao's many mistakes, he remains a very important symbol of the Communist Party in Xi Jinping's China. And as President Xi Jinping increasingly centralizes power, it is still not clear whether he will be a good or bad dictator. Repression at home and aggression abroad may not be a winning strategy.

Asia has also had some dictators who started strong, like the Philippines' Marcos and Indonesia's Suharto, but whose regimes deteriorated over time in terms of corruption and human rights. As dictators age, and their regimes hang on, it can be difficult for them to control the rapacious behavior of their families and cronies. Indeed, corruption which is difficult to control in any society is usually very much worse in non-democratic countries, as evidenced in the very low rankings of North Korea, Cambodia, Myanmar, Laos, Vietnam and China in Transparency International's Corruptions Perceptions Index.

Even the poster child for Asian benevolent dictatorship, Singapore, is facing its own challenges. Living in one of the world's very richest countries, Singapore's citizens should have every reason to be happy with their lot. Nevertheless, the People's Action Party (PAP), a creation of Lee Kuan Yew, which has governed since Singapore's independence, still goes to great lengths to win elections and retain its grip on power. The PAP "uses legal harassment to deter opposition leaders from seeking office, as well as the redrawing of district boundaries to minimize support for the opposition", as Freedom House reports.[37] And opposition parties are constrained by "a ban on political films and television programs, the threat of defamation suits, strict regulations on political associations, and the PAP's influence on the media and the courts … All domestic newspapers, radio stations, and television channels are owned by companies linked to the government." Bloggers are increasingly subject to legal suits and criminal charges. One outrageous case was that of Roy Ngerng Yi Ling who was ordered to pay over $10,000 in defamation damages to the prime minister for alleging corruption in the management of Singapore's retirement savings plan.

Although Singapore's elections have always been won by the PAP, to its great displeasure, the PAP's share of the national vote fell from over 75% in 2001 to barely 60% in 2011. Singapore's brilliant technocrats, who had engineered the Singaporean miracle, began to stumble and seemed aloof and out of touch with their "client population." Public concerns included the dramatic increase in immigration, a straining infrastructure, housing shortages, yawning inequality, and rising poverty. In a sign that the "House of Singapore" was nervous, the government called a snap election in September 2015, one year ahead of schedule, and with only nine days for campaigning. It was clearly seeking to exploit the wave of patriotism evident in the mourning of the passing of Lee Kwan Yew six months earlier ("the LKY effect"), and the extravagant celebrations of the 50th anniversary of Singapore's independence just one month before. The government was also seeking to "cash-in" on its policies to respond to popular concerns, like restricting migration and increasing social benefits. The government's strategy was very successful, as the PAP won a resounding victory, with some 70% of the popular vote.

Despite the PAP's impressive comeback, the next phase in Singapore's political development could be problematic. The PAP's current leader is Lee Hsien Loong, the son of Lee Kuan Yew, who has led the country since

2004, and will retire in the coming years, and there is no obvious replacement. At the same time, infighting has broken out in the Lee family over Lee Kuan Yew's estate, and in particular his family home. Lee Kuan Yew stated in his last will that it should be demolished after his death. Prime Minister Lee Hsien Loong has, however, been pushing to preserve it as a monument, against the wishes of his two younger siblings. In a statement on Facebook, these siblings declared they no longer trusted Lee Hsien Loong as a brother and a leader. "We have lost confidence in him," the pair said. They also claimed that they "have felt threatened by Hsien Loong's misuse of his position and influence over the Singapore government and its agencies to drive his personal agenda".

While this affair may seem like a mere bagatelle, it has captivated Singapore's citizens who are used to highly disciplined and strait-laced leadership from the Lee family. It also highlights how problematic even the most efficient family dictatorships can be. History, like that of Spain under Franco, shows that the passing of heroic leaders can be the moment for a decisive move toward democracy. No-one can replace people like Franco or Lee Kwan Yew. Prime Minister Lee Hsien Loong would be wise to open up Singapore's repressive system, and allow a real democracy to flourish, as Korea and Taiwan did. The PAP would likely continue to win elections, at least for many years.

## Why Democracy Matters, Even in Asia

The real lesson from Asia's successful economies like Japan, Korea, Taiwan, Singapore, Hong Kong and post-Mao China is that they all had strong, effective and meritocratic states, which built up their economies and shared the benefits of economic development with their citizens. It was not political repression that produced economic development. But even these states are now being challenged as societies are modernizing rapidly, and inequality is growing. Moreover, mature innovation-driven economies require a different type of governance from catch-up economies. Fundamentally, there is a great risk of political breakdown when the institutions of governance in authoritarian societies do not adapt sufficiently.

In this regard, there are many reasons why democracy matters for Asian development, even in China and Singapore. Continued economic development over time requires a process of creative destruction whereby new firms with new ideas and technologies can take a leading role in the economy, as firms that were successful in the past, but are no longer competitive, fade in importance or go bankrupt.[38] But creative destruction can be inhibited in authoritarian systems where there are close links between established business and political powers which protect inefficient companies, such as in China where state-owned enterprises and banks still play an important role in the economy. In short, a level playing field is necessary to foster creative destruction, and this is much more likely under an open democratic system.

In a similar vein, open democratic societies are more conducive to creativity and innovation, which are the principal drivers of all mature economies. As Michael Schuman has argued, "In order to be innovative, you need full access to information, a confidence to speak your mind and a willingness to take risks. Fear caused by political control doesn't foster an atmosphere conducive to free thinking."[39] Democratization in Korea has played a key role in enabling it to become a more innovative nation.

People like Lady Gaga, Mark Zuckerberg and Steve Jobs would find life difficult in China, as does Chinese artist Ai Weiwei who has spent long periods of time under house arrest for his politically inspired art. "Xi Jinping praises innovation in the abstract, but China's system is not set up to encourage innovation in practice" says Kerry Brown.[40]

Maintaining authoritarian regimes is also very, very costly. For example, social repression is very widespread in China, with typical targets being ethnic minorities like the Uighurs and Tibetans, journalists, academics, lawyers and artists. The upshot is that China spends more money on internal security than its military. Despite its friendly veneer, Singapore also invests vast resources controlling its society.

Non-democratic political systems are also prone to unstable leadership and regime transitions, which can be very destabilizing. In the past, this was a great problem in China. The country may have partly solved this issue by limiting presidents to two five-year terms. But even today, it is still a problem in China, where President XI Jinping has felt the need to eliminate his opposition figures in order to "consolidate power"—a process which has been underway ever since he took over the leadership, and with no immediate end in sight. And there are already signs that Xi Jinping may be planning to remain at the leadership of China after two-term limit. This shows that authoritarian regimes like China are fundamentally more fragile than they might appear. In contrast, Prime Minister Narendra Modi had a very smooth transition to power in India thanks to the country's democratic institutions.

Perhaps the most important reason why democracy matters is that, even if many upper- and middle-class Asians are happy with their lot, growing numbers of Asians, especially youth, are demanding freedom, rule of law, clean governance and democracy. You only have to look at the activism today in Hong Kong, Korea, Malaysia, Taiwan and Thailand, as well as many parts of China. And a simple conversation with a poor person in the street in India will reveal how proud Indians feel about their democracy, especially when compared with the case of China.

\* \* \*

One of the many consequences of Asia's flawed politics is that the region has become one of the centers of the global criminal economy. In the next chapter, we review Asia's involvement in counterfeiting and piracy, illegal drug production and trafficking, environmental crime, human trafficking and smuggling, corruption, money laundering and cybercrime.

## Notes

1. openDemocracy. An artist's duty: an interview with Ai Weiwei, 6 January 2014.
2. Economist Intelligence Unit. Democracy Index 2016: Revenge of the deplorables.
3. Reporters Without Borders. 2017 World Press Freedom Index.
4. Lipset, Seymour Martin. Some Social Requisites of Democracy: Economic Development and Political Legitimacy. The American Political Science Review Vol. 53, No. 1 (Mar., 1959), pp. 69–105.
5. Inglehart, Ronald and Christian Welzel. How Development Leads to Democracy: What We Know About Modernization. Foreign Affairs, March/April 2009.
6. Gurria, Angel. The OECD and Korea: Celebrating a milestone. OECD Observer, October 2016.
7. de Mesquita, Bruce Bueno and George W. Downs. Development and Democracy. Foreign Affairs, September/October 2005.
8. OECD. International Migration Outlook 2012.
9. Kurlantzick, Joshua. Southeast Asia's Regression from Democracy and Its Implications. Council on Foreign Relations, May 2014.
10. US Department of State. Country Reports on Human Rights Practices for 2015.
11. Xinhua. China issues report on U.S. human rights, 9 March 2017.
12. New Perspectives Quarterly. The China Model: A Dialogue between Francis Fukuyama and Zhang Weiwei. Fall 2011.

13. Fallows, James. China's Great Leap Backward. The Atlantic, December 2016.
14. Human Rights Watch. World Report 2016.
15. Goebel, Christian, and Lynette H. Ong. Social Unrest in China. Europe China Research and Advice Network, August 2012.
16. Chang, Gordon G. (2001). The Coming Collapse of China.
17. Pei, Minxin. 5 Ways China Could Become a Democracy. The Diplomat, 13 February 2013.
18. Pei, Minxin. Xi's war on corruption could hasten Chinese Communist Party's fall. Nikkei Asian Review, 4 June 2015.
19. Shambaugh, David (2016). China's Future.
20. West, John. Kim Dae-jung: A tribute. OECD Observer, November 2009.
21. Freedom House. Freedom in the World 2016.
22. Johnston, Donald. J. To the Miracle on the Han. OECD Observer, October 2016.
23. Reporters Without Borders. 2016 World Press Freedom Index.
24. Trade Union Advisory Committee to the OECD (TUAC). 20TH Anniversary of Korean OECD membership overshadowed by labour rights and freedom of assembly violations.
25. Denney, Steven. South Korea at a Crossroads. The Diplomat, 24 February 2017.
26. Villaseca, Matias. Bonsai Democracy: Looking Into the Evolution of Japan's Government. Research Discourse, Spring 2011.
27. The National Diet of Japan (2012). The official report of The Fukushima Nuclear Accident Independent Investigation Commission.
28. Repeta, Lawrence. Japan's Democracy at Risk—The LDP's Ten Most Dangerous Proposals for Constitutional Change. The Asia-Pacific Journal, Vol. 11, Issue 28, No. 3, 15 July 2013.
29. Sugimoto, Yoshio (2010). An Introduction to Japanese Society.
30. West, John. Is the Philippines about to realise its FDI potential? FDI-Intelligence, 1 December 2015.
31. US Department of State. Philippines 2015 Crime and Safety Report.
32. Heydarian, Richard Javad. The Philippines and America: A Tale of Two (Troubled) Democracies. The World Post, 24 October 2016.
33. OECD. Programme for International Student Assessment, 2015 Results.
34. Brookings. Kingdom at a crossroads: Thailand's uncertain political trajectory, 24 February 2016.
35. Kurlantzick, Joshua. The Mysterious Opening of Myanmar. Council on Foreign Relations, 4 December 2011.
36. Brookings. The struggle for democracy in Myanmar/Burma, 14 July 2015.
37. Freedom House. Freedom in the World 2016.

38. Acemoğlu, Daron, and James A. Robinson (2012). Why Nations Fail.
39. Schuman, Michael. Is democracy necessary for economic success? Time, 5 November 2010.
40. Brown, Kerry. Why China Can't Innovate. The Diplomat, 19 August 2014.

**Open Access** This chapter is licensed under the terms of the Creative Commons Attribution 4.0 International License (http://creativecommons.org/licenses/by/4.0/), which permits use, sharing, adaptation, distribution, and reproduction in any medium or format, as long as you give appropriate credit to the original author(s) and the source, provide a link to the Creative Commons license and indicate if changes were made.

The images or other third party material in this chapter are included in the chapter's Creative Commons license, unless indicated otherwise in a credit line to the material. If material is not included in the chapter's Creative Commons license and your intended use is not permitted by statutory regulation or exceeds the permitted use, you will need to obtain permission directly from the copyright holder.

CHAPTER 9

# Combating Asia's Economic Crime

We all enjoy buying fake Rolex watches, Nike shoes, Ray Ban sunglasses and Louis Vuitton handbags, as well as carvings from trafficked ivory, when we travel to China or Hong Kong. Some of our youth have fun experimenting with recreational drugs on their holidays to Bali or elsewhere.

But production and trade of counterfeit, pirated and other illicit goods are very serious matters. Such dirty business can endanger lives. Some of the traps are fake pharmaceuticals that make people sick or contribute to global microbial resistance and more virulent forms of disease, toys that harm children, baby formula that provides no nourishment or even endangers babies' health, medical instruments that deliver false readings and automobile parts that fail. Wildlife trafficking can destroy biodiversity and can trigger the spread of zoonotic disease, while a recreational drug habit is easier to start than to stop.

In addition, fake goods undermine our economy and employment as innovative individuals and companies see their good work stolen. Counterfeiting and piracy can impose additional costs for security and anti-counterfeiting technology, and affected companies can incur reputational damages. This robs them of their competitive advantage and discourages future efforts in innovation, thereby compromising long-term prosperity.

Organized criminal groups play an increasingly important role in the production and trade of fake, and other illicit goods, especially narcotics and wildlife products. Some profits from illicit trade finance terrorism and

© The Author(s) 2018
J. West, *Asian Century... on a Knife-edge*,
https://doi.org/10.1007/978-981-10-7182-9_9

other nefarious activities. Narcotics trade is one of the primary sources of revenue of the Taliban. Dirty trade also robs governments of tax revenues, results in regulatory and enforcement costs and undermines the integrity of public institutions.

Illicit trade has prospered alongside the rapid globalization of the world economy and represents the "dark side" of globalization as criminal groups often exploit states with weak capacity, law and institutions. And East Asia's vast number of special economic zones, which have very limited government regulation, are very fertile ground for illicit trade of all sorts.

In short, as Asia progressively becomes a major player in the global economy, so it is that Asia is at the center of the scourge of economic crime, and not only illicit trade.[1] In this chapter, we will examine several of the very many aspects of economic crime in Asia, namely counterfeiting and piracy, illegal drug production and trafficking in Asia environmental crimes, human trafficking and smuggling, corruption, money laundering and cybercrime.

## COUNTERFEITING AND PIRACY

Getting a handle on the production of counterfeit, pirated and other illicit goods is not easy. But the Organisation for Economic Co-operation and Development (OECD) has recently published two excellent reports that have estimates of international trade in such goods.[2,3] First, we look at counterfeit and pirated goods. The OECD estimates that world imports of counterfeit and pirated goods were worth $461 billion in 2013 or nearly half a trillion dollars. This amounts to around 2.5% of global imports, significantly higher than an estimate of $250 billion or 1.8% in an earlier 2009 study. This means that national and international efforts to tackle this problem have not been effective. In the case of the European Union (EU), up to 5% of imports are fakes. And since advanced countries are prime targets for fake imports, the US figure might be of a similar order.

China (including Hong Kong) is far and away the world's single biggest producer and exporter of counterfeit and pirated goods (including pharmaceuticals), accounting for 84% of estimated trade in fake goods. By comparison, China's share of global manufactured exports in 2013 was only 17%. China's e-commerce company, Alibaba, is notorious for its sale of counterfeit products. China is way ahead of the next most guilty country, which is Turkey with 3%. Four other Asian countries made into the top ten of offending countries, namely Singapore, Thailand, India and Pakistan.

But the reality of counterfeiting and piracy is much wider, as the OECD notes. Its study only deals with internationally traded counterfeit and pirated goods. It does not treat the issue of fake goods which are produced and sold within the same domestic market. There are millions of Asians and others who purchase counterfeit and pirated goods produced at home. This is a lower risk activity for the purveyors of fake goods, as it avoids customs controls. Furthermore, the OECD's estimate does not cover pirated digital products that are distributed via the Internet, which is a further drain on the formal economy. It only covers all physical counterfeit goods, which infringe trademarks, design rights or patents, and tangible pirated products, which breach copyright. As the OECD says, its data are largely "incomplete and limited", just like data on any clandestine activity. Its quantitative results only illustrate "certain parts of the phenomenon of counterfeiting and piracy".

Fake products crop up in everything from luxury items (like fashion apparel or deluxe watches), via intermediary products (such as machines, spare parts or chemicals) to consumer goods that have an impact on personal health and safety (such as pharmaceuticals, food and drink, medical equipment, or toys). While footwear is the most copied item, trademarks are infringed even on things like strawberries and bananas. And according to the United Nations Office on Drugs and Crime (UNODC), one-third of malaria medicines used in East Asia and sub-Saharan Africa are fake.

How does trade in counterfeit goods happen? Postal parcels are the top method of shipping fake goods, accounting for 62% of seizures over 2011–2013, reflecting the growing importance of E-commerce in international trade. Indeed, E-commerce has become a "major enabler for the distribution and sale of counterfeit and pirated tangible goods" according to the OECD.

Traffic in counterfeit and pirated goods usually goes through complex routes via major trade hubs like Hong Kong and Singapore and free trade zones such as those in the United Arab Emirates. Other transit points include countries with weak governance and widespread organized crime such as Afghanistan and Syria, but trade routes can change greatly from year to year as counterfeit gangs spot new weak points. In many cases, the proceeds of counterfeit trade go toward organized crime which are also involved in trafficking drugs, firearms and people.

The top countries whose companies had their intellectual property rights infringed were the US, whose brands or patents were affected by 20% of the knock-offs, then Italy with 15% and France and Switzerland with 12% each. Japan and Germany stood at 8% each followed by the UK and Luxembourg at 4% and 3% respectively. With China still being more of a copycat, rather than an innovation, nation, Chinese companies which suffered from fake production represented only 1% of total.

Massive efforts are required to promote "clean trade". National governments need to implement and enforce effective legislation, and to cooperate with other governments and international organizations, given the global nature of the problem. A multi-stakeholder approach involving partnerships with relevant business and civil society groups (including consumer protection advocates) is also necessary. In addition, educational and public awareness campaigns can play an important role.

But there are many factors which make tackling counterfeiting and piracy a daunting task, especially in the case where products are obviously fakes or even presented on the market as being fakes. After all, there is a strong demand for such goods in all our countries, especially by our youth. Why? Prices are usually much lower than for the genuine article and depending on the product, quality of the fake article can also be satisfactory. In this context, the growing gap between rich and poor and rising poverty in advanced OECD countries are just some of the factors driving such demand, especially when the risk of being prosecuted is usually low. Ignorance of the safety and security risks of consuming fake goods can be another factor.

What is much more worrying is the case where fake products are presented as being genuine, but their apparent high-quality results in consumers being deceived. In these circumstances, people unwittingly purchase counterfeit and pirated goods and are involuntarily exposed to the full range of product safety and security risks. The very big money to be made from counterfeit and pirated goods also means that implementing regulation and legislation, and especially their enforcement, remains a gigantic challenge. The criminal organizations behind today's counterfeiting and piracy are very nimble. In addition, with intellectual property playing an ever-growing role in our economies, there are more and more opportunities to produce counterfeit and pirated goods.

It was hoped that following China's membership of the World Trade Organisation in 2001, and rapid economic development, the Chinese government would begin to take intellectual property protection more seriously. Indeed, it is natural that improvements in institutions and governance in middle-income countries follow behind economic development. And as innovation becomes a more important component of China's growth story, it should have an interest in protecting intellectual property.

But despite repeated promises by government leaders, this has manifestly not occurred. Indeed, many Chinese officials seem to show no shame for their country's counterfeiting and piracy. As it seemingly pursues a grudge match against the West for its sufferings through its "century of humiliation", counterfeiting and piracy of Western products is often considered to be fair game. And with the Chinese economy currently struggling, and President Xi Jinping pushing a highly nationalist agenda, we cannot expect the Chinese government to invest much effort into protecting Western intellectual property.

One day, we may hope that China will become an innovation powerhouse, and will therefore have a stake in fighting counterfeiting and piracy. But even if China does eventually lift its game on counterfeit and pirated goods, it might well be replaced by India or Russia as the global capital for counterfeiting and piracy. International crime syndicates are very quick to change their business plans in response to new circumstances. Beyond counterfeit and pirated goods, there is a vast array of other illicit trade such as drug trafficking, and trade in wildlife, timber, art & cultural property, human organs, arms, diamonds, weapons, tobacco and alcohol. In the next section, we review drug trafficking, an area where Asia plays a major role on global markets.

## ILLEGAL DRUG PRODUCTION AND TRAFFICKING IN ASIA

Asia has long attracted recreational drug tourism to take advantage of opium and heroin produced in its infamous "Golden Triangle" region, spanning Myanmar, Laos and Thailand. But the region is now also following the Western world's descent into a drug crisis, as the consumption and production of methamphetamine grow rapidly. East and Southeast Asia may also be emerging as driver of the global market for "ecstasy". In short, Asia is a major player in this global drug trade, which was estimated at $320 billion in 2011 by Global Financial Integrity.[4] Indeed, global trade in illegal narcotics is perhaps the single largest black market worldwide and finances notorious transnational criminal organizations. Narcotics have an adverse impact on human health and well-being, while drug trafficking is usually accompanied by criminal violence that undermines state institutions and is often difficult to reverse.

Let's look at a few country cases, drawing on material from the US State Department's excellent International Narcotics Control Strategy Report,[5] and other sources.[6]

Myanmar is a major source of opium and exporter of heroin, second only to Afghanistan. Since the mid-1990s, Myanmar has also become a regional source for amphetamine-type stimulants. Production sites for heroin and methamphetamine are often co-located and are primarily situated along Myanmar's eastern borders in areas controlled by ethnic armed groups beyond the government's control. A general lack of capacity and resources hinders counternarcotics efforts, which are also hampered by extremely porous borders with India, Laos, China, Bangladesh and Thailand that continue to be exploited by traffickers. There are also informal reports that some senior government officials benefit financially from narcotics trafficking, and credible reports from NGOs and media that mid-level military officers and government officials are engaged in drug-related corruption.

Myanmar's northeastern neighbor, Laos is a major transport hub for amphetamine-type stimulants, opium and heroin, and is a major producer of opium. Indeed, the country sits at the heart of the regional drug trade in mainland Southeast Asia and shares remote and poorly controlled borders with Burma, Thailand, Cambodia, Vietnam and China. The US State Department reports that, ironically, economic development and the improvement in Laos' transportation infrastructure have created opportunities for the illicit drug trade to grow. Like Myanmar, Laos lacks the necessary capacity and resources to tackle narcotics production and trade, and corruption in Laos continues to plague law enforcement and government.

Highlighting the regional nature of Southeast Asia's illicit drug production and trade, crackdowns on drug trafficking in Thailand and China in recent years have pushed traffickers to use alternate routes, including through Cambodia. Indeed, the manufacturing, trafficking and use of illicit narcotics within Cambodia have escalated. Thailand and Vietnam are illicit drug transshipment points for local and international criminal organizations, while Indonesia is both a transshipment point and destination country for illegal drugs. Indonesia is a significant consumer of cannabis, methamphetamine and heroin.

Drug trafficking through Malaysia to supply both domestic and regional markets remains a problem. Nigerian and Iranian drug trafficking organizations continue to use Kuala Lumpur as a trafficking hub. The Philippines remains a transshipment point and destination country for large shipments of methamphetamine, with the trade being dominated by Chinese drug trafficking organizations.

China, which shares borders with most of the aforementioned Southeast Asian countries, is a significant destination and transit country for illicit drugs, as well as a major producer of synthetic drugs and drug precursor chemicals. Heroin is the most abused drug in China followed by synthetic drugs. Ethnic Chinese criminal groups control most large-scale drug and precursor chemical criminal activities in China, while there are a large and increasing number of transnational criminal organizations from other countries operating in China. North Korea is also believed to be a major source of methamphetamine in China. The Chinese government is making efforts to tackle its drug problem. However, the US State Department reports that China's collaborative law enforcement efforts with US law enforcement officials are often hindered by cumbersome bureaucracy that limits direct access to local Chinese counterparts.

As with counterfeiting and privacy, tackling Asia's illegal drug production and trafficking requires a multi-pronged strategy attacking both the demand and supply side of Asia's drug problem. Strong legislation and enforcement, buttressed by international cooperation, is necessary to tackle the traffickers who run the drug business. Demand reduction strategies must focus on the prevention of drug use, and treatment and rehabilitation of drug users.

But there is also the situation of the poor farmers who grow opium or cocaine because they are their only potential source of income. This is why it is also necessary to implement "alternative development" strategy which can provide sustainable alternative livelihoods to communities that cultivate illicit drug crops. As the UNODC has said the reality is that "drug crop growing areas are mostly areas where isolation and poverty are inherent and where farmers cultivate illicit drug crops because they are unable to obtain sufficient income from legal activities due to lack of markets, conflict, marginal land and absence of basic infrastructures." Indeed, there are hundreds of thousands of farmers affected by poverty, food insecurity, lack of land, instability who as a result engage in illicit drug cultivation.

Alternative development has brought about a significant decline in poppy cultivation in Thailand, which now accounts for only a negligible portion of total global opium cultivation, according to UNODC figures. The UNODC now supports and promotes sustainable alternative development programs and projects in countries like Laos and Myanmar. The focus is on helping small farmers with licit income generation activities to reduce their dependency on income from opium. But much more needs to be done, and much greater donor support is necessary.

## Environmental Crime

Keeping up with the Jones (or perhaps the Chans) is very much the obsession of Asia's nouveau riche, especially from China, Thailand and Vietnam. So what better thing to do than buying works of art made from precious elephant ivory. To feed your sophisticated appetite, some scaly anteater (pangolin), marine turtle or shark meat and fin are delicious. And to stay healthy, why not a dose of traditional medicine made from rhinoceros horn.

It is not surprising then that wildlife trafficking is now one of the most lucrative criminal activities, along with the global trade in narcotics, arms, counterfeits and humans. And it has more than doubled since 2007, reports the OECD. Sub-Saharan Africa has been the region most affected by Asia's rapacious appetite for wildlife. But it is not the only region affected. For example, Asian elephants, rhinos and big cat skins (tiger, leopard, snow leopard) are also suffering greatly from poaching.

According to the United Nation's Convention on International Trade in Endangered Species, some 1215 rhinos were killed in South Africa in 2014, a record high and ten-times the number of rhinos killed for their horn in 2009. In the last three years, poachers have killed 100,000 African elephants. The slaughter of wildlife is not just a matter of conserving biodiversity. In some countries, the reserves where these animals live are important sources of tourism revenues and employment. But tackling wildlife trafficking in sub-Saharan Africa is a daunting undertaking, as governments have few resource to patrol massive tracts of land. Violent confrontation with poachers also occurs regularly.

Wildlife trafficking is just one of the many forms of environmental crime that is endangering our planet and livelihoods.[7] Other environmental crimes include smuggling of ozone-depleting substances (ODS); illicit trade in hazardous waste; illegal, unregulated, and unreported fishing; and illegal logging and the associated trade in stolen timber. Root causes are primarily the low risks and high profits in a permissive environment as a result of poor governance and widespread corruption, minimal budgets to police, prosecution and courts, inadequate institutional support, political interference and low employee morale, minimal benefits to local communities and rising demand in particular in Asia.

The UN and Interpol estimate that environmental crime is now in the range of \$91–\$258 billion, 26% higher than the estimate of two years ago, and that it is growing at two to three times the pace of the global economy. More than half of this is due to illegal logging and deforestation.

Indonesia's rainforests have been victims of massive illegal logging since the late 1990s, and Indonesia has had the highest rate of deforestation in the world, with China's booming wooden flooring industry being a major beneficiary.[8] At one point, 80% of timber coming out of Indonesia was illegal, costing the government \$4 billion a year, around five times the annual health budget. This rape and pillage of Indonesia's environment have been masterminded and financed by the country's "timber mafia" who have been effectively above the law, another example of the endemic corruption of Indonesia's oligarchic economy. In more recent years, government action has managed to reduce, but not eliminate illegal logging. But Chinese timber dealers have merely switched their sourcing to Africa, while Vietnamese dealers switched to neighboring Laos.

Asia is also involved in many other forms of environmental crime. In 2013, UNODC reported that illegal trade in E-waste (discarded electrical or electronic devices) to Southeast Asia and the Pacific was estimated at \$3.75 billion annually or 1.5 times larger than the illegal trade in wildlife in the region. There is a large illegal trade in ODS principally involving China. China is also a major market for illegally harvested West Africa Rosewood.

Despite the fact that environmental crime poses a growing threat, it remains a low priority for the international enforcement community. For example, China accounted for nearly 80% of the reported seizures of illegal rhino horns in Asia between 2009 and 2013, despite a national ban on the illicit trade. This is wrong. As disturbing as each form of environmental crime is, perhaps the most disturbing aspect is that modern crime entrepreneurs and syndicates are now increasingly diversifying into several illicit activities and are globalizing their operations through transnational criminal networks, as the OECD has noted.

For example, criminal syndicates involved in human trafficking might also be active in the drug trade, illegal fishing, environmental crimes, arms trafficking, maritime piracy and tobacco smuggling. Distribution chains for trafficking in counterfeit tobacco are sometimes used for counterfeit pharmaceuticals and counterfeit currency. This business of illicit trade is also facilitated by corruption through all its various phases, while the profits are then laundered through tax havens, like Asia's seemingly clean cities of Hong Kong and Singapore.

As the OECD concludes, "This level of sophistication presents a substantial challenge to government law enforcement agencies and international institutions that are often unable to cooperate as rapidly as criminals can adapt their business practices to avoid identification."

## Human Trafficking in Asia

Asia has long been a global hub for human trafficking and smuggling, perhaps the most heinous of all crimes. Motivated by greed, traffickers and smugglers exploit poor, vulnerable people. They are able to prosper where governments are weak or uncaring, and in societies where respect for human rights and dignity is shallow. Tragically, virtually all countries are to various degrees sources, transit points and destinations for human trafficking and smuggling. And the efforts of governments and civil society to combat these vices vary greatly from country to country.

Human trafficking can take many forms as traffickers move people without their informed consent and exploit them along the way or at their final destination. For example, a young Asian lady may sign a contract with a migration agency to work as a maid in Saudi Arabia, only to find that when she arrives at her destination that she is actually working in a massage parlor in Dubai, that she owes a large financial debt to the agency, and that the agency has confiscated her passport to entrap her.

The many forms of human trafficking include forced labor, debt bondage, involuntary domestic servitude, forced child labor, trafficking of children for armed conflict or petty crime or forced begging, trafficking for sex, forced marriage and trafficking for organ removal. And some groups are particularly vulnerable to human trafficking like LGBT individuals, indigenous persons, refugees, women and children. Trafficking can occur both within countries (notably in the case of India) and through labor migration especially to the Middle East, like the example above.

In more technical terms, the US State Department defines human trafficking as "the act of recruiting, harboring, transporting, providing, or obtaining a person for compelled labor or commercial sex acts through the use of force, fraud, or coercion".[9] Human smuggling is different in that smugglers help people, with their consent, illegally cross borders for a payment, as we discuss later on.

Some 30 million of the world's 46 million victims of human trafficking (often referred to as "modern slavery") come from Asia, according to the 2016 Global Slavery Index. India tops the global list with over 18 million victims of modern slavery. The challenge of human trafficking in India is immense, with all forms of modern slavery present, especially intergenerational bonded labor, trafficking for sexual exploitation and forced marriage. Some 90% of India's human trafficking occurs within the country, with members of lower castes and tribes, religious minorities and migrant workers being the most vulnerable. Forced labor is India's most prevalent form of trafficking, especially in industries like brick kilns, carpet weaving, embroidery and textiles, forced prostitution, agriculture, domestic servitude, mining and organized begging rings.

The next most important Asian locations for human trafficking are China with over three million and Pakistan with over two million. Bangladesh (1.5 million), North Korea (1.1 million) and Indonesia (0.7 Million) also make it into the world's top ten. It goes without saying that the actual figures are bound to be far higher than these estimates which probably only scratch the surface. The UN estimates that some 64% of human trafficking in Asia is for forced labor, servitude and slavery, while 26% is for sexual exploitation (in Europe and Central Asia the figures are the inverse).[10] In Asia, 36% of trafficked victims are children, while 64% are adults. Trafficking victims from Asia can be found all around the world. While 72% of convicted traffickers are men, the share of women is 28%, much higher than the share of women convicted of crimes in general (10–15%).

The International Labor Organization estimates the illicit profits of forced labor to be $150 billion a year.[11] Many victims work in Asia's global value chains for industries like food, garments and technology, including in middle-income countries like Malaysia. In short, modern slavery is big business. Most countries in the Asia-Pacific exhibit a range of preconditions for modern slavery including weak rule of law, corruption, high levels of poverty, along with highly mobile unskilled labor forces who are dependent on remittances. Only two Asian countries, South Korea and Taiwan, are making very serious efforts to combat human trafficking, along with most advanced Western countries, according to the US Department of State. Asia's most notorious cases for human trafficking are North Korea, Thailand, Malaysia and China.

In North Korea, forced labor is part of the government's political repression. Some 80,000–120,000 people are held in prison camps in remote areas where they are subject to forced labor. The government has also sent 50,000 or more laborers to countries like Russia and China to earn much needed foreign exchange for North Korea's atrocious government, but not for the workers themselves.

In Thailand, there are three to four million migrant workers, mainly from Myanmar, Laos and Cambodia, some of whom are forced, coerced or defrauded into labor or sex trafficking in sectors like the sex industry, commercial fishing, forced begging, domestic work, manufacturing and agriculture. Indeed, Thailand is still notorious for slavery, trafficking, murder and corruption at all levels of government in its billion-dollar fishing industry, despite recent arrests and the threat of an EU-wide boycott. And social media is being used to recruit children and women into sex trafficking.

There are reports that some Thai officials are complicit in trafficking crimes and corruption undermines anti-trafficking efforts. Migrant workers are fearful of reporting trafficking crimes due to a lack of trust in government officials and a lack of awareness of their rights. According to the US State Department, the Thai government is not making significant efforts to fully comply with the minimum standards for the elimination of trafficking.

Most of Malaysia's trafficking victims come from its more than four million documented and undocumented foreign workers who mainly come from Indonesia, Bangladesh, the Philippines, Nepal and Myanmar. Many are subjected to forced labor or debt bondage by their employers, employment agencies or labor recruiters. Authorities report that large organized crime syndicates are responsible for some instances of trafficking. There are also reports alleging that some corrupt officials impede efforts to address trafficking crimes. Rohingya and other refugees lack formal status or the ability to obtain legal work permits, thus leaving them vulnerable to trafficking.

In China, trafficking is most pronounced among the large internal migrant population, who can be subject to forced labor in brick kilns, coal mines and factories. Chinese women and girls are recruited from rural areas and taken to urban centers by crime syndicates and local gangs. There are also reports of young girls being kidnapped from Vietnam and other countries for forced marriage to Chinese men in light of the China's "gendercide", which has resulted in a high male/female birth ratio. Other countries like Cambodia, Laos, Myanmar, Pakistan and Sri Lanka are also among the world's worst offenders when it comes to human trafficking.

Even seemingly civilized countries like Japan, Hong Kong and Singapore have human trafficking horror stories to tell. Japan has long been notorious for human trafficking for its sex industry. And despite pressure from the international community, sex trafficking remains endemic in Japan. Many women and children travel to Japan from Asia (especially the Philippines and Thailand) and elsewhere for employment or fraudulent marriage and are subjected to forced prostitution in bars, clubs, brothels and massage parlors. Traffickers strictly control the movement of victims using debt bondage, threats of violence or deportation, blackmail and other coercive psychological methods. Japanese men are also notorious for their sex tourism in neighboring Asian countries.

In Hong Kong, which has one of the highest densities of migrant domestic workers in the world, forced labor and exploitation are widespread, despite the efforts of the government to sweep the problem under the carpet, according to the Hong Kong-based Justice Center.[12] Some 17% of its study sample is subject to forced labor, which means that some 50,000 of Hong Kong's migrant domestic workers could be subject to forced labor. According to all reports, the situation of migrant domestic workers is fairly similar in Singapore.

Most countries have laws and policies to protect possible victims and prosecute offenders from human trafficking. But overall, there are still very few convictions, highlighting the gross inadequacy of enforcement of these laws and policies. According to the UN, only 40% of countries reported having ten or more yearly convictions, with nearly 15% having no convictions at all. This is unbelievable given the prevalence of human trafficking in Asia. The 2016 Global Slavery Index has highlighted in particular the cases of Hong Kong, Japan, Malaysia and Singapore which are countries, despite their great wealth, have done little to respond to the challenge of human trafficking. As to Thailand and Indonesia, they appear to have strong responses on paper, but these are often poorly implemented or are hampered by high levels of corruption. In contrast, the Philippines is one country that, when national economic capacity is taken into account, is making strong efforts with limited resources.

At the regional level, there are also initiatives like the Coordinated Mekong Ministerial Initiative involving Cambodia, China, Laos, Myanmar, Thailand and Vietnam. And regional organizations like the Asian Development Bank (ADB) and United Nations Economic and Social Commission for Asia and the Pacific (UNESCAP) have human trafficking programs. But despite their good intentions, these initiatives rely on national governments for implementation and enforcement.

## Human Smuggling

Human smuggling is different from trafficking in that smugglers help people, with their consent, cross borders illegally for a payment, as we mentioned above. It is a very risky venture for these political and economic refugees in light of the uncertain welcome they receive at their destination. But even when they consent to being smuggled, many people also suffer great abuses at the hands of their nefarious smugglers who coerce, force or even abduct them into being smuggled, who don't inform them of the physical risks involved, and who abuse and extort them during their journey. Thus, most smuggled people also become victims of human trafficking as well, as many aspects of their journey are imposed without their consent.

Perhaps the most tragic cases of human smuggling in Asia are the Rohingya Muslims escaping persecution in Myanmar.[13] The Rohingya is an ethnic group of over million people living primarily in Myanmar's western Rakhine State. After decades of discrimination, the government stripped the Rohingya of their citizenship in 1982, leaving them stateless. The government considers them illegal migrants from Bangladesh, and refuses to use the word Rohingya. They are referred to as "Bengalis". Anti-Muslim propaganda has become part of the regular nationalistic discourse. Even Nobel Peace Prize winner Aung San Suu Kyi refuses to say anything in support of the Rohingya. There are now hundreds of thousands of Rohingya displaced in Bangladesh, Thailand, Malaysia and Indonesia.

Since 2012, the Rakhine state's Buddhist majority, assisted by religious leaders, government officials, and state security forces have engaged in widespread violence against the Rohingya, who are perhaps the world's most persecuted people.[14] Hundreds have been killed, and homes and businesses destroyed. There have been claims of ethnic cleansing and even genocide. Over 150,000 Rohingya now live in virtual concentration camps where they lack access to health care, education and employment. Efforts by international organizations and civil society to provide assistance are often impeded by Myanmar authorities. This situation has led many Rohingya to risk their lives and flee by boat to neighboring countries, usually Malaysia, facilitated by Myanmar security forces and human smugglers (some Bangladeshis escaping poverty at home are part of these boat trips). The UN High Commissioner for Refugees (UNHCR) estimates there have been 160,000 Rohingya maritime departures to neighboring countries since 2012.

They were typically transported to Thailand, where they were put in camps. Smugglers then demand a ransom before smuggling further by land to Malaysia. But if this extortion doesn't work, Rohingyas are often killed. A number of mass Rohingya graves have been found in Thailand and Malaysia. These smuggling operations are reportedly arranged through well-organized transnational networks of smugglers and traffickers, usually with the complicity or involvement of corrupt government officials.

The human tragedy of the Rohingya refugees reached a head in 2015.[15] Indonesia, Malaysia and Thailand towed smugglers' boats back out to sea. And when the Thai government announced a crackdown on smuggling in early 2015, many boats were abandoned at sea by their crews, leaving passengers at sea for weeks. Many Rohingya died. Eventually, following international criticism, Malaysia and Indonesia allowed the Rohingya to come ashore (Thailand refused), on the condition that they only stay one year, before being resettled in third countries. Since mid-2015, much fewer Rohingya have been leaving Myanmar, in part because of a crackdown on smugglers.

More recently, in 2017, the Rohingya have been victims of a cruel military operation that the UN human rights chief, Zeid Raad Al Hussein, said "seems a textbook example of ethnic cleansing". More than 600,000 Rohingya Muslims fled to neighboring Bangladesh.

The attitude of the Myanmar government toward the Rohingya population is reprehensible. The international community, which has been pressuring the government to be more humane, should be more forceful. But Myanmar is in the midst of a delicate transition to democracy, and the West is still seeking to woo the government away from the clutches of China.

The Rohingya refugee crisis cries out for effective regional cooperation to address the issue. Most regrettably, it has highlighted yet again how ineffectual Association of Southeast Nations (ASEAN) is when confronted with real challenges. Southeast Asian countries must cooperate to establish measures to combat human smuggling and trafficking, and to protect people from human rights abuses from smugglers and traffickers. A lot more could also be done at the national level. Both Thailand and Malaysia are experiencing labor shortages, and could readily absorb large inflows of Rohingya migrants.

The crisis also highlights the apparent unwillingness of China, which has not been visible at all, to make a positive contribution to Asian regional problems—despite its massive buildup of naval and other maritime assets in the region, and also despite its desire to be a regional hegemon in Asia.

Our brief overview of human trafficking and smuggling in Asia can only leave one feeling deeply despondent about Asia. Economic development without human development makes no sense. And Asia's human development lags well behind its spectacular economic development. In particular:

- Japan, the region's first economic mover, has never taken human trafficking and smuggling seriously, and is now moving backward through its bogus intern program.
- Hong Kong and Singapore, Asia's current leaders in terms of GDP per capita, treat their maids and other low-skilled migrants abominably.
- Malaysia and Thailand are two economies that have enjoyed great economic success, but are at the bottom of the barrel in terms of human trafficking and smuggling.
- China has pretensions of becoming a great power, but is totally bereft of ethical and moral leadership when it comes to human trafficking and smuggling.
- The Rohingya crisis in Myanmar highlights the fractured and fragile state of the country's society and politics, and how ineffectual ASEAN is in dealing with regional problems.

We will now turn to another type of economic crime, that of corruption.

## CORRUPTION IN ASIA

Back in 1974, the Hong Kong-based Far Eastern Economic Review wrote "If you want to buy a Sherman tank, a Red Cross blanket, or simply speed up the installation of a telephone, there is probably no easier place to do just that than in Asia—if you are willing to part with some cash, that is.[16]"

And over 40 years later, after major transformations to Asia's economy, society and politics, things may not have improved very much.

Indeed, Asia would still be one of the most corrupt places on the planet, according to Transparency International (TI), an activist group that works together with governments, businesses and citizens to stop the abuse of power, bribery and secret deals. Only six Asian economies make it into the world's top 50 cleanest economies in TI's Corruption Perceptions Index— Singapore (7th), Hong Kong (15th), Japan (20th), Bhutan (27th), Taiwan (31st) and Brunei (41st).

But as Alan Greenspan, former Chairman of the US Federal Reserve, once remarked, "Corruption, embezzlement and fraud are all characteristics that exist everywhere! It is regrettably the way human nature functions, whether we like it or not."[17] Another simple observation is that as economies become more sophisticated, so also does their corruption become more sophisticated. And that while petty corruption is endemic in poorer countries like India, richer countries tend to be plagued by grand corruption, the abuse of high-level power that benefits the few at the expense of the many. What could be more corrupt than all the shenanigans that take place in Washington DC?

What exactly do we mean by corruption? TI defines corruption as the abuse of entrusted power for private gain. So when a government official, who is working for the nation's citizens, or a corporate employee who is working for his company's shareholders, fills their pockets with money, they are guilty of corruption. But as we will discuss, corruption can take very many other forms.

Is corruption really such a problem? Many will argue that some of Asia's most successful economies, like China and India, are also among the most corrupt and that before them Japan and Korea also suffered from great corruption during their high-growth periods. It may indeed be true that corruption payments can help get things done (facilitation payments) and promote economic development. But as economies become more sophisticated, corruption acts as a deterrent to investment and development. Corruption also drives the yawning inequality in Asia which is fracturing societies, it undermines the integrity of public institutions which is essential for good governance, and can ultimately lead to social and political instability, as was evident, for example, in the Tiananmen Square incident in 1989. Well-educated, middle-class populations will not tolerate corruption forever.

## Japan's Institutionalized Corruption

As any visitor to Japan can tell you, this country seems to be entirely squeaky clean. And the US State Department has noted "The direct exchange of cash for favors from government officials in Japan is extremely rare." But as the State Department also notes, there is much more going on behind the scenes—"the web of close relationships between Japanese companies, politicians, government organizations, and universities has been said to foster an inwardly-cooperative business climate that is conducive to the awarding of contracts, positions, etc. within a tight circle of local players."[18] One important factor greasing the wheels of collusion in Japan is that of "amakudari" whereby government officials retire into top positions in Japanese companies, frequently in industries that they once regulated, and where they can pressure former colleagues for favors—most notably in the agriculture, construction, whaling and banking sectors. Some have even remarked that the situation in Japan could be described as "institutionalized corruption".

In 2016, Japan also received a scolding from the OECD for its paltry efforts in the global fight against foreign bribery.[19] Indeed, since 2002, the OECD has continuously urged Japan to strengthen its efforts to fight bribery by Japanese companies in their foreign business activities, and implementation of the Convention on Combating the Bribery of Foreign Public Officials in International Business Transactions. However, Japan has only prosecuted the incredibly low number of four cases of "foreign bribery" since 1999. The OECD has also repeatedly urged Japan, to no avail, to amend the Anti-organised Crime Law so that companies and individuals convicted of bribing foreign public officials cannot keep their illegal proceeds, including by laundering them, as required by the OECD convention.

Japan seems to have had a never-ending series of high-level corruption cases which continue to this very day. For example, in 2011, it was revealed that Olympus had the longest-running loss-hiding arrangement in Japanese corporate history, while in 2013 the Mizuho Bank was discovered to have loaned money to organized crime groups ("yakuza"). And just in 2016, the Japanese Government's Minister for Economic Revitalization, Akira Amari, resigned over a cash-for-favors bribery scandal. In short, there is much more to squeaky clean Japan than meets the eye. And as I have seen firsthand, there is no country which better at stonewalling and fending off international pressure to do the right thing. As we discussed in the previous chapter, Korea shares many similarities with Japan in terms of cozy relationships between government and business fostering corruption.

## Malaysia's Crime of the Century

Malaysia is a country that once promoted the idea that Asian values are different from Western values, that Asians appreciate order and harmony, while Westerners appreciate personal freedom, and that other so-called Asian values include saving and thriftiness, insistence on hard work, respect for leaders and family loyalty. But as the current corruption scandal involving Malaysian Prime Minister Najib Razak demonstrates, such assertions of Asian values are invariably little more than attempts by authoritarian leaders to justify non-democratic forms of government.

Corruption in various forms has always been part of the Malaysian landscape, even if it is less rapacious than in some other Asian countries. According to an Ernst & Young survey, 39% of respondents say that bribery or corrupt practices happen widely in Malaysia, which is nearly double the Asia-Pacific average of 21%.[20] Corruption and inefficient government bureaucracy would be two of the most problematic factors for doing business in Malaysia reports the World Economic Forum.[21] Corruption is prevalent in state-owned enterprises, the logging industry, public procurement, the judicial system, arranging the delivery of public services and acquiring business and import licenses.[22] Moreover, an intricate system of patronage and vote-buying, together with repression of political opponents, has enabled Malaysia's ruling political party coalition, known as the Barisan Nasional, to win all the nation's elections since independence in 1957.

Although most Asian polities are indeed held together through networks of corruption, Malaysian Prime Minister Najib went one step too far with the creation of sovereign wealth fund, 1Malaysia Development Bhd (1MBD). This fund, established in 2009, was ostensibly designed to drive sustainable economic development by forging strategic global partnerships and promoting foreign direct investment. But it has unfolded into a tawdry tale of deep corruption and shady transactions including an alleged payment of $700 million into Prime Minister Najib's personal bank account, bond sales of $6.5 billion by Goldman Sachs, financing the Hollywood film "The Wolf of Wall Street" and investments in plush luxury properties, private jets and paintings, and payments to cover gambling debts—most involving dubious people connected to Najib.

The US, Swiss and Singaporean governments have been hot on the trail of this shady affair, as billions of dollars were allegedly laundered through their financial systems. The US Department of Justice alleged that $3.5 billion was misappropriated from 1MDB. Former US Attorney-General Loretta Lynch described the affair as "the largest kleptocracy case" in US history. Former Malaysian Prime Minister Mahathir Mohamad has called on Najib to resign. Najib has arranged the assistance of China to help bail out 1MDB by selling some of its assets to Chinese companies. Many now worry about the leverage will now have over Malaysian politics.

As Najib has been desperately struggling to hang on to power, he sacked his deputy Muhyiddin Yassin and replaced the former attorney-general over critical comments they made about the scandal. The new attorney-general cleared Najib of any wrongdoing after investigations by the Malaysian Anti-Corruption Commission. Large street protests, mainly by Chinese Malaysians, against Prime Minister Najib have taken place, with some activists being arrested. The government has cracked down on reporting of the 1MDB scandal, blocking access to certain online news portals and targeting media groups and journalists.

The 1MDB affair is also a product of the dirty and violent struggle to hang on to power waged by the Barisan Nasional. Malaysia's politics starting going off the rails almost two decades ago when Deputy Prime Minister Anwar Ibrahim fell out of favor with then Prime Minister Mahathir Mohamad. In 1998, Anwar was convicted of sodomy, and given a nine-year prison sentence. In 2004, the verdict was overturned, and Anwar was released from jail. Years later, he was charged and acquitted again, and then yet again in 2014 he was convicted and given a five-year sentence. It is widely believed that the sodomy charges were politically motivated and that this is merely a case of persecution of the highly talented Anwar, who is seen as a threat to the ruling party.

The Malaysian opposition coalition, led by Anwar, came close to achieving a majority in parliament in 2008 and won several state elections. Anwar's opposition then won a majority of the popular vote in 2013, while the BN held onto power through a campaign of dirty tricks. Indeed, it has been reported that some 1MDB funds would have been used by the Barisan Nasional to help ensure its victory in the 2013 elections. With the next elections due in 2018, Najib has also been trying to turn the affair into an ethno-patriotic issue, arguing that support for the government represents support for Islamic Malaysia, and that Malays must fight against the ethnic Chinese-dominated opposition. Najib still retains strong support among the ethnic Malay community, but not among the Chinese and Indian communities. Indeed, despite the 1MDB affair, Najib has recently led BN to emphatic victories in a state election and two by-elections. And many are betting that Najib will call snap elections and try to capitalize on his continuing popularity among the Malay ethnic group.

The case of 1MDB highlights how successful, soft-authoritarian regimes can be highly vulnerable to corruption due to their weak institutions, and to repression by ruthless governments which seek to defy popular pressure for good governance and democracy. The only hope is that Malaysian civil society can exert sufficient pressure on the Barisan Nasional regime to bring about democratic change, with rule of law and freedom of speech, assembly and association. For the moment, Malaysia is in a state of creeping authoritarianism.

China is also suffering from rampant corruption, but its government now has a vigorous campaign to fight corruption, which it sees as an existential threat to Communist Party rule of China.

## China's Cancerous Corruption

Corruption was not a major problem in Mao Zedong's China, from 1949 to 1976. But with the subsequent opening of the economy, corruption has exploded like a cancer through China's polity, economy and society. China's very impressive infrastructure development has fueled widespread graft. Urbanization has been associated with land grabs from poor Chinese citizens by local government officials who offer minimal compensation. State-owned enterprises, most of which operate in highly protected markets, have been milked for money by executives. Local government officials often collude with local business to rip off what they can. Government officials frequently extract bribes in administrations like taxation, customs, land, construction, judiciary, police, public procurement, natural resources and general public services. Corruption has been rife in the People's Liberation Army, where large bribes are paid for promotion casting serious doubts on how powerful the People's Liberation Army really is.

Misinvoicing of China's international trade has facilitated massive illicit financial outflows (to the tune of more than $1 trillion over the decade to 2013[23]). The proceeds of economic crime are laundered, notably through Hong Kong, to disguise their criminality. The 2015 chemical explosions which killed over 170 people and injured hundreds of others in Tianjin highlighted how safety regulations are routinely flouted. Violation of regulations is the major cause of China's food safety problems. Despite widespread concerns about China's environment, environmental laws are frequently not enforced. The police sometimes collude with organized crime in the management of prostitution, gambling and drugs. Members of the Communist Party received favored treatment in many aspects of their lives. If you want a good hospital bed, privileged medical treatment, a place for child in a good school, or most anything, graft payments will help make things happen.

Most corruption in China would be graft, according to William H. Overholt, such as when officials take kickbacks for doing their job, like for building a road.[24] China's system of economic growth performance targets has provided officials with a strong incentive to get things done, even if they are corrupt. Such graft is much less debilitating for the economy than pure corruption where money is diverted but things don't get done, such as in the cases of India and the Philippines. How could such corruption spread so quickly through the Chinese economy? Much of the reason is because the Chinese government freed up markets in the economy, but did not complement such liberalization with well-enforced regulations and institutional development.

Public outrage at corruption has also been a long-running affair. The 1989 Tiananmen Square protests were mainly motivated by public concerns about corruption. In the subsequent period, government efforts to combat corruption had some success, particularly for petty corruption. You are now much less likely to be hit up for a few dollars (or renminbi) by low-level government officials. But corruption exploded again during the regime President Hu Jintao, from 2002 to 2012 when reform efforts slowed. The government's mega stimulus package in response to the global financial crisis provided fresh opportunities for corruption. The revelation by the New York Times in 2012 that the family of Premier Wen Jiabao has hidden riches of at least $2.7 billion was symbolic of the rampant corruption that had spread through China.[25]

It was against this background that in late 2012 new Chinese President Xi Jinping launched an anti-corruption campaign as the centerpiece of his reform program, along with a "Disciplinary Code" to improve the ethics of Communist Party officials. In explaining the need to combat corruption, President Xi stressed that the Communist Party risks "losing the trust and support of the people ... In our vigorous campaign against corruption, we have punished both tigers and flies—corrupt official—

irrespective of ranking, in response to our people's demand. This has nothing to do with power struggle. In this case, there is no House of Cards."[26] Indeed, Xi sees corruption as a potential existential threat to the Communist Party's one-party rule in China, especially since the Chinese public considers official corruption as the country's biggest problem.[27] Xi has much to be concerned about—a major reason why Mao Zedong's Communist Party was able to beat the Nationalist Kuomintang in the Chinese Civil War was because of the latter's rampant corruption.

Many have been arrested and punished over the past five years, with the biggest catches being: former security czar, Zhou Yongkang; former chief of staff of former President Hu Jintao, Ling Jihua; former Minister of Railways, Liu Zhijun; and former Vice Chairmen of the Central Military Commission, General Xu Caihou and General Guo Boxiong. According to one report, 1880 officials, including 184 tigers, would have been sentenced for corruption.[28] The Chinese government has also spread its campaign overseas, putting pressure on foreign governments to repatriate fugitives. In 2015, China reportedly provided the US government a list of 150 corrupt Chinese officials believed to be hiding in the US. China's most-wanted economic fugitive Yang Xiuzhu surrendered in November 2016. And to stimulate popular support for the anti-corruption campaign, the government produced an eight-part television series, "Always on the Road", which features confessions of convicted high-level officials.

Despite what President Xi said, most analysts believe that the anti-corruption campaign has been important for Xi in terms of eliminating political rivals and facilitating his consolidation of power. Indeed, the anti-corruption campaign has been conducted in a very selective way—a large share of convicted officials are linked to Zhou Yongkang, and no "princelings[29]" have been prosecuted. And a vast array of China's vested interests—like managers of state-owned enterprises and banks who sit on the Chinese Communist Party's (CCP) Central Committee—have not been tackled by Xi's anti-corruption campaign. Although Xi's anti-corruption drive has merely scratched the surface, he has exposed how thoroughly corrupt the whole system (and the CCP) has become. It is a complex system of patronage which holds the CCP together.

Many expected that the anti-corruption campaign would only last a year or two, but it now seems to have morphed into a never-ending campaign. But five years after the launch of the anti-corruption campaign,

China is doubling down on fighting corruption. A major message of the 2016 October's Communist Party plenum was more discipline; punishment with tougher penalties and zero tolerance, regardless of position. China set up new anti-corruption body to oversee all public servants as it intensifies battle against graft.

There has also been much debate the effectiveness of the anti-corruption campaign. It is difficult to see how such deeply entrenched corruption can be solved by a campaign like that of President Xi which seems to attack the symptoms rather than the root causes of corruption. Experience shows that all countries are vulnerable to corruption, and the only effective way of controlling corruption is by allowing freedom of the press, civil society watchdogs, independent anti-corruption commissions, rule of law and accountability through elections.

There is none of that in Xi's China. The CCP, not the state judiciary, decides who is and is not corrupt. According to Human Rights Watch, the CCP has a secretive detention system which is uses torture to extract confessions from corruption suspects.[30] For its part, the CCP itself is opaque and accountable to no-one. Media and civil society activists who speak up on corruption are arrested. And it is clear that Xi is using the anti-corruption campaign as a means of eliminating political enemies and rivals. But it also seems that the deeper the anti-corruption campaign digs, the more enemies Xi has. Despite the shock-and-awe facade of the anti-corruption campaign, analysis by the Financial Times suggests that the statistical probability of being punished for corruption are slim—fewer than 0.5% of Chinese officials were prosecuted, while most people believe that a majority of officials have been corrupt some time in recent years.[31] And according to most reports, corruption still remains widespread in China.

For the moment, it seems that the anti-corruption campaign is having an adverse effect on the economy, as the luxury and entertainment sector is being hit. The campaign has also forced local officials to become highly risk averse and unwilling to attempt policy innovations on the ground. China's local officials now prefer to sit on their hands. Doing nothing is the safest strategy.

## Mongolia's Corruption Curse

In many ways, Mongolia has everything going for it. After being a satellite state of the former Soviet Union for much of the twentieth century, Mongolia regained its independence with the end of the Cold War. A relatively peaceful political revolution in the early 1990s ushered in a multi-party democracy and open society which have remained in place. Mongolia is an enormous country, more than twice the size of France, but only has a population of three million people. And it is blessed with vast reserves of copper, gold, coal, molybdenum, fluorspar, uranium, tin and tungsten deposits. True, Mongolia experienced great upheavals as the breakup of the Soviet Union saw its trade decline by 80%. But Mongolia was also perfectly placed to be benefit from the commodity super cycle driven by China, which is now the destination for the vast majority of its exports.

However, despite much hype about the Mongolian "wolf economy", this country of so much promise is being dragged down by massive corruption. According to the Gan Business Anti-corruption Portal, corruption is a high risk in the judicial system, in land, tax and customs administrations, in public procurement, and also when acquiring public licenses, permits or utilities. And Mongolia's mining sector would also be highly vulnerable to corruption. Mongolia's corruption problems have long been a topic in domestic political debates, and with international investors and donors. But it is not clear that things are improving. In its 2016 Investment Climate Statement on Mongolia, the US State Department noted with concern that "the opportunities for corruption have increased at both the 'petty' or administrative and 'grand' or elite levels."

Mongolia's corruption is greatly weakening its attractiveness as an investment destination, is fracturing its society and weakening its fragile political institutions. Its culture of corruption has also fed its love–hate relationship with foreign investors, which has destabilized the economy. And as Jargal Dambadarjaa, an Ulaanbaatar-based commentator, has argued, corruption is feeding Mongolia's debt problems. While economic growth virtually ground to a halt in 2016, the fiscal deficit reached 18% of GDP, up from 8% in the previous year, and public debt exceeded 90% of GDP by year-end. The Mongolian government also made some large borrowings on international markets in recent years to finance infrastructure, but is now faced with more than $1 billion in debt repayments in 2017 and early 2018. Mongolia's increasingly precarious finances led credit rating agencies Moody's and Standard & Poor's, to downgrade Mongolia's sovereign rating in August 2016.

The country's mounting double deficits prompted the new government led by Prime Minister Erdenebat Jargaltulga to turn to the IMF, the ADB and other donors for rescue loans. But Mongolia has too many friends coming to its rescue when greater discipline is necessary to get its house in order. Mongolian friends like the Japan, US, UK and Australia are very keen to support this fledgling democracy which is landlocked between the two non-democratic giants of China and Russia. The Mongolian government was also keen to avoid seeking extra support from China, following an earlier currency swap agreement to support its currency.

There is hope that when Rio Tinto's Oyu Tolgoi mine, the world's largest underdeveloped reserve of copper, and some other mines get into full production swing, that Mongolia will turn the corner and realize its great potential. But another scenario is that increasing resource revenues will only fuel more corruption.

Mongolia needs to desperately kill its corruption curse and build the institutions for a successful young democracy. If it doesn't, it will be trapped in the competition between China and Western countries for its attention. And ultimately, Western donor fatigue could set in, and Mongolia could find itself being bought out by communist China, and losing its democracy forever. This would be a sad ending to one of democracy's great hopes.

## LESSONS FROM CLEAN SINGAPORE

Singapore would be Asia's least corrupt country, ranking seventh in TI's Corruption Perceptions Index 2015, well ahead of 15th placed Hong Kong and 20th placed Japan. What can we learn from this bastion of authoritarian capitalism?

In private discussions with Asit K. Biswas of the National University of Singapore, the late Prime Minister Lee Kuan Yew recalled that corruption was once commonplace in Singapore's colonial civil service.[32] When his People's Action Party came to power, it made anti-corruption policies a key priority in order to attract foreign investment and foster economic development. As Jon S.T. Quah has analyzed, this required eliminating both the opportunities and incentives for corruption.[33]

In his insightful analysis, Professor Quah suggested a number of lessons from Singapore's success in fighting corruption, including: (1) commitment of the political leadership, especially Prime Minister Lee Kuan Yew—indeed, anyone found guilty of corruption must be punished, regardless of his status or position in society; (2) anti-corruption measures must be comprehensive, not piecemeal, to prevent loopholes, and must be constantly reviewed; (3) there are a number of government ministries and agencies which are particularly vulnerable to corruption, notably like customs, immigration, internal revenue, traffic police and the above all the anti-corruption agency, and which require special attention for eliminating the opportunities for corruption; and (4) it is important to pay civil servants competitive salaries to reduce the incentive for corruption. Today, Singapore's politicians and civil servants are among the very best paid in the world.

Singapore has shown Asia, and the rest of the world, that it is possible to virtually eliminate corruption. Indeed, Chinese President Xi Jinping is inspired by his perception of the Singapore model—a war on corruption, a crackdown on dissent, and pro-market economic reforms—which he hopes would allow the Communist Party to retain its monopoly on political power.

But there is much more to the Singapore model than that.[34] Singapore allows opposition political parties and holds elections, even if they are far from free elections. This allows the public to express their point of view and hold the government somewhat accountable. Indeed, the 2011 national elections saw a 6% swing against the ruling party, which recorded its lowest score since independence. Singapore also rates very highly when it comes to the rule of law. And so it was that with his strong leadership, limited democracy and the rule of law that Lee Kuan Yew was able keep the predatory appetite of Singapore's elite under control.

## Money Laundering in Asia

When it comes to money laundering (i.e., concealing the identity of criminal proceeds so they appear legitimate), Asia is even much worse shape than it is for corruption. Not one Asian economy makes it in the world's cleanest 50 countries of the 149 surveyed by the International Centre for Asset Recovery. Indeed, nine Asian economies make it into the worst 50, namely Cambodia, Myanmar, Nepal, Laos, Sri Lanka, China, Vietnam,

Pakistan and Thailand. Seemingly respectable ones like Taiwan, Malaysia, Hong Kong and Japan only make it into the middle of the pack.

The very many reported cases, as well as the Panama Papers, highlight the prominence of Hong Kong as a hub for money laundering. As one of the world's leading financial centers, it has facilitated the massive rise of illicit financial flows from China through middlemen entities that set up companies, foundations and trusts to help clients hide their wealth. According to the Panama Papers, Hong Kong has the most offshore companies surpassing the UK and Switzerland as the economy with the most offshore companies. Hong Kong's crime proceeds can be generated from a vast array of activities like drug trafficking, smuggling and illegal gambling. In a similar vein, Singapore's role as an international financial center makes it vulnerable to money laundering, all the more so given position as a haven of sophistication in Southeast Asia, a region riddled with organized crime and large-scale corruption.

According to Banker's Academy, "Money laundering in Japan is a persistent problem." And the US State Department reports that Japan continues to face substantial risk of money laundering by organized crime, and that there has been an increase in financial crimes by citizens of West African countries, such as Nigeria and Ghana, who reside in Japan. Drug trafficking, fraud, loan sharking (illegal money lending), remittance frauds, the black market economy, prostitution and illicit gambling are the main sources of laundered funds.

## CYBERCRIME

Asia has also become a major theater for global cybercrime. This was highlighted in 2016 when cyber criminals used the Philippines and a SWIfT code to steal $81 million from the account of the Bangladesh central bank at the Federal Reserve of New York. But unfortunately, the majority of cyber attacks in Asia go unreported. This actually increases the region's vulnerability to cybercrime, as it feeds the perception that the cyber threat is lower than it actually is.

Cybercrimes are vast in scope—from hacking, data theft and espionage, identity theft, malware, ransomware, phishing, spamming, content-related crime like child pornography, copyright and trademark-related offenses and fraud. Cybercrime is also facilitating many traditional crimes like human trafficking, drug dealing, corruption and money laundering.

Cybercrime attacks in the Asia-Pacific have increased dramatically, according to ThreatMetrix. Business revenues lost to cyber attacks in Asia came to over $80 billion in the 12 months to September 2015, according to the professional services company Grant Thornton. Some 28% of organizations in Asia were hit with an advanced cyber attack in the second half of 2015, double the world average, according to FireEye, an American security company. For the first time, Asian enterprises have identified cybercrime as a critical business risk, according to Aon's 2017 Global Risk Management Survey. Reflecting the gravity of cybercrime in Asia, Microsoft has opened Cybercrime Satellite Centers in Tokyo, Beijing and Singapore.

To reduce its vulnerability to cybercrime, Asia needs to improve cybersecurity awareness, especially in the business sector, to strengthen cyber regulations and their enforcement, and above all, to take international cooperation much more seriously, in light of the trans-border nature of cybercrime. Fortunately, the US and China, two top sources of cybercrime, are now cooperating closely. Australia is also cooperating closely with China, Singapore and Thailand on combating cybercrime in Asia.

\* \* \*

Can Asian countries live together in peace and harmony is the question we ask in the next chapter. The relative stability of postwar Asia, led by the US, is being shaken by the rise of China, as China is now engaged in a bitter power struggle with the US and its Asian allies for the political leadership of Asia. We review some aspects of China's relations with the US, Japan, Taiwan, Hong Kong, North Korea and Southeast Asia, and the many of the manifold tensions.

## Notes

1. United Nations Office on Drugs and Crime. Transnational Organized Crime in East Asia and the Pacific: A Threat Assessment. 2013.
2. OECD (2016). Trade in Counterfeit and Pirated Goods: Mapping the Economic Impact. 2016.
3. OECD (2016). Illicit Trade: Converging Criminal Networks.
4. Global Financial Integrity (2011). Transnational Crime in the Developing World, Jeremy Haken.

5. US State Department. 2016 International Narcotics Control Strategy Report.
6. United Nations Office on Drugs and Crime. World Drug Report 2015.
7. UNEP and Interpol (2016). The rise of environmental crime. A UNEP-Interpol rapid response assessment.
8. Environmental Investigation Agency (2008). Environmental Crime: a threat to our future.
9. US Department of State. 2016 Trafficking in Persons Report.
10. United Nations Office on Drugs and Crime. Global Report on Trafficking in Persons 2014.
11. International Labour Organisation. Profits and Poverty: The Economics of Forced Labour.
12. Justice Centre (2016). Coming Clean—The prevalence of forced labour and human trafficking for the purpose of forced labour amongst migrant domestic workers in Hong Kong.
13. Freedom House. Myanmar's Muslim Minority: The Plight of the Rohingya, 8 September 2015. Russell Raymond.
14. US Department of State. Atrocities Prevention Report, 17 March 2016. Targeting of and Attacks on Members of Religious Groups in the Middle East and Burma.
15. Amnesty International (2015). Deadly journeys: The refugee and trafficking crisis in Southeast Asia.
16. Far Eastern Economic Review (Hong Kong), 6 September 1974.
17. Economist's View. Alan Greenspan versus Naomi Klein, 26 September 2007.
18. US Department of State. 2015 Investment Climate Statement—Japan.
19. OECD. Japan must make fighting international bribery a priority, 30 June 2016.
20. Ernst & Young. Building a more ethical business environment Asia-Pacific Fraud Survey 2013.
21. World Economic Forum. Global Competitiveness Report 2016–2017.
22. GAN Business Anti-corruption Portal. Malaysia Corruption Report.
23. Global Financial Integrity. Illicit Financial Flows from Developing Countries: 2004–2013.
24. Overholt, William H. The politics of China's anti-corruption campaign. East Asia Forum Quarterly April–June 2015.
25. New York Times. Billions in Hidden Riches for Family of Chinese Leader, David Barboza, 25 October 2012.
26. Chinese President Xi Jinping Addresses the American Public, 22 September 2015.
27. PewResearchCenter. Corruption, Pollution, Inequality Are Top Concerns in China, 24 September 2015.

28. ChinaFile. Catching tigers and flies. Accessed 6 December 2016.
29. Descendants of early Communist revolutionaries.
30. Human Rights Watch. China: Secretive Detention System Mars Anti-Corruption Campaign, 6 December 2016.
31. Financial Times. China anti-corruption campaign backfires, 10 October 2016.
32. Biswas, Asit K., Cecilia Tortajada and Augustin Boey. Corruption, Economic Development and Poverty Alleviation. Asian Century Institute, 15 May 2016.
33. Quah, Jon S. T. Corruption in Asia with special reference to Singapore: Patterns and Consequence. Asian Journal of Public Administration. Volume 10, 1988.
34. Pei, Minxin. The Real Singapore Model. Project Syndicate, 26 March 2016.

**Open Access** This chapter is licensed under the terms of the Creative Commons Attribution 4.0 International License (http://creativecommons.org/licenses/by/4.0/), which permits use, sharing, adaptation, distribution, and reproduction in any medium or format, as long as you give appropriate credit to the original author(s) and the source, provide a link to the Creative Commons license and indicate if changes were made.

The images or other third party material in this chapter are included in the chapter's Creative Commons license, unless indicated otherwise in a credit line to the material. If material is not included in the chapter's Creative Commons license and your intended use is not permitted by statutory regulation or exceeds the permitted use, you will need to obtain permission directly from the copyright holder.

CHAPTER 10

# Can Asian Countries Live Together in Peace and Harmony?

"If the US would only leave Asia, we Asians could all live together in peace and harmony," a group of over 40 Chinese students said in response to my question. But when I reported this exchange back to another one of my classes, the Americans in the group instantly retorted that "Asia would descend into war if ever the US left Asia to itself—Asians hate each other."

I was shocked at both the sharpness of the two reactions and the unanimity of the feelings of each of the two groups of students. So I invited a Chinese professorial colleague to lunch to see her reactions. She almost jumped in responding: "Why must the US have a system of alliances with so many Asian countries surrounding China? The US is not an Asian country. The US is just encircling China, trying to hem us in. It is trying to stop China's rise. It sees China's rise as a threat. The US just wants to remain Asia's hegemon."

These revealing comments highlight the great power transition under way in Asia—from a US-led region to perhaps a China-led one. Asia's post-World War 2 geopolitics are being shaken by the rise of China, and China is now engaged in a bitter power struggle with the US and its Asian allies for the political leadership of Asia. At this stage, the US seems to be losing its hold over Asia, something which will likely accelerate under the Trump administration. China has signed up most Asian countries to its new initiatives like the Asian Infrastructure Investment Bank (AIIB) and the Belt and Road Initiative (BRI), which the US and Japan have boycotted. China is also proving very effective at subjugating many of its neighbors through its market, financial and military power. For its part, the US is distracted by the Middle East, Russia and the circus of Washington, and has difficulties being consistent from one administration to another.

China's burgeoning domination of Asia is incongruous in many ways. When compared with Japan, Korea, Taiwan, Hong Kong and Singapore, China's economy is inferior in terms of GDP per capita, and economic, business and technological sophistication. Its citizens suffer from human rights abuses, widespread restrictions on freedom, censorship of information and dubious official propaganda. And its government is neither democratic nor transparent, and is shrouded in secrecy and is accountable to no one but itself.

But China does have size on its side thanks to its enormous population. This means that it has the world's biggest economy in purchasing power parity terms, the largest foreign exchange reserves and the highest military expenditure in Asia. China is also the most important trading partner of virtually all other Asian economies. And it is not shy to assert its political and military power, even it means breaking international law to which it has signed up.

The Chinese are also motivated by an enormous belief in their destiny. As former US Secretary of State, Henry Kissinger, once said, "The Chinese think of themselves as having always been on top and that there was only an interruption of a hundred years in which the West exploited its momentary weakness. And in their mind, they are reclaiming their traditional position."[1] In short, China has great economic weight and motivation, which it has transformed into economic, political and military power.

No one can be sure how the future will unfold and what the "new normal" will be. Traditional military conflict cannot be ruled out, though perhaps not between China and the US. American business is hooked on the Chinese market, and US diplomatic and military leaders would not want to put this at risk. The US also needs Chinese cooperation on issues like North Korea, counter-terrorism, cyber-security, Iran and, depending on the administration, climate change. And both sides seem very conscious of the futility and massive costs of a possible military conflict.

But despite the size of its market and military, China has very few friends in Asia, and the potential is enormous for conflict with Japan, Taiwan, Hong Kong, Vietnam and especially India. And China has been the ultimate guarantor of North Korea, Asia's greatest security risk.

The relative peace that Asia has enjoyed these past seven decades has been key to the region's economic renaissance. But as we discuss in this chapter, a peaceful future in Asia cannot be taken for granted. Indeed, the ability of Asians to live together in peace and harmony will perhaps be the most important determinant of a successful Asian Century.

How did we get into this situation? What are Asia's hot spots? And what will the future hold?

## US and Asia During the Cold War

The Chinese communist government's giant military parade on Tiananmen Square on 3 September 2015 to celebrate the 70th anniversary of the "Victory of the Chinese People's War of Resistance Against Japanese Aggression" was a grotesque affair with perfectly goose-stepping soldiers and a massive display of new military equipment, including the DF-21D, the so-called carrier killer anti-ship ballistic missile. It was also a sham. The US, along with China's nationalist army (the Kuomintang—KMT), was responsible for bringing an end to Japan's aggression and to the Pacific side of World War 2—the Communist Party had virtually nothing to do with it.

In fact, China's communists were fortunate that the KMT had invested so much energy in fighting the Japanese that they could then easily beat the diminished KMT in the subsequent Chinese Civil War, which ended in 1949. Another major event that shaped Cold War relations in East Asia was the Korean War which saw the peninsula divided between North Korea, supported by China and the USSR, and South Korea, supported by the US and its allies, from war's end in 1953.

As the ultimate victor of World War 2, the US faced a complex post-war geopolitical landscape. Asia's only great power, Japan, was not only defeated, it was virtually destroyed. The process of decolonization in Asia was beginning, leaving many new nations to fend for themselves. This period also witnessed the onset of the Cold War with countries like Japan, South Korea, the Philippines, Taiwan and Thailand lining up on the American side, and China, North Korea and the USSR on the other side. Reflecting these Cold War politics, Taiwan occupied China's seat at the United Nations (UN), the IMF, World Bank and other international organizations, with the People's Republic being virtually sidelined.

The US government was very keen to provide its allies with security. But the US did not want to give them a blank check to start wars and entrap it in parochial conflicts. The US needed to control these allies. So the US created a bilateral "hub-and-spoke" alliance system in Asia, which provided its Asian allies with security, but kept them under control. Quite deliberately, it did not create an "Asian NATO", because the US did not have sufficient trust in its Asian allies. For their part, these Asian countries did not have any need for an Asian NATO once the US had provided them with sufficient security through tight bilateral agreements. In the case of Japan, at the time Asia's most important country, the US occupying powers went further, and virtually created a new nation, a democracy, with a constitution that renounced to right to wage war.[2]

The alliances with Japan, South Korea, the Philippines and Thailand remain in place to this very day (the US also has a close military partnership with Singapore). In 1979, the US switched its allegiances and recognized mainland China as "one China" rather than Taiwan. But the US did not totally abandon Taiwan. It implemented new security obligations through the US Taiwan Relations Act which states that "the United States will make available to Taiwan such defense articles and defense services in such quantity as may be necessary to enable Taiwan to maintain a sufficient self-defense capabilities." This legislation is designed to deter both China from invading Taiwan and Taiwan from unilaterally declaring independence.

As the US system of alliances provided security to its Asian friends, it also underpinned the exceptional economic development that these countries would experience. But the US provided even greater support to its Asian friends. In the immediate post-war years, they received financial assistance to help reconstruct their economies. They benefited from the stability and open markets fostered by the new multilateral economic system, including most notably the UN, IMF, World Bank and the GATT (which would become the World Trade Organisation). The export-driven development of Japan, Hong Kong, Korea, Singapore and Taiwan would also benefit greatly from the substantial openness of US markets to exports from these countries. It is important to stress that as generous as the American actions might seem, they were substantially motivated by geopolitics. After years of World War 2, and with the emerging Cold War, the US had as much interest in promoting peace, stability and security as anyone.[3]

Perhaps one of the most important developments in the post-war period was that, despite the violent war, Japan was able to reestablish peaceful and friendly relations with most of its former adversaries. For example, on the 70th anniversary of the end of World War 2, on 2 September 2015, US President Barack Obama said:

"The end of the war marked the beginning of a new era in America's relationship with Japan. As Prime Minister Abe and I noted during his visit in April, the relationship between our two countries over the last 70 years stands as a model of the power of reconciliation: former adversaries who have become steadfast allies and who work together to advance common interests and universal values in Asia and globally. Seventy years ago this partnership was unimaginable. Today it is a fitting reflection of our shared interests, capabilities, and values, and I am confident that it will continue to deepen in the decades to come."[4] Japanese Prime Minister Shinzo Abe's visit to Pearl Harbour in late 2016 was also emblematic of the reconciliation and friendship between the US and Japan. It may also have been motivated by Abe's fear that President Trump will downplay the US–Japan Alliance.

In a similar spirit, Australia's former Prime Minister Tony Abbott told Japan's Shinzo Abe, when these two prime ministers met at an East Asia Summit in Brunei in 2013. "As far as I'm concerned, Japan is Australia's best friend in Asia and we want to keep it a very strong friendship."[5] There are now only a few Asian nations with which Japan now has poor relations, notably China, North Korea and South Korea. Efforts by the US to prod Japan and South Korea to bury the hatchet, notably over Japan's forced employment of Korean "comfort women", are still struggling to achieve durable results.

On a visit to Japan in 2015, Germany's Chancellor Angela Merkel had some wise advice on post-war reconciliation when she spoke of Germany's readiness "to face our history openly and squarely", but also of the "generous gestures of our neighbours". In other words, post-war reconciliation requires efforts on both sides. And regrettably, anti-Japanese sentiment is a still an important tool in domestic politics in China, and North and South Korea.

Overall, the US played a major role in fostering the rapid and peaceful development of its allies and friends in the post-war period, including the successful democratization of Korea and Taiwan. The US would also make a major contribution to China's development, when it finally opened up its economy.

## Rehabilitation of China

Although China was substantially isolated from the West and the rest of Asia, over the years from 1949, the People's Republic of China worked hard to secure international recognition and support for its position that it, not Taiwan, was the sole legitimate government of all China, including Hong Kong, Macau and Taiwan. Thus, a growing number of Western countries recognized the People's Republic of China, starting with Switzerland, Sweden, Denmark and Finland in 1950. Other important milestones along the way included recognition by Canada (1970), UK (1972), Japan (1972) and Australia (1972). A major turning point occurred when Taiwan, which had occupied China's seat at the UN since 1945, was effectively expelled on 25 October 1971, with its seat being taken over by the People's Republic of China. Indeed, the People's Republic took over the China seat in all international organizations.

But the most important event in the rehabilitation of the People's Republic was the visit to China in 1972 by US President Richard Nixon and National Security Advisor Henry Kissinger, and the subsequent, in 1979, formal recognition of the People's Republic by the US, and its severing of relations with Taiwan. At China's insistence, the US also adhered to the "One-China Policy" by which there is only one China, and Taiwan is considered a renegade province which must in time be reunited with the motherland.

While the US was keen to join forces with China against the USSR in the Cold War of the day, it was also motivated by Nixon's belief that China should be brought into the international system. In 1967 Nixon wrote "Taking the long view, we simply cannot afford to leave China forever outside the family of nations, there to nurture its fantasies, cherish its hates and threaten its neighbours.... There is no place on this small planet for a billion of its potentially most able people to live in angry isolation."[6] In more recent years, US President Obama emphasized that his administration welcomes China's peaceful rise, and believes that a strong and prosperous China is one that can help to bring prosperity and stability to the region and the world.

From the moment of US recognition of People's Republic of China, through various administrations, US policy was always designed to support the revival of the Chinese economy, even if there have been ups and downs, like the Tiananmen Square Massacre. Another major step took place in 2000, when President Bill Clinton signed into law the U.S.–China

Relations Act which granted permanent normal trade relations to China, against stiff opposition from labor and human rights groups. This facilitated China's entry into the World Trade Organization in 2001. Prior to passage of the bill, China was subject to an annual review of its trade status with the US.

There were of course powerful US business interests supporting the normalization of trade relations between the US and China. But President Clinton believed that there were also powerful political interests when he said: "…many of [China's leaders] believe that we honestly don't want their country to assume a respected place in the world. If … we turn our backs on them, it will confirm their fears." He also said: "Membership in the WTO, of course, will not create a free society in China overnight or guarantee that China will play by global rules. But over time, I believe it will move China faster and further in the right direction, and certainly will do that more than rejection would."[7]

While China's dramatic economic transformation since 1978 owes a great deal to the reforms initiated by Deng Xiaoping, China has benefited greatly from the openness of the US economy, which is vastly more open than the Chinese economy. Today, China is the US' largest supplier of merchandise imports and the third largest market for US merchandise exports. US goods and services trade with China totaled an estimated $659.4 billion in 2015, with the US having a goods and services trade deficit with China of $336.2 billion in 2015.[8]

The US is becoming a very important destination for China's outbound investment, with Chinese companies investing a record $45.6 billion of foreign direct investment (FDI) in 2016. This threefold increase from 2015 is helping Chinese companies acquire technology, knowhow and brands, and penetrate US markets. It is estimated that the US has received over $100 billion in FDI from China since the year 2000.[9] Since Chinese outbound investment is a relatively new phenomenon, the stock of US investment in China is very much higher.

Another point of point of access to US knowledge is through the 330,000 Chinese students studying in the US in 2016, accounting for over 30% of the US' international students. China has also become a massive source of tourist revenues for the US. In 2016, 3 million Chinese tourists visited the US, and with $33 billion in visitor spending, they were by far the US' most important source of tourist dollars. And according to the 2010 census, there are some 3.8 millions of Americans of Chinese descent, reflecting the openness of America's society.

In sum, the US has contributed greatly to the development of the Chinese economy. But as China's rise has progressed, the US economy has become increasingly dependent on China, which has reduced US' political leverage over China.

As we discussed in Chap. 4, trade and investment with Japan has been another factor driving the Chinese economy forward. But friendly relations between these countries took a turn for the worse after the Tiananmen Square massacre, thereby destabilizing the foundations for peace and harmony in Asia.

## Japan, from Chinese Friend to Foe

Japan has been the subject of growing Chinese vitriol these past few years. The dispute over the contested Senkaku/Diaoyu Islands has only increased. Despite Japan's manifold apologies for its atrocious war crimes in World War 2, China keeps questioning Japan's sincerity, and requests more and more apologies. The Chinese government seeks every opportunity it can to humiliate Japan.

At the same time, the actions of the Japanese government have not helped. Visits by Japanese Prime Minister Shinzo Abe and other leading government figures to the Yasukuni Shrine which honors among others Japanese war criminals have incensed not only China but also Korea. Comments by right wing Japanese political figures which question the veracity of events like the Nanjing Massacre and other Japanese wartime violence only add fuel to the fire. But what is also clear is that the Chinese government is actively promoting anti-Japanese sentiment, especially through grotesque television dramas. And as China regularly whips itself up into a frenzy over Japan, it is perhaps easy to forget that China's modern anti-Japanese sentiment is only a recent phenomenon.

During the 1970s and 1980s, China and Japan actually had good relations. In 1972, Mao Zedong told Prime Minister Kakuei Tanaka that his apologies for Japan's wartime aggression were not necessary, and expressed gratitude for Japan's help in defeating Chiang Kai-shek's KMT national army. Also in 1972, in a joint communiqué signed by Premier Zhou Enlai, China magnanimously renounced its right to war reparations, satisfying itself with Japan's acceptance of "responsibility for serious damage caused to the Chinese people through war." And following Deng Xiaoping's historic visit to Japan in 1978, relations between the two countries improved greatly. Japan played a key role in the take-off of the backward Chinese economy through financial assistance, corporate investments and technology transfer.

But things changed quickly after the 1989 Tiananmen Square Massacre, even though Japan was the first country to restore high-level relations with China following the diplomatic rupture with advanced countries. One lesson that the Chinese leadership drew from the Tiananmen Square incident was that the Communist Party needed to make greater efforts to promote nationalism to improve support for the Party. So under the leadership of Jiang Zemin, China embarked on a massive campaign of patriotic education. Students and citizens were taught how the Communist Party was leading China's recovery from its "century of humiliation" (from the opium wars to the end of the civil war in 1949). And at the heart of this patriotic education was anti-Japanese propaganda, since Japan was the country that inflicted the most suffering on China. As academic Minxin Pei has argued, the official anti-Japanese campaign has left deep scars: "Chinese state media and history textbooks have fed the younger generation such a diet of distorted, jingoistic facts, outright lies, and nationalistic myths that it is easy to provoke anti-Western or anti-Japanese sentiments."[10]

There have been other factors that have weakened China's burgeoning friendship with Japan. With the end of the Cold War and the dissolution of the USSR, China and Japan lost a common enemy which had helped unite them. And with its rapid development, China increasingly believed that it had less need for Japanese aid, investment and technology.

Is there any hope that China and Japan could bury the hatchet and have friendly relations?

It is very difficult to see a positive way out in the immediate future, even though it is ultimately in the interests of both countries to have good relations. The Chinese government has invested so much political energy in its anti-Japan propaganda that it would be difficult for it to back down. With its shaky economy and obvious political fragility, we are likely to see more, not less, Chinese nationalism. And China's anti-Japan propaganda has also emboldened Japan's right wing, which seeks to minimize Japanese wartime atrocities. It is also fostering "apology fatigue", especially among Japanese citizens born after the war.

Over the past couple of years, there has been a little softening of the rhetoric between the two countries. They regret the unfortunate economic costs of the "war of words", especially as Japanese investment in China has fallen dramatically over the past few years. Both leaders have met at international events. But it will likely require generational change in both countries, and probably democracy and freedom of the press in China, for real reconciliation to ever take place between the two countries.

As reconciliation will take a very long time, Asian neighbors and indeed the whole world must stay prepared for Northeast Asia remaining one of the world's political hotspots. Indeed, as Japan's Akiko Fukushima has argued, the security environment in Northeast Asia has seriously worsened over past decade with China's military buildup, the thickening of its presence in the South and East China Seas and North Korea's missile testing. This was the motivation for Japan's new security strategy, released in 2013, by which it has shifted from a passive and reactive approach to a proactive one.[11]

Like Japan, Taiwan is another country which, through its trade and investment, has made a major contribution to China's development. But since the election in 2016 of Tsai Ing-wen of the pro-independence Democratic Progressive Party (DPP) to presidency of Taiwan, the Taiwan Straits have become another one of Asia's hotspots.

## Taiwan and China: It's Complicated

China still regards Taiwan as a renegade province, which must be reunified with the mainland under the banner of its "one-China policy", even though it is almost seven decades since Chiang Kai-shek's Chinese Nationalist Party (KMT) fled to Taiwan after losing the China's Civil War in 1949. Today, China's claims seem anachronistic, as Taiwan's GDP per capita is more than three times that of the mainland, and Taiwan has been a successful democracy since the early 1990s in sharp contrast to the increasingly authoritarian China. But China's claims to Taiwan are only intensifying in tandem with its growing economic power. The growing impatience of Chinese President Xi Jinping was palpable when he said that the "Taiwan issue cannot be passed on from generation to generation."

Taiwan is one of Asia's most democratic countries. Its citizens have a choice between two major political parties with different policy agendas. The KMT supports Beijing's one-China policy, and has had very good working relations with Beijing. The DPP is a pro-independence party which Beijing detests. In recent years, there has also been a real and meaningful alternance of power between these two parties, in contrast to Japan which has been dominated by the Liberal Democratic Party. Chen

Shui-bian of the DPP was Taiwan's President from 2000 to 2008, and was followed by Ma Ying-jeou of the KMT from 2000 to 2016. And then following widespread dissatisfaction with the KMT, Madame Tsai Ing-wen of the DPP was elected president, the first female head of state or government in a Chinese territory.

Why would Taiwanese citizens elect the DPP's Madame Tsai and risk the wrath of China's assertive leaders?

The return of the KMT to the presidency in 2008 under Ma Ying-jeou ushered in a golden age of relations between Taiwan and China. Official contacts with Beijing, which had been on hold since 1999, were revived. A free trade agreement between China and Taiwan was signed in 2010. Tourists from Mainland China were permitted to visit Taiwan starting in 2008, with more than ten million Chinese tourists traveling to Taiwan since that time. Overall, more than 20 economic, academic and cultural agreements were signed between Taipei and Beijing under Ma's watch. Underpinning this rapprochement was the "1992 Consensus" by which both sides commit to the principle of "One China", even if they may interpret that principle differently. Notwithstanding these positive developments, Taiwan is substantially shut out of most international organizations and free trade agreements because of pressure exerted by Beijing on the international community. Taiwan only has formal diplomatic relations with a very few countries, 21 mainly small, poor countries at last count.

To the great dismay of Beijing, this period of closer economic linkages saw the two sides drifting apart politically. There was widespread popular discontent in Taiwan, especially among youth, as the public was experiencing rising inequality, high cost of living and declining opportunity. There was a widespread perception that while the Taiwanese business sector benefited from closer linkages with China, ordinary citizens suffered, as business increasingly moved production facilities, and hence jobs, from Taiwan to the lower-cost mainland.

Ma himself became deeply unpopular. There were public concerns about the growing dependence of Taiwan on China, as Ma has been "selling out" Taiwan to the mainland. These feelings came to a head in 2014, when students and activists ("the sunflower movement") occupied the national parliament for three weeks to block the approval of a free trade agreement, and again when students protested against China-friendly changes to curriculum guidelines in Taiwanese schools. These developments took place in a context where the vast majority of Taiwanese citizens now feel a greater attachment to their distinct Taiwanese identity rather than to a Chinese identity. Generational change is fundamentally transforming Taiwan's society and politics, and a majority of its citizens have no interest in unification with China.

It was against this background that Madame Tsai Ing-wen won Taiwan's presidential elections on 16 January 2016 as a representative of the pro-independence DPP, with her inauguration taking place on 20 May. China's communist government has always had a deep allergy to the DPP because it fears that it could declare independence. Indeed, Beijing has long threatened military intervention should Taiwan seek to declare independence. Thus the victory of Tsai Ing-wen was a defiance of Beijing's playbook. Taiwan's citizens should have appreciated the benefits of closer economic and person-to-person linkages under the KMT. Ironically, the increase in person-to-person contacts between China and Taiwan seems to have emphasized their differences for the Taiwanese.

Through the presidential election campaign and subsequently, Tsai Ing-wen refused to adhere to the 1992 Consensus and say that Taiwan and China are part of one country. Rather, she tried to dance a fine line between the pro-independence elements from her party and the incessant demands from Beijing that she commit to the one-China policy. Her standard formulation was that she supports the "status quo", meaning neither independence nor reunification, a position which is supported by the majority of Taiwanese people. But this is not good enough for Beijing which does not trust Tsai Ing-wen and the DPP. Beijing continues trying to bully her into formally accepting the 1992 Consensus on one-China.

Since Tsai's election victory, Beijing has been tightening the screws on Taiwan, employing "megaphone diplomacy" to tell Tsai what to do, stopping all official contacts with Taiwan, encouraging some of Taiwan's diplomatic partners to sever relations with Taiwan, pressuring third countries to repatriate alleged Taiwanese criminals to China, pressuring international organizations to withhold invitations to meetings, and sharply reducing the number of mainland tourists visiting Taiwan.

It is clearly Beijing's intention to undermine the government of Tsai Ing-wen, something which is supported by Taiwan's pro-Beijing business elite. But Beijing's actions may also stiffen the backbone of Taiwanese citizens, especially its youth. Clearly, what is required is a period of trust-building between the two sides. Looking to the longer term, Beijing needs to learn the merits of soft power. Playing hardball is certainly no way to win the hearts and minds of the people of Taiwan. But it has seen a strengthening in the already warm relations between Taiwan and Japan.

Any desire of Taiwanese citizens for the reunification of their country with mainland China is frittering away in tandem with growing interference of Beijing in the affairs of Hong Kong, another source of political instability in Asia.

### Hong Kong and China: It's Even More Complicated

After more than 150 years of British colonial rule, Hong Kong was returned to China in 1997. It was to be governed under the "One country, two systems" principle for the next 50 years. Hong Kong could retain a "high degree of autonomy" for its domestic legal and economic system, while China assumed control of Hong Kong's foreign affairs and interpretation of Hong Kong's Basic Law, a mini-constitution negotiated between the British and Chinese governments.

This was seen to be a "win-win" solution. Hong Kong citizens would keep the many freedoms they enjoy. The Chinese economy would continue to benefit from Hong Kong's role as an important gateway to the global economy thanks to its sophisticated financial, legal and logistics sectors, and its sound rule of law, and advanced education system. And both China and Hong Kong would have 50 years to adapt to each other.

But there has been a progressive deterioration in relations between the Hong Kong population and Beijing in recent years, and Beijing is now openly flouting the Basic Law. There are very many factors which have been driving a wedge between Hong Kong and Beijing. Despite Beijing's reputation for meritocracy and wisdom, its choices for Hong Kong's Chief Executive have been anything but meritocratic or wise. Tung Chee-hwa, the first Chief Executive chosen by Beijing, was widely considered to be incompetent and was deeply unpopular with the Hong Kong public. In 2003, some 500,000 Hong Kongers protested against Tung, who ultimately resigned in 2005, three years into his second five-year term. In February 2017, the second Chief Executive, Donald Tsang, was sentenced to 20 months in prison for corruption, becoming Hong Kong's highest-ranking official to be jailed. The third Chief Executive, Leung Chun-ying, mismanaged Hong Kong's growing social unrest, and did not seek a second term. Beijing has great hopes for Carrie Lam, who was elected as the new Chief Executive in March 2017.

Hong Kong has experienced growing social unrest in recent years, most notably through the "Occupy Central" and "Umbrella Revolution" pro-democracy protests, about the method for choosing future chief executives. Based on the Basic Law and commitments from Beijing, Hong Kong's Chief Executive was scheduled to be elected by universal suffrage from 2017. But Beijing insisted that it choose the election candidates. It insisted that chief executive candidates must "love China and love Hong Kong". Protesters wanted an open nomination process for candidates.

Ultimately, in 2015 pro-democracy members of Hong Kong's Legislative Council ("LegCo") rejected a bill supporting Beijing proposals for the 2017 Chief Executive elections, and Hong Kong's Chief Executive is still not elected via universal suffrage. Relations between Hong Kong and Beijing deteriorated further in 2016 when anti-establishment candidates won 29 out of 70 the Lego seats, including many new faces from the post-Occupy political movement. Beijing then expelled two of these new pro-independence lawmakers from LegCo for "insincere oath-taking" when they severely criticized Beijing.

Although Beijing is very keen for Hong Kong's new Chief Executive, Carrie Lam, to greatly improve relations between the territory and Beijing, this will be a great challenge. In March 2017, Lam was elected by an 1194-member Election Committee, representing only 0.16% of Hong Kong's population. Lam, a former Chief Secretary for Administration, was Beijing's preferred candidate, but not the preferred candidate of the Hong Kong population. That was former Financial Secretary John Tsang. But Beijing intervened to pressure Election Committee members to vote for Lam.

Hong Kongers see the "hand of Beijing" interfering more and more in Hong Kong affairs, in defiance with the Basic Law. Hong Kong's freedom of the press freedom has been in sharp decline, as the number of physical attacks on journalists has increased. Academic freedom and university autonomy are now increasingly compromised in Hong Kong. There have been cases of academics, who are seen as critical of Beijing, being demoted or coming under attack by pro-Beijing media. China's pervasive political influence over Hong Kong was evident in the 2015 extraterritorial abductions, apparently orchestrated by the Chinese government, of booksellers and others who offended Beijing.

Hong Kong's protests were not only inspired by a desire for democracy. They also reflected a broader feeling of popular discontent concerning the cost of living and housing, poverty and inequality, air pollution and the growing presence of mainland tourists, migrants and business. Way back in 2009, then Chinese Premier Wen Jiabao raised the issue of Hong

Kong's "deep contradictions" when he pushed then Chief Executive Donald Tsang to do better in maintaining "Hong Kong's harmony and stability", to little effect.

Hong Kongers can see that its government's policies are stacked in favor of the territory's pro-Beijing business elite. More fundamentally, Hong Kong society is becoming deeply polarized between pro- and anti-Beijing camps. Increasing numbers of youth have no desire to live under Beijing's rule and favor independence of the territory.

Beijing and Hong Kong leaders have blamed "foreign intervention" (meaning US and UK) for stoking up social unrest, reflecting their state of denial of the genuine grievances of Hong Kong citizens, and divisions in Hong Kong society. In fact, Hong Kong's churches played a quiet but important role in the city's protests, offering food and shelter to demonstrators, with some organizers and supporters citing Christian values as inspiration in their fight. "Christians, by definition, don't trust communists," said Joseph Chan, a political-science professor at Chinese University of Hong Kong.

In his speech in 2017 on the occasion of the 20th anniversary of Hong Kong's return to China, China's President Xi Jinping made clear that protests in support of democracy or independence are unacceptable: "Any attempt to endanger China's sovereignty and security, challenge the power of the central government and the authority of the Basic Law of the HKSAR or use Hong Kong to carry out infiltration and sabotage activities against the mainland is an act that crosses the red line, and is absolutely impermissible ... making everything political or deliberately creating differences and provoking confrontation will not resolve the problems.[12]" As Beijing becomes more assertive in its relations with Hong Kong, the UK, the country which agreed the Basic Law with Beijing, is very reluctant to criticize Beijing, as it does not wish to upset the strong business and political relationship between China and the UK.

In all likelihood, Hong Kong will continue to be another growing flash point for Beijing to manage. But the biggest flashpoint in China's sphere of influence is North Korea.

## NORTH KOREAN IMBROGLIO

North Korea and the US are locked in a stalemate in their struggle over North Korea's growing nuclear threat. How did we land in this imbroglio? Is there a way out? Where is China in this imbroglio?

No one should blame North Korea for equipping itself with adequate self-defenses. Every country does that. And following the end of the Korean War in 1953, North Korea had more reason to worry than most countries, being "a shrimp among whales". It was indeed surrounded by the giants of the Soviet Union and China, and enemies like South Korea, Japan and the US with its military bases in these latter two countries.

And as the South Korean economy grew rapidly through the 1970s and 1980s, North Korea felt even more vulnerable with its stagnating centrally planned economy. It was during the 1980s that North Korea reportedly began acquiring nuclear technology with lots of help from friends like Pakistan, China and the Soviet Union.

The end of the Cold War and the 1990s was a major turning point in North Korea's modern history. It suffered greatly from the loss of financial support from the Soviet Union, natural disasters and economic mismanagement which led to a massive famine with over 300,000 people dying (it did however benefit from out-of-work Russian rocket scientists who sought work in North Korea). And then Kim Il-sung, the founding father of North Korea, died in 1994, and was succeeded by his eccentric and fun-loving son, Kim Jong-il.

The Kim dictatorship was spooked by the democratization and adoption of market economics in Russia, and Soviet satellites in Central and Eastern Europe, and Mongolia. The reunification of East and West Germany also exacerbated North Korea's fear of a US desire to reunify North and South Korea.

The lesson that North Korea drew from the end of the Cold War was that rather transforming into a market economy and democracy, it should double down on efforts for regime survival. So it invested heavily in its military capabilities both to act as a deterrent to potential aggressors and to extract economic concessions from the US, Japan and South Korea. North Korea also maintained firm control over the economy (the self-reliance or "juche" philosophy), in contrast to China's market opening.

The US interventions in Iraq, Afghanistan and Libya only confirmed the vulnerabilities that the Kim regime felt, and vindicated its policy of building up nuclear weapons. As a North Korean official once said, "the US would not have invaded Afghanistan if it had nuclear weapons."

Over the past two decades or so North Korea has been playing cat and mouse with the international community over its development of ballistic missiles and nuclear weapons. Following each nuclear test or missile launch, the UN Security Council declares its condemnations, and imposes trade and financial sanctions on North Korea, but nothing changes. "Six-party talks" involving North Korea, South Korea, China, Japan, US and Russia were held from 2003 to 2009. But North Korea sabotaged and walked away from these diplomatic efforts to bring a halt to North Korea's development of nuclear weapons.

Today, the Chinese government is immensely irritated by North Korea, and sees great dangers in its volatile behavior. But China has played a crucial role in the development of the North Korean menace. Some 90% of North Korea's trade is with China, which is also responsible for the lion's share of its foreign investment. China also hosts thousands of North Korean workers, most of whose wages goes back to the North Korean regime. North Korea is highly dependent on Chinese aid, especially for food and energy.

The Chinese government has allowed North Korean state-owned enterprises to operate in China. They very often buy materials and goods from Chinese and international companies, and then export them to North Korea. Then there are Chinese enterprises like the Dandong Hongxiang Development Company which have been helping North Korea procure raw materials for nuclear weapons. And Chinese banks reportedly hold some of the Kim family assets. At the UN Security Council, China always pushes for moderation and loopholes in sanctions on North Korea. China routinely condemns North Korea's actions and urges it to comply with UN resolutions. But it has never implemented US sanctions seriously.

Why would China support such a heinous regime? It's a question of strategic buffers. As Beijing looks out toward the Pacific Ocean, it feels encircled by a string of US allies—from South Korea and Japan to Taiwan and the Philippines. In other words, the Chinese see North Korea as a critical protective buffer for them against the US.

So China does not want a regime change that would see the US and China battling for control of the Korean peninsula. The last thing that China wants is a failed nuclear state on its border, with the prospect of millions of poor refugees flooding into the country. It is also fearful that regime change could result in a reunification of North and South Korea, with the new state aligned with the US, and American troops sitting directly on its border.

China is of course not the only friend of North Korea. The Pakistan Energy Commission has reportedly sold nuclear materials to North Korea, some of which they have initially bought from China. The recent murder of Kim Jong-nam has highlighted the close links between Malaysia and

North Korea. And Myanmar's military reportedly has close ties with Pyongyang.

US–North Korean relations have been on a downward slide for many years. But North Korea's rogue activities took a dramatic turn for the worse with the ascension of Kim Jong-un to North Korea's leadership, following the death of his father, Kim Jong-il, in 2011. The new 30-something-year-old dictator, with no direct military or governmental experience, has had to consolidate and assert his leadership to win the necessary loyalty of the military. This has meant eliminating all possible rivals, including his uncle and most recently his half-brother, Kim Jong-nam, as well as accelerating his missile and nuclear program. Kim Jong-un conducted two nuclear tests and more than 20 ballistic tests in 2016 alone. And already, he has greeted Donald Trump with a flurry of missile launches in 2017.

After Donald Trump won the US presidential election, outgoing President Barack Obama warned Trump that the first major challenge he would face was North Korea. Indeed, North Korea is widely perceived to be the greatest threat to security, stability and peace in Asia and the rest of the world. Today, North Korea could attack South Korea, Japan, the US base in Guam, and probably even the US mainland with nuclear and other missiles.

The bellicose Donald Trump, surrounded by ex-army generals in his Cabinet, may not be the coolest head for dealing with North Korea. The Trump team announced that the era of Obama's "strategic patience" is over. That all options are on the table, including the military option. The possibility of taking out Kim Jong-un has also been raised. In other words, it is hardly surprising that Kim should have upped the ante in 2017.

The Trump team believes that by ratcheting up the pressure, as the UN did in 2017, North Korea can be forced to give up its nuclear weapons, and to engage dialogue. But the evidence suggests that the more North Korea feels cornered, the more it will still stick to its nuclear weapons. North Korea sees the US and US-supported South Korea as being the principal threats to its security.

Trump had a successful first summit with President Xi Jinping in April 2017 and seemed to have enlisted his support to help control North Korea. However, it only took a couple of months for Trump to realize that China is reluctant to seriously tackle North Korea for fear of destabilizing the regime, despite agreeing to new, tougher UN sanctions.

Chinese President XI Jinping seems equally fearful of Donald Trump as of Kim Jong-un. He is pushing both sides to de-escalate tensions and engage in dialogue. Both China and Russia are arguing for a "double-freeze", whereby North Korea would stopping testing weapons, and the US and South Korea would stop their military exercises. At the same time, China is cutely claiming that the North Korean problem is a problem between the US and North Korea, and does not involve China.

Some experts argue that a grand deal is the only hope—freeze or elimination of North Korea's nuclear program in return for economic assistance, a guarantee that the US would not seek to overthrow the regime and a formal peace treaty. But the level of distrust between the US and North Korea is so great that it is difficult to imagine such a grand deal being agreed. It also seems clear that the US will ultimately have to accept North Korea as a nuclear power, and live with that, as it did with China many decades ago. It will also have to accept that unification of the Korean peninsula under South Korea would never be accepted by China, and is not a realistic option.

Although China wants political stability on the Korean peninsula, it is also very keen that any resolution of the North Korean problem results in a weakening of the US position in Asia—such as by a reduction in the US commitment to defend South Korea through a cut or even removal of US troops from the South. Even though there is no love lost between China and North Korea, the North will have done China a great favor if it manages to weaken the alliance between US and South Korea.

Trade is another factor which is working in China's favor. South Korea is becoming increasingly dependent on the Chinese market. And, depending on the outcome, Donald Trump's threat to renegotiate or even abolish the US-Korea Free Trade Agreement could help tilt South Korea's trade further toward China. The South China Sea is another area where China has stolen a march on the US and its partners, and will remain a strategic flashpoint for at least some time to come.

## CHINA SNAFFLES THE SOUTH CHINA SEA FROM ITS SOUTHEAST ASIAN NEIGHBORS

Myriad countries surround the South China Sea, namely China, the Philippines, Vietnam, Brunei, Malaysia and Taiwan. It is thus not surprising that since time immemorial these same countries should have had overlapping claims to these waters, their reefs, islands and atolls, including the Spratly Islands, Paracel Islands and Scarborough Shoal. The South China Sea is a massive 1.4 square million miles, an area the size of Mexico and larger than the Mediterranean Sea.

In 1947, China issued a map of its claims, which encompassed about 90% of the entire South China Sea. This claim has come to be known as the "nine-dash-line", which reflects the pictorial representation of China's claim. In 2009, China submitted a diplomatic note to the UN including the nine-dash-line on a map. This overlaps with claims by the Philippines, Vietnam, Malaysia, Indonesia and Brunei. According to the UN Convention on the Law of the Sea (UNCLOS), to which China is a signatory, countries have special access to marine resources, including fisheries, oil and gas, in the area up to 200 nautical miles from their shores, called exclusive economic zones. Most of the South China Sea is very much further from China than that distance.

In 2012, China forcibly seized control of the previously unoccupied Scarborough Shoal during a standoff with the Philippine Navy. The Scarborough Shoal is only 100 miles from the Philippines, but 500 miles from China. Under a 2012 deal mediated by the US, China and the Philippines promised to withdraw their forces from the shoal until a deal over its ownership could be reached. The Philippines complied with the agreement and withdrew. China, however, did not abide by the agreement and maintained its presence at the shoal, effectively militarizing it. Then Philippine President Benigno S. Aquino III later compared China's behavior to Nazi Germany's annexation of Czechoslovakia.

With no other recourse, the Philippines took China to a UNCLOS tribunal. China boycotted the tribunal's proceedings on the basis that it had indisputable sovereignty over its claimed area and that the tribunal did not have the authority to deal with this matter. Reflecting its indignation and contempt for the Philippine challenge, China embarked on massive construction exercise in the South China Sea, building or expanding at least seven artificial islands, some with airports on which military aircraft can land.

This was clearly a ploy to create "facts on the water", which are irreversible. It is dubbed the great wall of sand by senior US officials. In 2014, China also deployed a deep-sea oil rig within Vietnam's exclusive economic zone, leading to a drawn out dispute. President Obama's reluctance to stand up to Beijing during the early stages of its blatant land reclamation activities in the South China Sea only emboldened Beijing to continue with its buildup and militarization of artificial islands. And the US' subsequent freedom of navigation exercises through the South China Sea are a case of "too little/too late".

What is at stake in the South China Sea? According to the US Department of Energy, there would be 11 billion barrels of oil in the South China Sea, and 190 trillion cubic feet of natural gas. It is also a very rich fishing ground, which is now most regrettably being depleted. Some $5.3 trillion worth of international trade passes through the South China Sea, about 30% of global maritime trade. And $1.2 trillion of this is US trade. Japan and Korea also rely heavily on the South China Sea for their supply of energy and other raw materials, and also as an export route. Some 60% of Australia's trade passes through the South China Sea. Not surprisingly, non-claimants want the South China Sea to remain as international waters, rather than being privatized by China. Circumnavigating the South China Sea would drive up commercial shipping costs.

More fundamentally, the international rule of law is at stake. China is a country that has benefited from the multilateral system, but is now seen by most to be flagrantly flouting this very system. As former French Defense Minister Jean-Yves Le Drian said: "If the Law of the Sea is not respected today in the South China Sea, it will be threatened tomorrow in the Arctic, the Mediterranean or elsewhere." Vladimir Putin and other authoritarians are watching.

The UNCLOS arbitration tribunal accepted 14 of the 15 claims by the Philippines. In particular, it ruled that there is no legal basis for any Chinese historic rights within the nine-dash line. The tribunal also ruled that none of the disputed maritime features in the Spratly Islands, including Scarborough Shoal, Gaven Reef and Fiery Cross Reef, are islands under the law of the sea (they are instead "rocks"). Thus, they do not result in entitlements to a 200 mile exclusive economic zone or continental shelf. In other words, Scarborough Shoal—the scene of the standoff between the Philippine Navy and China—is within the Philippines' maritime domain, rather than China's. The tribunal also found that China's land reclamation and island-building activities had caused irreparable damage to the coral reef ecosystem and breached the UNCLOS treaty. And in the case of Scarborough Shoal, China breached the treaty by undertaking land reclamation without the authorization of the Philippines.

China is legally bound by the UNCLOS decision, by virtue of being a signatory to the treaty. But there are no enforcement mechanisms, and China never had any intention of respecting the judgment. The Chinese government lambasted the tribunal's judgment, claiming that it is part of an American conspiracy. On the Philippine side, there were great public celebrations in this nation that is tired of being bullied by more powerful nations.

But the UNCLOS decision was delivered just a matter of days after Rodrigo Duterte assumed the presidency of the Philippines, following the six-year term of Benigno Aquino III. While Aquino's foreign policy was closely aligned with the US, its treaty ally, Duterte has shifted course to an "independent" foreign policy. His firebrand and colorful personality was in evidence when he visited China in 2016 and said "I announce my separation from the United States, both in military but economics also … America has lost it." He announced the Philippines would align itself with China and Russia.

Duterte's approach has been to seek cooperation rather than conflict with China over the South China Sea. Indeed, as he garnered $24 billion worth of investment and financing agreements from China, he has clearly sought to use the South China Sea as a bargaining chip with China. China has allowed Philippine fishermen to return to the Scarborough Shoal. Meanwhile, China has only accelerated its constructions and militarization of its artificial islands.

Perhaps realistically, Duterte said "We cannot stop China from doing its thing. Even the Americans were not able to stop them … So what do you want me to do? Declare war against China?" The Chinese government is surely celebrating that this Scarborough Shoal incident has enabled it to drive a wedge between the Philippines and the US which had hitherto been the closest of allies. Malaysia, another important claimant to the South China Sea, has also been silent following another large signing of trade deals. The only Asian country left challenging China in the South China Sea seems to be Vietnam.

The new US administration of President Trump has made many feisty comments regarding China's actions in the South China Sea. Secretary of State Rex Tillerson even said that US would prevent China from accessing its own artificial islands in the South China Sea. And even though this region is a long, long way from Washington, the US does have enduring interests in the dispute, namely, freedom of navigation and overflight, support for the rules-based international order and the peaceful resolution of disputes. But it seems hardly likely that President Trump will invest too much political capital in this dispute, when most of the claimants are no longer fighting for the issue, and when he has bigger fish to fry with China.

In sum, China has achieved a stunning victory in the South China Sea over its Southeast Asian neighbors and weakened ASEAN in the process. And while the US may have kept its powder dry for possible future conflicts, its inaction seems to have only emboldened China and weakened the credibility of the US as a security partner in East Asia.

## China Fractures ASEAN

ASEAN, the Association of Southeast Asian Nations, represents Asia's most successful effort at regional cooperation and integration. But it is now being increasingly fractured and dominated by China.

China was already on the minds of ASEAN's founding fathers in 1967 when the governments of Indonesia, Malaysia, the Philippines, Singapore and Thailand decided to join forces. Security was of paramount importance during this Cold War period, when ASEAN was concerned about the threat of communism coming from China and Vietnam. During the 1960s, Mao Zedong supported communist insurgency movements in Southeast Asia. Over the years, ASEAN has gradually expanded with the membership of Brunei (1984), Vietnam (1995), Laos and Myanmar (1997) and Cambodia (1999).

Though huddling between Asia's giants of China and India, with their billion-plus populations, ASEAN is an important regional player. Its population of 622 million is almost double America's 320 million and also more than the European Union's (EU) 506 million. As a group, ASEAN is an economic powerhouse, being the world's seventh biggest economy. And while ASEAN has not grown as quickly as China or India, the group has been one of the world's fastest-growing markets with an annual average growth rate of 5.1% from 2000 to 2013. Indonesia, with a population of 260 million, accounts for almost 40% of ASEAN's GDP.

With the end of the Cold War and the emerging globalization of the world economy, ASEAN was transformed into an important organization for economic cooperation, as well as political and social–cultural cooperation. The ASEAN Free Trade Area was signed in 1992, and now includes all ten ASEAN members. Building on this, in 2015 the ASEAN Community came into force with economic, political–security and socio-cultural pillars.

With international squabbling, rather than cooperation, being the currency in Northeast and South Asia, ASEAN has become an effective meeting ground and fulcrum for Asian cooperation. Six other regional partners—China, Japan, Korea, Australia, New Zealand and India—have free trade agreements with ASEAN, and talks are under way to transform them into a single undertaking, the Regional Comprehensive Economic Partnership (RCEP).

ASEAN takes a leading role in security dialogue in Asia through the ASEAN Regional Forum (ARF), which was established in 1994, and now includes 27 members. The ARF is unique in that North Korea is a member, and its 2017 meeting provided an important opportunity for discussions with the North on its nuclear and missile programs. ASEAN is also in a leadership position of the East Asia Summit which is a regional leaders' forum for strategic dialogue and cooperation on key challenges facing the East Asian region.

While concern about the threat of Chinese communism was a key motivator for the creation of ASEAN, China has since become a leading partner of the ASEAN countries, in many cases now overtaking Japan, which had previously been the leading partner. China is ASEAN's most important trading partner, with the least developed countries of Cambodia, Laos, Myanmar and Vietnam being the most reliant on Chinese trade. China is the most important source of FDI in Cambodia, Laos and Myanmar, and the second most important in Vietnam, even though it is not yet a major investor in ASEAN overall. China has also been investing heavily in infrastructure in ASEAN countries bordering China, namely Laos, Myanmar and Vietnam. And Chinese tourists are now flooding ASEAN countries, bringing much-appreciated revenues.

In short, China's rise is exerting a powerful pull over ASEAN economies and politics, and the Chinese government now routinely tries to lord it over ASEAN in their regular meetings. China's contempt for ASEAN was on full display in a 2010 meeting in Hanoi, Vietnam, when China's then foreign minister Yang Jiechi famously said "China is a big country and you are small countries and that is a fact" (Yang was subsequently promoted to the Chinese State Council). Many cite this comment as the trigger for US President Obama's pivot to Asia.

China's divide-and-rule of ASEAN has been in full evidence as it succeeded in pressuring several ASEAN countries to refrain from supporting the decision of the arbitration tribunal of the UNCLOS in favor of the Philippines and against China. For the moment, China seems to have bought off the claims of Malaysia and the Philippines with packages of trade, investment and assistance. Brunei is too small to stand up to China. Only Vietnam is seriously attempting to push China back.

Throughout this process, ASEAN has been totally ineffective at working as a group to counter China's claims to the South China Sea. For example, Cambodia, Beijing's most loyal stooge, has blocked or watered down mentions of the South China Sea dispute in ASEAN ministerial communiqués, which are agreed by consensus. Laos and Malaysia have also been weak on the South China Sea issue due to Chinese pressure. And Thailand has been moving into Beijing's orbit as the US has criticized the role of the military in Thai politics and the deterioration in human rights, following the 2014 military coup.

A possible South China Sea code of conduct between ASEAN and China has been talked about since 2002, but China has always used stalling tactics. Now that China has achieved its goal of seizing the South China Sea, discussions are now back under way, but are moving slowly, as China rushes ahead with its construction and militarization. And while the Philippines and Vietnam have pushed for a legally binding code, China is insisting on a non-binding code. China will not accept an independent dispute settlement mechanism. And above all, China prefers bilateral negotiations to resolve all disputes, so it can play the carrots and sticks game to submit smaller countries to its will.

As China seeks to create a sphere of influence in East Asia, ASEAN is becoming a casualty of China's realpolitik.[13] A strong and united ASEAN could protect the region's interests in the South China Sea and elsewhere. But it is in China's interest to have a weak and divided ASEAN, and China is succeeding famously in this regard.

The US has long had close relations with most ASEAN countries. But there was some fallout between the US and Malaysia, the Philippines and Thailand during the Obama administration. And Donald Trump paid no attention to Singapore's warning about the importance of the Trans-Pacific Partnership (TPP). Overall, the general feeling in ASEAN is that the US' interest in and commitment to the region is waning. While Japan is becoming more active and competing with China for regional influence, it has difficulty vying with China. In particular, China's AIIB and the BRI are proving to be very important instruments for strengthening relations between Beijing and individual ASEAN countries.

## China's Leadership for Asian Infrastructure

Massive investments in infrastructure have been a major element in China's development strategy. They have also become the key instrument for China's efforts to re-shape international cooperation in Asia and beyond.

Under Chinese leadership, AIIB opened for business in 2016. This initiative was motivated by the US Congress' delays in approving an increase in the weight of China and other emerging economies in the IMF and World Bank. It was also inspired by China's feeling that the multilateral international system was still too dominated by the West.

The Obama administration pressured all of its friends and allies not to join the AIIB. The US saw it as a competitor for the US-led World Bank and the Japan-led Asian Development Bank (ADB). But ultimately the UK broke ranks, and was then followed by virtually all other advanced and emerging economies. At last count the AIIB had 56 member countries. Japan and the US are the only major countries to have not signed up. And in acts of contrition, the World Bank and ADB are now cooperating very closely with the AIIB.

The new bank's lending may be only slowly getting off the ground, but it already has more members than the ADB and its authorized lending limit is also higher than the ADB's. The new competition from the AIIB has seen the ADB streamline its lending procedures and rush to approve new lending. Overall, the AIIB is seen as great success for Chinese leadership in Asia and the multilateral system more generally. After all, Asia's infrastructure needs are enormous, some $1700 billion a year in investments in power, transport, telecommunications and water through 2030, according to ADB estimates. For its part, the US is seen have egg on its face from its strategic blunder in opposing the AIIB. If the US really wanted China to become a responsible stakeholder in the international system, it should never have opposed China's initiative to create the AIIB.

While the rivalry between the ADB and the AIIB is capturing international attention, the biggest race to finance Asia's infrastructure is between Japanese and Chinese national institutions. Lending by the Japan Bank for International Co-operation and the Japan International Co-operation Agency dwarfs that of the ADB, while the China Development Bank and the Export-Import Bank of China together lend many times what the AIIB will lend when it hits cruising speed.

"This funding race has many upsides," says Robert Wihtol of the Manila-based Asian Institute of Management. "The competition is increasing the total financing available for Asian infrastructure. And having numerous financial institutions increases the scope for joint financing, which can spread the risk inherent in large projects."

Mr. Wihtol cautioned, however, that the race to finance Asia's enormous infrastructure also has its downsides. "Geopolitical rivalries can see projects of questionable value get rapidly approved, without proper preparation or cost-benefit analysis, thereby saddling borrowers with burdensome debt, as we have seen in Sri Lanka," he says. "And there are many examples of lenders not taking sufficient account of sovereign risk, most notably in the case of Venezuela. In this context, the advantage of multilateral banks like ADB and AIIB is that they conduct thorough risk analysis and due diligence."[14]

## Belt and Road Initiative for a Sinocentric Asia

The BRI is another Chinese initiative to improve infrastructure, notably across Eurasia. In the eyes of many, however, it is also an initiative that seeks to advance China's hegemonic ambitions in Asia.

It was in 2013 that Chinese President Xi Jinping launched his BRI with the aim of connecting major Eurasian economies through infrastructure, trade and investment. This initiative is a key element in Xi's "China Dream" for the great rejuvenation of the Chinese nation, and for China to become the paramount Asian country. Xi has invited BRI partners to join a "Community of Common Destiny".

The BRI comprises two main elements — the Silk Road Economic Belt and the 21st Century Maritime Silk Road. The Silk Road Economic Belt will be a network of high-speed railways, roads, pipelines and utility grids which will provide improved connections between China and Central Asia, parts of South Asia, the Middle East and ultimately Europe. This will reduce China's sense of vulnerability due to its reliance on Straits of Malacca and the South China Sea for its energy imports from the Middle East. The Maritime Silk Road will create ports and other infrastructure to better connect China with Southeast Asia, South Asia, the Middle East, East Africa and Europe (China already owns the Greek port of Piraeus).

Six major economic corridors are planned, including the New Eurasian Land Bridge, China–Mongolia–Russia, China–Central Asia–Western Asia, Indo-China Peninsula, China–Pakistan and Bangladesh–China–India–Myanmar. Some 68 countries, representing 55% of world GDP and 70% of world population, have signed up to the BRI.[15]

The financing needs of the BRI will be enormous. China's total investment in the BRI over the next decade is expected to reach $1.6 trillion, according to preliminary estimates by the China International Capital Corporation. This exceeds by many times the capital of the ADB, the AIIB, the New Development Bank and China's Silk Road Fund, which will only play small roles in the overall financing. Much of the funding will come through loans from the China Development Bank and other Chinese state-owned banks.

The BRI has a different model from other regional economic initiatives. For example, agreements like the RCEP and TPP mainly concern trade liberalization and policy reform, whereas the BRI focuses on improving infrastructure connectivity. Further, the BRI is not an organization like the EU or a multilateral agreement like the RCEP or TPP. It is a Sinocentric "hub-and-spoke" arrangement of bilateral agreements between China and each of the participating countries. And these are only political, not legal, agreements. This means that China, as the dominant partner in each of these agreements, will have a tremendous ability to set agendas and advance its own interests.

In this sense, the BRI is not only inspired by the legendary trade along the Silk Road, but as David Arase once remarked, it is a "backward looking vision of the future" which seeks to recreate a Sinocentric regional order from the past.[16] But the BRI is clearly the signature project of President Xi, and will remain a very high priority during his presidency, even if it is unwieldy and perhaps overly ambitious.

The BRI has generated mixed reactions. Many have welcomed China's bold initiative, which promises to help address Asia's massive infrastructure deficit, and which could provide a much needed boost to economic growth through the market integration it will foster. And through the BRI China is proving to be a more reliable partner than the US, which abandoned the TPP after several years of hard work by all the negotiating countries.

However, the ratings agency Fitch has also highlighted the risks for China's banking sector emanating from the BRI (also known as OBOR, "one belt, one road").[17] "OBOR is driven primarily by China's efforts to extend its global influence and relieve domestic overcapacity", notes Fitch, and "there is a risk that projects ... could fail to deliver expected returns." Fitch has doubts that China's banks can identify profitable projects— "After all", says Fitch, "Chinese banks do not have a track record of allocating resources efficiently at home, especially in relation to infrastructure projects." "Meanwhile, local politicians have an incentive to associate themselves with marquee projects. This subjugation of market forces means there is a heightened risk of projects proving unprofitable."

The asymmetries of size and power between China and the participating countries make the BRI unique and challenging. As countries like the Philippines, Vietnam and Japan have discovered in recent times, disagreements with China can lead to punishment by the Chinese government in the form of reduced market access and diplomatic exclusion. China will not accept the role of international tribunals to resolve disputes, such that international law will not play a role in BRI.[18] And China's assertive behavior in the East and South China Seas has only made BRI partners suspicious of its motives.

The benefits for partner countries can be questionable, as most BRI infrastructure projects will be financed by Chinese state-owned banks, and built by state-owned Chinese companies, using Chinese workers and suppliers. Partner countries can be left with an enormous debt to the Chinese banks, sometimes for projects of dubious value.

On the ground, China has been running into opposition. The upgrade of Sri Lanka's deep-sea port in Hambantota saw street protests and opposition by legislators because of the perceived generous concessions to China. As the port quickly became a loss-making white elephant, the government was forced to look for a way out, which eventually took the form of a debt-to-equity swap granting state-controlled China Merchant Holdings control of the port and a 99-year concession to develop its operations.[19] There have also been reports of the Chinese People's Liberation Army's navy using this commercial port for visits of military submarines.[20]

What are the prospects for the BRI looking forward? According to Paul Keating, former Australian Prime Minister, and now advisor to the China Development Bank, "What we're going to see is a reasonably obvious economic colonisation of the 50-odd states between the western border of China up to at least western Europe."[21]

The BRI will no doubt encounter many hiccoughs along the way, and its full ambitions may never be fully met. But the attractiveness of Chinese money to finance Asia's massive infrastructure deficit will be irresistible to many countries, even if it means becoming part of China's sphere of political influence.

One hiccough for China's BRI has been the frictions that it has generated with India, Asia's other behemoth.

## Chinese and Indian Frictions

China has joined forces with India's arch enemy, Pakistan, to build the China–Pakistan Economic Corridor. This initiative is a bold package of investment projects ($44½ billion or about 16% of Pakistan's GDP), in energy and transport infrastructure, financed by Chinese loans and FDI. The Corridor is a "flagship project" which will link the Chinese city of Kashgar to the Pakistani port of Gwadar, thereby potentially connecting the Silk Road Economic Belt with the Maritime Silk Road, which would enable China's energy imports from the Middle East to circumvent the Straits of Malacca.

The IMF has issued warnings about the project and its management. It noted that Pakistan's current account deficit could widen during the investment phase, and that over the longer term, Pakistan will need to manage the repatriation of profits and loan repayments of Chinese investors. As the IMF also warns sharply, "There is a need to ensure sound project evaluation and prioritization mechanisms based on effective cost-benefit analysis … The procurement process should be transparent and competitive, and there is a need to ensure transparency and accountability in project management and monitoring."[22]

India has several profound concerns about the Economic Corridor. During a 2015 visit to Beijing, Indian Prime Minister Narendra Modi reportedly told Chinese leaders that China–Pakistan Economic Corridor is "unacceptable" because it passes through Pakistan-occupied Kashmir, an area claimed by India. India fears that Pakistan's port of Gwadar could become a Chinese naval base, rather than a commercial hub.

Beyond the China–Pakistan Economic Corridor, India has many understandable concerns now that China's quest for regional dominance seems to have extended to the Indian Ocean, after conquering the South China Sea. In particular, India fears being encircled in the Indian Ocean by Chinese-financed ports. China now has a majority stake in Sri Lanka's Hambantota port, which straddles the world's busiest east-west shipping route. Bangladesh has inked memorandums of understanding with two Chinese companies for the construction of components of the Payra deep-sea port. China is reportedly seeking an 85% stake in the strategically important deep-sea port of Kyauk Pyu in Myanmar on the Bay of Bengal. And the Maldives has leased an island close to Malé airport to a Chinese company for 50 years.

As India's former Defense Minister, Pallam Raju, once remarked, there is a need for more information sharing regarding the BRI. "China is not necessarily a benign power, and it should be more transparent," said Mr. Raju.[23] So it was not entirely surprising that when China hosted a BRI Summit in May 2017, India should boycott this meeting which brought together leaders and officials of 130 countries, 68 of which had already signed on to the Initiative. The Indian government reiterated its objections, namely that it includes projects in land belonging to India, it could push smaller countries into crushing debt cycles, it could destroy the ecology and disrupt local communities, and that China's agenda was unclear, suggesting that the BRI was more about enhancing its political influence, not just its physical networks.

Concerns over the BRI come on top of seven decades of on-again, off-again frictions between China and India. There are several border disputes along their shared 3500 km border, and China claims the Indian state of Arunachal Pradesh as its own. The two nations fought a war in 1962, which China won decisively, and there have been several other conflicts and skirmishes. The most recent dispute occurred in mid-2017, when India responded to Bhutan's cry for help as China was found to be building a road in an area disputed by Bhutan and China. The two great powers then spent over two months facing each other in a military standoff.

There have been many other factors driving frictions between Asia's two great powers. India sees China as a source of regional instability through its support for Pakistan, and in particular its nuclear weapons program. India was never happy about China's annexation of Tibet, which it had considered an important strategic buffer. For its part, China is not happy that its nemesis, the Dalai Lama, lives in India, where he has set up a Tibetan government in exile in the city of Dharamshala. In more recent years, trade and investment ties between China and India have boomed, and China has become India's largest trading partner. But the balance has been heavily in China's favor. More generally, Chinese media and commentators often have a condescending attitude toward India, and the perceived inefficiencies of its chaotic democracy.

It is not surprising that in recent years India has pivoted its foreign policy toward forging partnerships with the US, Japan and Southeast Asia. For example, the navies of India, Japan and the US undertake a joint annual exercise, "Exercise Malabar". And India's Look East policy seeks to cultivate relations with Southeast Asia as a counterweight to the strategic influence of China.

As we have argued, India's economic size will progressively challenge China's over the course of the twenty-first century and will likely result in an intensification of frictions between these two great Asian powers. And the Indian Ocean could well become a theater for future conflict.

China's growing assertiveness in East Asia instigated US President Barack Obama's "pivot" to Asia.

## Obama's Pivot to Asia

The election of Barack Obama promised a new phase in America's relationship with Asia, following George Bush's costly decade of Middle East wars. In a speech in Tokyo in 2009, the first year of his presidency, he billed himself as "America's first Pacific president" (he was born in Hawaii), promising the nations of Asia "a new era of engagement with the world based on mutual interests and mutual respect".

Obama was very right to focus on Asia. With some 60% of US trade being with the Pacific region, Asian maritime and regional security are vital US interests. Japan and China are the biggest foreign holders of US Treasury Securities, with Hong Kong, Taiwan and India also being important investors. And the US has long-standing security ties with Japan, Korea, the Philippines, Thailand, Taiwan and Singapore, with a combined 80,000 troops stationed in Japan and Korea.

Asian Americans, which now make up 6% of the nation's population, are also America's fastest-growing and most successful migrant group—their average household income is some 30% higher than Americans overall. China, India and Korea account for over half the foreign students in the US, with Vietnam, Taiwan and Japan also being in the top 10. Japan, China and Korea are among the top 10 source countries for foreign tourists in America. All these factors generate deep human and emotional connections between the US and Asia.

It was perhaps not surprising that in 2011 President Obama should decide to deepen his engagement through his "pivot" to Asia. The US pivot was an attempt at a longer term strengthening of America's already deep engagement with the Asia-Pacific region, in light of the region's growing importance, and also in light of the reverberations from the rise of China. On the military side, it was planned that by 2020, the US navy would reposture its forces from today's roughly 50–50% split between the Pacific and the Atlantic to about a 60–40 split between those oceans. In the economic area, the TPP was the key piece. Obama's defense secretary

Ashton Carter once said that the "TPP is as important to me as another aircraft carrier."

President Obama's pivot to Asia was subject to much criticism. Its initial emphasis was on the military dimension. Some argued that Obama's pivot reflected the US desire to "contain" China, and that by exacerbating strategic rivalry, the US actually provoked China's subsequent assertive behavior, notably in the South China Sea. Others argue that it was all talk and no action, with very few substantive results.

US bilateral relations with other Asian countries were a mixture of sweet and sour through the Obama administration. President Obama had bromances with Manmohan Singh and especially Narendra Modi, the two Indian prime ministers who overlapped with his presidency. They had a lot in common, coming from the world's two largest democracies, and sharing a concern about China's assertive behavior. Economic and military cooperation also strengthened greatly Vietnam, a member of the TPP. Washington also lifted its decades-long embargo on selling lethal arms to Vietnam, despite the war history between the two countries. The Obama administration fostered a warm relationship with Myanmar and its de facto leader Aung San Suu Kyi, even though there were great concerns about the country's appalling treatment of its Rohingya minority.

At the same time, Obama oversaw a cooling of relations with a number of countries. In the case of Thailand, the 2014 coup and the failure of the military to restore democracy, together with growing human rights abuses, led to strained relations with one of America's closest friends in Asia. Thailand's military government has since moved closer to China. Obama had made great efforts to foster warm relations with Malaysia, a moderate Muslim country, for its help in fighting radical Islamic terrorism. In 2014, he even played golf with Malaysian Prime Minister Najib Razak in Hawaii. But the US Justice Department's lawsuit concerning Malaysia's corrupt sovereign wealth fund, 1MDB, saw a fading of the friendship.

After a strengthening in US–Philippines military cooperation under President Aquino, the new Philippine President Rodrigo Duterte distanced his country from the US, following its criticism of human rights abuses in the country's murderous war against drugs. In the case of both Malaysia and the Philippines, Beijing has been able to step into the gap left the US and assuage objections to its military buildup in the South China Sea by through generous trade, investment and aid packages. Despite America's infatuation with Myanmar's Aung San Suu Kyi, she is also cultivating close links with China. And like his predecessors, Obama was unable to put a halt to North Korea's missile and nuclear arm development. And lastly, Obama's Asian diplomacy was guilty of one really big blunder, its opposition to the Chinese-led AIIB.

Despite the great promise of America's first Pacific president, and his pivot to Asia, America's footprint in the region weakened during the Obama presidency. Competing with China for Asian friendships is increasingly difficult for the US. Short-term imperatives in the Middle East, Russia and Washington will also always draw US attentions away from the longer term strategic importance of Asia. The Chinese provide lots of financial and infrastructure to buy friendships, which the US does not do. China also uses trade as an extension of their foreign policy, and is not concerned about ethical issues like corruption and human rights.

Ever since Nixon's trip to China in 1972, American policy elites had believed that encouraging China's participation in the global economy and global governance would result in China becoming a responsible stakeholder in the post-war multilateral system, and becoming "more like us". In this context, the Obama administration was also the time when America discovered that democracy, rule of law and human rights were not coming to China any time soon, as the Chinese Communist Party under President Xi Jinping was tightening its grip on power. Moreover, even though China had been a great beneficiary of the post-war order, in tandem with its rise in power, China is intent on challenging the post-war order, and pushing America out of Asia.

A deterioration in US–China relations under the Obama administration set the stage for China to become the whipping boy of Donald Trump's presidential election campaign.

## Trump's Potshots at Asia

During the election campaign and before his inauguration, Donald Trump had much to say about Asia and China in particular. As we have discussed above, Trump was very critical of trade relations with China, the TPP, China's military island-building program in the South China Sea and its lack of help to contain North Korea. Trump also threatened to make Japan and Korea pay more for the US military troops and assets that are defending them, and suggested that they could acquire nuclear weapons so that they could assure their own defense. Trump also questioned the "One-China Policy", and spoke by telephone with Taiwan President Tsai Ing-wen.

The Trump administration moved quickly into action on the Asian front, as it withdrew the US from the TPP. At the same time, Trump's rhetoric on trade policy has been evolving and softening, as he is now arguing for both free and fair trade. He is concerned about the lack of reciprocity in trading relations, and would now like US trade policy to focus on bilateral, rather than multilateral deals, to secure better market access. Despite the softening in Trump's trade rhetoric, there remains a strongly protectionist undercurrent, as Trump's overriding trade policy goals are reducing the US' bilateral trade deficits (notably with China, Japan and Korea), and bringing back manufacturing jobs to America.

To the great disappointment of China and the rest of the international community, President Trump has also withdrawn the US from the Paris Climate Change Agreement, which relied on strong US–China cooperation. China and the EU are now positioning themselves as global leaders in the fight against climate change, despite China's appalling domestic environment, and the poor environmental performance of China's investments in Africa and Latin America.

Trump officials reaffirmed the US commitment to its alliances with Japan and Korea, while Trump himself indicated his support for the "One-China Policy" in a telephone conversation with Chinese President Xi Jinping. This is seen to have been a big back down for Trump, as Xi reportedly refused to talk with him until Trump honored the One-China Policy.

Trump had a successful first summit with President Xi Jinping in April 2017, and seemed to have enlisted his support to help control North Korea. However, it only took a couple of months for Trump to realize that China is reluctant to seriously tackle North Korea for fear of destabilizing the regime. The XI-Trump honeymoon was then over, almost as quickly as it started, when the Trump administration announced sanctions against Chinese entities for their dealings with North Korea, also announced actions against China's alleged dumping of steel exports, gave a green light for a $1 billion arms sale to Taiwan, and sailed a US destroyer through the Chinese-occupied South China Sea. And Trump's launching in August 2017 of an investigation into China's alleged theft of US intellectual property has deeply troubled the Chinese government, and raised the specter of a possible trade war between China and the US.

It also seems that Donald Trump's administration is planning to defy Winston Churchill's advice that "to jaw-jaw is always better than to war-war". His 2017 budget proposal involves increasing funding to the US military by 9%, while cutting the State Department's diplomacy and foreign aid by a combined 28%, and also the Environment Protection Agency by 31%. "There is no question that this is a hard-power budget; it is not a soft-power budget," said Mick Mulvaney, the director of the Office of Management and Budget. While the US Congress is seeking to restore funding for these agencies, Trump's budget proposals certainly set the tone for his administration's approach to international relations. Trump's hard-power approach to international relations was soon evident in its approach to North Korea. Indeed, North Korea has been virtually the sole focus of Trump's Asia policy.

Countries like China, India and the Philippines which rely heavily on migrants' remittances could suffer from President Trump's tightening of migration policies. These three countries account for almost all of America's 1.5 million illegal migrants coming from Asia, and 13% of all illegal migrants. Asia could also be hit by a tightening up of H1-B visas, of which India is the principal beneficiary.

President Donald Trump's working assumption is that Asia has been "ripping off" America in different ways. For their part, many Asian countries also have concerns about the US. The big policy switch-around from one administration to another can undermine the reliability of the US as a partner. For example, in an interview before the US elections, Singapore's Prime Minister Lee Hsien Loong said that a failure to ratify the TPP "would be a very big setback for America". "Your standing goes down with many countries around the world," Lee said. "After you have gotten Vietnam to join, after you have gotten Japan to join, after Japanese Prime Minister Shinzo Abe has made very difficult arrangements on agriculture, cars, sugar, and dairy. Now you say, 'I walk away, that I do not believe in this deal.' How can anybody believe in you anymore?"[24]

In Australia, arguably the US' most loyal ally, commentators are calling for a rethink of the country's historic relations with the US. For example, Australia's former foreign minister Gareth Evans has said that Trump is "manifestly the most ill-informed, under-prepared, ethically challenged and psychologically ill-equipped president in US history" and that Australia should reduce its dependence on the US alliance and accept China as a legitimate "global rule maker". And as former Washington Post reporter, Paul Blustein, has remarked, it is certainly clear that "this administration has no respect for international institutions."

Overall, following the election of Donald Trump, Asia is now faced with a likely deterioration in key factors that have driven its development—an open US market, a relatively benign security environment and a stable global economic system. More generally, the US election campaign and the turmoil of the Trump administration have greatly undermined the credibility of the US as an indispensable strategic power in Asia. Its moral ascendancy and soft power have been greatly diminished. At the same time, China is now the most important economic partner of most Asian countries, is providing much assistance and financing infrastructure without any policy conditionality and seems like a steadier, more reliable partner.

## The Future of Peace and Harmony in Asia

The relative peace that Asia has enjoyed these past seven decades has been key to the region's economic renaissance. But the future of peace in Asia cannot be taken for granted. Asia is in the midst of a great power transition, as China is becoming the region's dominant power, and the US is receding. But this transition may not be smooth, as it involves a power struggle between these two giants, which are both burdened by immense domestic fragilities and weaknesses while they try to assert their regional and international leadership at the same time.

The great power transition under way is of historic proportions. As Singapore's founding father and intellectual giant Lee Kuan Yew once cautioned, "the size of China's displacement of the world balance is such that the world must find a new balance. It is not possible to pretend that this is just another big player. This is the biggest player in the history of the world.[25]" And yet, for the first three decades of its high growth period, China kept a relatively low profile in international politics. Chinese leaders heeded the caution of great leader Deng Xiaoping that China should "observe calmly; secure our position; cope with affairs calmly; hide our capacities and bide our time; be good at maintaining a low profile; and never claim leadership". This is widely known as the "hide and bide" strategy.

But following the outbreak of the global financial crisis in 2008, and especially since the ascension of Xi Jinping to Chinese leadership in 2012–2013, China has been doing much less hiding and biding. Its new assertive posture is evident in its aggressive behavior toward Japan, its annexation of the South China Sea, its divide-and-rule tactics vis-à-vis ASEAN, its economic sanctions against countries like Korea and the Philippines, its interference in Hong Kong affairs and its disrespect for the political choices of Taiwan's citizens. Its new leadership has also been manifest in initiatives like the AIIB and the BRI.

The new assertive China is most evident in its posture vis-à-vis the US. Chinese President Xi has been overtly trying to push the US out of East Asia and position China as the region's paramount power. In arguing for "a new security cooperation architecture", Xi quite pointedly expressed his view on the role of the US in Asia when he said that "strengthening military alliances with a third party does not benefit the maintenance of regional security … it is for the people of Asia to run the affairs of Asia, solve the problems of Asia and uphold the security of Asia. The people of Asia have the capability and wisdom to achieve peace and stability in the region through enhanced cooperation."[26]

These developments have led some analysts to argue that the great power struggle between the US and China is pushing them to war. As Graham Allison has recalled, more than 2400 years ago, the Athenian historian Thucydides offered a powerful insight: "It was the rise of Athens, and the fear that this inspired in Sparta, that made war inevitable."[27] According to Allison, when a rising power rivals a ruling power, like Athens and Sparta, and Germany and Britain a century ago, the contests often end badly. Indeed, in 12 of 16 cases over the past 500 years, the result was war. "When the parties avoided war, it required huge, painful adjustments in attitudes and actions on the part not just of the challenger but also the challenged," wrote Allison.

Quite predictably, there has been much debate about the prospects for war between China and the US. Some argue that the dense trade, investment, finance and people-to-people relations between the two countries mean that war between the two countries would be too costly for both sides. But similarly close relations did not stop Germany and Britain from going to war a century ago. Another line of argument is that today China is so militarily inferior to the US. But if China's Communist Party were faced with an existential threat, such as over Taiwan or in the future even the South China Sea, it may fight for its life. And looking ahead, the balance of power between the Chinese and American militaries will narrow quickly over the coming decades, and the US military will likely remain more thinly spread across the globe, while China's remains more concentrated in East Asia.

Would China and the US be willing to make the huge, painful adjustments in attitudes and actions in order to avoid war? For his part, Chinese President Xi Jinping seemed rather stubborn when he argued "There is no such thing as the so-called Thucydides Trap in the world. But should major countries time and again make the mistakes of strategic miscalculation, they might create such traps for themselves.[28]"

There are however reasons to believe that the possibility of traditional military war between the US and China is highly unlikely. Both sides are well aware that there would be no winners. Indeed, the potential for mutually assured destruction between two nuclear powers virtually rules out a full-blown military war.

The progressive fading of the US' influence in Asia could also reduce the possibility of conflict between China and the US. Over time, issues like the South China Sea and even Japan's Senkaku Islands could seem less and less important. They are, after all, just bunches of rocks, reefs, shoals and islets in seas which are an awfully long way from Washington.

Against that, there is always the risk of accidental conflicts spiraling out of control. Several naval accidents involving the US Navy in 2017, which fortunately did not involve Chinese ships, highlight how easily accidents can occur in Asia's highly congested shipping lanes. And possible economic stagnation could see the Chinese government promote nationalism more aggressively, and resort to military adventurism as a diversionary tactic.

All things considered, the US and China seem destined to remain "frenemies", that is, both friends and rivals. In addition to the dense trade, investment, finance and people-to-people relations that bind the US and China together, the US needs China's cooperation on issues like North Korea, counter-terrorism, cyber-security, Iran and, depending on the administration, climate change. But as in recent times, rather than traditional military conflicts, we should expect conflicts in the areas of trade, intellectual property, international rule of law and cyber to be constantly bubbling, with even greater explosions from time to time. The likely inability to put an end to such conflicts will undermine the prospects for an Asian Century.

As China progressively displaces the US as Asia's hegemon, it will become ever more necessary for Asian countries to cooperate better together. The US has operated like a boxing referee who holds old enemies apart. However, as we have discussed in this chapter, Asia is bristling with tensions involving China on the one hand, and Japan, Taiwan, Hong Kong, North Korea, the South China Sea, ASEAN and India. And Chinese initiatives like the AIIB and the BRI are not seen with a friendly eye by all regional players.

The most likely source of conflict in Asia could be between China and India or Japan, two countries that are unlikely to buckle under China's ambitious regional designs. Indeed, while Asian Century hype has focused substantially on the rise of China, India's population will surpass China's as early as 2022, and could be some 50% higher than China's by 2100. And if current trends continue, India's economic size could overtake China's sometime in the second half of this century. Such a power shift could foster political instability in Asia, especially since India has more friends in Asia than does China.

Avoiding conflict for Japan may ultimately require political reconciliation with former adversaries. This is no easy task as the Chinese and Korean governments have invested so much in anti-Japanese nationalism, rather than looking to the future and fostering reconciliation.

Possible conflicts between Asian countries could do much to derail the prospects for an Asian Century. And the great risk for the US is being dragged into these conflicts between Asian countries, more than a straight head-on conflict with China.

## Notes

1. Henry Kissinger on China, Nixon and OBL CBS NEWS, 4 June 2012.
2. Cha, Victor Cha (2016). Powerplay: The Origins of the American Alliance System in Asia.
3. Buchanan, Ian. Is regional economic integration enough? The search for "Wave 3" growth. Asia Pathways, 11 December 2012.
4. Barack Obama. Statement by the President on the 70th Anniversary Commemorating the End of World War II in the Pacific. The White House, 2 September 2015.
5. ABC. Prime Minister Tony Abbott holds first formal meeting with Japanese PM Shinzo Abe, 10 October 2013.
6. Nixon, Richard M. Asia After Viet Nam. Foreign Affairs, October 1967.
7. President Bill Clinton. Speech on China Trade Bill, 8 March 2000.
8. Office of the US Trade Representative.
9. Rhodium Group. China Investment Monitor.
10. Pei, Minxin. Everything You Think You Know About China Is Wrong. Foreign Policy, 29 August 2012.
11. Lowy Institute. Conference by Professor Akiko Fukushima of Aoyama Gakuin University and the Tokyo Foundation on 7 February 2017.
12. Full text of President Xi Jinping's speech on "one country, two systems" and how China rules Hong Kong. South China Morning Post, 1 July 2017.

13. Khoo, Nicholas. Why ASEAN is in Disarray in the South China Sea. The National Interest, 7 October 2016.
14. West, John. Race to finance Asia's infrastructure heats up. FDI Intelligence, 10 May 2017.
15. Jinchen, Tian. "One Belt and One Road": Connecting China and the world. McKinsey&Company, July 2016.
16. Asian Development Bank Annual Meeting, Frankfurt 2016. City of Sustainability. The Chinese One Belt One Road Initiative: Asian Perceptions.
17. Fitch Ratings. China's One Belt, One Road Initiative Brings Risks, 25 January 2017.
18. Arase, David. China's two Silk Roads: implications for Southeast Asia. Institute of Southeast Asian Studies, 22 January 2015.
19. Financial Times. Chinese investment adds to Sri Lankan debt pile, 24 February 2017.
20. Gunasekara, Shiyana. Sri Lanka Suffers from China's Indian Ocean Strategy. Asia Pacific Bulletin, 21 February 2017. East-West Center.
21. Asia-Pacific Banking and Finance. "Keating's China bank plans 'economic colonisation'," 27 February 2017.
22. IMF. Pakistan. Twelfth and Final Review under the extended arrangement, request for waivers or nonobservance of performance criteria, and proposal for post-program monitoring, 13 September 2016.
23. Asian Development Bank Annual Meeting, Frankfurt 2016. City of Sustainability. The Chinese One Belt One Road Initiative: Asian Perceptions.
24. Bremmer, Ian. Singapore PM Lee Hsien Loong on America's Declining Influence in Asia. Time Magazine, 26 October 2016.
25. Allison, Graham and Robert Blackwill. Interview: Lee Kuan Yew on the Future of U.S.–China Relations. The Atlantic, 5 March 2013.
26. Xi Jinping. New Asian security concept for new progress in security cooperation. Remarks at the Fourth Summit of the Conference on Interaction and Confidence Building Measures in Asia, 21 May 2014.
27. Allison, Graham. The Thucydides Trap: Are the U.S. and China Headed for War? The Atlantic, 24 September 2015.
28. Xi Jinping, Speech on China–U.S. Relations, Seattle, 25 September 2015.

**Open Access** This chapter is licensed under the terms of the Creative Commons Attribution 4.0 International License (http://creativecommons.org/licenses/by/4.0/), which permits use, sharing, adaptation, distribution, and reproduction in any medium or format, as long as you give appropriate credit to the original author(s) and the source, provide a link to the Creative Commons license and indicate if changes were made.

The images or other third party material in this chapter are included in the chapter's Creative Commons license, unless indicated otherwise in a credit line to the material. If material is not included in the chapter's Creative Commons license and your intended use is not permitted by statutory regulation or exceeds the permitted use, you will need to obtain permission directly from the copyright holder.

# PART III

# Looking Ahead

CHAPTER 11

# What Next for the Asian Century?

In this book, we have argued that Asia is suffering from stunted economic development, despite the rapid growth in recent decades. No major Asian economy has managed to achieve full catch-up to world leaders like the US and Germany in terms of GDP per capita, or economic, business and technological sophistication.

Asia is also suffering from stunted social development. Half of Asia's population is stranded between poverty and the middle class, living in a zone of vulnerability and precarity. Middle-class Asia remains a myth, even if Asian lives have improved immeasurably in tandem with rapid economic development. And the middle class is receding in advanced countries like Japan and Korea along with rising inequality and poverty.

Asia may have become a powerful force in the global economy and politics. But this is mainly thanks to the enormous populations of countries like China, India and Indonesia, not because of economic, business and technological sophistication. Large populations have given these countries economic, market and financial weight, which has been transformed into economic, political and military power. These countries remain, however, fragile superpowers.

To some extent, Asia's current predicament of stunted economic and social development is not surprising. As countries like even Bangladesh have demonstrated, you only have to get a few things right to break out of low-income status and to reduce extreme poverty. But to realize a nation's full economic and social potential, and become a high-income economy with a middle-class society, requires addressing a more complex set of challenges.

## CAN ASIA RISE TO THE CHALLENGE?

The prospects for an Asian Century will depend on how Asia responds to the seven challenges identified in this book: (1) getting better value out of global value chains, (2) making the most of urbanization's potential, (3) giving all Asians a chance, (4) solving Asia's demographic dilemmas, (5) fixing Asia's flawed politics, (6) combating Asia's economic crime and (7) living together in peace and harmony.

If Asia were able to successfully tackle our seven challenges for an Asian Century, over time it would be able to achieve advanced economies and middle-class societies. Indeed, many have projected massive benefits from such a "Goldilocks scenario". For example, the Asian Development Bank once projected that an additional 3 billion Asians could enjoy living standards similar to those in Europe today, and the region could account for over half of global output by the middle of this century.[1] But in the six years since the ADB painted this rosy picture, very few of the policy reforms necessary for realizing an Asian Century have been implemented. And as Asia's economy and politics have become more fragile and uncertain, there is little prospect of dramatic reforms being implemented.

Indeed, our overall assessment is that Asian governments are unlikely to have either the political courage or wisdom to tackle the above seven challenges with great vigor. The case of Japan, which has postponed necessary reforms for over two decades, is salutary. Its latest reform program, dubbed Abenomics, has left the whole international community underwhelmed. Even the polite and diplomatic IMF called for Abenomics to be "reloaded", some four years after it was launched.[2]

In a similar context, Korean big business has a stranglehold over the nation's politics, and is resisting a crucial opening of the economy to more market forces. Shamefully, Korea's corporate governance lags behind countries like Thailand, Malaysia and India, countries which are much less advanced, as well as Singapore, Hong Kong, Japan and Taiwan. And corruption in business and politics is deep and endemic, as evident in the corruption scandal that engulfed the now-impeached President Park Geun-hye and Samsung in 2016–2017.

China, which proudly aspires to Asian leadership, seems afraid of the possible disruptive effects of reform, and has postponed its promise of allowing market forces to play a "decisive role" in the economy. Instead, for some time now, China has resorted to unsustainable debt-financing to intoxicate the economy. This will not drive China's productivity and innovation capacities up the development ladder.

## THE DONALD TRUMP COLLISION

Colliding with our seven challenges for an Asian Century is the arrival of Donald Trump to the leadership of the US. Trump's America will also shape the contours of a possible Asian Century. We are now seeing a deterioration in some key factors that have driven Asia development—an open US market, a relatively benign security environment, and a stable global economic system.

Many observers speculate that Trump will not survive a year or two or beyond his first term. This is far from certain. His rise to the presidency was equally improbable. But even post-Trump, we should not assume a return to the US as a promoter of open markets and globalization, and a friend of democratic partners and the liberal international system. America has been struck by a wave of populism, and in particular nationalism (make America great again), nativism (secure our borders) and protectionism (protect American workers),[3] which is unlikely to go away anytime soon.

American society has become polarized by inequality, a product of globalization and rapid technological change. And support for multilateral free trade is now withering on the vine. There is very little chance that the US would sign up again to the TPP in the foreseeable future. Further, nationalism and military fatigue from more than 15 years of war mean that US has much less enthusiasm for maintaining his system of alliances and partnerships. And the US government seems more distracted than ever by the Middle East and Vladimir Putin's designs on Europe, and is paralyzed by Washington's shenanigans.

The US' influence in Asia is declining, in the context of the great power struggle between China and the US, and this decline will likely accelerate under Trump's administration. The US is losing ground to China, especially in Southeast Asia which is increasingly becoming a Chinese sphere of influence. And China is increasingly asserting its military power in the East and South China Seas, and the Indian Ocean, and through initiatives like the Belt and Road Initiative, and the Asian Infrastructure Investment Bank. But China is not a promoter of open markets, good governance and international rule of law, key elements that are necessary for realizing an Asian Century. Rather, state capitalism, authoritarian governance and Sinocentric bilateralism are China's currency.

This power shift is epochal. Following the end of World War 2, the US became Asia's leading power as it provided assistance to rebuild war-torn countries, open markets that enabled export-oriented growth, an international system that facilitated development and a security blanket to its allies. The US also remade Japan from an expansionist, militaristic nation into a pacifist democracy, encouraged successful democratization in Korea and Taiwan and promoted open market economics, human rights and the rule of law. The waning of America's positive influence will have profound effects on Asia.

## A World with Increasingly Divergent Interests

Even if Asia continues to muddle through, in some decades time, the region could account for around half the world economy, far outstripping the West in total economic weight, thanks mainly to its enormous population, as organizations like the Asian Development Bank, OECD and PWC have projected. After all, Asia accounts for some 55% of the world's population, while the West (as represented by members of the OECD) only accounts for 18%. Three of the world's four biggest economies could be Asian—China, India and Indonesia—with the West only represented by the US at third place.

Even in these circumstances, no major Asian economy would have approached world leaders like the US and Germany in terms of GDP per capita, or economic, business and technological sophistication. For example, in one report PWC projects that in 2050 US GDP per capita would still be double that of China (compared with four times in 2016) and would be triple that of India (compared with nine times in 2016).[4] Moreover, Asia could remain a democratic desert, with not one full democracy, and with continuing widespread human rights abuses and restrictions on personal freedoms. In other words, Asia would have the world's greatest economic weight and be a leading economic and political power, but would remain a pygmy in terms of economic, social and political development.

Needless to say, the incongruities of such a scenario could generate even greater geopolitical tensions than we see today.

These incongruities would test the capacity of the international community to cooperate on issues like open trade and investment, democracy and human rights, climate change, protection of intellectual property rights, economic crime, international rule of law, law of the sea and natural disasters. Why? Because forging consensus and working together requires shared interest and values, and a culture of cooperation and trust. As the

UN Security Council has proved time and again, when great powers have fundamentally divergent interests, it is very difficult to achieve anything. In fact, a world with even larger emerging economies, together with relatively smaller highly developed countries, could be a recipe for international instability.

## Risks of Conflict and Crisis

Beyond these incongruities, there are endless possibilities of economic, social, political and military crises in Asia—mostly due to the likely failure to deal with our seven challenges for an Asian Century.

We have argued that the US and China are unlikely to engage in a traditional military conflict, although the naval collisions involving the US Navy in 2017 show how easily accidents can occur, and possibly spiral out of control. They seem destined to remain "frenemies", that is both friends and rivals, with conflicts taking place in the areas of trade, intellectual property, international rule of law, and cyber, rather than on the battlefield.

As China progressively displaces the US as Asia's hegemon, it will become ever more necessary for Asian countries to cooperate better together. However, Asia is bristling with tensions involving China on the one hand, and Japan, Taiwan, Hong Kong, North Korea, the South China Sea, ASEAN and India on the other. The most likely source of conflict in Asia could be between China and India or Japan.

While Asian Century hype has focused substantially on the rise of China, India's population will surpass China's as early as 2022, and could be some 50% higher than China's by 2100. And if current trends continue, India's economic size could overtake China's sometime in the second half of this century. Such a power shift could foster political instability in Asia, especially since India has more friends in Asia than does China. And avoiding conflict for Japan will ultimately require political reconciliation with former adversaries, China and South Korea, something which is not on the cards any time soon.

Any such conflicts between Asian countries could do much to derail the prospects for an Asian Century. And the great risk for the US is being dragged into these conflicts between Asian countries, more than a straight head-on conflict with China.

Economic crisis is also stalking several Asian countries, most notably Japan and China with their massive debt problems. And anti-globalization populism could break the most important driver of Asia's rapid development, open trade and investment. Social crisis could happen in India, Indonesia and the Philippines with their bulging youth populations, if they are unable to find decent jobs. Multi-ethnic countries like India and Indonesia could easily descend into violence as groups suffering from discrimination, prejudice and persecution mobilize themselves against dominant elites. And as natural disasters and environmental problems increasingly hit Asia's overcrowded and badly planned cities, social crises will also accelerate.

Continued authoritarian politics and social repression in China, North Korea and Vietnam could provoke political crises as citizens demand cleaner and democratic government. Social unrest is already rampant in China, and North Korea has thousands of regime opponents locked away in secret gulags. Further, the corruption crisis that engulfed former South Korean President Park Geun-hye shows how fragile even Asia's most advanced countries can be.

Today, Asia is sitting on a knife edge. The potential of the region to generate good and happy lives for its citizens is enormous. But the requirements of success and the risks of failure are equally enormous. We cannot be sure of "what's next for the Asian Century". Indeed, anything could happen, and complacency of the region's elites could be the Asian Century's greatest enemy.

## Notes

1. Asian Development Bank (2011). Asia 2050: Realising the Asian Century.
2. IMF. How to Reload Abenomics, August 2, 2016.
3. McGann, James G. 2016 Global Go to Think Tank Index Report.
4. PWC. The Long View: How will the global economic order change by 2050?, February 2017.

**Open Access** This chapter is licensed under the terms of the Creative Commons Attribution 4.0 International License (http://creativecommons.org/licenses/by/4.0/), which permits use, sharing, adaptation, distribution, and reproduction in any medium or format, as long as you give appropriate credit to the original author(s) and the source, provide a link to the Creative Commons license and indicate if changes were made.

The images or other third party material in this chapter are included in the chapter's Creative Commons license, unless indicated otherwise in a credit line to the material. If material is not included in the chapter's Creative Commons license and your intended use is not permitted by statutory regulation or exceeds the permitted use, you will need to obtain permission directly from the copyright holder.

# Index[1]

**NUMBERS AND SYMBOLS**
1Malaysian Development Berhad (1MDB), 80, 266, 267, 311
1MDB, *see* 1Malaysian Development Berhad

## A
Abe, Shinzo, 30, 102, 145, 157, 202, 204, 227, 283, 286, 314, 318n5
Abenomics, 29, 30, 121n26, 156, 202, 203, 227, 324
ADB, *see* Asian Development Bank
Ai Weiwei, 146, 213, 243, 244n1
AIIB, *see* Asian Infrastructure Investment Bank
Alibaba, 105, 110, 248
Amnesty International, 86n31, 207, 208, 211n47, 276n15
Apple, 10, 32, 40, 91, 94, 105, 107, 116, 117, 121n11, 122n29, 122n50, 123n51, 153, 155
ASEAN, *see* Association of Southeast Nations
Asian Century, 1–5, 7–14, 23, 57, 84, 85, 114, 122n48, 151n37, 180, 185, 197, 277n32, 281, 317, 318, 323–328
Asian Development Bank (ADB), 4, 15n6, 21, 23, 34, 52n3, 52n5, 58, 69, 71, 72, 75, 85n2, 86n11, 86n18, 86n27, 120n1, 137, 139, 140, 144, 150n24, 209n6, 210n26, 259, 272, 304–306, 319n16, 319n23, 324, 326
Asian Infrastructure Investment Bank (AIIB), 3, 24, 36, 133, 139, 279, 303–306, 312, 316, 317, 325
Association of Southeast Nations (ASEAN), 12, 14, 48, 49, 51, 100, 103, 104, 115, 261, 262, 301–303, 315, 317, 319n13, 327
Australia, 2, 7, 11, 15n3, 25, 41, 49, 73, 83, 97, 100, 101, 103, 108, 126, 137, 163, 166, 167, 169, 216, 231, 272, 275, 283, 284, 299, 302, 314

---

[1] Note: Page numbers followed by 'n' refer to notes.

© The Author(s) 2018
J. West, *Asian Century... on a Knife-edge*,
https://doi.org/10.1007/978-981-10-7182-9

## B

Bangladesh, 7, 11, 42, 44, 62–65, 69, 70, 72, 76, 82, 92, 95, 116, 118–120, 123n55, 128, 134, 135, 154, 162, 163, 166, 185–187, 215, 237, 252, 257, 258, 260, 261, 274, 305, 308, 323

Belt and Road Initiative (BRI), 5, 24, 36, 103, 279, 303, 305–307, 309, 316, 317, 325

BPO, *see* Business Process Outsourcing

BRI, *see* Belt and Road Initiative

Business Process Outsourcing (BPO), 44, 112, 113, 189, 229

## C

Cambodia, 11, 69, 92, 94–98, 100, 103, 105, 106, 121n17, 121n18, 128, 189, 207, 215, 240, 252, 258, 259, 273, 301–303

Chaebol, 23, 30–35, 224, 225

China, 19, 35–41, 49–52, 58, 91, 100, 106–111, 126, 129–133, 154, 169–174, 184, 192–194, 213, 218–225, 248, 267–270, 279, 284–286, 288–307, 323

China's one-child policy, 160, 192

Climate change, 4, 6, 10, 40, 72, 137, 140–143, 217, 280, 313, 317, 326

Corruption, 12, 14, 31, 34, 43, 46, 47, 50, 51, 53n24, 55n73, 61, 78, 80, 87n36, 98, 110, 114, 118, 121n19, 123n53, 139, 147, 175, 215, 220–222, 224–226, 228–231, 233, 235, 240, 241, 244, 245n18, 248, 252, 254–259, 262–265, 267–274, 276n22, 276n27, 277n32, 277n33, 291, 312, 324, 328

## D

Dalai Lama, 3, 170, 171, 181n18, 309

Dalits, 70, 80, 178, 179, 181n25, 188

Democracy, 1, 11, 13, 22, 31, 42, 43, 45, 46, 48, 51, 74, 80, 81, 134, 145, 147, 150n17, 166, 167, 196, 200–202, 208, 210n34, 210n35, 213–219, 221–230, 233–236, 238–240, 242–244, 244n2, 244n4, 244n5, 244n7, 244n9, 245n17, 245n26, 245n28, 245n32, 245n36, 246n39, 261, 267, 271–273, 282, 288, 292–294, 309, 311, 312, 326

Demography, 188, 189

Deng Xiaoping, 51, 93, 121n9, 192, 218, 221, 240, 285, 286, 315

Duterte, Rodrigo, 217, 230, 231, 300, 311

## E

Economic crime, 12, 13, 247–275, 324, 326

Economist Intelligence Unit (EIU), 19, 38, 54n40, 86n14, 150n5, 151n41, 213, 244n2

Education, 9, 20, 26, 28, 43, 46–49, 51, 54n57, 57–59, 61, 62, 64, 67, 69, 71, 73–76, 97, 99, 107, 110, 125, 127, 132, 144–147, 149, 151n34, 155, 159–162, 165, 167, 169, 172, 178, 179, 181n26, 185, 186, 188, 190, 191, 193, 197, 199, 201, 204, 207, 209n9, 209n10, 214, 228, 232, 239, 240, 260, 287, 291

Environment, 6, 7, 13, 21, 101, 113, 127, 136, 140–145, 157, 158, 178, 190, 192, 205, 220, 231, 254, 255, 268, 276n20, 288, 313–315, 325

## F

FDI, *see* Foreign direct investment
Foreign direct investment (FDI), 27, 31, 44, 46, 49, 53n13, 54n65, 79, 96, 97, 100, 108, 109, 121n17, 121n26, 204, 229, 232, 245n30, 265, 285, 308, 319n14
Foxconn, 10, 27, 44, 91, 116

## G

Global financial crisis, 37, 63, 113, 220, 268, 315
Global value chains (GVC), 10, 38, 46, 49, 91–120, 128, 131, 132, 143, 149, 196, 232, 257, 324
GVC, *see* Global value chains

## H

Hong Kong, 3, 8, 11, 12, 14, 20, 22, 26, 34, 52, 61–63, 66, 73–75, 79, 82, 84, 94, 95, 98, 99, 104, 111, 115, 128, 129, 135, 137, 143–149, 185, 186, 190, 191, 193, 198, 202, 205, 215, 220, 242, 244, 247–249, 256, 259, 262, 263, 267, 272, 274, 275, 276n12, 276n16, 280, 282, 284, 291–297, 310, 315, 317, 318n12, 324, 327
Hukou, 130–133, 150n11
Human rights, 9, 11, 13, 40, 57, 74, 75, 77–82, 115, 153, 155, 160, 166, 168–170, 174–177, 181n20, 181n23, 193, 208, 214, 216, 217, 219–221, 229–231, 234, 235, 237, 240, 244n10, 244n11, 245n14, 256, 261, 280, 285, 303, 311, 312, 326
Human Rights Watch, 79, 80, 86n32, 98, 120, 121n21, 123n57, 154, 155, 173, 179, 180n4, 181n12, 181n25, 181n26, 181n27, 270, 277n30

## I

IMF, *see* International Monetary Fund
India, 3, 21, 41–45, 58, 92, 125, 133, 135–138, 154, 177–180, 185, 187–189, 213, 249, 280, 323
Indonesia, 2, 8, 11, 14, 20, 24, 25, 27, 28, 34, 45–50, 58, 60–63, 69–71, 75, 76, 82–84, 86n26, 95, 99, 100, 103, 104, 106, 111, 126, 134, 135, 138–140, 154–156, 167–169, 180n4, 185–187, 215, 232, 240, 252, 255, 257–261, 298, 301, 323, 326–328
Inequality, 2, 9, 29, 42, 45, 52n7, 53n20, 54n52, 59, 61, 62, 66, 68, 85n10, 86n17, 114, 132, 140, 148, 191, 201, 210n27, 216, 220, 224, 232, 241, 263, 276n27, 289, 292, 323, 325
Innovation, 10, 15n9, 28, 33, 35, 38, 39, 51, 66, 106–108, 110, 111, 122n33, 122n34, 122n41, 127, 140, 143–147, 155, 195, 203, 204, 242, 243, 247, 250, 251, 270, 325
International Monetary Fund (IMF), 1, 30, 31, 37, 39, 45, 52n7, 53n22, 53n38, 54n52, 61, 85n7, 85n9, 99, 150n25, 188, 196, 203, 209n8, 210n27, 210n39, 272, 281, 282, 304, 308, 319n22
Internet, 9, 40, 51, 57, 67, 75–78, 86n28, 86n29, 138, 146, 172, 214, 216, 219, 220, 222, 235, 237, 249
iPhone, 91, 105, 120n1, 128

ISIS, *see* Islamic State
Islamic State (ISIS), 48, 92, 121n8, 231

## J
Jack Ma, 84, 110
Japan, 1, 19, 25–30, 59, 61, 67, 68, 91, 126, 154, 156–159, 183, 200–205, 213, 225–228, 250, 264, 265, 279, 286–288, 323

## K
Kissinger, Henry, 280, 284, 318n1
Korea (South Korea), 12, 14, 25, 31, 34, 53n29, 96, 154, 207, 209n13, 209n14, 210n24, 210n30, 210n43, 211n47, 245n25, 257, 281–283, 294–297, 323, 324, 326

## L
Laos, 11, 97, 156, 215, 240, 251, 252, 254, 255, 258, 259, 273, 301–303
Lee Hsien Loong, 7, 241, 242, 314, 319n24
Lee Kuan Yew, 41, 51, 54n46, 66, 240–242, 272, 273, 315, 319n25
Lesbian, gay, bisexual and transgender (LGBT), 10, 11, 153–156, 256
Lewis turning point, 128, 143
LGBT, *see* Lesbian, gay, bisexual and transgender

## M
Mahbubani, Kishore, 2, 15n1, 57, 66, 85n1, 86n15

Malaysia, 8, 11, 20, 28, 34, 46, 47, 49, 50, 63, 75, 79, 80, 82–84, 95, 96, 99, 101, 103, 106, 116–118, 123n52, 128, 138, 145, 154, 162, 215, 216, 229, 240, 244, 252, 257–262, 265–267, 274, 276n22, 295, 297, 298, 300, 301, 303, 311, 324
Middle class, 3, 9–12, 45, 52, 57–85, 115, 131, 140, 153, 160, 206, 209, 214, 221, 235, 238, 243, 263, 323
Middle-income trap, 7, 21, 80, 128, 232
Migration, 11, 59, 131, 132, 161, 169, 172, 185, 191, 197, 202, 206, 211n45, 216, 221, 241, 256, 314
Modi, Narendra, 42–44, 70, 80, 189, 243, 308, 311
Mongolia, 11, 95, 154, 215, 271, 272, 294, 305
Moon Jae-in, 34, 103, 225
Myanmar, 11, 63, 72, 76, 77, 82, 99, 100, 103, 154, 166, 215, 217, 232, 235–240, 245n35, 245n36, 251, 252, 254, 258–262, 273, 276n13, 296, 301, 302, 305, 308, 311

## N
Natural disasters, 9, 13, 14, 57, 61, 71, 72, 81, 118, 125, 126, 140–143, 161, 204, 227, 294, 326, 328
North Korea, 4, 6, 11, 12, 14, 20, 22, 25, 27, 32, 40, 42, 77–79, 215, 217, 223, 225, 240, 253, 257, 258, 275, 280, 281, 283, 288, 293–297, 302, 312–314, 317, 327, 328

INDEX   333

**O**
Obama, Barack, 3, 4, 6, 15n2, 109, 142, 155, 220, 237, 283, 284, 296, 298, 302–304, 310–312, 318n4
OECD, *see* Organisation for Economic Cooperation and Development
Oligarchy, 45–48, 230
One-China policy, 5, 6, 284, 288, 290, 312, 313
Organisation for Economic Cooperation and Development (OECD), 23, 27–29, 31–33, 36, 38, 42, 43, 47, 49, 53n13, 53n16, 53n20, 53n21, 53n30, 53n34, 53n36, 53n37, 54n51, 54n55, 54n61, 54n62, 54n65, 55n67, 55n68, 58, 68, 73–75, 83, 85n3, 86n16, 86n17, 86n25, 86n26, 87n39, 99, 100, 111, 120, 120n3, 121n6, 121n25, 121n28, 122n43, 122n44, 122n45, 123n55, 123n58, 123n59, 143, 147, 150n4, 151n32, 156, 157, 181n7, 195, 196, 198–202, 208, 210n23, 210n28, 210n32, 210n33, 214, 223, 224, 232, 244n6, 244n8, 245n20, 245n22, 245n24, 245n33, 248–250, 254–256, 264, 275n2, 275n3, 276n19, 326

**P**
Pakistan, 11, 25, 62, 63, 69, 72, 76, 77, 82, 134, 141, 154, 160, 162–165, 185, 215, 240, 249, 257, 258, 274, 294, 295, 305, 308, 309, 319n22
Paris Climate Change Agreement, 4, 6, 10, 142, 313
Park Geun-hye, 14, 31, 34, 145, 222–224, 324, 328

Philippines, 1, 11, 14, 34, 40, 48, 50, 59, 62, 70, 71, 76, 77, 82–84, 99, 100, 103, 112, 113, 122n46, 134, 154, 156, 158, 167, 185–187, 189, 191, 199, 202, 206, 215, 217, 228–232, 240, 245n30, 245n31, 245n32, 253, 258, 259, 268, 274, 281, 282, 295, 297–303, 307, 310, 311, 314, 315, 327
Politics, 1, 9, 12, 14, 22, 23, 30, 31, 35, 40, 43, 48, 93, 111, 115, 157, 191, 201, 208, 209, 210n35, 213–244, 262, 263, 266, 276n24, 283, 290, 302, 303, 323, 324, 328
Pollution, 36, 70, 106, 134, 140–142, 145, 151n27, 151n28, 164, 276n27, 292
Poverty, 9, 10, 29, 38, 42, 45, 48, 50, 52, 52n6, 54n49, 57, 59–62, 64–72, 79, 80, 83, 95–98, 117, 118, 125, 127, 132–135, 138, 139, 148, 150n22, 159, 165–167, 169, 172, 178, 188, 189, 191, 197 199, 201, 214, 219, 229, 231, 232, 235, 237, 239, 241, 250, 253, 257, 261, 276n11, 277n32, 292, 323

**R**
Rana Plaza, 116, 119, 120, 123n56, 135
RCEP, *see* Regional Comprehensive Economic Partnership
Regional Comprehensive Economic Partnership (RCEP), 10, 100, 103, 104, 302, 306
Rohingya, 63, 166, 237, 258, 260–262, 276n13, 311

## S

Samsung, 14, 23, 27, 32, 34, 222, 224
Sen, Amartya, 42, 54n53, 160, 181n9, 193, 209n19
Singapore, 1, 7, 8, 11, 15n1, 20, 22, 24, 26–28, 34, 41, 47, 49, 51, 52, 54n46, 57, 61–63, 66, 67, 73, 82, 83, 85, 94, 95, 98–101, 103, 104, 111, 128, 137, 140, 143–149, 153–156, 177, 185, 186, 190, 191, 198, 202, 205, 215, 221, 240–243, 249, 256, 259, 262, 263, 272–275, 277n33, 277n34, 280, 282, 301, 303, 310, 314, 315, 319n24, 324
Slum, 10, 64, 69, 127, 132–139, 141, 142, 150n22
South China Sea, 4, 6, 14, 40, 41, 133, 219, 297–308, 311–313, 315–317, 319n13, 325, 327
Sri Lanka, 11, 82, 154, 174–177, 215, 258, 273, 305, 307, 308, 319n20

## T

Taiwan, 1, 5, 6, 8, 10, 12, 14, 19, 20, 22, 27, 28, 34, 52, 61, 73, 94, 96, 98, 100, 103, 105, 114, 117, 128, 143, 145, 154, 185, 186, 188, 190, 191, 213–215, 221, 240, 242, 244, 257, 263, 274, 275, 280–284, 288–291, 295, 297, 310, 312, 313, 316, 317, 324, 326, 327
Thailand, 1, 8, 11, 20, 27, 34, 46, 47, 49, 50, 62, 63, 75–77, 79, 80, 82–84, 86n25, 94–96, 99, 103, 106, 128, 138, 145, 154, 185, 193, 195, 196, 206, 210n25, 215, 217, 229, 231–235, 244, 245n34, 249, 251–254, 257–262, 274, 275, 281, 282, 301, 303, 310, 311
TI, *see*.Transparency International
Tibet, 170, 171, 181n18, 309
TPP, *see* Trans Pacific Partnership
Trade, 4, 23, 50, 91, 99–103, 128, 169, 223, 247, 285, 325
Trans Pacific Partnership (TPP), 4, 5, 7, 10, 30, 49, 50, 99–101, 103, 104, 118, 121n13, 303, 306, 310–314, 325
Transparency International (TI), 31, 53n24, 55n73, 98, 118, 121n19, 123n53, 147, 240, 263
Trump, Donald, 1, 4–8, 10–13, 15n7, 21, 30, 34, 36, 40, 99–103, 115, 122n49, 142, 155, 216, 225, 230, 239, 279, 283, 296, 297, 300, 303, 312–315, 325, 326
Tsai Ing-wen, 5, 288–290, 312

## U

Uighurs, 10, 79, 170–174, 243
UN, *see* United Nations
United Nations (UN), 1, 45, 54n58, 60, 72, 77, 79–81, 87n34, 96, 120n2, 126, 134, 149n1, 150n13, 155, 160–163, 168, 175–177, 179, 181n10, 181n19, 181n20, 181n23, 181n24, 185, 187, 204, 207, 208, 209n4, 209n7, 211n46, 230, 237, 254, 255, 257, 259, 261, 281, 282, 284, 294–296, 298
United States (US), 1–3, 15n7, 15n8, 19, 28, 63, 91, 115, 120n1, 121n27, 122n40, 142, 157, 189, 214, 248, 279, 281–283, 300, 323
Urbanization, 10, 44, 120, 125–149, 163, 186, 190, 193, 196, 197, 214, 267, 324

US Department of State, 53n15,
    53n31, 86n33, 210n37, 244n10,
    245n31, 257, 276n9, 276n14,
    276n18
USAID, 11, 155

**V**

Vietnam, 8, 11, 14, 21, 25, 28,
    49–52, 70, 73, 76, 77, 79, 82,
    92, 95–97, 101, 103, 106, 128,
    138, 154, 160, 167, 189, 191,
    202, 206, 215, 232, 240, 252,
    254, 258, 259, 273, 280, 297,
    298, 300–303, 307, 310, 311,
    314, 328

**W**

WHO, *see* World Health Organization
Widido, Joko ("Jokowi"), 46
Womenomics, 28, 156, 158, 159,
    181n8, 203
World Bank, 1, 20, 36, 43, 46, 50,
    52n2, 53n35, 54n49, 54n54,
    54n59, 54n64, 55n70, 55n74,
    58, 60, 85n4, 85n7, 96, 98,
    120n3, 121n13, 121n14,
    121n16, 121n22, 139, 147,
    150n19, 150n21, 281, 282,
    304
World Economic Forum, 39, 43,
    53n26, 54n43, 54n56, 55n71,
    98, 118, 121n23, 123n54, 145,
    147, 151n38, 156, 165, 181n6,
    181n16, 232, 265, 276n21
World Health Organization (WHO),
    141, 151n28, 209n5
World Justice Project, 55n72, 98,
    121n20, 121n24, 147, 165
World Trade Organization (WTO), 1,
    2, 5, 49, 99, 102, 103, 107,
    120n3, 121n4, 250, 282, 285
WTO, *see* World Trade Organization

**X**

Xi Jinping, 3, 6, 15n4, 35, 40, 41, 51,
    74, 77, 78, 102, 114, 130,
    146–148, 171, 173, 219, 220,
    240, 243, 251, 268, 273,
    276n26, 288, 293, 296, 297,
    305, 312, 313, 315, 316,
    318n12, 319n26, 319n28

The manufacturer's authorised representative in the EU is Springer Nature Customer Service Centre GmbH, Europaplatz 3, 69115 Heidelberg, Germany. If you have any concerns regarding our products, please contact ProductSafety@springernature.com

Printed and bound by CPI Group (UK) Ltd, Croydon, CR0 4YY

23/03/2026

02076663-0012